TruthQuest History

Pursuing the vast breadth and depth of the

Age of Revolution II
(America/Europe, A.D. 1800-1865)

in a chronological investigation
enlivening its history, art, culture & ideas
and probing the spiritual truths of history!

By Michelle Miller

Grades 5-12
(Younger Students May Participate)

To Jeanna Riness,
whose hard work, encouragement, and prayerfully
carried me through this project.
May I not be *too* jealous of the family
who gets this fabulous young woman as a daughter-in-law!

TruthQuest History is not affiliated with the "TruthQuest Inductive Study Bible."

Print Version: ISBN 978-0-9752908-5-9 Published in the United States of America

TruthQuest History/ThinkWrite, L.L.C.
PO Box 2128, Traverse City, MI 49685-2128
www.TruthQuestHistory.com info@TruthQuestHistory.com

We would love to have you join our online discussion group. Simply send an email to:
HIStoryQuesters-subscribe@YahooGroups.com

Notes for Dad & Mom:

"How does one 'do' TruthQuest History?
Isn't it just a lot of words and booklists?
It looks too easy.
Are my kids just supposed to read?
Aren't they going to 'do' something?
Where are the activities and the daily lesson plans?
How will I know if they're learning anything?"

Good questions! They show your spirit of excellence. But you are leaving *regular history* behind.

"Regular history. What do you mean by that?
History is history! It's the people and events of the past.
It's the story of mankind."

Is it? Where did you get that definition?

"Are you crazy? I went to school. I sat through many a history class.
That's what we studied!"

Ah, but this is where I must challenge you, as I've been challenged. We only *think* that's what history is, because that's what was in our history books. So, we were learning not only the history they taught us, but also the *definition of history* they taught us. As Christian adults, though, we must hold every definition up to His blazing light. Is history indeed the story of mankind? Could the secular minds that birthed our history textbooks also have had a secular definition of history itself? Is it possible?

"Okay, okay! You yak a lot. Just let me think."

Gladly. That's just what I hope you'll do. Please think about history in a brand new way, for it is *not* first the story of mankind, but of the One who *made* mankind! Yes, only the Lord Creator could *initiate* all life and the laws that govern life. He towers over all human existence. Thankfully, He chose to make us in His image; thus He gave us the potential for impact which flows from how we *respond* to His preeminence and truths. And, He lets us participate in His plans for this earth!

God's initiation and our response...that's history. To the degree that we believe and obey truth, to that degree our lives are blessed, our nations free and healthy, our science beneficial, our laws wise, our businesses prospering, and our art glorious. Each of these spheres of life cannot be understood without grasping the spiritual issues at their base. Again I say, *now that's history!*

“ Then that means...er, that means the opposite is true! ”

You hit the nail on the head! For a couple hundred years now, western civilization has put God on the sidelines of life, so most history is taught as the story of mankind, as if people were the "prime force" of the universe, as if they were the makers of themselves and of truth. How presumptuous! But there's more! After Darwin, little reason was seen to learn about the past; folks believed they were moving—on their own power—toward a perfect future. Since then, history has become a dull, meaningless "obligation." (No wonder it was so boring!) It should be a *personal* encounter with the King of the Universe, the Maker of our souls! It should be one of the most inspiring, personal, real, and intimate topics because it hooks us up with the truths that make life work! And our practical-minded boys *especially* need to know that history is about *right now*...about truth and power and law and right and good government...and all the other things for which this world is secretly hungering. Now *that's* something into which kids can pour their energies and ambitions!

“ I admit that my history classes were dull and meaningless, but I never wanted to say that to my kids. ”

Well, isn't it good to know all that's behind you? Because history *is different* than what you were taught, you can teach history in a *different way* than you were taught. You won't need the artificial motivations of "questions at the end of the chapter" and multiple-choice tests. Why? Because you're not giving your kids dead material. Their eyes won't glaze over. Real truth is a spark that lights its own fire! You are free to convey truth to your kids in the way the Bible often does: through narrative (true *story*); not a recitation of dry facts. Hence, the copious booklists in this guide, and the happy fact that your children's "history time" will be spent basking in great reading. Since all your children can learn together, they will play it, eat it, dream it, and talk it. Besides, as Jeremy Jackson put it: *history is philosophy* [beliefs] *teaching by example.* All these great books give lots of great examples. But...

“ What do you mean 'but?' That was sounding good! ”

All that good reading will still be mere humanistic fluff unless your kids have first been "primed" to look for the deep spiritual issues at work in the lives of all those people and events they're reading about. Otherwise, your child will just be impressed by the human heroics. Ooh, more humanism, even though well-meant! That's where this guide's commentary comes in (the emboldened text). You'll see that a paragraph or two introduces each new topic. It does that "priming" for you, and incrementally and subtly weaves together the deepest issues of this era of history. By the end of the guide, the veil will lift. History will be truly connected. The key importance of God and of beliefs will be seen, and the consequences of truth and untruth will be personally grasped by your children. If you, Mama and Papa, can just read the emboldened text too, you'll find yourself much better able to lead—and enjoy—vivid and profound conversations with your kids on some of the most important topics in life...and isn't that why we're teaching? (It isn't absolutely necessary, but it's great if you can!) To help your kids think deeply, *ThinkWrite* exercises focus their seeking and synthesizing. (Sample answers are provided for you in Appendix 1.)

"OK. So what about Day One. Tell me how I should plan each week."

Well, that's up to you. But you mustn't panic! Remember, this history is a new kind of history. You'll see that it takes on a life of it's own. You'll gather the little kids on the couch to read aloud to them, or you'll have kids sprawled around (or sitting in an orderly row) as each is absorbed in their books. At dinner time or while driving to piano lessons you'll have the most fascinating conversations, guaranteed! Older students can more deeply research special topics. Yes, this can be enough. It's that simple.

But you may want more, as befits your style. You can arrange special bi-weekly or monthly evenings where you gather as a family, or with other families, to give oral reports, put on skits, show off projects, and eat "historical" food. You can all talk about what you've learned. Believe me. Your mother-in-law will be thunderstruck by the good, deep stuff flowing out of your child's heart! You can do narrations, or enjoy the new companion resources created by *A Journey Through Learning* to work with each *TruthQuest History* guide: the Binder-Builder,™ Map/Timeline/Report Packages, and Notebooks now offered at our website (www.TruthQuestHistory.com). You can draw, paint, sculpt, or build Lego towers. You can "publish" a newspaper reporting on "breaking news" and mail it to friends and family. (Many ideas are shared on our online discussion loop.) Or, you can do none of the above. You can simply immerse in and discuss great living books (as listed in this guide, for example), a favorite of ours!

You'll be spending a great deal of time in this era, and the learning (both factual and ideological) will be quite impressive. You won't need any tests to show that your kids are learning; they'll be living what they learn, playing what they learn, talking what they learn, and praying what they learn!

As for overall planning, it's good to jot down a general plan. How many years do you have left with your students? How many historical eras do you need to cover? (There is a *TruthQuest History* guide for each era.) If you have plenty of time, you can "play" this guide by ear (knowing that the content of this guide has been carefully planned) and go at the rate of interest in your students, allowing time for greater or lesser depth as you feel led...*or* you can divide the number of units in this guide by the number of months you have available, and then see to it that you get through them in a timely fashion. Either way is fine.

You know what's best because you're the one seeking God's design for your family. He certainly doesn't have a one-size-fits-all-plan for children! No, He made each one uniquely, and has a specific design for their lives; how and what they learn is an important part. You get to sense and implement that for your children. Far be it from us, then, to schedule your day!

Enough said.

~~~ ~ ~~~
~~~

Let me just close, then, with a few "housekeeping" details:

1.) Be assertive! Feel free to skip topics as you deem best. I've even mentioned some that can be safely omitted. So why do I include them at all? Because each child is unique. He may need to know something others do not. I've included as much as possible. The executive decisions are up to you!

2.) All worrying about acquiring listed books is hereby outlawed! You can see that I've listed oodles...so you have as many choices as possible. Certainly, you're *not* supposed to read each book on each topic. It's a smorgasbord; enjoy some delicious options, but don't eat all! Your library will have more choices (especially with the interlibrary loan service), and great books can be found in church libraries, private/parochial school libraries, and even in the youth literature collections held by some colleges' education departments. Many older classics are available for free, online viewing. But don't try to be such a "good mother" that you bore your kids to tears by reading a million books on each topic! Wondering which books to select? Probably, the older the book, the more Judeo-Christian is its outlook, but there *are* new books which are very good, especially in the picture book section.

3.) Books which were known or deemed to be *in-print* at the time of this writing are marked with an asterisk. (*) The asterisk does *not* mean it is a "preferred" book, as is often assumed.

4.) We will often refer to a handful of books of three types:

a) "spines" which offer thorough, narrative coverage of this era's history for the sake of families who like to follow such...either with, or instead of, the many topic-specific books we also cite, especially when the latter cannot be procured;

b) "insight" books that explore key issues/events which expose spiritual truths;

c) "snapshot" books which give a quick peek at an era in order to build up a "50-000-foot-view" of world history generally.

d) These resources are all cited in this guide's booklists *before* a dashed line (--------), followed by the topic-specific books. You *definitely* can use this *TruthQuest History* guide *without* reading any of these references because it does not lead you through a required set of books, but instead helps you use whatever is at hand.

e) Editions of some "spines" vary; please see www.TruthQuestHistory.com/spine if your version numbers its chapters differently than those we reference in this guide.

"Spines"

**Story of the Great Republic*, by H.A. Guerber (Nothing New Press, 2002) Gr. 3-7
**This Country of Ours*, by H.E. Marshall (Doran, 1917) Gr. 3-8

**Island Story*, by H.E. Marshall (Frederick Stokes, 1920) Gr. 3-8
**Sweet Land of Liberty*, by Charles Coffin (Maranatha Publications) Gr. 5-12

This is the sequel to the very important *Story of Liberty*. The hardback reprint uses the original title: **Old Times in the Colonies.*

**Basic History of the United States: Vol. 2 & 3*, by Clarence Carson Gr. 9-12

"<u>Insight books</u>"

**From Sea to Shining Sea for Children* <u>and</u> **Sounding Forth the Trumpet for Children* Gr. 1-5

by Peter Marshall & David Manuel (Revell, 1993 and 1999, respectively)

Some folks appreciate this book's attempt to see God's hand in history; others do not. Strongly northern point of view in regard to Civil War issues.

**From Sea to Shining Sea* <u>and</u> **Sounding Forth the Trumpet* Gr. 6-12

by Peter Marshall & David Manuel

Some folks appreciate this book's attempt to see God's hand in history; others do not. Strongly northern point of view in regard to Civil War issues.

**How Should We Then Live?* by Francis Schaeffer [book or video format] Gr. 9-12

This is, in my opinion, one of the most important resources that older students—and their parents!—will ever encounter.... Its various chapters are cited throughout the entire *TruthQuest History* series.

"<u>Snapshot books</u>"

**Story of the World: Volume 3*, by Susan Wise Bauer (Peace Hill Press, 2003) Gr. 3-6

Some families enjoy this book's scope, so ask us to cite it; others seek different worldview; so, parental decision.

5.) What happens if you can't find a book on a topic? Be creative! Use an encyclopedia or some other general resource, and *many* books are now available for free, online reading. Hey, when you decide to use "living books" (to learn through real literature), you're automatically committed to using whatever you can find. That's true no matter which curriculum guide you choose. See why I list so many books here? I'm trying to increase your chances of finding gems. A ***copyrighted*** list of books cited in this guide is also included in Appendix 2. It may ***not*** be copied for others, but you may make a copy to keep in your purse during book hunts.

6.) Don't forget you're the boss! You decide which topics, books, and films are appropriate for your family. I would have to live a thousand years to read all the books in this guide, so you know I've not personally read every book listed here. I have selected those from more reliable authors, publishers, or periods. Remember, the grade levels marked on the booklists denote estimated independent reading, *not recommended* reading, level. Only you, the parent, know best!

7.) Some kids have favorite book series, so the series names are in parentheses in the listings.

8.) Searches through your library's database will usually work *only* if you do *not* use a book's subtitle. So why did I include them in the booklists? They give a glimpse of the book's content. But few library databases include subtitles, so don't nullify your searches by including them.

9.) One last thing...*enjoy!*

TruthQuest History: Age of Revolution II (America/Europe, 1800-1865)

Table of Contents

TruthQuest History

Age of Revolution II
(America/Europe, A.D. 1800-1865)

By Michelle Miller

TruthQuest History: Age of Revolution II

America/Europe, 1800-1865

1 Onward and Upward!

Onward and upward!
The sky's the limit!
Forward, march!

"What's this?" you ask. "A pep rally?" No. Then again, maybe it *is!* For many people who lived during the 1800s, life was a giant pep rally. These catchy phrases were their cheers! Can you guess why?

Here's a hint: look backward! In fact, if you've been with us chronologically, you know we're watching the consequences of western civilization's *fork in the road*, which occurred during the Renaissance and Reformation.[1] The people then had *real* needs—personal, social, and spiritual—but they sought answers in two completely different places!

As you recall, Renaissance[2] thinkers said that a deeper awareness of the greatness of mankind was the answer, and that through mankind's fabulous senses and reason, people could fully figure out life, morality, and truth. The role of religion in these matters was increasingly denied. Ah, *humanism*.

Humanism

Others knew that the opposite was true: people were hurting because they were too *far* from the Lord and His truths, even if the church had been powerful then! Their renewed pursuit of God and direct study of the Bible led to what is called the *Reformation*, a time when many new Christian churches were begun. Others stayed within their beloved Catholic church to inject renewal there. Don't worry about the many denominations of the church. Here's the key: people were being urged by the reformers to dig deeper into the Bible. And that always has impact!

So whether in the era of the Renaissance and Reformation, or in the original Garden of Eden, or right now, mankind answers the question: God first or humans first? It's an individual question, but past history shows us, interestingly enough, that whole civilizations have tended to answer the same, generation after generation, as their nations have moved toward the inevitable consequences of that belief.

What's so amazing about the Renaissance and Reformation era is that European beliefs split in two. Some said *God first!* Some said *man first!* Ever since—in Europe and her colonies (America, Canada, Australia, etc.)—there has been a battle for the minds of the rulers, pastors, artists, teachers, writers, judges, philosophers, musicians...and the next generation!

That's why history isn't about facts; it's about the truth and how we respond to it. *Individual* beliefs. Decisions. Forks. *Unavoidable* forks! No, not silverware. *Forks in the road!*

Each person develops a worldview (basic beliefs). The most important questions we answer are these, so I call them the *Big 2*

1 Approximately 1400-1600.

2 *Renaissance* means *re-birth*. It was a time when people wanted to rebirth the classic elements of ancient Greek and Roman culture, which focused on human ability and authority. For many, this included a desire for a pre-Christian way of life.

Beliefs: Who is God? Who, then, is mankind? The Renaissance, while not saying so directly, implied that mankind is his own god (*Big Belief #1*), and can thus decide itself how people (*Big Belief #2*) are to be treated. The Biblical worldview says the opposite: the Lord is God; He alone can determine right and wrong. And because He lovingly created mankind (and died to redeem us!), each person has worth and rights based in God and is to be treated with respect. *Whoa, what a difference!*

And the gap widens! While God is the same yesterday, today, and forever, and while the principles of His Word are unchanging,[3] humanism built increasingly arrogant philosophies, arts, and sciences on its basic position that mankind is the center of all.

You know what, though? We're going to keep this simple. Let's focus on one belief that helps summarize the 1800s, the one that made it a giant pep rally! Ready? On the edge of your seat? Breathless? Suspense getting to you? Here it is—*progress!*

Yup. The humanists believed that mankind was perfecting himself. Sure, people could look back at history and see a booboo or two, but that's when the church was calling the shots, they said, and before people "realized" how "powerful" they were. Now, they cried, mankind, using his great intelligence, was going to emerge victorious over all problems! Onward and upward! Forward, march!

How did humanists come to this *enormous* conclusion? Easy. Just look at their *Big Belief #1:* mankind is his own god, and gods are perfect, or are headed that way. When God was flushed from society, so too was His unflattering declaration that mankind is fallen and needs salvation.
In fact, Jean Jacques Rousseau (called *Father of the Enlightenment*, a period in the later 1700s when people supposedly "saw the light") said man was born not as a sinner, but as a *noble savage*. Pure, simple, uncivilized. He said it was institutions like the church and government which ruined people. (You already know his beliefs contributed greatly to the bloody French Revolution of the late 1700s, because we covered that in the last unit.)

Again I say, *Whoa, what a difference!* Think of it. The Reformation had reminded everyone of the Bible's claim that all are sinful, that all are under God's higher law, but that this law protects us by restraining our own sin natures and those of others. Even though this law actually yields freedom, you have to admit this Biblical worldview sounds pretty drab next to those humanist cheers: *Onward and upward! We are gods!* (I would like to point out, however, that worldviews ought to be chosen for their accuracy, not their appeal.)

Sit up now. Miss this, and you'll just be wasting your history time for the rest of this year! Earlier, I used the word *progress* to explain this new Enlightenment belief that mankind was getting better and better! What other word describes the increasing improvement of something? You're right. *Evolution!* You've got to get this: a hundred years *before* Charles Darwin, humanists believed that mankind was becoming perfect, that he was evolving!

I want to simultaneously say two things about this, but can only express the thoughts one at a time. You *must* weave them together in your heart and mind though.

3 Heb. 13:8, Ps. 119:89, Mt. 5:18, I Pet 1:25.

First, do you have any idea what a revolution this caused? I don't mean a revolution of guns and swords, but of ideas and words! The whole *prime force* of the universe was no longer God; it was man. Everything had to be rethought in terms of man's godhood: history, religion, ethics, government, art, science, economics, and even mankind's physical and mental being!

You can guess the humanistic thinkers of the 1800s were busy. So much was written, so many ideas were introduced, so many artworks expressing these ideas were created, and they had such a profound impact on society, that this whole guide can cover just 65 years of history!

Yes, revolutions with guns would follow this revolution of ideas, because *ideas have consequences*, as they say. But we're not so sappy as to think things are only important when they get to the gun stage. We know it's the hidden ideas of the world—the beliefs of the heart—that are most important.

Secondly, this new belief in evolutionary progress would impact Christianity in a titanic battle! Here's why. If mankind was evolving toward perfection, religion could be seen as something that had been necessary for a time, a time when mankind was weaker and *needed* those beliefs, when his mind had only evolved far enough to think in those terms. But now, Voltaire (another Enlightenment thinker) said Christianity was out-of-date. It was a fetter that limited mankind to just one expression of supreme power and high principles. Mankind was ready to go beyond this to an awareness of the general sense of "God-ness" in the universe and people generally. From that point on, Christians have had the difficult task of trying to call mankind to something he deems primitive.[4] Is it any wonder modern Christians are often dubbed in the media as Neanderthals, and our suggestions are treated with utter disgust?!

With these ideas, the Bible could no longer be considered the supreme, authoritative, and personal revelation of a divine God; it could only be a collection of myths told by mankind in a lower stage of evolution. Scholars spent much time looking for "errors" (they had already decided they existed) to help everyone accept this devaluing of the Bible. This spawned an anti-Biblical sort of *higher criticism* led by Julius Wellhausen, a German theologian. The bottom line was the "evisceration[5] of Christianity, leaving it a mere religion, without life, without hope, without authority."[6] Yet, "religion still continued in Europe. There were still large churches, burning candles, beautiful choirs, lovely stained glass windows, congregations.... What was gone was the spiritual life. The Bible was only empty pages written by men who were now dead, rather than the revelation of the living God."[7]

It's shocking how rapidly Christians who were plagued with intellectual pride flocked to these ideas, especially theologians and pastors—the shepherds of the flock! Of course the sheep followed too...and the soul was cut out of Europe. America was *not* exempt from this onslaught, but frequent revivals, thankfully, kept it from completely overrunning the nation. Where only a fraction of Europeans consider themselves

---

4 Jeremy Jackson, *No Other Foundation: The Church Through Twenty Centuries* (Westchester, IL: Cornerstone, 1980) 238.

5 *Evisceration* literally means to have the guts cut out! Strong speech for a strong idea!

6 Dave Breese, *Seven Men Who Rule the World from the Grave.* (Chicago: Moody Press, 1990) 96.

7 Breese 97.

fully sold out to the God of the Bible, many Americans do. (Don't let that sound like a proud statement or one telling you to relax. On the contrary, as you'll see throughout this unit!)

You've heard *nature abhors a vacuum*. The empty, soulless churches didn't *stay* empty. A "natural religion" seeped in; it was *called* Christianity, but was *very* different. People still talked about God, but He was no longer Master, Creator, and Savior. He was merely the capital "N in Nature."[8]

Natural religion

Though the world often denies the significance of spiritual things, a lot of time is spent refuting them! Much of Europe's literature during the 1800s described the tension between Christianity and the new natural religion. World-famous thinkers like Kant and Hegel also tried to mothball Christianity in the attic of the 1800s by saying it only represented the increasing waves of mankind's history or by saying spirituality was outside the realm of reason and sensory input. All this was said in a way which caused people to dismiss it.

I don't usually cite readings in the middle of our discussions, but these fit precisely here. If you're old enough, can you consider them right now?

**Seven Men Who Rule the World from the Grave*, by Dave Breese, Ch.6 — Gr. 8-12
This is a *very* important book, I think.

No Other Foundation: The Church Through Twenty Centuries, Ch. 17 by Jeremy Jackson — Gr. 11-12
Too difficult for most students, but it's so profound that I always mention it, just in case...

8 Jackson 193.

But that's not the whole story, of course. Even though the past failures of the church had opened the door to humanism, and even though many Christians were so busy pursuing "personal peace and affluence" (as Francis Schaeffer puts it) that they ignored the real needs of people around them, God was still busy doing what He's always doing—lovingly working to draw mankind to Himself. And that's the *real* saga of history! The good news is that when evil comes in like a flood, God raises a standard against it![9]

So, we're not just going to watch the humanist juggernaut. We'll also see that where people of the 1800s chose to pursue God and His real-life principles, revivals arose and feet were put to faith. As God desired to spread Christianity, you'll see humble people cross deserts, mountains, oceans, and their back fence to share in God's work. They would extend its life-giving, freedom-inducing influence in capitals and congresses, in parishes and parliaments. They would tackle the greatest injustices of the day. Remember, one must *determine* to really live *in* Him to have the power to be Christ-like at home, work, school, and in society at large, especially in free societies which offer so many options!

Do you see the deep issues swirling below the surface of the 1800s? We can *certainly* call the 1800s an "Age of Revolution!" Each individual, and the nations they make up, faced that fork in the road: what to believe, *whom* to believe? We get to see where both these roads led. Put on your travelin' shoes!

9 Isaiah 59:19

2 America's Early Republic

As you know, *TruthQuest History* usually intersperses European and American history, but this guide will be a bit different. Why? Well, have you had a new baby born into your family? Then you know the intensity of those first years of development. America went from being an infant nation in the year 1800 (with almost everyone living within 50 miles of the Atlantic coast)...to having folks spread all the way to the Pacific Ocean! Those western lands didn't even belong to America when the century opened. That's a lot of growth and change! By the middle of the century, America was already headed for a massive civil war. That's a lot of history...and we're going to cover it. But plenty was happening in Europe too. Britain's Industrial Revolution, Napoleon's gruesome wars, and the ongoing impact of spiritual issues in Europe would lead to many significant "forks in the road" on *both* sides of the pond! I can't mention them all now; but I can tell you that when we come to those *forks*, you'll see the graphic on the right. That will help you see how powerfully history is affected by people's spiritual beliefs! Ready? Let's dive in.

~~~~~

***Hum, hum, hum. Whir, whir, whir.* Can you hear America purring along in the early 1800s? "Whew!" these early Americans might have said. "The Revolutionary War is over, we're on our own, the Indians are further west, and we have a good Constitution, as well as high-falutin' presidents. Let's get busy building our farms and shops!"**

It *was* a nice time for America. A hard-fought battle *had* been won. The honoring of God's supremacy and Biblical principles by key leaders (even if not personally Christians) *had* yielded limited government, wise laws, and individual freedom. This, in turn, allowed opportunity, confidence, inventiveness, private property, free enterprise, and safety. These things make for prosperity! As one American historian, Clarence Carson, said:

> *Governments were restrained that individuals might be free....The story of America after 1789*[10] *until well into the 20th century, is not so much the story of the doings of government as of people generally. It is the story of freed individuals working, building, growing crops, building factories, clearing the land for farms, organizing churches, providing for families, and doing all those things that make up the warp and woof of life. They did this singly as individuals, as families, and in voluntary groups.*[11]

Or, as Thomas Jefferson so eloquently put it:

> *A wise and frugal Government, which shall restrain men from injuring one another, shall leave them otherwise free to regulate their own pursuits of industry and improvement, and shall not take from the mouth of the labor the bread it has earned. This is the sum of good government...*[12]

---

10 Date of the ratification of the U.S. Constitution.

11 Clarence B. Carson, *The Beginning of the Republic—A Basic History of the United States, Volume 2* (Wadley, AL: American Textbook Committee, 1984) 111, 118.

12 Carson 157.
~~~~~

Doesn't that sound blissful? Limited government and free enterprise! What a great beginning. No wonder America was so vivacious! She was confidently seeking her way in the old aristocratic world, even though Britain expected her to act like a naughty child now wanting back into Mama's good graces. While, due to the help given during the American Revolution, France thought surely the United States would be an obedient puppy. But the early presidents were having none of that. They had fought long and hard to be independent and were going to keep it that way!

> We aren't specifically studying the lives of the first three presidents (Washington, Adams, and Jefferson) because they were so intensely intertwined with the American Revolution, and were thus thoroughly covered in the last *TruthQuest History* unit. If you weren't with us, be certain you meet these important men!

In the spirit of national excitement that swept America during this *Early Republic* era, a brand new capital city was forged out of a swamp and named for George Washington, of course. Fabulous buildings were erected in the middle of wilderness. John Adams was the first president to preside there.

2a Early Republic era

These books give a general overview of the era, but you needn't worry; we'll cover key events separately throughout. It is always good for older students to read Carson's book though.

**Basic History of the United States: Vol. 2*, by Clarence Carson, Ch. 9a-d — Gr. 9-12

Year of the Horseless Carriage: 1801, by Genevieve Foster — Gr. 4-9
Precious, broad overview of the early 1800s, but it is too rare to be actively sought.

First Book of the Founding of the Republic, by Richard Morris (First Books) — Gr. 6-12

Young United States, by Edwin Tunis — Gr. 7-12
This book features amazingly detailed illustrations and text.

Fiction/Historical Fiction

Julia Ann, by Rachel Varble — Gr. 7-12
I've not seen this story of a girl growing up in early Washington, D.C.

2b New capital city, Washington, D.C.

These books focus on the building of Washington. See below for "tour" books of the capital city.

Story of the U.S. Capitol, by Marilyn Prolman (Cornerstones) — Gr. 1-6

**Story of the White House*, by Natalie Miller (Cornerstones) — Gr. 1-6

**Child's History of Art*, by Hillyer & Huey (*Architecture* section, Ch. 26) Gr. 2-8
We cite the 1951 edition (published by Appleton); if your version differs, please see www.TruthQuestHistory.com/spine for help in cross-referencing.
OR *Young People's Story of Architecture: Gothic-Modern*, pp. 84-89

**Building the Capital City*, by Marlene Brill (Cornerstones) Gr. 3-6

**Capital*, by Lynn Curlee Gr. 3-7
Building of Washington, D.C.

**Capitol*, by Andrew Santella (Cornerstones) Gr. 3-7

Mr. Jefferson's Washington, by Esther Douty (Garrard How They Lived) Gr. 3-8

Washington, D.C., by Howard K. Smith (Landmark Giant) Gr. 6-12
Only the first chapters deal with the founding of the city.

Capital Capital City: 1790-1814, by Suzanne Hilton Gr. 7-12

Capital for the Nation, by Stan Hoig Gr. 8-12

Fiction/Historical Fiction

Washington Adventure, by Stockton Banks Gr. 4-10
I've not seen this story of a boy who discovers a land swindler in early Washington as the White House is being built.

2c Art of the Early Republic

Art of the New American Nation, by Shirley Glubok Various

2d "Tour" of current Washington, D.C.

These books take a "tour" around current Washington, D.C. Many are available and the modern era is not the focus of this guide, so I've cited only a few. Since these are quick peeks, they tend to be for the young, but anyone can browse!

**Capital! Washington, D.C., from A to Z*, by Laura Melmud Gr. K-3

**Inside-Outside Book of Washington*, by Roxie Munro Gr. K-3

**Story of the White House*, by Kate Waters Gr. 1-4

This is Washington, D.C., by Miroslav Sasek Gr. 2-5

**Washington, D.C.: A Scrapbook*, by Laura Lee Benson Gr. 2-8

**Washington, D.C.*, KIDS Discover magazine, March, 1997 Gr. 2-10

**City! Washington, D.C.*, by Shirley Climo Gr. 3-6

3 *Land-a-Rama!* Lewis & Clark, Louisiana Purchase, and a Haitian!

Americans knew the nation was growing. Then, Thomas Jefferson was able to acquire the Louisiana Purchase from a French ruler named Napoleon. We'll talk a lot more about Napoleon later, but you must know now that he had, at first, no intention of selling French lands in North America. Soon, though, he was engaged in an expensive drive to conquer Europe, and he lost control of Haiti—his stepping stone to the American lands—due to an amazing slave revolt led by Toussaint-L'Ouverture.[13] Needing cash, Napoleon suddenly decided to sell the Louisiana Territory...and Mr. Jefferson was a very willing buyer!

The Louisiana Purchase was much more than what we now call Louisiana. In fact, it was a good chunk of the land west of the Mississippi River and thus almost *doubled* the size of America! Jefferson then sent two groups to explore it: Lewis & Clark, and later, Zebulon Pike. Of course, this brings up the issue of the Indians who lived on that land. We'll talk about that later too.

3a Louisiana Purchase (1803)

Naturally, Lewis and Clark will be mentioned in materials about the Louisiana Purchase, but in the next section we'll cite resources specifically about their great expedition. Parents, please remember that editions of some "spines" vary; please see www.TruthQuestHistory.com/spine if your version numbers its chapters differently than those we reference in this guide. Those not using spines needn't be concerned.

**From Sea to Shining Sea for Children*, by Marshall & Manuel, Ch. 5 Gr. 1-5

**Story of the World: Volume 3*, by Susan Wise Bauer, Ch. 32a Gr. 3-6

Some families enjoy this book's scope, so ask us to cite it; others seek different worldview; so, parental decision.

13 Carson 2:189.

**Story of the Great Republic*, by H.A. Guerber, Ch. X — Gr. 3-7

**This Country of Ours*, by H.E. Marshall, Ch. 66-68 — Gr. 3-8

**From Sea to Shining Sea*, by Marshall & Manuel, pp. 321-330 — Gr. 6-12

**Basic History of the United States: Vol. 2*, by Clarence Carson, Ch. 10b-c — Gr. 9-12

Continent for Sale, by Arthur Groom (Winston Adventure) — Gr. 3-9
Thrilling tale of the real contribution made by two teenagers who overheard plans to sabotage the Purchase! My kids loved this!

**Louisiana Purchase*, by Gail Sakurai (Cornerstones of Freedom II) — Gr. 3-9

Louisiana Purchase, by Robert Tallant (Landmark) — Gr. 3-9

**Louisiana Purchase*, by Elizabeth Jaffe (Let Freedom Ring) — Gr. 4-8

**Louisiana Purchase*, by Michael Burgan (We the People) — Gr. 5-8

Story of the Louisiana Purchase, by Mary Kay Phelan — Gr. 5-12

**What's the Deal?* by Rhoda Blumberg — Gr. 6-12

Fiction/Historical Fiction

Flag on the Levee, by Manly Wade Wellman — Gr. 7-12
Life in Louisiana after Purchase, but before statehood; I thought I'd slip it in here.

3b Lewis & Clark Expedition (1804-1806)

There are many books on the expedition, so I'll just list a sampling. Use whatever is available!

**Story of the World: Vol. 3*, by Susan Wise Bauer, Ch. 32a — Gr. 3-6
Some families enjoy this book's scope, so ask us to cite it; others seek different worldview; so, parental decision.

**Picture Book of Lewis and Clark*, by David Adler — Gr. K-2

**My Name is York*, by Elizabeth Van Steenwyk — Gr. K-3
True story of Negro slave who was on the journey.

Adventures of Lewis and Clark, by Ormonde de Kay (Step-Up Books) Gr. 1-3

**Lewis and Clark: A Prairie Dog for the President*, by S. Redmond (Step into...3) Gr. 1-3
This is a cartoon-y telling of the items, including a prairie dog, sent back to Jefferson.

**Story of the Lewis and Clark Expedition*, by R. Conrad Stein (Cornerstones) Gr. 1-4

Lewis and Clark, by Elizabeth Montgomery (Garrard World Explorer) Gr. 1-5

**Meriwether Lewis*, by Charlotte Bebenroth (Childhood) Gr. 1-6

Will Clark, by Katharine Wilkie (Childhood) Gr. 1-6

Bill Clark: American Explorer, by Sanford Tousey Gr. 2-5
Another of Tousey's incredible, colorful, and rare biographies.

**Lewis and Clark*, by Steven Kroll Gr. 2-5

**Back of Beyond*, by Andy Bowen (Creative Minds) Gr. 2-7

**How We Crossed the West: Adventures of Lewis & Clark*, by Rosalyn Schanzer Gr. 2-7

**Off the Map*, edited by Peter & Connie Roop Gr. 2-8
Abridged version of Lewis & Clark's own journals.

Lewis and Clark, by Madge Haines & Leslie Morrill (Makers of America) Gr. 3-7

**Lewis and Clark Expedition*, by Richard Neuberger (Landmark) Gr. 3-9

**Seaman: Dog Who Explored the West with Lewis & Clark*, by Gail Karwoski Gr. 4-7

**Meriwether Lewis*, by Janet & Geoff Benge (Heroes of History) Gr. 4-10
Some Benge books are being put into audio format also.

**Of Courage Undaunted*, by James Daugherty Gr. 4-12
This is a very respected book on the topic, I'm told.

Adventures of Lewis and Clark, by John Bakeless (NorthStar) Gr. 5-12

Adventures of Lewis and Clark, by John Bakeless (North Star) Gr. 6-12

**Meriwether Lewis and William Clark*, by D. Petersen (People of Distinction) Gr. 6-12

*_Incredible Journey of Lewis and Clark_, by Rhoda Blumberg Gr. 7-12

Caution! I was just warned that this contains a section on personal relationships between some of the explorers and the Indian women.

George Shannon: Young Explorer with Lewis and Clark, by Virginia Eifert Gr. 9-12

Fiction/Historical Fiction

*_Great Expedition of Lewis and Clark_, by Judith Edwards Gr. 2-5

This is a fictionalized account supposedly told by a real member of the expedition.

We Were There with Lewis and Clark, by James Munves (We Were There) Gr. 3-8

*_My Travels with Capts. Lewis and Clark, by George Shannon_, by K. McMullan Gr. 4-10

Fictional diary of young expedition member.

*_Bold Journey_, by Charles Bohner Gr. 4-12

I've had wonderful families tell me this is a very good story.

*_Journal of Augustus Pelletier_, by Kathryn Lasky (My Name is America) Gr. 5-9

The tone of this series is not appreciated by many families. Happily, there are many books about Lewis & Clark so you have many other choices. I've not read this one.

Magnificent Adventure, by Emerson Hough Gr. 8-12

Supposedly based on fact, Aaron Burr tries to foil Lewis & Clark.

Film

*_Lewis & Clark_, produced by Ken Burns Unknown

3c Activities

*_Lewis and Clark Expedition Coloring Book_ (Dover) Various

*_Lewis and Clark for Kids_, by Janis Herbert Various

This book contains info on the expedition along with 21 hands-on activities.

3d Sacajawea (Sacagawea)

There are many more books on Sacajawea than I can list here, especially since I don't know which of the newer books are too politically correct. You're sure to find something on your library's shelves! Don't hesitate to consider the historical fiction recommendations below; these books have tried to follow history very closely.

**Picture Book of Sacagawea*, by David Adler — Gr. K-2

Sacajawea, by Virginia Voight (See and Read) — Gr. K-2

**Sacajawea: Her True Story*, by Joyce Milton (All Aboard 3) — Gr. 1-3

Value of Adventure: Sacajawea, by Ann Johnson (ValueTales) — Gr. 1-4

Sacajawea: Indian Guide, by Wyatt Blassingame (Garrard Am. Indian) — Gr. 1-5

**Sacagawea*, by Flora Seymour (Childhood) — Gr. 1-6

**Sacagawea*, by Liselotte Erdich — Gr. 2-6

Sacajawea: Guide to Lewis and Clark, by Jerry Seibert (Piper) — Gr. 2-8

**Land Beyond the Setting Sun*, by Tracy Leininger (Beautiful Girlhood) — Gr. 3-8
A biography about Sacajawea from a Christian author.

Lost Children of the Shoshones, by Evelyn Nevin — Gr. 3-9
Sacajawea's childhood abduction, which put her in the path of Lewis & Clark.

**Truth about Sacajawea*, by Kenneth Thomasma — Gr. 5-10

Winged Moccasins: The Story of Sacajawea, by Frances Farnsworth (Messner) — Gr. 5-12

Fiction/Historical Fiction

**Streams to the River, River to the Sea*, by Scott O'Dell — Gr. 5-12
Gripping novel based on Sacajawea's journey.

**Girl of the Shining Mountains*, by Peter & Connie Roop — Gr. 7-12
I've not read this new novel; Sacagawea looks back on the expedition five years later.

3e Seaman, dog on the Lewis & Clark Expedition

**Seaman's Journal*, by Patricia Eubank — Gr. 1-3

**Dog of Discovery*, by Laurence Pringle — Gr. 3-6

**Lewis and Clark and Me: A Dog's Tale*, by Laurie Myers — Gr. 3-7

Scannon: Dog with Lewis and Clark, by Adrien Stoutenberg & L.N. Baker — Gr. 3-8
Scholars previously thought Seaman's name was Scannon.

**Seaman: Dog Who Explored the West with Lewis & Clark*, by Gail Karwoski — Gr. 4-7

**Captain's Dog*, by Roland Smith — Gr. 5-8

3f Toussaint-L'Ouverture and the Haitian slave uprising (1802)

**Story of the World: Vol. 3*, by Susan Wise Bauer, Ch. 30 — Gr. 3-6
Some families enjoy this book's scope, so ask us to cite it; others seek different worldview; so, parental decision.

**Toussaint L'Ouverture*, by Laurence Santrey — Gr. 2-6

**Toussaint L'Overture*, by Walter Dean Myers — Gr. 3-6
I've not seen this book illustrated by a famous artist of the Harlem Renaissance.

Slave Who Freed Haiti, by Katharine Scherman (Landmark) — Gr. 4-10

Toussaint: Black Liberator, by Ronald Syme — Gr. 4-10

Black Patriot and Martyr by Ann Griffiths (Messner) — Gr. 7-12

Fiction/Historical Fiction

**Roving Commission*, by G.A. Henty — Gr. 7-12

3g Zebulon Pike

Zeb Pike, by Augusta Stevenson (Childhood) — Gr. 1-6

Zebulon Pike, by Faith Knoop (Real People) — Gr. 3-7
This antique is very rare.

Pike of Pike's Peak, by Nina Brown Baker — Gr. 3-8

**Zebulon Pike: Explorer of the Southwest*, by William Sanford & Carl Green Gr. 4-7

Zebulon Pike: Soldier and Explorer, by Barbara Witteman (Let Freedom Ring) Gr. 4-8

Zebulon Pike, by Bern Keating Gr. 4-12

Zebulon Pike: Soldier and Explorer, by Leonard Wibberley Gr. 7-12

Fiction/Historical Fiction

As the Crow Flies, by Cornelia Meigs Gr. 7-12

4 Barbary Pirates

Why, those perky Americans even went after (1801-1805) the Barbary pirates of the North African coast who were demanding bribes of anyone wanting to travel in their area of the Mediterranean! President Jefferson had to make the decision. You may have heard of Stephen Decatur; he was one of the heroes of this early American naval engagement. You certainly need not invest much time in this topic; you may have noticed I didn't even give much commentary on it. It is adventurous reading though.

**Story of the Great Republic*, by H.A. Guerber, Ch. XI-XII Gr. 3-7

**Basic History of the United States: Vol. 2*, by Clarence Carson, Ch. 10a Gr. 9-12

\--------

Stephen Decatur: Fighting Sailor, by Wyatt Blassingame (Garrard Discovery) Gr. 1-5

Stephen Decatur, by Bradford Smith (Childhood) Gr. 1-6

**Story of the Barbary Pirates*, by R. Conrad Stein (Cornerstones) Gr. 2-7

Story of Stephen Decatur, by Iris Vinton (Signature) Gr. 3-9

**American Adventures*, by Morrie Greenberg, Ch. 4 Gr. 3-10

**Barbary Pirates*, by C.S. Forester (Landmark) Gr. 3-12
This is now being reprinted, and Forester is a good author!

To the Shores of Tripoli, by Berta Briggs (Winston Adventure) Gr. 3-12
True story of teens' contribution to the Barbary War.

Commodore Bainbridge, by James Barnes — Gr. 5-12

This antique is too rare to be sought, but enjoy it if you have it!

Fiction/Historical Fiction

Plenty of Pirates, by Elisabeth Meg — Gr. 4-12

Fact-based, Barbary pirates force a boy to Constantinople.

Jack Darby, Able Seaman, by John Clagett — Gr. 5-10

Consul's Daughter, by Ann Schlee — Gr. 7-12

Fact-based, an American consul's daughter is caught in the Battle of Algiers.

When Guns Thundered at Tripoli, by Charles Finger — Gr. 8-12

Some lovely books are set during the early 1800s, but they don't fit into any one section, so I will mention them here. They are based on the girlhood of Laura Ingalls Wilder's grandmother, Charlotte, and I have been told they feature wonderful spiritual values. This **Charlotte Years* series is by Melissa Wiley. Some families have enjoyed going with Mrs. Wiley back another generation, to Charlotte's mother when a girl, Martha. These **Martha Years* books are set in Scotland in the late 1700s, but do mention America a bit. Enjoy!

And you'll laugh over the true story of a giant cheese sent to President Jefferson!

**Big Cheese for the White House*, by Candace Fleming — Gr. 1-4

5 Alexander Hamilton & Aaron Burr

In 1804, also during Thomas Jefferson's presidency, there was a famous duel between two national leaders. We covered Alexander Hamilton in the previous unit, so you have probably read about his significant effort to stabilize America's finances during the Early Republic era and I won't mention all the resources again here. Aaron Burr was eventually branded as a traitor. (This topic can be considered optional.)

**Story of the Great Republic*, by H.A. Guerber, Ch. XIIIb — Gr. 3-7

Alec Hamilton: The Little Lion, by H.B. Higgins (Childhood) Gr. 1-6
Covers Hamilton's childhood, which was *before* the Revolutionary War, so you may not want to go back that far in time at this point in our study of history.

**Duel! Burr and Hamilton's Deadly War of Words*, by Dennis Fradin Gr. 2-4
A new picture-book on the topic with powerful illustrations!

Alexander Hamilton and Aaron Burr, by Anna & Russel Crouse (Landmark) Gr. 3-12

Library *Wide World of Aaron Burr*, by Helen Orlob Gr. 5-12

Aaron Burr, by William Wise Gr. 7-12

Amazing Alexander Hamilton, by Arthur Orrmont (Messner) Gr. 7-12

**Aaron Burr and the Young Nation*, by Scott Ingram (Notorious Americans) Gr. 7-12

Soldier, Statesman, Defendant: Aaron Burr, by Jeannette Nolen (Messner) Gr. 7-12

Theodosia: Daughter of Aaron Burr, by Anne Colver Gr. 7-12

**Pistols and Politics: Alexander Hamilton's Great Duel*, by August Greeley Unknown

Fiction/Historical Fiction

River Pirates, by Manly Wade Wellman Gr. 5-12
Story is mostly about Mississippi adventure, but includes Burr's conspiracy.

Strange Island, by Marion Havighurst Gr. 5-12
Young girl is involved in Aaron Burr's conspiracy.

6 Napoleon

We've mentioned a man named Napoleon, but we've not really met him. We've seen a little naval tussle with the Barbary pirates, but there were much greater doings at sea...and they were courtesy of Napoleon! Yes, Napoleon and his mighty ambitions rolled over vast tracts of Europe. But don't forget, our eyes are not chiefly on famous people and events, but on the Lord and His truths at work in the nations. Do you remember that we're specifically exploring the long-term impact of the divergent paths of the Renaissance and Reformation? Yes, in the last *TruthQuest History* guide, we saw that Biblical Reformation ideals contributed largely to the American Revolution while humanistic Renaissance ideals contributed largely to the French Revolution (both of which occurred in the late 1700s).

We've just seen some early chapters of America's post-revolutionary history; now we'll view France's. It's not a pretty picture. Post-revolutionary France was in utter chaos; proud humanism had performed on the world stage... and flopped!

Why did the French Revolution flop? It's hard to recap briefly, but we can generally say that with only their Enlightenment *Big 2 Beliefs* (which did not include a respect for God as God, or the preciousness of God's creation of others), the French people had no solid base on which to engineer an appropriate overthrow of the king's tyrannical power. Nor (in large part due to the then-current church's lack of Biblical teaching) did they know God's guidelines for establishing good government once the king had been ousted. Thus, the French Revolution had been little more than a bloodbath. Such anarchy provided the perfect opportunity for someone like Napoleon—well, *exactly* like Napoleon—to be welcomed by order-hungry Frenchmen.

Anarchy
Tyranny

Napoleon's power grab doesn't surprise *TruthQuest History* veterans who've learned that continued bad government yields two eventual endings: 1) anarchy and then tyranny, or, 2) just immediate tyranny. As we've said, France's revolution was little more than anarchy, so tyranny could not be far behind! Few in late-1700s France would have guessed the tyrant would be a short little Corsican who was just a lowly officer in the French army and who also believed the Enlightenment's claims that *liberté*, *fraternité*, and *égalité* could be had without God. Yet, this little man would become one of the biggest characters in history—Napoleon Bonaparte!

There certainly was nothing "little" about his military genius, though. He won stupendous battles for France, and this military glory warmed French hearts and massaged the national ego. "Surely," the French people murmured, "this man can bring order to our chaos." But their feeling-based decisions, their ignorance of important Biblical truths, and their humanistic denial of Jeremiah 17:9 (which warns that the heart is deceitfully wicked, who can know it?) all led them to place Napoleon in power, much to his egotistical delight, *without* any pre-planned restraints on his authority, *without* any wise checks-and-balances, and *without* any limits. This was the absolute opposite of the Reformation focus, and it reminds me of the completely true saying: *power corrupts, and absolute power corrupts absolutely*. The French would live (and die) to see that axiom lived out in full color...the bright red color of blood!

Napoleon probably meant well at first; humanists usually do. Indeed, most European churches had long been "baptizing" Enlightenment thinking. Thus, many of Napoleon's early policies *seemed* helpful. But who could retain a humble servant-heart *with* an entire nation at his feet and *without* valid acknowledgment of a higher King, Lawmaker, and Judge? Is it any wonder

ThinkWrite 1: "Gimme the crown!"

As you sort through Napoleon's life, look for his *Big 2 Beliefs*. Remember, the last French king before their revolution said: *I am the state.* Was Napoleon's outlook any different? Why did he believe that he had the right to so much power, and to take so many lives?

Napoleon had the audacity to seize the crown from the pope's hands and instead coronate himself as emperor? (Do *ThinkWrite 1* while studying Napoleon.)

The time of Napoleon's rule is thus known as *The Empire*. So impactful were his years of reign and conquest (think of the Egyptian campaign) that you'll see completely new styles in clothing (ever heard of the Empire waistline?), art, and decoration! Painting Napoleon was a huge part of Jean Louis David's artistic career, for example, and Empress Josephine sponsored Redouté, the botanical painter of flowers. (Speaking of Napoleon's Egyptian campaign, though, don't forget it was Napoleon's longing to be like Alexander the Great that led him to the Land of the Nile. Interestingly, it was one of Napoleon's soldiers who found there the Rosetta Stone, the carved writing on which allowed Mr. Champollion to finally unlock the mystery of hieroglyphics!)

England was rightfully concerned! In just a few years, Napoleon had amassed one of the largest European empires ever to exist. He was even marching troops far, far, far away into the heart of Russia! That takes guts, but it turned out to be....well, I won't tell you directly, since it's one of the most dramatic stories in history! England quickly decided Napoleon had to be stopped, for they preferred to be the dominant power, or at least to have a balance of power. The battles between the two great nations and their allies are *still* legendary. Ever heard of the Battle of Trafalgar or Austerlitz or Waterloo, for example? You'll be fascinated with this meteoric story of maneuvering and strategy, as well as despair, courage, and victory!

But how did it all end for Napoleon? Glory or infamy? And why is a devastating personal humiliation still called one's *Waterloo*? What became of France? Do you think Napoleon would be surprised to discover how little his life *really* impacted history? Let's find out!

6a General overview

We'll list general biographical items here, as well as books on the breadth of his military campaigns. More topic-specific items, such as those regarding his Egyptian or European campaigns, will be listed further below. Please beware that because these are youth books, they will tend to accentuate the "positives," and make him out to be a dazzling and dashing military hero. It is hard for children not to form their first opinions of him under this emotion. So, please help your kids see past the surface "glory" (which was very temporary, especially compared to eternity!) to the reality of life under his rule, for those who survived it...

**Story of the World: Vol. 3*, by Susan Wise Bauer, Ch. 28, 33 — Gr. 3-6

Some families enjoy this book's scope, so ask us to cite it; others seek different worldview; so, parental decision.

**Island Story*, by H.E. Marshall, Ch. XCVII-XCIX — Gr. 3-8

Napoleon and the Battle of Waterloo, by Frances Winwar (Landmark) — Gr. 3-10

√ Library:
· Napoleon / Leslie McGuire
· Napoleon / Paul Johnson

***Stories of Napoleon Told to the Children*, by H.E. Marshall — Gr. 4-7
A vintage classic, now being reprinted.

Men of Power, by Albert Carr, Ch. 4 — Gr. 5-12

***Age of Napoleon*, by Harry Henderson (World History) — Gr. 7-12

Napoleon, by Manuel Komroff (Messner) — Gr. 7-12

True Story of Napoleon, by Anthony Corley — Gr. 7-12

Young Napoleon, by Leonard Cooper — Gr. 7-12

Military Life of Napoleon, by Trevor Dupuy — Gr. 8-12

***Napoleonic Wars*, by Thomas Streissguth — Gr. 9-12

Fiction/Historical Fiction

***Napoleon & Josephine: The Sword and the Hummingbird*, by G. Hausman — Gr. 7-12
I've not read this novel of Napoleon and his wife.

Sapphire Pendant, by Audrey Beyer — Gr. 7-12
This older novel is designed for girls.

6b Egyptian campaign and the Rosetta Stone

It was actually in 1799 that one of Napoleon's soldiers bumped into the Rosetta Stone. Because it contained writing in both ancient Greek and hieroglyphics, it gave scholars a chance to decode Egypt's old language. You may not need to take time to learn about the race to decode hieroglyphics, but it's an interesting story! I was able to see the actual Rosetta Stone at the British Museum in London. What a thrill!

Giraffe that Walked to Paris, by Nancy Milton — Gr. 1-6
This wonderful story actually takes place after Napoleon, but shows the relationship of France and Egypt precipitated by Napoleon.

King's Giraffe, by Mary Jo & Pete Collier — Gr. 2-7
Same as above book.

***Seeker of Knowledge: The Man Who Deciphered...*, by James Rumford — Gr. 2-7

library ✓ ***Riddle of the Rosetta Stone*, by James Cross Giblin — Gr. 5-12

**Mystery of the Hieroglyphs*, by Carol Donoughue Gr. 6-12

Man Who Could Read Stones, by Alan Honour Gr. 8-12

Fiction/Historical Fiction

**At Aboukir and Acre*, by G.A. Henty Gr. 7-12
Horatio Nelson's brave resistance to Napoleon's dreams for Egyptian conquest.

6c Napoleonic Wars: Horatio Nelson, Battle of Trafalgar, Peninsular War, etc.

Hero of Trafalgar, by A.B.C. Whipple (Landmark) Gr. 3-10

**British Redcoat of the Napoleonic Wars*, by Martin Windrow (Soldiers...) Gr. 4-10

**(Great Battles and Sieges:) Trafalgar*, by Richard Balkwill Gr. 5-10

Story of Britain, by R.J. Unstead, pp. 272-276 Gr. 5-12
Use especially if you've been following English history in this book throughout previous *TruthQuest History* guides.

Battle of Austerlitz, by Trevor Dupuy (Macmillan Battle Books) Gr. 7-12

Battle of Trafalgar, by Alan Villiers (Macmillan Battle Books) Gr. 7-12

Sabres of France, by James Finn Gr. 7-12
I believe this is gives a concise history of the Napoleonic Wars. It is a companion book to Sir Arthur Conan Doyle's *Glorious Hussar* (see below).

True Story of Lord Nelson, by Richard Houghton Gr. 7-12

Young Nelson, by Ronald Syme Gr. 7-12

Military Life of Napoleon, by Trevor Dupuy Gr. 8-12

**Napoleonic Wars*, by Thomas Streissguth Gr. 9-12

Fiction/Historical Fiction

Brave Soldier Janosh, by Victor Ambrus Gr. 1-3
A fun legend of Hungarian soldier who alone routs Napoleon.

Emperor and the Drummer Boy, by Ruth Robbins — Gr. 1-6

A fact-based story of a shipwrecked drummer boy who meets Napoleon.

First Adventure at Sea, by Ida Rifkin — Gr. 2-6

American ships get involved with French-English struggle at sea.

Castors Away! by Hester Burton — Gr. 5-12

A family finds a drowning soldier and gets involved in the French-English battles.

Dangerfoot, by Antony Brown — Gr. 5-12

A boy gets involved in the Napoleonic Wars and a fight for cannon.

**By Conduct and Courage*, by G.A. Henty — Gr. 7-12

Boy has adventures with Horatio Nelson.

**Complete Brigadier Gerard*, by Sir Arthur Conan Doyle — Gr. 7-12

Fact-based novel from famed author on General Gerard, one of Napoleon's top men. The various Brigadier Gerard stories can be found under many titles, including a one-time compilation entitled *Glorious Hussar.* I've not read any.

**Flying Ensign*, by Showell Styles — Gr. 7-12

Two books reprinted in one, young Englishman fights Napoleon's forces in Spain.

**Midshipman Quinn Collection*, by Showell Styles — Gr. 7-12

Quinn's various naval adventures bound in one thrilling volume!

**With Moore at Corunna*, **The Young Buglers*, and **Under Wellington's Command* — Gr. 7-12

all by G.A. Henty

These three books follow the adventures of a young man serving in the British army under the Duke of Wellington in what is known as the Peninsular War. Their mission was to help Spain and Portugal overthrow the rule of Napoleon's brother, who had been placed over them.

Captain of Foot, by Ronald Welch — Gr. 8-12

Another in a series following an English family through the centuries; this one finds the hero fighting with English troops against Napoleon in Spain.

Society of Foxes, by Patrick O'Connor/Leonard Wibberley — Gr. 9-12

I've heard this is a humorous story of spies during the Napoleonic era.

**Captain Hornblower* series, by C.S. Forester — Parental decision

This famed trilogy—comprised of **Beat to Quarters*, **Ship of the Line,* and **Flying Colours*—is set during the Napoleonic Wars. I do not know the moral content of these novels, but I see them recommended by reputable sources. Extracts, which may be more age appropriate, were published as: **Hornblower Takes Command* and **Hornblower in Captivity.*

6d Napoleon's invasion of Russia

Napoleon's invasion of Russia in 1812, the Russian response (I don't want to tell you about it here, it's just too moving), and the subsequent French retreat make one of the most heart-wrenching stories in military history! I'll just say this: nearly 500,000 French soldiers left for Moscow; only 20,000-40,000 returned. These events were the setting for Tolstoy's massive tome, War and Peace, *and Tchaikovsky's stunning musical celebration of the Russian role: "1812 Overture." Please, please listen to it, and have your students listen for the French national anthem inserted; it's the musical story of this extremely intense event!*

Retreat from Moscow, by E.M. Almedingen — Gr. 7-12

Fiction/Historical Fiction

Marvelous March of Jean François, by John Raymond — Gr. 2-6

Kindle **Through Russian Snows*, by G.A. Henty — Gr. 7-12

**War and Peace*, by Leo Tolstoy — Parental decision

This large novel is so time-consuming that few families would probably find it a beneficial assignment. I've not read it and am thus unaware of its age-appropriateness. There is a film version starring Henry Fonda and Audrey Hepburn.

6e Napoleon's last hurrah: the Hundred Days, Battle of Waterloo, and final exile

**(Great Battles and Sieges:) Waterloo*, by Philip Sauvain — Gr. 4-10

Story of Britain, by R.J. Unstead, pp. 277-280 — Gr. 5-12

**Battle of Waterloo*, by David Pietrusza (Battles of the Nineteenth Century) — Gr. 7-12

Napoleon's Hundred Days, by Patrick Pringle — Gr. 7-12

Battle of Waterloo, by Manuel Komroff (Macmillan Battle Books) — Gr. 8-12

Fiction/Historical Fiction

Betsy's Napoleon, by Jeannette Covert Nolan — Gr. 7-12

A girl meets Napoleon during his St. Helena exile.

Kindle – **One of the 28th*, by G.A. Henty — Gr. 7-12

A young soldier fights at Waterloo.

Violet for Bonaparte, by Geoffrey Trease — Gr. 7-12

**Les Misérables*, by Victor Hugo — Various

Powerful novel grippingly portrays the torturous life of common Frenchman during the Napoleonic cataclysm and aftermath. It comes in many versions (some abridged), and is available both on film and in audio. The *Focus on the Family Radio Theater* presentation is excellent!

**Count of Monte Cristo*, by Alexandre Dumas — Parental decision

Original novel has mature content; edited adaptations also exist. Exiled Napoleon plays a part in this classic story. It is available in various film versions and on audio.

6f Talleyrand

It is not necessary to study Talleyrand, but since his name will come up, I thought you'd want to know he was Napoleon's foreign minister and that he helped reestablish the Bourbon dynasty upon Napoleon's banishment.

Talleyrand, by Manuel Komroff (Messner) — Gr. 7-12

6g Napoleon's family...and horse!

Some of Napoleon's extended family members lived, at one point, in America!

Empress Josephine, by Marguerite Vance — Gr. 4-12

Life of Napoleon's wife by an esteemed author.

Horses of Destiny, by Fairfax Downey — Gr. 4-12

Learn about Napoleon's own horse!

More than a Queen: Josephine Bonaparte, by Frances Mossiker — Gr. 7-12

Bewitching Betsy Bonaparte, by Alice Curtis Desmond — Gr. 8-12

Life of an American woman who married Napoleon's brother.

Fiction/Historical Fiction

Scarlet Oak, by Cornelia Meigs — Gr. 5-12

A boy gets involved with Joseph Bonaparte on his estate in America.

6h Jean Louis David & Redouté

David, famed for his classical paintings of Napoleon, was fired by the same passions for regaining the glories of ancient Greece and Rome.[14] Most any art book will show some of David's works. Redouté had more scientific interests, especially botany.

Redouté: The Man Who Painted Flowers, by Carolyn Croll — Gr. 2-5

Child's History of Art, by Hillyer & Huey (*Painting* section, Ch. 22a) — Gr. 2-8
OR *Young People's Story of Fine Art: Last Two Hundred Years*, pp. 10-17
This chapter discusses Jean Louis David.

6i Activities

**Napoleon and Josephine Paper Dolls*, by Tom Tierney — Various
You may also like one just about clothes of the era: **Empire Costumes Paper Dolls.*

7 War of 1812

The European powers weren't ready to make room for America in the family of nations quite yet, though! The big boys on the block, France and Britain, had little respect for American naval rights...especially since they were at war with each other, as you've just discovered. Each country tried to keep America (and other nations) from trading with their enemies, and this was a major economic and political blow. America's grievances with the British were especially acute because they were stopping American ships and taking sailors right off the boats!

Furthermore, the British began supporting Tecumseh, a Shawnee chief, in his effort to unite several Indian tribes (some of them age-old enemies) in resisting American expansion. Yes, the British weren't above exploiting the frontier violence in their attempt to destabilize their former American colony. Since Canada was still a British colony, the Canadian governor naturally participated in these efforts,[15] and the stage was set for a great battle. William Henry Harrison, governor of the Indiana Territory, was sent to lead American forces against Tecumseh at the Battle of Tippecanoe (1811). Things were really heating up!

James Madison, who had long been enmeshed in these issues as Secretary of State to President Jefferson, was now president himself. He was not inclined to war, but finally

14 Gill Rowley (editor), *The Book of Music* (Englewood Cliffs, NJ: Prentice-Hall, 1978) 36.
15 Richard Morris, *Encyclopedia of American History* (New York: Harper & Brothers, 1953) 139.

decided America must act.[16] The War of 1812 officially began! Britain was now fighting both Napoleon and America! Mr. Carson makes some interesting comments thereupon:

> *The United States was not well prepared for war, nor was the war effort well coordinated. Congress was better at passing resolutions than raising revenue or armies. Except for Andrew Jackson, and perhaps one or two more, there were no bold and capable military commanders of high rank in the country. The navy was the most efficient and well commanded branch of the service, but it was small and hardly a match for the British fleet. The political leaders were hardly accustomed to mustering the goods and people for military purposes. Certainly, President Madison was more adept at the arts of restraining government than he was in mobilizing the country for* war.[17]

Interestingly, folks in different parts of the country had different views of and goals for the war. For example, Tecumseh's activities had many more westerners in favor of military retaliation, and many southerners hoped to gain Florida, especially since raiding Indians sought refuge in Spanish Florida.[18] (Andrew Jackson was militarily active during and after the war in the Floridas; his victory at the Battle of Horseshoe Bend in 1814 over the Creek Indians and a later treaty would lead to Florida becoming part of the United States shortly after war in 1819.) Then there were the easterners; though not great proponents of the war generally, they did want their ships and sailors safe from British seizure.[19]

British support for Tecumseh's moves against American settlers adds weight to the claim that Britain had hoped of regaining her former American colony, thus this war is sometimes called the "Second American Revolution." Since Canada was a British possession at the time, much of the American military—such as it was—was pointed in the Canadian direction. Was the acquisition of Canada an actual American goal? Mr. Carson says:

> *It should be kept in mind...that Canada was the only place where British forces could be attacked by land. Britain controlled the seas, and there was no other way to reach either her possessions or Britain. Undoubtedly, settlers in the West would have liked to have Britain entirely out of North America, but it does not follow that the purpose of the war was to acquire Canada.*[20]

Whatever your view, battles were fought on and around the Great Lakes between America and British Canada. In fact, the northern frontier was a key area in the war effort, but once Napoleon was (temporarily) beaten back in Europe, British troops were freed for an assault on America's eastern coast. It was then that the Battle of Fort McHenry found Francis Scott Key in the harbor writing a poem which became our national anthem, and Dolley Madison had to hurry precious items out of the White House before British torches could char them.

As if all that weren't interesting enough, the war's last conflict occurred *after* a peace treaty (the Treaty of Ghent) had already been signed...but word had not yet arrived! So Andrew Jackson, along with Pirate Lafitte, fought the Battle of New Orleans! Mr. Carson wryly comments:

---

16 Morris 140.
17 Carson 2:197.
18 Carson 2:192.
19 Morris 140.
20 Carson 2:196.

The greatest American victory of the war came two weeks after the signing of the treaty that was supposed to end the fighting, but it stood as a symbol for more than a century of the welcome an invading army might expect in America.[21]

Hmmm. Well, I dare not tell more. You'll want to find out yourself. Have at it!

7a General overview

**From Sea to Shining Sea for Children*, by Marshall & Manuel, Ch. 7-8 — Gr. 1-5

**Story of the World: Vol. 3*, by Susan Wise Bauer, Ch. 32b, 33b — Gr. 3-6
Some families enjoy this book's scope, so ask us to cite it; others seek different worldview; so, parental decision.

**Story of the Great Republic*, by H.A. Guerber, Ch. XIIIa, XIV-XVII — Gr. 3-7
Ch. XIIIa discusses trade conflicts occurring in Jefferson's term which would eventually lead to the War of 1812.

**This Country of Ours*, by H.E. Marshall, Ch. 69-70 — Gr. 3-8

**From Sea to Shining Sea*, by Marshall & Manuel, Ch. 6-7 — Gr. 6-12

**Basic History of the United States: Vol. 2*, by Clarence Carson, Ch. 10d — Gr. 9-12

**War of 1812*, by Andrew Santella (Cornerstones of Freedom II) — Gr. 3-7

**(First Book of the) War of 1812*, by Richard Morris (First Book) — Gr. 3-8
This was the original entry in the First Book series by this title.

**War of 1812*, by Carl Green — Gr. 4-7

1812: The War and the World, by Walter Buehr — Gr. 4-10
His books are usually quite interest.

**War of 1812*, by Kathlyn & Martin Gay (Voices from the Past) — Gr. 5-8

**War of 1812*, by Alden Carter (First Book) — Gr. 5-12

War of 1812, by Donald Lawson — Gr. 6-12

---

21 Carson 2:200.

**1812: The War Nobody Won*, by Albert Marrin — Gr. 7-12

Marrin is usually a very good choice; I've not read this, but would look for it first!

Story of the War of 1812, by Colonel Red Reeder — Gr. 7-12

Reeder attempts to give readable, narrative, flowing tale of the war.

Mr. Madison's War: 1812, by Noel Gerson (Messner/Milestones) — Gr. 8-12

Dawn's Early Light, by Walter Lord — Gr. 10-12

This book focuses on the last year of the war. Because of its length, it may be too in-depth for our purposes here. Content unknown; reputedly knowledgeable author.

Battles of the War of 1812* **and **Soldiers of the War of 1812* by Diane & Henry Smolinski — Unknown

7b President James Madison & Dolly Madison

You may have covered Madison in our last unit since he was involved in the Revolution and Constitution, so be selective about what you cover now. There are many book series on the US presidents; there is no need to mention each one here. As for Mrs. Madison, you will see variations in the spelling of her name, Dolly or Dolley. I couldn't begin to list all the books on this famous First Lady, either, but there is no need; you'll have no difficulty finding something to read.

Dolly Madison: Famous First Lady, by Mary Davidson (Garrard Discovery) — Gr. 1-5

**James Madison*, by Mike Venezia (Getting to Know the US Presidents) — Gr. 1-5

Dolly Madison, by Helen Monsell (Childhood) — Gr. 1-6

James Madison: Statesman and President, by Regina Kelly (Piper) — Gr. 2-8

**Dolley Madison*, by Jean Patrick (History Makers) — Gr. 3-6

Dolly Madison, by Jane Mayer (Landmark) — Gr. 3-8

**Unfading Beauty*, by Tracy Leininger (Beautiful Girlhood) — Gr. 3-8

A biography of Dolley Madison from a distinctly Christian series.

**Dolley Madison*, by Myra Weatherly — Gr. 6-12

James Madison, by Susan Clinton (Encyclopedia of the Presidents) — Gr. 6-12

Dolley Madison, by Jeannette Covert Nolan (Messner) — Gr. 7-12

Great Little Madison, by Jean Fritz — Gr. 7-12

Father of the Constitution: James Madison, by Katharine Wilkie *et al* (Messner) — Gr. 8-12

**Dolley Madison: Her Life, Letters, and Legacy*, by H. Shulman & D. Mattern — Unknown

**James Madison*, by Brendan January (Encyclopedia of the Presidents II) — Unknown

**James Madison*, by Andrew Santella (Profiles of the Presidents) — Unknown

**James Madison: Creating a Nation*, by Zachary Kent — Unknown

Activities

**What Was Cooking in Dolley Madison's White House?* by Tanya Larkin — Various

7c Tecumseh and William Henry Harrison

**Tecumseh: Shawnee War Chief*, by Jane Fleischer — Gr. 1-5

Tecumseh: Shawnee Warrior-Statesman, by James McCague (Garrard Am. Ind.) — Gr. 1-5

**William Henry Harrison*, by Mike Venezia (Getting to Know the US Presi...) — Gr. 1-5

Tecumseh, by Augusta Stevenson (Childhood) — Gr. 1-6

**William Henry Harrison*, by Howard Peckham (Childhood/Young Patriots) — Gr. 1-6

Story of Tecumseh: Shawnee Chief, by Zachary Kent (Cornerstones) — Gr. 2-6
This was in-print very recently and is in most public libraries.

**Tecumseh: Shawnee Leader*, by Susan Gregson (Let Freedom Ring) — Gr. 3-6

Indians Wars and Warriors—East, by Paul Wellman, Ch. 9 (North Star) — Gr. 3-10

Tippecanoe and Tyler Too, by Stanley Young (Landmark) — Gr. 3-12

Tecumseh: Shawnee Rebel, by Robert Cwiklik (N. Am. Indians of Achievement) — Gr. 5-10

**William Henry Harrison*, by Stephen Otfinoski (Encyclopedia of Presidents) — Gr. 5-12

Tecumseh: Destiny's Warrior, by David Cooke (Messner) — Gr. 7-12

**Tecumseh: Chief of the Shawnee*, by C. Ann Fitterer (Our People) Unknown
I've only read about this book, so can't give a precise grade recommendation.

**Tecumseh*, by Rachel Koestler-Grack Unknown

Fiction/Historical Fiction

Zachary, the Governor's Pig, by Bruce Grant Gr. 3-10
Story of a boy and his pig who are involved in the war.

**Millie Cooper's Ride: A True Story from History*, by Marc Simmons Middle Grades
Girl offers to ride for help through hostile territory when fellow Missourians are faced by Indians allied with British. It looks like this is for middle grades.

Red Pawns, by Leonard Wibberley Gr. 5-12
Fictional boy helps William Henry Harrison fight Tecumseh; this author is usually exciting!

**Loon Feather*, by Iola Fuller Gr. 10-12
Older girls may enjoy this novel of Tecumseh's daughter while she lived on Mackinac Island, Michigan.

7d Battles on the Great Lakes and Oliver Hazard Perry

Oliver Hazard Perry, by Laura Long (Childhood) Gr. 1-6

**Laura Secord's Brave Walk*, by Connie Brummel Cook Gr. 2-5
Fact-based, a woman in Canada overhears plans for an American attack and must get word to the Canadian army!

Captive Island, by August Derleth (Aladdin's American Heritage) Gr. 3-8

General Brock and Niagara Falls, by Samuel Adams (Landmark) Gr. 3-10

Battle of Lake Erie, by F. Van Wyck Mason (North Star Books) Gr. 4-12

**Capture of Detroit*, by Pierre Berton Gr. 4-12
Written from Canadian perspective; first in a series. Since America was aggressive about attacking Britain in Canada (it was a strong base of operations for them), the Canadians have a point!

Oliver Hazard Perry, by Alfred Fenton Gr. 5-12

**Defenders*, by Robert Livesay (Discovering Canada) Unknown
The online info on this book did not specify which aspect of the war it covers.

Fiction/Historical Fiction

Adventure at the Mill, by Barbara & Heather Bramwell (Buckskin) Gr. 2-8
Buckskin series brings Canadian history to life. Here, a Negro boy mysteriously appears at a southern Ontario farm while Father is off fighting in the War of 1812.

Scout Who Led an Army, by Lareine Ballantyne (Buckskin) Gr. 2-8
Buckskin series brings Canadian history to life. In this fact-based book, 19-year-old Billy Green's knowledge of the Ontario woods helps in an important battle in 1813.

**Once on This Island*, by Gloria Whelan Gr. 3-10
Exciting adventures and responsibilities of kids left on farm on Mackinac Island, Michigan while their father is away soldiering. We've had some wonderful vacations there, and I would think of this story! My youngest son would take his plastic sword up to the ruins of Fort Holmes...and I would again remember the real battles there!

Candle in the Night, by Elizabeth Howard (there are two authors by this name) Gr. 4-10
The British attack Detroit!

Great Rope, by Rosemary Nesbitt Gr. 4-10
I've not seen this story of an Oswego, New York boy's bravery during the war.

Guns Over Champlain, by Leon Dean Gr. 4-10
Boy gets involved in fighting on Lake Champlain.

Danger at Niagara, by Margaret Goff Clark Gr. 5-12
Boy must hurry with an important alert!

Ensign Ronan, by Leonard Burgoyne Gr. 5-12
Chicagoans will like this story; it tells of the role of Fort Dearborn during the war.

7e *Old Ironsides*

This storied ship gained much of its fame during the War of 1812.

Story of Old Ironsides, by Norman Richards (Cornerstones) Gr. 2-7

**Old Ironsides*, by David Weitzman Gr. 3-8
The drawings in this book are amazingly detailed. Very attractive!

Old Ironsides, by Harry Hansen (Landmark) Gr. 3-9

Eagle of the Sea, by Bruce Grant Gr. 3-12

Fiction/Historical Fiction

So Proudly She Sailed, by Olga Cabral Gr. 3-12

7f British attack on Washington, D.C. (August 1814)

**Story of the Burning of Washington, D.C.*, by R. Conrad Stein (Cornerstones) Gr. 1-5

Burning of Washington, by Mary Kay Phelan Gr. 8-1

Fiction/Historical Fiction

A Wish on Capitol Hill, by Esther Brady Gr. 3-10

**Washington City is Burning*, by Harriette Robinet Gr. 4-9
White House slave girl is involved with slaves using the war as a cover for escape.

7g Battle of Fort McHenry and Francis Scott Key's *Star-Spangled Banner*

**Francis Scott Key and the "Star Spangled Banner,"* by Lynea Bowdish Gr. K-3

**Star-Spangled Banner*, by Catherine Welch (On My Own) Gr. 1-3

**Flag Maker*, by Susan Bartoletti Gr. 1-4
Wonderful story of Mary Pickersgill, who with her daughter sewed flag seen by Mr. Key. Girls, especially, will enjoy this one.

Francis Scott Key: Poet and Patriot, by Lillie Patterson (Garrard Discovery) Gr. 1-5

Francis Scott Key, by Augusta Stevenson (Childhood) Gr. 1-6

**Star-Spangled Banner*, by Peter Spier Gr. 1-6
Don't miss this nicely illustrated version of the words of the anthem.

**By the Dawn's Early Light*, by Steven Kroll — Gr. 2-6

This newer book is beautifully illustrated.

**National Anthem*, by Patricia Quiri (True Book) — Gr. 2-6

**Our Flag was Still There*, by Tracy Leininger — Gr. 2-6

I've not actually seen this new book from a homeschool mother, but I've been told that her books are very good, and this appears to be for younger age group.

**Story of the Star-Spangled Banner*, by Natalie Miller (Cornerstones) — Gr. 2-6

**Francis Scott Key: Patriotic Poet*, by Susan Gregson (Let Freedom Ring) — Gr. 3-6

**Star-Spangled Banner*, by Deborah Kent (Cornerstones II) — Gr. 3-8

Flag for the Fort, by Carl Carmer — Gr. 4-8

Based on the life of the real girl who helped sew the flag watched by Key.

Broad Stripes and Bright Stars, by Marion Marsh Brown — Gr. 4-12

amazon – **Francis Scott Key*, by David Collins (Sower) — Gr. 4-12

This biography illuminates the Christian beliefs of Key.

library - several books on the topic

Fiction/Historical Fiction

Sunrise Over the Harbor, by Louise Mandrell & Ace Collins — Gr. 3-6

Star-Spangled Rooster, by Bruce Grant — Gr. 3-10

Funny story of a rooster at Fort McHenry.

Amazon – *Star-Spangled Banner*, by Neil & Anne Swanson — Gr. 5-12

"Thrilling story of boy who lived the words of our national anthem," the cover says.

7h General eastern seaboard/Atlantic naval action

Army of Two, by Polly Curren — Gr. 1-4

The Bates sisters help out!

**Cornstalks and Cannonballs*, by Barbara Mitchell — Gr. 1-4

Don't miss this book! A whole town fights the English navy.

*_American Army of Two_, by Janet Greeson — Gr. 1-5

Don't miss this! Another version of the *true* story of the two heroic Bates sisters!

*_Abigail's Drum_, by John Minahan — Gr. 2-5

Yet another story about two girls managing the lighthouse under British attack.

Army in Pigtails, by Harriet Evatt — Gr. 2-5

The Bates sisters help out in this adorable older book too. Rare, but good.

Fiction/Historical Fiction

American Twins of 1812, by Lucy Fitch Perkins — Gr. 1-6

Too rare to be actively sought (I'm not sure of its geographical setting).

Capture at Sea, by Audrey Beyer — Gr. 1-6

Two American boys are captured by the British navy.

Sea Lady, by J.F. Batchelor — Gr. 2-5

A Connecticut boy is fascinated with shipping during the War of 1812.

*_Battle for St. Michaels_, by Emily McCully — Gr. 3-5

Can a fast-running girl help her Maryland town defend itself against the British?

At the Sign of the Golden Anchor, by Ruth Langland Holberg — Gr. 4-10

New England children grow up during the war.

Black Falcon, by Armstrong Sperry — Gr. 4-12

Another exciting naval tale from this great author!

Boatswain's Boy, by Robert DuSoe — Gr. 4-12

Sailor boy is kidnapped and placed on British ship.

Secret on the Potomac, by Eleanor Nolen — Gr. 4-12

A boy and girl help out!

Cape May Packet, by Stephen Meader — Gr. 5-12

American father and son work as privateers. Meader's books are usually tops!

*_Clear(ed) for Action!_ by Stephen Meader — Gr. 5-12

Acclaimed author brings story of boy impressed into British navy. It was originally entitled *Clear for Action*. Bethlehem Books is reprinting four Meader books (including this one) in a combo entitled *Cleared for Action!*

Gold-Lined Box, by Marjory Hall — Gr. 5-12
War mars the life of a Maryland teen, but she attempts to save the life of her father.

Lanterns Aloft, by Mary Andrews — Gr. 5-12
A boy's adventure on the Maryland coast.

Storm Canvas, by Armstrong Sperry — Gr. 5-12
Boy is on a ship which dares to face a British blockade! Well-known author.

7i Southern action

We'll include the acquisition of Florida, which occurred just after the War of 1812. The Seminole War will be covered later.

**Basic History of the United States: Vol. 2*, by Clarence Carson, Ch. 10e — Gr. 9-12

Fiction/Historical Fiction

Long Hunt, by Charlie May Simon — Gr. 5-12
Very good! Boy searches for father who is away fighting Seminoles and British.

7j Battle of New Orleans, Andrew Jackson, and Pirate Lafitte

A treaty conference in Ghent, Belgium agreed to end the war, but news did not arrive in time to prevent the Battle of New Orleans, which saw the heroics of Andrew Jackson and Pirate Jean Lafitte. Books about Andrew Jackson will tell of his role in the Battle of New Orleans, but they will be listed later, when Jackson is studied separately.

Flag for Lafitte, by Frederick Lane (Aladdin's American Heritage) — Gr. 3-8
This is a terrific series from yesteryear!

Pirate Lafitte and the Battle of New Orleans, by Robert Tallant (Landmark) — Gr. 3-9
The Landmarks are also terrific, usually! Many families try to collect them.

**New Orleans*, by King David (Battlefields Across America) — Gr. 5-10

Battles for New Orleans, by F. VanWyck Mason (NorthStar) — Gr. 5-12

Battle of New Orleans, by Donald Chidsey — Gr. 8-12
More in-depth than is necessary for most students.

**New Orleans*, by King David — Unknown

Fiction/Historical Fiction

Lafitte the Pirate, by Ariane Dewey — Gr. 1-4
Funny tall tales about Jean Lafitte.

Open Gate, by Wilma Pitchford Hays — Gr. 2-6
Boy and girl of New Orleans live through the battles there.

Little Maid of New Orleans, by Alice Turner Curtis — Gr. 3-8
Classic older fiction.

We Were There with Jean Lafitte, by Iris Vinton (We Were There) — Gr. 3-8

A Spy in Old New Orleans, by Anne Emery — Gr. 3-12

**Twins, the Pirates and the Battle of New Orleans*, by Harriette Robinet — Gr. 4-7
Brothers, just rescued from slavery by their father, find themselves in the middle of the Battle of New Orleans. I've not seen this, but it sounds interesting!

**If Pigs Could Fly*, by John Lawson — Gr. 5-8
I've only read about this online, but it is supposedly a fun tall-tale that culminates at the Battle of New Orleans. I cannot speak to its content, but it might be worth checking.

8 Science and Industry

With a victory over mighty Britain in the War of 1812, America was about to burst its buttons with pride. The *Second American Revolution* was over, and America was still standing strong. Many people owned their own land (a tremendously important right) and could pursue their own labors and crafts. This made for a strong middle class, which is crucial to any nation's health. Thus began an even greater period of peace, prosperity, and pride that has been called the *Era of Good Feelings*...but feelings were about to get *gooder!*

Why? Before I answer, let me ask you to settle into your chair, because you've got to first dig into your memory for two important truths. (They *are* in your memory, right?) The first one we discussed at the beginning of this guide. We said America's constitution protected freedom and free enterprise. These *vital* principles allowed individuals to pursue their personal dreams with creativity, confidence, *and* with

> ### *ThinkWrite 2: "Free?"*
>
> Find a good definition of free enterprise, but then go beyond to give a quick explanation for the basis of that freedom as we've discussed. Can you see how it contributes to scientific and industrial creativity?

capital (land, tools, or extra money which can be used to produce income). Hard work and ingenuity *would* pay off. Mr. Carson reveals the forgotten fact that this freeing focus on the individual was partly based on Christianity! Since individual freedom requires individual responsibility, though, each person *must* find the right basis for their beliefs and decisions. Americans even had to decide their beliefs about free enterprise, which some families may want to study at this time also. (Begin *ThinkWrite 2* now.)

You've got to remember something else, from further back, which brings Europe back into the picture. Do you recall the bubbling surges of creativity and discovery wrought by the Reformation's rediscovery of the Bible's insights and freedoms? Now, also recall the Renaissance's self-confidence and intellectualism. These powerful forces upwelled into the Scientific Revolution, remember? Well, it began to bear fruit in the early 1800s!

That means it's *fork time!* Whenever you have a bunch of brand new scientific discoveries, you've got decisions to make too! How should these new discoveries be used? That answer depended entirely on the *Big 2 Beliefs* of those harnessing the discoveries. Would the Creator remain supreme, or would mankind's discoveries "prove" man's "right" to supremacy (*Big Belief #1*)? Would these powers be used to benefit mankind, or abuse, exploit, and dehumanize him (*Big Belief #2*)? It's ironic—and sad—that our modern society portrays God as the enemy of science and deems itself a scientific god, when in fact mankind only discovers what God invented! Science reveals *His* intelligence, power, creativity, and intricacy, and only when His truths are obeyed can the power of science be wisely harnessed...for there *was* great power in these new discoveries. Now scientists and inventors had more impact on the world than conquerors and kings! *That's* quite a switch from earlier history. Think about it!

Well, the treasure trove of scientific truths unearthed during the *Scientific Revolution* began to be applied to real-life needs. This spawned the *Industrial Revolution!* (Is it any wonder we call this unit the *Age of Revolution?* We've discussed four revolutions already!) Yes, the *Machine Age*, as it's sometimes called, had begun. It started in Britain in the later 1700s, as we mentioned in the last *TruthQuest History* unit, but I promised we'd study it now, when its incredible impact on Europe and America could more fully be seen.

We will thoroughly examine the Industrial Revolution, but I'd like you to also see the chain of discoveries which led to it. Please, too, take special note of the personal qualities of perseverance and industriousness which characterized these great achievers. Naturally, no one can study all these great men and women, but you can select a few. (Do note that all American children should be familiar with Eli Whitney, and most everyone should know of James Watt.) Here's my Hall of Fame, and so many more could be added!

Scientists/Mathematicians:

Lord Rutherford (physics)
Joseph Priestly (chemistry)
Luigi (Aloisio) Galvani (electricity)
Humphry Davy (chemistry)
William & Caroline Herschel (astronomy)
Alessandro Volta (electricity)
John Dalton (chemistry)
Carl Gauss (math/astronomy)
Jöns Berzelius (chemistry)
Hans Oersted (electromagnetism)
André Ampère (electricity)
Michael Faraday (chemistry/electromagnetism)
George Ohm (electricity)
Friedrich Wöhler (organic chemistry)
Justus von Liebig (chemistry)

Inventors/Engineers:

Richard Trevithick (steam engine)
James Watt (steam engine)
Eli Whitney (lots!)
Montgolfier brothers (hot air balloon)
Robert Fulton (submarine/steamboat)
Henry Shrapnel (ammunition)
Samuel Slater (rebuilt textile machine)
George Stephenson (locomotive)
Augustin Fresnel (lighthouse lamp)
John Macadam (hardtop roads)
R.T. Laënnec (stethoscope)
Charles Babbage (early computer)
Ada Byron Lovelace (early computer)
Samuel Colt (revolver)
Samuel Morse (telegraph)
Elias Howe (sewing machine)
John Deere (plow)
Cyrus McCormick (mechanical reaper)
James Hargreaves (spinning jenny)
Charles Goodyear (vulcanized rubber)
L.J.M. Daguerre (photography)

Ah, so many choices, so little time. Before you begin, though, *please* let me mention here what we're *not* going to study right now: we won't cover the social aspects of the Industrial Revolution yet. Why do I mention this? Because most books about the Industrial Revolution also discuss the problems associated with it, such as child labor, poor working conditions, etc. As a Christian, though, I disagree with the usual secular view of these problems, their real causes, and their solutions. We'll discuss all that in upcoming sections, so if you find a book about the Industrial Revolution—maybe even one of these cited here—which covers more than just the lives of the key scientists and inventors, please defer reading those sections until we've had a chance to pursue a Biblical view of these issues. Right now, our focus is solely on the science and invention. Let's dig in!

8a General overview

These resources offer a glimpse of multiple scientists/inventors or follow the general history of scientific discovery. Resources on individual scientists/inventors will be cited alphabetically below. Don't hesitate to independently seek information on particular fields of interest, such as computers, photography, or aviation.

**Child's History of the World*, by V.M. Hillyer, Ch. 77 Gr. 1-4

We cite the 1924 original throughout *TruthQuest History*. This chapter (Ch. 77) is also cited in the next *TruthQuest History* guide, since its time-range overlaps. If your version differs, www.TruthQuestHistory.com/spine may help in cross-referencing.

**Story of the World: Vol. 3*, by Susan Wise Bauer, Ch. 27 — Gr. 3-6

Some families enjoy this book's scope, so ask us to cite it; others seek different worldview; so, parental decision.

**Story of the Great Republic*, by H.A. Guerber, Ch. XIIIc — Gr. 3-7

**Island Story*, by H.E. Marshall, Ch. XCVI — Gr. 3-8

**Basic History of the United States: Vol. 2*, by Clarence Carson, Ch. 9e — Gr. 9-12

This section discusses the politics of the *Era of Good Feelings* and the emphasis on limited government; in that regard, the section fits our topic here. It also alludes to events, such as the Missouri Compromise, which we'll discuss later.

**How Should We Then Live?* by Francis Schaeffer, Ch.7 and pp. 113-119 — Gr. 9-12

This resource is always *terribly* important! Please note that Video Episode #6 is the same as Ch. 7 of the book, so either will serve.

\--------

**Great Bridge-Building Contest*, by Bo Zaunders — Gr. 1-4

Lemuel Chenoweth didn't build his bridge until 1850, but *he was self-taught*, and thus captures the spirit of discovery we are discussing now! Besides, there isn't a better place to list the book later, and I wouldn't want you to miss it. Amazing, and well-told!

Picture History of Great Inventors, by Gillian Clement — Gr. 2-7

**Champions of Invention;* **Champions of Mathematics;* <u>and</u> **Champions of Invention* by John Hudson Tiner — Gr. 3-7

**Early American Industrial Revolution*, by Katie Bagley (Let Freedom Ring) — Gr. 3-8

This covers only the American phase. It may deal with child labor, labor unions, and other issues which we'll discuss later. Right now our focus is on the people of science and invention, not the Industrial Revolution as a social movement, so I'm not sure which, if any, sections are pertinent here, since I've not seen the book.

**Mathematicians are People Too: Vol. 1 and 2*, by L. & W. Reimer — Gr. 3-10

The short chapters in these books are really fascinating.

Famous Mathematicians, by Frances Stonaker — Gr. 3-10

**Industrial Revolution*, by Mary Collins (Cornerstones) — Gr. 4-8

This seems to be in the new Cornerstones II series which is for older students. It may deal with child labor, labor unions, and other issues which we'll discuss later. Right now our focus is on the people of science and invention, not the Industrial Revolution as a social movement, so I'm not sure which, if any, sections are pertinent here, since I've not seen the book.

*_History Makers of the Scientific Revolution_, by Nina Morgan (History Makers) Gr. 4-9

*_Mystery of the Periodic Table_, by Benjamin Wiker Gr. 4-9

Someone is reprinting this, so it must have an engaging, narrative style! It contains chapters on Priestly, Lavoisier, etc.

Bright Design, by Katherine B. Shippen Gr. 5-12

This book is truly fascinating. In quite interesting narrative, it relates the gradual discoveries made in the fields of electricity, atomic theory, and general physics...and how these discoveries built upon each other. It includes chapters on many of the people listed above, such as John Dalton, about whom little else has been written for youth.

*_Invention_, by Lionel Bender (Eyewitness) Gr. 5-12

This coffeetable-type book doesn't offer narrative history (which is usually necessary for deeper learning) but instead features fascinating photos of objects related to invention.

amazon *_Men of Science, Men of God_, by Henry Morris Gr. 5-12

Most of the biographical sketches in this book are too short to serve as research, but make for inspiring browsing since the long-overlooked role of Christian scientists is brought to light.

amazon *_Smithsonian Visual Timeline of Inventions_, by Richard Platt Gr. 5-12

Intriguing! The graphic layout quickly shows the timing of various inventions.

Story of Britain, by R.J. Unstead, pp. 268-271 Gr. 5-12

Famous Scientists, by William Stevens Gr. 6-12

Story Behind Great Inventions, by Elizabeth Montgomery Gr. 6-12

*_Story of Inventions_, by Michael McHugh & Frank Bachman Gr. 6-12

This is one of the Christian Liberty books.

*_21 Great Scientists Who Believed the Bible_, by Ann Lamont Gr. 7-12

Another book which provides spiritual background on various scientists.

Romance of Physics, by Keith Irwin Gr. 7-12
Romance of Chemistry, by Keith Irwin Gr. 7-12

Both of these books are intriguing narratives (my son couldn't stop reading!) about the drama and interconnectedness of unfolding discovery.

Scientists Behind the Inventors, by Roger Burlingame Gr. 7-12
Inventors Behind the Inventors, by Roger Burlingame Gr. 7-12

These connect pure science with process of invention. They may help practical, mechanical, applied-science students appreciate the contribution of pure sciences.

Twelve Pioneers of Science, by Harry Sootin Gr. 7-12

From Spinning Wheel to Spacecraft, by Harry Neal (Messner/Milestones) Gr. 9-12

Mechanical Age: Industrial Revolution in England, by Celia Bland (World Hist) Gr. 9-12

Covers the scientific/engineering aspects, as well as the social and religious; I've not seen it and not aware of its viewpoint on these important matters. Right now our focus is on the people of science and invention, not the Industrial Revolution as a social movement, so I'm not sure which, if any, sections are pertinent here.

**Industrial Revolution*, by Sara Wooten (People at the Center of...) Unknown

I've not seen this. Apparently, it deals with labor union issues that we'll discuss later. Right now our focus is on the people of science and invention, not the Industrial Revolution as a social movement, so I'm not sure which, if any, sections are pertinent here.

**Industrial Revolution Almanac*, by James & Elizabeth Outman Unknown

I've not seen this. Apparently, it deals with labor union issues that we'll discuss later. Right now our focus is on the people of science and invention, not the Industrial Revolution as a social movement, so I'm not sure which, if any, sections are pertinent here.

8b Nathaniel Bowditch

**Carry On, Mr. Bowditch*, by Jean Lee Latham Gr. 4-12

Fascinating account of an amazing navigator, mathematician, and astronomer. His works are still in use today! This has long been a *favorite* book. My husband was very moved by it when reading to my kids, and he says "don't miss it!"

8c Samuel Colt

Colt is famous for his revolver which revolutionized the making of guns...and so much more!

Teenagers Who Made History, by Russell Freedman, Ch. 3 Gr. 4-12

Samuel Colt and His Gun, by Gertrude Winders Gr. 5-12

You may also find it as *Sam Colt and His Gun*.

8d Humphry Davy

Humphry Davy and Chemical Discovery, by Elba Carrier (Immortals of Science) Gr. 7-12

8e John Deere

You are probably familiar with John Deere's name, but do you know his story? If you could "see" how hard it was to break up the ground before Deere, you'd better appreciate his contribution to the millions of farmers!

**John Deere*, by Margaret Hall (Lives and Times) Gr. 1-3

John Deere, by Margaret Bare (Childhood) Gr. 1-6

**Pioneer Plowmaker: A Story about John Deere*, by David Collins (Carolrhoda) Gr. 2-7

8f Michael Faraday

Faraday was an especially important contributor and a strong Christian!

**Michael Faraday*, by Anita Ganeri (What Would You Ask...) Unknown
I've listed this book first because I get the impression it's for younger readers.

Michael Faraday: Apprentice to Science, by Sam & Beryl Epstein Gr. 2-7

Coils, Magnets and Rings: Michael Faraday's World, by Nancy Veglahn Gr. 3-8

**Michael Faraday*, by Stewart Ross (Scientists Who Made History) Gr. 4-6
The publisher claims this is for Grades 4-6.

**Michael Faraday*, by Ann Fullick (Groundbreakers) Gr. 5-7
The publisher claims this is for Grades 5-7.

Michael Faraday, by Harry Sootin (Messner) Gr. 6-12

Michael Faraday and the Electric Dynamo, by C. May (Immortals of Science) Gr. 7-12

**Michael Faraday: Creative Genius*, by Martin Gutnik Gr. 7-12
The text looks somewhat dry, and this secular book may not cover his strong faith.

Quest of Michael Faraday, by Tad Harvey Gr. 7-12

Young Faraday, by Patrick Pringle Gr. 7-12

Amazon **Michael Faraday: Father of Electronics*, by Charles Ludwig Gr. 8-12
Ludwig has included Faraday's strong Christian beliefs.

8g Robert Fulton

How amazing it this guy?! He wasn't just a famous inventor, but was also a fine artist! Napoleon asked him to build a submarine, and he worked on early torpedoes for the British Navy.

**Story of the Great Republic*, by H.A. Guerber, Ch. XIIIc Gr. 3-7
Was also cited in our General Overview above, but it mostly relates to Fulton.

**Robert Fulton*, by Jennifer Gillis (Lives and Times) Gr. 1-3

Robert Fulton, by Ruby Radford (See and Read) Gr. 1-3

Robert Fulton, by Joanne Henry (Garrard Discovery) Gr. 1-5

Robert Fulton, by Marguerite Henry (Childhood) Gr. 1-6

**Head Full of Notions*, by Andy Bowen (Carolrhoda Creative Minds) Gr. 2-7

Watt Got You Started, Mr. Fulton? by Robert Quackenbush Gr. 2-7
Fun dual story of both Watt and Robert Fulton. I bet most libraries have it still!

Child's History of Art, by Hillyer & Huey (*Painting* section, Ch. 29a) Gr. 2-8
OR *Young People's Story of Fine Art: Last Two Hundred Years*, p. 77
Yes, Fulton also produced artwork, and it is covered in this lovely old book.

**Robert Fulton: From Submarine to Steamboat*, by Steven Kroll Gr. 3-6

Boat Builder, by Clara Ingram Judson Gr. 3-8

Robert Fulton and the Steamboat, by Ralph Hill (Landmark) Gr. 3-8

Robert Fulton, by Elaine Landau (First Books) Gr. 4-7

First Steamboat on the Mississippi, by Sterling North (NorthStar) Gr. 5-12
May be about the role of Nicholas Roosevelt, but we'll tuck it here with Fulton.

**Robert Fulton*, by Lola Schaefer — Unknown

**Robert Fulton: The Steamboat Man*, by Carin Ford (Famous Inventors) — Unknown

Library: Robert Fulton: from submarine to steamboat by Steven Kroll

8h Carl Friedrich Gauss

Carl Friedrich Gauss: Prince of Mathematicians, by W. Schaaf (Immortals....) — Gr. 8-12

8i William & Caroline Herschel

This brother-sister duo discovered Uranus, binary stars, and infrared solar rays.

King's Astronomer, by Deborah Crawford — Gr. 5-12

Amazon *Sweeper of the Skies*, by Frances Higgins — Gr. 6-12

Shows the contribution of William's sister, an astronomer in her own right.

8j Elias Howe

Elias Howe, by Jean Corcoran (Childhood) — Gr. 1-6

8k R.T. Laënnec

Amazing Stethoscope, by Geoffrey Marks — Gr. 3-12

Above All a Physician, by Jeanne Carbonnier — Gr. 9-12

8l Justus Liebig

Liebeg: Master Chemist, by Louis Kuslan — Gr. 7-12

8m Ada Byron Lovelace

Ada was not only a contributor to the later development of the computer, but was the daughter of the famous poet, Lord Byron.

Ada Byron Lovelace: The Lady and the Computer, by Mary Dodson Wade — Gr. 5-12

8n Cyrus McCormick

McCormick's machine hugely increased the effectiveness of agriculture!

Cyrus McCormick, by Lavinia Dobler (Childhood) — Gr. 1-6

Wheat Won't Wait, by Adele Nathan (Aladdin's American Heritage) — Gr. 3-8

**Cyrus McCormick and the Mechanical Reaper*, by Lisa Aldrich — Gr. 5-12

Reaper Man, by Clara Ingram Judson — Gr. 6-12

Amazon *More than Conquerors*, edited by John Woodbridge, pp. 328-331 — Gr. 7-12

This is a compendium of short biographies of Christian heroes.

8o Samuel F.B. Morse

You already know about Morse and his telegraph, and thus Morse Code—all of it amazing. But did you know Morse was also a famous painter too? You will probably recognize his best-known painting!

**Story of the Great Republic*, by H.A. Guerber, Ch. XXV — Gr. 3-7

Only the latter half of the chapter covers Morse; the first half discusses topics we'll hit in greater depth elsewhere in this guide.

**Samuel Morse*, by Margaret Hall (Lives and Times) — Gr. 1-3

Samuel F.B. Morse: Artist-Inventor, by Jean Lee Latham (Garrard Discovery) — Gr. 1-5

Samuel Morse, by Dorothea Snow (Childhood) — Gr. 1-6

Quick, Annie, Give Me a Catchy Line! by Robert Quackenbush — Gr. 2-7

Mr. Quackenbush's stories usually have some humor injected!

Child's History of Art, by Hillyer & Huey (*Painting* section, Ch. 29a) — Gr. 2-8

OR *Young People's Story of Fine Art: Last Two Hundred Years*, p. 77

Yes, Morse was also esteemed painter; his artwork is covered in this lovely old book.

Singing Wire, by Mark Miller (Winston Adventure) Gr. 3-9

True story (with amazing contributions from young people) jumps ahead in time to tell of the first trans-continental telegraph.

Samuel Morse, by Mona Kerby (First Book) Gr. 4-7

Medals for Morse: Artist and Inventor, by Jean Lee Latham (Alad. Am. Heritage) Gr. 4-12

Samuel Morse and the Telegraph, by Wilma Pitchford Hays Gr. 4-12

Amazon **Samuel F.B. Morse*, by John Tiner (Sower) Gr. 5-12

The biographies in this series always include the subject's Christian walk.

**Samuel F.B. Morse: Inventor and Code Creator*, by Judy Alter Unknown

Library - Inventors and Their Discoveries by Richard Hozar

8p Joseph Priestly

Joseph Priestly: Pioneer Chemist, by Rebecca Marcus (Immortals of Science) Gr. 7-12

8q Samuel Slater

Slater is another important figure for Americans since he brought the new English discoveries to the U.S.

Samuel Slater's Mill, by Christopher Simonds (Turning Points) Gr. 4-10

Samuel Slater's Mill and the Industrial Revolution, by Christopher Simonds Gr. 5-10

Slater's Mill, by F.N. Monjo Gr. 5-12

Industrial Genius: Samuel Slater, by Lewis Miner (Messner) Gr. 8-12

Fiction/Historical Fiction

Nicholas Arnold, Toolmaker, by Marion Lansing Gr. 4-12

Fictional apprentice works for Eli Whitney and Samuel Slater.

8r George Stephenson

Stephenson's locomotives had a big impact on industrial development in England, as well as on transportation!

Railway Engineer: George Stephenson, by Clara Ingram Judson — Gr. 4-12

8s Richard Trevithick

I'm surprised more has not been written about the great contribution of Mr Trevithick's steam engine.

Year of the Horseless Carriage: 1801, by Genevieve Foster — Gr. 4-9

8t Alessandro Volta

Alessandro Volta and the Electric Battery, by Bern Dibner (Immortals of Science) — Gr. 7-12

8u James Watt

Mr. Watt is another especially important contributor. Students should be familiar with him!

Library – *Watt Got You Started, Mr. Fulton?* by Robert Quackenbush — Gr. 2-7

Fun dual story of both Watt and Robert Fulton. I bet most libraries have it still!

**James Watt*, by Neil Champion (Groundbreakers) — Gr. 5-7

**James Watt: Master of the Steam Engine*, by Anna Sproule (Giants of Science) — Gr. 5-12

James Watt: Inventor of a Steam Engine, by Robert Webb (Immortals of...) — Gr. 7-12

(James Watt:) The Man Who Transformed the World, by William Crane (Messner) — Gr. 7-12

Kindle- James Watt by Andrew Carnegie

8v Eli Whitney

Like Mr. Slater, Mr. Whitney played a crucial role in the Industrial Revolution in America.

**Eli Whitney*, by Margaret Hall (Lives and Times) — Gr. 1-3

**Eli Whitney*, by Ann Gaines (Discover the Life of an Inventor) — Gr. 1-4

Eli Whitney: Great Inventor, by Jean Lee Latham (Garrard Discovery) Gr. 1-5

I read this aloud to my daughter.....and ached for all books to be this wholesome and inspiring for children.... Really fine!

Eli Whitney, by Dorothea Snow (Childhood) Gr. 1-6

**Maker of Machines: A Story about Eli Whitney*, by Barbara Mitchell (Creative...) Gr. 2-7

Eli Whitney: Master Craftsman, by Miriam Gilbert (Makers of America) Gr. 3-7

**Eli Whitney: American Inventor*, by Katie Bagley (Let Freedom Ring) Gr. 3-8

Eli Whitney and the Machine Age, by Wilma Pitchford Hays Gr. 3-8

Story of Eli Whitney, by Jean Lee Latham (Aladdin's American Heritage) Gr. 3-8

This must be wonderful, because it is a usually-great series, and Latham's other book on Whitney, which I discussed above was outstandingly wholesome and inspiring.

Eli Whitney, by Judy Alter (First Book) Gr. 4-7

Eli Whitney: Founder of Modern Industry, by Wilma P. Hays (Immortals of Eng.) Gr. 8-12

Fiction/Historical Fiction

Amazon - *Nicholas Arnold, Toolmaker*, by Marion Lansing Gr. 4-12

Fictional apprentice works for Eli Whitney and Samuel Slater.

Library - Several, including Eli Whitney by Catherine A. Welch

8w Miscellaneous

**First Air Voyage in the United States*, by Alexandra Wallner Gr. 1-4

George Washington and the First Balloon Flight, by Edmund Lindop Gr. 2-5

Also cited in the last guide, but relates to our topic here, and was very close to 1800.

8x Free Enterprise

Wow! Such an important topic to be tucked in this odd spot! Most families have already studied this or will study it in a separate economics unit. Nevertheless, it is too important to overlook, so I will cite a few resources here. Keep in mind that one of the most important books on the topic, The Wealth of Nations, *was written by Adam Smith of Scotland in 1776, just prior to the time period we're studying now. Thus, it was just at this time that Smith's ideas were really having impact!*

Biblical Economics in Comics, by Vic Lockman Gr. 6-12

***Whatever Happened to Penny Candy*, by Richard Maybury Gr. 7-12

***Economics in One Lesson*, by Henry Hazlitt Gr. 9-12

***Wealth of Nations*, by Adam Smith Gr. 11-12
Few students have time to tackle this *important* book, but some may want to browse!

***Age of Uncertainty*, Ch. 1, by John Kenneth Galbraith Parental decision
I hesitate to mention this book due to the author's worldview. Yet, a discerning student may be able to glean the beneficial information. It is certainly written with great wit!

9 Industrial Revolution

Yes, the Industrial Revolution is rightfully titled. It *did* turn life upside down, both in Europe and in America. Its unparalleled productivity and efficiency allowed the poor to purchase necessities only dreamed of by their ancestors! Railways and canals linked farms with cities, boosting trade and communication! The cities were growing at a frenzied pace, since countryfolk were pouring in to work for cash in the new factories. (This urban growth was more rapid in Europe, where there was less economic freedom, and thus less prosperity. American men resisted working in factories, so U.S. workers were usually single women, poor children, and, later, immigrants.) Whole new communities, such as Lowell, Massachusetts, were built as factory towns.

Are you grasping what a big deal this was? Society (American and European) was moving from being only rural and agrarian (agricultural) to being industrial and urban! For example, New York City's population grew from 60,000 in 1800 to almost 1,000,000 by 1860.[22] **As cities swelled, more political power shifted there since representative government is based on population. Spiritual, cultural, and relational roots weakened when people left their family farms, rural communities, local stores, small-scale workshops, and familiar little churches. It was easy for inappropriate ideas of *progress* to puff up the industrial leaders. Here are some comments made by two men who saw the changes come to America:**

> *We are no longer to remain plain and simple republics of farmers.*[23]

> *There are certain causes which have acted with peculiar energy in our generation, and which have improved the condition of the mass of society with a degree of rapidity heretofore altogether unknown....Who is so familiarized to the sight even now, as to look without wonder and amazement on a long train of cars, full of passengers and merchandise, drawn along our valleys, and the sides of our mountains themselves with a rapidity that holds competition [with] the winds? (Daniel Webster)*[24]

22 Douglas T. Miller, *Then was the Future* (New York: Knopf, 1973) x.
23 Miller 1.
24 Miller 2-3.

Imagine, if you'd previously done everything by hand, as had been done for millennia, how much you'd be amazed and energized by all these powerful tools and the prosperity they generated! Americans, especially, were busy dreaming, risking, inventing, pioneering, and achieving, for their efforts would pay off, thanks to free enterprise. What a new thing this was! For previous centuries, people had been locked into a rigid class structure, where greater work usually only yielded benefit only to one's feudal lord!

> *ThinkWrite 3: "Moolah!"*
>
> What does God say about wealth? Don't stop when you've found a few Bible verses that support your preconceived notions. Instead, look for the full counsel of God!

Yes, prosperity! That meant it was decision time...and each individual's spiritual foundation determined the decisions made. Earlier history has shown us that mankind's tendency is to use his power and wealth to make a "kingdom" for himself. Would the newly rich (*nouveau riche*, as the French said it) in America and Europe make the same mistake, or would they be accountable to God with their money and priorities, showing a correct *Big Belief #1?* Would they use their wealth to bless others, showing a correct *Big Belief #2?* Remember, God doesn't disdain wealth; in fact, He often is free to dispense it when His principles are obeyed! He *does*, however, demand it be used Biblically and unselfishly. It was another *big* fork in the road. (Begin *ThinkWrite 3.*)

The Industrial Revolution affected various nations differently. The distinctive American response can be seen in the contemporary comment below:

> *This state of incessant excitement gives to the American an air of busy inquietude...which, in fact, constitutes their principle happiness.*[25]

That observation has got to make us Americans smile...or grimace, for we still seem to be characterized by a love of busyness. Unfortunately, we're known by a couple other traits as well: a focus on material things (*materialism*) and being self-made (which hints at an overly independent attitude). These characteristics were so much a part of the 1800s, that we find the term *self-made* to have been coined by an American leader (Henry Clay) in 1832!

> *The idea of rising "from rags to riches" was common. President* [Andrew] *Jackson, having started as an orphan and being clearly self-made, was a fitting symbol for the age.*[26]

A foreign traveler made this comment:

> *Americans boast of their skill in money making; and it is the only standard of dignity, and nobility, and worth.*[27]

---

25 Miller 20.
26 Miller 4.
27 Miller 4.

Hmm. *Self-made man.* The "rags to riches" dream eventually became so idealized in America—and to some degree in the other industrialized nations too—that many who lived merely comfortable lives somehow felt they'd failed![28] Let's think about that for a second. It *is* Biblical to care for your family without unnecessarily relying on others, but being "captain of one's own ship" is taking it too far...though many did just that. Why? Well, for many, they felt it was the next step in their evolutionary progress! In other words, they felt completely responsible for their own success. (How many times did the Israelites do the same thing?) This silently nudged God off the throne (*Big Belief #1*), and a spiritual hardening, over-independence, arrogance, and materialism thus became widespread. Of course, *Big Belief #2* changed also. So you see an increasingly insensitive use of others in the drive for financial success, especially when the potential for profit created by the Industrial Revolution was so great!

Yes, too many employers cared little for their employees' safety, dignity, wages, and health, as you'll soon see. Women and children worked long and hard in factories. Immigrants on big engineering jobs were pushed like poor animals. Especially in Europe—where conditions were worse because virtually all land was owned by a few aristocrats and there was thus little opportunity for others to advance—the plentiful supply of desperate workers put little pressure on employers to improve. Amazingly, in spite of all that, the new industrial workers were seldom "worse off than in the previous agrarian situation."[29] That fact gives us a good look at fallen human nature: the powerful tend to take advantage of those less powerful. At least, the Industrial Revolution offered opportunity to more people, especially those who were hard-working innovators. There were some who knew God's principles for the workplace; would they speak out? What would happen?

Good question! Especially because it allows me to hit my favorite point. Actually, I'll have Francis Schaeffer—the great Christian historian and philosopher—explain it to you!

> *The churches could have changed things in that day if they had spoken with clarity and courage. The central reason the church should have spoken clearly and courageously on these issues is that the Bible commands it. Had the church been faithful to the Bible's teaching about the compassionate use of wealth, it would not later have lost so many of the workers. And if it had spoken clearly against the use of wealth as a weapon in a kind of "survival of the fittest," in all probability this concept as it came into secularized science* [later with Darwin and others] *would not have been so automatically accepted.*[30]

You see, some really nasty ideas were floating around at the time. The first said that the world was too populated and that hard times would eliminate the weak. Indeed, some human thinkers considered this elimination a necessary step in the flow of *progress!* Worse yet, this played right into another bad idea—*utilitarianism*—which said situations should be measured only by the usefulness (utility) of their outcomes. That gave the hardhearted factory owners (thought not all were hardhearted) a chance to say their harshness was useful since it eliminated those who couldn't progress *and* made for more useful profits.

---

28 Miller 23.
29 Francis Schaeffer, *How Should We Then Live?* (Old Tappan, NJ: Revell, 1976) 116.
30 Schaeffer 117.

ThinkWrite 4:
"What does the Big Boss say about being a boss?"

What does the Bible say to employers...*and* employees too? (Isn't it neat that God cares about people's jobs?!)

Wow! The believing church—the Body of Christ—needed to fire back some truth, for God strongly emphasizes the worth of each individual and the need for employers and employees to be kind and humble. The amazing thing is that many of the problematic factory owners were actually churchgoers who should have been hearing that message! But too many churches had chosen humanistic, natural religion, remember? They bought into the humanist lie that people should remake the world with their *own* ideas for society and business, and they dispensed that untruth in many a Sunday sermon. They should instead have been exhorting their listeners with God's already-established truth and encouraging them to self-government—the personal *decision* to abide by Biblical wisdom! (Begin *ThinkWrite 4* now.)

Self-government

I think there was another reason the harsh factory owners were not convicted, and we alluded to it earlier: conditions for the poor weren't any worse than they'd always been. Therefore, too few saw the problem. It's no excuse, though, to say "it's always been this way." What matters is how God says it *ought* to be! Pursuing that higher goal moves a society toward the richness and security of God's great principles! So, the question for us is this: are *we* blindly ignoring problems to which we've become accustomed? Are we even taking time out of our busy lives to notice problems and seek His solutions? Let's ponder one of my theme verses (please allow me to here use a paraphrase because it especially captures the thought for the youngest students) for *TruthQuest History:*

> *The church, you see, is not peripheral to the world; the world is peripheral to the church. The church is Christ's body, in which he speaks and acts, by which he fills everything with his presence. (Eph. 1:22-23, Message)*

The church is called to leadership in this world, and cannot wriggle out of its God-given place of authority. If the church itself is utilitarian and materialistic, it will lead the world to be likewise. You needn't be a rocket scientist to realize that if many new industrialists weren't being self-governing, and if the church wasn't preaching God's standards and speaking out for the exploited, a terrible void developed. Humanists were able to vilify Christianity, embarrass the church, and, significantly, claim leadership instead. Of course, humanists (by definition) oppose the Bible's clear teaching on mankind's sin nature and on his spiritual nature; they also refute the superiority of God's principles. Thus, their humanistic "solutions" are merely legal, political, and/or economic, and do not yield the deep and permanent change which comes only with the embracing of spiritual truth and renewal.

Want an example? Then watch, for the spiritual-social problems which flourished during the Industrial Revolution received a humanistic response in most of the western nations. Humanists looked to government—not Biblical truth—to control the evil actions of various people, so you will find a mass of government regulations and the resultant economic snafu.

And, to this day, you will all-too-often find a deep bitterness between *labor* and *management*, as folks separated into adversarial factions and looked to massed human power to solve their problems. Of course, whenever we reject God's power, we must marshal our own, such as it is...which means that the longer we reject His solutions, the more complicated our problems become, and by now the situation is quite sticky. Just remember that God's way would have instead brought cooperation, freedom, and prosperity.

Don't forget! Most secular books on this topic, such as you'll find at your library and as I've had to list here, will be steeped in the humanistic, politically correct view that Big Business is made entirely of evil moneygrubbers, while all workers are abused paragons of humanity. It is a virtually Marxist view, as you'll later see, but you know that people of *all* strata need the Lord to act rightly and lovingly!

That said, I'm happy to report that some folks *did* make enormous sacrifices on behalf of the downtrodden. Some of these reformers (we'll meet them later) acted out of Biblical principles; some did not. Oh how I wish I could have told you the whole church had led the charge!

**Story of the World: Volume 3*, by Susan Wise Bauer, Ch. 31 Gr. 3-6
Some families enjoy this book's scope, so ask us to cite it; others seek different worldview; so, parental decision. This chapter focuses on the Industrial Revolution in Britain, and then shows how it spread to the United States.

**Kids During the Industrial Revolution*, by Lisa Wroble Gr. 2-4

**Life in a New England Mill Town*, by Sally Isaacs (Picture the Past) Gr. 2-4

**Working in the First Factories*, by Patrice Coupry Gr. 3-8

**Early American Industrial Revolution*, by Katie Bagley (Let Freedom Ring) Gr. 3-8

**Industrial Revolution*, by Mary Collins (Cornerstones) Gr. 4-8
This seems to be in the new Cornerstones II series which is for older students.

**Mill*, by David Macaulay Gr. 4-10
A don't-miss book! See the inner workings of a mill with fantastic drawings!

Factories, by Leonard Everett Fisher (Nineteenth Century America) Gr. 4-12

**Industrial Revolution*, by John Clare (Living History) Gr. 4-12
I love this series because it features costumed reenactors showing real life.

*_Industrial Revolution_, by Andrew Langley (See Through History) Gr. 4-12

*_Industrial America_, by Kitty Shea (We the People) Gr. 5-12

Story of Britain, by R.J. Unstead, pp. 281-287 Gr. 5-12

Then Was the Future, by Douglas Miller, Ch. 1-4 (Living History Library) Gr. 8-12
Real letters, documents, etc.

*_History through the Eyes of Faith_, by Ronald Wells Gr. 9-12

Mechanical Age: Industrial Revolution in England, by Celia Bland (World Hist) Gr. 9-12
This book covers the scientific/engineering aspects, as well as the social and religious; I've not seen it and not aware of its viewpoint on these important matters.

*_Industrial Revolution_, by Sara Wooten (People at the Center of...) Unknown

*_Industrial Revolution Almanac_, by James & Elizabeth Outman Unknown

Fiction/Historical Fiction

*_Bobbin Girl_, by Emily McCully Gr. 2-5
Picture book; worker sees labor unions develop in Lowell, Massachusetts.

Whistle for the Crossing, by Marguerite de Angeli Gr. 2-7
This is a nice story set on the early trains.

*_So Far From Home: Diary of an Irish Mill Girl_, by Barry Denenberg (Dear Am.) Gr. 3-8
I'm mentioning this fictional diary _not_ because I'm recommending it, but precisely because I've been told this volume is particularly depressing and refers to superstitious future-telling.

Glorious Conspiracy, by Joanne Williamson Gr. 5-12
Good author tells gritty story of the Early Republic and Industrial Revolution. Does have strong opinion against Alexander Hamilton.

Engine and the Gun, by James Barbary Gr. 8-12
Good, fact-based novel; a young man tries to get industrial knowledge into America to help the American Revolution. This was also cited in our previous guide, but because it captures the excitement of the Industrial Revolution—a topic we didn't have time to meaningfully discuss then—I'm also including it here.

Pat and the Iron Horse, by Polly Angell Gr. 8-12
I've not seen this story of a poor Irish immigrant laboring on the Erie Railroad.

10 Revival...and Why it was Needed!

In spite of the new industrial tensions, the Era of Good Feelings was still in full swing in America. The glow of pride had not yet faded from the victory over mighty Britain in the War of 1812. It *was* pretty amazing! Then there was the suppression of Tecumseh's Indian alliance. Remember? He had tried to unite many tribes in the Deep South and trans-Appalachian areas.

Their defeat and that of the tribes aiding the British along the Old Northwest frontier opened many new lands to white settlers. More growth. But, aha! Do you see our next fork-in-the-road logo? Hope I didn't catch you snoozing? Well, wake up, because Americans had a decision to make. Would all these events make them feel like *Superman?* The answer to this burning question would determine many things, including how would they would deal with the Native-American Indians.

I'll give you a hint about the *Superman* issue: lots of Americans already found themselves thinking that ol' religion just wasn't necessary for people as stunningly capable as themselves. They were *self-made men*, don't ya' know? They had *progressed!* They didn't seem to need God or other people either, for when the stony soil of their New England farms wore out, or when Southerners tired of picking cotton for some plantation owner at paltry wages, and when the government was practically giving away land further west, they clomped over to that new wilderness with seldom a concern about being near a church (or quickly building one). Spiritual connection and accountability just didn't matter much. These two issues had been so important to the first Pilgrims...that is until their lives got easier and they could make more money on the bigger farms available further afield. It's pretty hard to make God a priority when you're totally focused on getting ahead, and that's something we struggle with today!

The church, though, has to take major responsibility for this spiritual cooling, for due in large part to the emphasis on rationalism in Europe (as we've discussed in earlier *TruthQuest History* guides), theology was getting dusty, musty, and over-intellectualized....or, in a word: lifeless. Yes, that's it! It no longer applied to *real life*, and Americans are way too practical to waste time on pomp and fluff. The church couldn't have picked a worse time to become a theological fussbudget, for the flattering humanism of the French Enlightenment—which had already inundated European society and had been peddled in the U.S. by people like Thomas Paine—was now being taught in many universities. Alas, it was even penetrating the seminaries where it had a new name: Unitarianism. Boston, which had been the fountainhead of Puritan godliness, was now headquarters for this natural religion. Ah, it all seemed *so* sophisticated!

Of course, the Lord was not ignoring this. He has always worked to draw people to Himself, both as individuals and as nations! Some God-fearing Americans started praying and revivals sprang up. Naturally, there was some human error added in, but there were still significant revivals in three areas: 1) Kentucky—where circuit-riding preachers slogged

through sleet and heat to keep the spiritual fires burning; 2) Boston—where Lyman Beecher (father of a famous family) took on Unitarianism and coldhearted industrialists; and, 3) western New York—where Charles Finney let rip!

The same process may have been occurring other nations. You lovely folk who are Canadian, Australian, English, etc., can of course feel free to study your own spiritual heroes!

**From Sea to Shining Sea for Children*, by Marshall & Manuel, Ch. 3-4, 13 Gr. 1-5
**From Sea to Shining Sea*, by Marshall & Manuel, Ch. 3-5, 13 Gr. 6-12

**Hero Tales: Volume II*, by Dave & Neta Jackson, pp. 33-43 Gr. 3-6
This chapter covers Peter Cartwright.

Fire Upon the Earth, by Norman Langford, pp. 185-188 Gr. 4-12

Peter Cartwright: Pioneer Circuit Rider, by Nancy Veglahn Gr. 5-12

They Rode the Frontier, by Wyatt Blassingame Gr. 6-12

**Charles Finney*, by Bonnie Harvey (Heroes of the Faith) Gr. 6-12

**Ambassadors for Christ*, edited by John Woodbridge, pp. 50-55 Gr. 7-12
This is a compendium of short chapter biographies on Christian heroes.

**Charles Finney*, by Basil Miller (Men of the Faith) Gr. 9-12

Great Evangelical Preachers of Yesterday, by James MacGraw Gr. 11-12
There are chapters on both Peter Cartwright and Francis Asbury.

No Other Foundation: Church Through Twenty Centuries, by J. Jackson, Ch. 16 Gr. 11-12
This book is too hard for most students, but has such valuable insights!

Fiction/Historical Fiction

**Abandoned on the Wild Frontier*, by Dave & Neta Jackson (Trailblazer) Gr. 3-9
Fictional boy meets the real Peter Cartwright, a famous circuit rider.

11 Pioneers Head West...and South...and North!

Remember, many new lands were open to settlement after the defeat of Tecumseh's alliance and the other Indians siding with the British in the War of 1812. Another wave of pioneers

headed deeper into the far-western areas of New York, the far-western areas of the Deep South, the land between the Appalachians and the Mississippi River, and the Old Northwest areas of Indiana, Illinois, Michigan, Wisconsin, etc.

We will thoroughly discuss the Indians these pioneers met and displaced later in this unit, not because that's when they become important. On the contrary, it is then that we have a fuller context to understand their culture and the new challenges which faced them.

Actually, we can also explore the farm life of the early 1800s for those who remained in the settled areas of the nation, for whether one was pioneering or staying put, the chores and joys were quite similar. Those of you in Canada, Australia, and New Zealand will naturally prefer to study the settlers of this same era in your own country. Let's head out!

11a General overview

**From Sea to Shining Sea for Children*, by Marshall & Manuel, Ch. 2 Gr. 1-5
**From Sea to Shining Sea*, by Marshall & Manuel, Ch. 2 Gr. 6-12

**Basic History of the United States: Vol. 3*, by Clarence Carson, pp. 81-84 Gr. 9-12

True Book of Pioneers, by Mabel Harmer (True Books) Gr. K-3

**If You Grew Up with Abe Lincoln*, by Ann McGovern Gr. 1-6
This doesn't really discuss Lincoln, as much as it shows life for children of his era. Of course, your children haven't yet "met" Lincoln in this unit. They will!

**Frontier Village: A Town is Born*, by C. Chambers (Adv. in Frontier Am.) Gr. 2-6

**Adventures of the Waterways*, by Edith McCall (Frontiers of America) Gr. 2-8
This was originally titled *Pioneers on Early Waterways.*

**Seasons Sewn*, by Ann Paul Gr. 2-8
This precious book uses quilt patterns to reveal the yearly flow of pioneer life.

Pioneer Stories for Boys, by C. Richard Schaare Gr. 3-7
This book is unusually designed and illustrated, so is good for reluctant readers, but its rarity makes finding a copy very unlikely.

First Book of Pioneers, by Walter Havighurst (First Books) Gr. 3-8

Flatboat Days on Frontier Rivers, by James McCague (Garrard How They Lived) Gr. 3-8

To Be a Pioneer, by Paul Burns — Gr. 3-8

Ladd of the Big Swamp, by Cecile Matschat (Winston Adventure) — Gr. 3-9
Families move into the Okefenokee.

**Frontier Home*, by Raymond Bial — Gr. 3-10
Photographs show reality of pioneer life in this striking book.

Frontier Leaders and Pioneers, by Dorothy Heiderstadt — Gr. 3-10
Chapter biographies on many pioneers.

**Diary of an Early American Boy*, by Eric Sloane — Gr. 4-12
This book, based on a diary actually kept by Noah Blake, warmly reveals life on an 1800s farm. Excellent!

Famous Pioneers, by Franklin Folsom — Gr. 4-12
Chapter biographies on many pioneer leaders.

Heroines of the Early West, by Nancy Wilson Ross (Landmark) — Gr. 4-12

**Pioneer Sampler*, by Barbara Greenwood — Gr. 4-12
This is a much-loved look at the intricacies of pioneer life!

Solomon Juneau, Voyageur, by Marion Lawson — Gr. 5-12
The story of the explorer who helped settle what is now Milwaukee.

Westward Adventure, by William O. Steele — Gr. 6-12
This well-known book tells the story of six pioneers.

**Frontier Living*, by Edwin Tunis — Gr. 7-12
Detailed survey with meticulous drawings; save portion on plains pioneers for later.

Old Wilderness Road, by William O. Steele — Gr. 8-12

Big Sky: An Edition for Younger Readers, by A.B. Guthrie — Gr. 9-12
An abridged version of a well-known story of buffalo hunters in wild Mississippi territory during the 1830s and 1840s; I've not read this.

Sketches of America Past, by Eric Sloane — Various
Three books in one, about pioneer tools, woodworking, etc.; meticulous drawings.

**Children of the Frontier*, by Sylvia Whitman — Unknown

Fiction/Historical Fiction

**Daniel's Duck*, by Clyde Robert Bulla — Gr. K-2

Granny, Baby, and the Big Gray Wolf **and** *Granny and the Desperadoes*, by P. Parish Gr. K-2

**Least of All*, by Carol Purdy — Gr. K-3
Don't miss this story of a Vermont farm girl who earnestly desires to read the Bible.

**Ox-Cart Man*, by Donald Hall — Gr. K-4
Tender book shows the yearly cycle of 1800s farm life.

Dancing Tom, by Elizabeth Coatsworth — Gr. 1-3
An Ohio boy loves his pet pig.

Hannah's Farm, by Michael McCurdy — Gr. 1-3
Hard work during the seasons on a New England farm; strongly illustrated.

Here Comes the Mystery Man, by Scott Russell Sanders — Gr. 1-3
An Indiana pioneer family looks forward to the peddler's visit.

**Hog Music*, by M.C. Helldorfer — Gr. 1-3
What fun!

**Log Cabin Quilt*
**Log Cabin Christmas*
**Log Cabin Church*, all by Ellen Howard — Gr. 1-3
These stories tell of a pioneer family in Michigan.

**Sewing Quilts*, by Ann Turner — Gr. 1-3
As usual, Turner's book is wonderfully poignant!

**Warm as Wool*
**Aurora Means Dawn*
**Floating House*, all by Scott Russell Sanders — Gr. 1-3
Truly wonderful stories about Ohio pioneers.

Josiah True and the Art Maker, by Amy Littlesugar — Gr. 1-4
Connecticut farm family enjoys traveling artist in 1817.

**Nothing Here But Trees*, by Jean Van Leeuwen — Gr. 1-4
The story of a warm family carving a place in the Ohio wilderness. Nice.

**Swamp Angel*, by Anne Isaacs Gr. 1-4

Rip-snorting fun in this tall tale about a gigantic frontier woman!

Caroline and Her Kettle Named Maud, by Miriam Mason Gr. 1-5

Set in Michigan. Sequel, *Caroline and the Seven Little Words*, is for slightly older readers.

Flatboats and Wagon Wheels, by Mildred Comfort Gr. 1-5

The story of Ohio pioneers.

Susannah: The Pioneer Cow, by Miriam Mason Gr. 1-5

The beloved cow of a Virginia family heads to Indiana behind the wagon.

Next Spring an Oriole* **and **Night of the Full Moon*, by Gloria Whelan Gr. 1-6

These good stories find a Michigan pioneer girl making friends with local Indians.

Miney and the Blessing, by Miriam Mason Gr. 2-5

A young girl learns that life is harder when the men are away.

Little Jonathan, by Miriam Mason Gr. 2-6

Young Indiana pioneer boy wants to be bigger.

Secret of the Rosewood Box, by Helen Fuller Orton (set in Michigan) Gr. 2-6

**Abigail*, by Portia Sperry Gr. 2-8

Indiana pioneer girl gets a beloved doll.

**Away Goes Sally* and **Five Bushel Farm*, by Elizabeth Coatsworth Gr. 2-8

Trilogy begins with **Fair American*, the story of a boy arriving in America after fleeing the French Revolution of the late 1700s.

Shoes for Matt, by Elsa Falk Gr. 2-8

Pioneer boy works and plays hard in Wisconsin Territory.

Phebe Fairchild: Her Book, by Lois Lenski Gr. 3-7

I've not seen this, so am guessing on the age recommendation, but it is the story of a Connecticut girl in the 1830s and her love for songs and rhymes.

Two Logs Crossing, by Walter Edmonds Gr. 3-7

New York boy traps furs in wilderness.

**Adventure in the Wilderness;* **Earthquake in Cincinnati;* **Trouble on the Ohio River* Gr. 3-8

by various authors (American Adventure #13-15)

These volumes in a new Christian series by various authors are set in early Cincinnati and include topics such as an earthquake and a drought.

Buffalo Knife, by William O. Steele Gr. 3-8
Family has harrowing flatboat journey through Chickamauga territory.

Hester & Timothy, Pioneers, by Ruth Langland Holberg Gr. 3-8
More Wisconsin Territory adventure.

By Wagon and Flatboat, by Enid LaMonte Meadowcroft Gr. 3-9
This story is actually set in 1789, but if you missed it, you'll enjoy it now.

Hello, the Boat, by Phyllis Crawford Gr. 3-10
A family heads to Ohio on a flatboat.

**Jessica's First Prayer*, by Hesba Stretton (Lamplighter) Gr. 3-10
Folks speak highly of the character in this old tale, as the heart of a miserly man is softened by a young girl.

**A Gathering of Days*, by Joan Blos Gr. 3-12
This is a beloved book set in New England.

Lone Hunt, by William O. Steele Gr. 3-12
The last bison in Tennessee is killed.

Blueberry Corners, by Lois Lenski Gr. 4-8
Tale of the rather rugged life of New England farmers.

Treasure in the Little Trunk, by Helen Fuller Orton Gr. 4-8
Pioneer family heads to western New York state.

**Brothers of the Heart*, by Joan Blos Gr. 4-10
Crippled Michigan pioneer boy bonds with Indian widow.

**Hitty: Her First Hundred Years*, by Rachel Field Gr. 4-10
A doll sees American history in this much-beloved book. Most girls won't want to miss this one!

Merrie's Miracle, by Florence Musgrave Gr. 4-10
I've not seen this story of the more educated settlers in Ohio's Western Reserve.

Proving Years, by Cateau de Leeuw Gr. 4-10
Ohio pioneer tale.

Great Turkey Drive, by Charles Wilson Gr. 4-12
Farm boy must drive thousands of turkeys to Boston.

**They Loved to Laugh*, by Kathryn Worth Gr. 4-12
Warm story of an orphan girl taken in by a southern Quaker family.

**Journey to Nowhere*; **Frozen Summer*; **Road to Home*, all by Mary Jane Auch Gr. 5-10
A girl and mother in western New York struggle with their new life.

Dark and Bloody Ground, by Phyllis Fenner Gr. 5-12
Another of Fenner's short story collections, this one being about pioneers.

Far-Off Land, by Rebecca Caudill Gr. 5-12
A girl pioneer and her family on a Cumberland River flatboat.

Fish Hawk's Nest, by Stephen Meader Gr. 5-12
Can coastal New Jersey boy stop smugglers? Meader's books are usually top-notch.

Gunsmith's Boy, by Herbert Best Gr. 5-12

Hearthstone in the Wilderness **and** *Homespun*, both by Erick Berry Gr. 5-12
These two stories are set in New York state.

Jonathan Goes West, by Stephen Meader Gr. 5-12
Pioneer boy follows his father on the long journey to Illinois. Another Meader!

Journeyman* **and **Hue and Cry*, by Elizabeth Yates Gr. 6-12
Moral author illuminates New England farm life in the early 1800s.

A-Going to the Westward, by Lois Lenski Gr. 7-10

Attack at Fort Lookout, by Red Reeder Gr. 7-12
Adventure on the northwest frontier.

Chicago: Big-Shouldered City, by Regina Kelly Gr. 7-12
After the War of 1812, a soldier from Fort Dearborn helps build Chicago.

Hills Stand Watch, by August Derleth Gr. 7-12
Pioneering in Wisconsin.

Some Plant Olive Trees, by Emma Sterne Gr. 7-12
I've not seen this story of Napoleonic refugees making a new life in Alabama.

Song of the Voyageur, by Beverly Butler Gr. 7-12
I've not read this; girl from the east faces life in the Wisconsin Territory.

Sweet Land of Michigan, by August Derleth — Gr. 7-12

Michigan boy helps survey the territory.

Who Rides in the Dark? by Stephen Meader — Gr. 7-12

Upper New England adventures. Yup, another Meader!

11b Activities

**History Alive Through Music: Westward Ho!* by Diana Waring — Various

This audio features real songs sung by the pioneers!

**Pioneer Days Lapbook with Study Guide*, by AJTL/Michelle Miller — Various

"A Journey Through Learning" asked me to write text for their fun lapbook about pioneers heading west. Especially if you're not already doing the AJTL binders/notebooks for this *TruthQuest History: Age of Revolution II* guide, you may enjoy this topical project. Available at www.TruthQuestHistory.com/studies.

**Pioneer Days*, by David C. King — Various

An activity book with projects, games, and recipes.

**Pioneer Recipes*, by Bobbie Kalman — Various

**Skillet Bread, Sourdough, and Vinegar Pie*, by Loretta Frances Ichord — Various

12 Native Peoples

Now that we have a sense of the widespread movement of pioneers into native areas, it's time to officially meet the Indians (if you're American or Canadian, or the aborigines, if you're Australian) and ponder the conflict for land. We'll do so gingerly, for these are complex and emotionally explosive topics. One thing is certain: God loved each individual native as much as the white people who displaced them. It being a Christian nation who forced them from their homes, it's easy to see why many Indians viewed the Lord as only the "white man's god." This is an utter tragedy....

So much philosophical "stuff" has been added to our view of native culture that it's hard for us to look back accurately. The best thing is to seek God's perspective. I think it's fair to say, though, that we Americans can see some Indian tribes who sensed truths about the Creator and had a sense of living nobly by heeding their consciences.[31] This is

31 I'm not sure exactly where to credit this thought I read years ago. Sorry!

understandable since Scripture says He is revealed in everything He has made, so men are without excuse. We can also see, though, that other tribes embraced dark beliefs, making their cultures harsh and/or morbid.

As we probe this further, we must tackle an intricate idea, so you must think carefully and patiently. I'll begin by saying that if you view real photographs of Indians and their culture, you'll see they were more shockingly primitive than is presented in modern films and books. Why? It's partly due to the current popularity of the Enlightenment's belief in the *noble savage*, which we mentioned in the introduction to this guide. People of this persuasion idealize native peoples as ultimate humans and often frown upon missionary work. They point to the few mission works which toiled to make natives first into Americans or Brits rather than Christians.

Back to our point...the pioneers are sharply criticized for their alteration of Indian culture. But is it *possible* that God wanted some things to change? Now, I most certainly *do not* know the mind of God, so keep in mind that I'm *only* presenting *possibilities!* What we can know is that God wanted the Indians to hear the good news of Jesus Christ. Did He also, for example, want an end to the killing a wife when her husband died, as some tribes decreed?

Think back to the Old Testament, where we observe God dealing with pagan societies. He did give the Israelites land which belonged to pagans (actually all land is His!), *but* the Israelites were to be a spiritual light and testimony to the former residents. In that sense, God's judgment was redemptive: it brought to the pagans neighbors who knew blessed truths about Him. Sadly though, the Israelites too often became lulled by the peace and prosperity of their new land, quickly forgetting their ministry to others. *If* the American situation was similar (though I'm *not* saying America is a modern Israel), God may have meant for white settlers to benefit Indian culture in some way, but most Americans flunked as badly as the Israelites. Why?

I'll hazard my own opinion here, but before you deem me an egocentric crackpot who thinks every culture ought to be like mine, hear me out. My *guess* is that God meant for *both* the white settlers and the Indians to benefit from contact with each other. If that is the case, it seems that many whites failed to both give and receive appropriately because they confused something very important.

What is that "something?" Well, I must once again ask you to patiently think this all through before you make judgment! Here goes....

Because God is completely right and best, then in whatever aspects a human culture embraces His basic truths, those aspects (and only those) of that culture are right and best. Thankfully, the American culture had embraced *some* of God's truths....not because it was American, or white, or previously European, but only because God had been graciously working to that end as He does with every nation. The pioneers, seeing that *some* aspects of their Judeo-Christian culture were *righter* and *better* could easily find aspects of pagan

Indian culture which were *not* right and were *not* best. Here, though, is where the big mistake was made, in my opinion. Instead of that comparison remaining specific and impersonal, it became generalized and personal: *all* aspects of Indian life were denigrated (thus whites didn't learn what the Indians might have been able to teach us), and many individual whites began feeling they were more valuable persons than individual Indians. This is WRONG! God never mandates racism! He always loves all individuals. In fact, I'm guessing He actually enjoys the aspects unique to each culture (whichever aspects are wholesome), because they are part of our God-created humanness. He loves individuality, both personally and nationally.

First, though, we must first face another clear area of American failure: a lack of integrity. Treaties, which are covenants between peoples, were constantly broken by Americans who justified this blatant illegality (they forgot *lex rex*—law is king!) by declaring the Indians as sub-human, as discussed above. (By the way, you'll later see injustices against the slaves defended in much the same way). We know that cheating and lying could not possibly have been God's way for interfacing with the Indians, even *if* it was God's will for the pioneers to access Indian lands.

There is something else I wonder about: the lands held by most tribes were vast beyond description. Would there have been room for both pioneers and Indians if a Christian brotherhood had developed? Was that God's will? Possibly. We'll never know though, for the Indians were continuously forced to much less habitable lands further west...and the separation between white Americans and Indians, and Australians and aborigines, is *still* dreadfully deep. I guess the remaining question, then, is what does the Lord want done now?

Let's meet an early justice (1801-1835) of the Supreme Court who decided some Indian legal issues, and who virtually defined (the Constitution left room for implementation) the role of the Supreme Court as we still know it today.

Sidebar: John Marshall, Chief Justice

**From Sea to Shining Sea for Children*, Ch. 6
by Marshall & Manuel
**From Sea to Shining Sea*, Ch. 9
by Marshall & Manuel

John Marshall (See and Read) by Patricia Miles Martin	Gr. 1-3
John Marshall (Childhood) by Helen Monsell	Gr. 1-6
**John Marshall*, by Stuart Kallen	Gr. 3-5
John Marshall, by Teri Martini	Gr. 3-10
John Marshall, by Alfred Steinberg	Gr. 9-12
John Marshall, by Caroline Tucker	Gr. 9-12
**Chief Justice*, by C. Wetterer	Unknown

We'll now get to know those Indian tribes in areas newly being penetrated by the American pioneers, while you non-Americans can study the same process in your own lands. Please let me mention to American students, though, that at the end of this section we'll also glimpse the Seminole War, the Black Hawk War, and we'll meet Sequoyah—the brilliant and persevering Cherokee who created their written language and provided other leadership. (If you're ever thinking of giving up on a project, just think of his determination!) Just be on guard: the Enlightenment *noble savage* idea is in most books about native peoples!

12a General overview

In previous the TruthQuest History guide, we studied the Indians of the eastern seaboard. In the next guide, we'll focus on the Indians of the Great Southwest, Great Northwest, and the Great Plains. At this time, we're learning of the Indians outside the original thirteen colonies, but still east of the Mississippi River. Here is just a sampling of resources.

**American Indian Prayer Guide*, by Danette Maloof — Various

I've not seen this, but have heard many folks say they enjoy meeting and praying for various tribal groups specifically. I believe it is from Intercessors for America. Because of its positive spiritual approach, I'll give it special mention first!

North American Indians, by Marie Gorsline — Gr. K-2

True Book of Indians, by Teri Martini — Gr. K-3

Indians: The First Americans, by Patricia Miles Martin (Stepping-Stone) — Gr. 1-5

Meet the North American Indians, by Elizabeth Payne (Step-Up) — Gr. 1-5

Famous Indian Tribes, by William Moyers — Gr. 1-6

**Indian Crafts*, by Keith Brandt — Gr. 1-6

**Native Americans*, by Gallimard Jeunesse (First Discovery) — Gr. 2-4

**American Indian Families;* **American Indian Food;* **American Indian Games*, etc. by Jay Miller (True Books) — Gr. 2-6

Indian Tribes of America, by Marion Gridley — Gr. 3-9

Indian Fishing and Camping, Indian Hunting, Indians at Home, Indian Games and Crafts, Indian Sign Language, etc., by Robert Hofsinde — Gr. 3-12

Real Book about Indians, by Michael Gorham — Gr. 4-10

American Indian, by Sydney Fletcher — Gr. 4-12

Nice illustrations.

American Indian Story, by May McNeer — Gr. 4-12

Book of Indians, by Holling Clancy Holling — Gr. 4-12

Rare, but beloved book. Two sections on each tribe: the first delivers interesting factual coverage, the second creates a fictional Indian character of that tribe and shows him/her in their culture, religion, etc. Because of good writing, kids will relate strongly with character, so be sure they are mature enough to see tribe's religion (or rosy representation of it, since author is trying to write cheerful book for children) without feeling drawn to the beliefs.

Indian Harvests, by William Grimm — Gr. 4-12
Interesting look at plants the Indians used, but beware of drawing on cover.

**North American Indian*, by Doug Murdoch (DorlingKindersley) — Gr. 4-12
A photographic display of Indian articles.

Red Man in Art, by Rena Coen — Gr. 4-12

American Indian , by Oliver LaFarge — Gr. 5-12

Indians, by Edwin Tunis — Gr. 6-12

Indians as the Westerners Saw Them, by Ralph Andrews — Gr. 7-12
This book features very authentic photographs of actual Indians.

**Two Little Savages: Two Boys Who Lived as Indians and What They Learned* — Unknown
by Ernest Thompson Seton
This relates the amazing activities of two boys!

Audio

**Origin of the Indians*, by Richard "Little Bear" Wheeler — Various

Fiction/Historical Fiction

**Small Wolf*, by Nathaniel Benchley (I Can Read) — Gr. K-1

**Red Fox and His Canoe*, by Nathaniel Benchley (I Can Read) — Gr. K-2

**Good Hunting, Blue Sky*, by Peggy Parish — Gr. K-2

Indians, Indians, Indians, by Phyllis Fenner — Gr. 3-12
Collection of interesting short stories; some families speak highly of Fenner's books.

12b Activities, cooking, crafts & art

Parents should determine suitability, safety, and interest levels.

**Food and Recipes of the Native Americans*, by George Erdosh — Various

Foods the Indian Gave Us, by Wilma Pitchford Hays — Various
How to plant, harvest, and cook the Indian way.

**Indian Tribes of North America Coloring Book* (Dover) Various

Indians Knew, by Tillie Pine Various

Fun look at Indian skills and science with projects, also showing how we accomplish the same things now.

**Indians of the Past and Present Coloring Book*, by Connie Asch Various

Let's Be Indians, by Peggy Parish Various

Fun activity book, especially for the youngest students, by the author of the *Amelia Bedelia* books.

**More than Moccasins: A Kid's Activity Guide*, by Laurie Carlson Various

Fun hands-on projects!

**Native Americans*, by Andrew Haslam (Make It Work! History) Various

Fun hands-on projects!

North American Indians, by Susan Purdy Various

**Traditional Native American Arts & Activities*, by Arlette Braman Various

12c Geographical settings of various tribes

If you would like to focus on Indian tribes which originally occupied a specific area, such as your state, please see the list below. Resources on these specific tribes, where available, will be listed further below. Information on all these tribes should also be found in the general resources listed above.

New York . . . . Iroquois
Ohio . . . . Shawnee
Michigan . . . . Ottawa, Potawatomie, Ojibwa/Chippewa
Illinois . . . . Illiniwek, Sauk & Fox, Miami, Potawatomie
Indiana . . . . Miami
Wisconsin . . . . Kickapoo, Menominee, Ojibwa, Potawatomie, Sauk & Fox, Winnebago
North Carolina . . . . Cherokee, Catawba, Tuscarora
South Carolina . . . . Santee
Tennessee . . . . Chickasaw
Georgia . . . . Creek
Alabama . . . . Alibamu, Choctaw, Creek
Mississippi . . . . Chickasaw, Choctaw, Natchez
Louisiana . . . . Caddo, Natchez
Arkansas . . . . Arkansas
Missouri . . . . Osage

12d Cherokee and the Trail of Tears

**Story of the World: Vol. 3*, by Susan Wise Bauer, Ch. 38a — Gr. 3-6
Some families enjoy this book's scope, so ask us to cite it; others seek different worldview; so, parental decision.

**Trail of Tears*, by Joseph Bruchac (Step Into Reading 5) — Gr. 2-4

**Cherokee*, by Richard Gaines (Native Americans) — Gr. 2-5

Cherokee, by Emilie Lepthien (New True Books) — Gr. 2-5

**If You Lived with the Cherokee*, by Peter & Connie Roop — Gr. 2-6

**Story of the Trail of Tears*, by R. Conrad Stein (Cornerstones) — Gr. 2-6

**Cherokee*, by Andrew Santella (True Books, American Indians) — Gr. 3-6

**Cherokee Indians*, by Bill Lund — Gr. 3-7

Cherokee Indians, by Sonia Bleeker — Gr. 3-12

**Trail of Tears*, by Sally Isaacs (American Adventure) — Gr. 4-7
Yet another series named *American Adventure*, but this is a new, non-fiction series.

Trail of Tears, by Marlene Brill — Gr. 5-12

Fiction/Historical Fiction

**Soft Rain: A Story of the Cherokee Trail of Tears*, by Cornelia Cornelissen — Gr. 3-8
I've not read this new book about the Trail, but see that it features a young girl and mother who must make the arduous journey alone since the soldiers forced them to leave family members and necessary supplies behind, alas.

Trail to Oklahoma, by Jim Booker — Gr. 4-9
I've not seen this book, but have heard others recommend it.

**On the Long Trail Home*, by Elizabeth Stewart — Gr. 6-10
I've not read this new novel, but it reportedly has very jarring plot elements.

Cherokee Boy, by Alexander Key — Gr. 7-12

12e Chippewa (See: Ojibwa)

12f Choctaw

Choctaw, by Emilie Lepthien (New True Books) Gr. 2-5

**Long March*, by Marie-Louise Fitzpatrick Unknown
True story of the later Choctaw effort to raise funds for the Irish during their potato famine even though the Choctaw were suffering themselves. I've not read this.

12g Creek

**Three Little Indians*, by George Stuart, Section 1 Gr. 1-4

**Creek*, by Barbara Gray-Kanatiiosh Gr. 2-5

**Creek Nation*, by Allison Lassieur Unknown

12h Iroquois

You probably studied Iroquois in the previous TruthQuest History unit, so we won't go into great depth here.

Iroquois, by Irene Estep Gr. 1-4

**Iroquois*, by Richard Gaines (Native Americans) Gr. 2-5

**Iroquois*, by Virginia Driving Hawk Sneve Gr. 2-5
I've not seen this and am not actually sure of the age recommendation.

**If You Lived with the Iroquois*, by Ellen Levine Gr. 2-6

**Iroquois Indians*, by Bill Lund Gr. 3-7

Indians of the Longhouse, by Sonia Bleeker Gr. 4-12

Story of Hiawatha Various
The original, by Henry Wadsworth Longfellow, is for older students. Allen Chaffee wrote an abridged version for Grades 2-6, but there are others, I would think. This story does contain dark elements of Indian religion.

Fiction/Historical Fiction

**Little Runner of the Longhouse*, by Betty Baker Gr. K-3

12i Menominee

Menominee, by Joan Kalbacken (New True Books) Gr. 2-5

12j Ojibwa/Chippewa, Ottawa, and Potawatomie

**Legend of Sleeping Bear*, by Kathy-jo Wargin Gr. 1-4
Real legend of Ojibwa Indians (contains Indian religion) about my home area!

Chippewa, by Alice Osinski (New True Books) Gr. 2-5

**Ojibwa Indians*, by Bill Lund Gr. 3-7

**Nishnawbe*, by Lynne Deur Gr. 3-8

**Life in an Anishinabe Camp*, by B. Kalman & N. Walker (Native Nations) Gr. 4-9

**Nations of the Western Great Lakes*, by Kathryn Smithyman (Native Nations) Gr. 4-9

Chippewa Indians, by Sonia Bleeker Gr. 4-12

Ottawa, by Elaine Landau (First Books) Gr. 5-12

Potawatomi, by Suzanne Powell (First Books) Gr. 5-12

William Warren, by Will Antell Gr. 5-12
Rare, but if it's in your library, you'll find the story of an Ojibwa who was elected as a U.S. representative at a time when Indians couldn't vote!

**Potawatomi*, by Karen Gibson (Native Peoples) Unknown

**Potawatomi of Wisconsin*, by Damon Mayrl Unknown

Fiction/Historical Fiction

**Birchbark House*, by Louise Erdrich Gr. 3-8?

I've not read this book and have heard comments both in favor of it and concerned about its mystical Indian elements, so I cannot advise you regarding this story of an Ojibwa girl on an island in Lake Superior during the year 1847 and the many joys and challenges she faces.

Potawatomie Indian Summer, by E. William Oldenburg Gr. 5-10

Caution: contains light mention of magic as modern kids go back in time to visit Potawatomie village in Michigan, but otherwise gives vicarious sense of Indian life.

12k Sauk & Fox

You'll also see "Sauk" spelled as "Sac."

**Sac and Fox*, by Nancy Bonvillain Gr. 5-12

12l Shawnee

**Shawnee*, by Alice Flanagan (New True Books) Gr. 2-5

Shawnee Indians, by Sonia Bleeker Gr. 3-12

Shawnee, by Elaine Landau (First Books) Gr. 4-10

**Shawnee Indians*, by Terrance Dolan (Jr. Lib. of Am. Indians) Gr. 4-12

**Shawnee*, by Petra Press Unknown

Fiction/Historical Fiction

White Feather, by Ruth Eitzen Gr. 1-4

A Quaker family in Ohio tries to make peace with the Shawnee. Looks very nice!

12m Tuscarora

Tuscarora, by Jill Duvall (New True Books) Gr. 2-5

12n Early Indians

If you want to jump back further in time, you may study the Indians, such as the Mound Builders, who were ancestors of the Indians of the 1600s. However, I recommend caution when selecting books on this topic due to the darkness and death-focus in their pagan religions. Also, there can be an evolutionary mind-set. Please consider most of these books as relevant, not recommended.

**Journey to Cahokia*, by Albert Lorenz — Gr. 1-4
This book shows a warm family, with colorful illustrations; religion not emphasized.

Mound Builders, by William Scheele — Parental decision
Mr. Scheele does seem to have a real interest in and knowledge of his subject.

Earliest Americans, by William Scheele — Parental decision

Talking Bones, by William O. Steele — Parental decision

Cliff Dwellers of Walnut Canyon, by Carroll Fenton & Alice Epstein — Parental decision
This one doesn't "appear" to be quite as dark, but I've not read it.

Fiction/Historical Fiction

Chula: Son of the Mound Builders, by William Bunce — Parental decision

12o Seminole War

Andrew Jackson, whom we'll study later, made it his personal mission to subdue the Seminole Indians from Florida, which was purchased from Spain in 1819. There were various phases to this conflict; we've grouped them here. You'll want to meet Osceola, a key Seminole leader.

Osceola, by Marion Gridley (See and Read) — Gr. 1-3

Osceola: Seminole War Chief, by Wyatt Blassingame (Garrard Am. Indians) — Gr. 1-5

**Seminoles*, by Virginia Driving Hawk Sneve — Gr. 1-5

Osceola, by Electa Clark (Childhood) — Gr. 1-6

**Seminole*, by Richard Gaines (Native Americans) — Gr. 2-5

Seminole, by Emilie Lepthien (New True Books) Gr. 2-5
This is probably in most libraries still.

Osceola: Seminole Leader, by Ronald Syme Gr. 2-6

**Seminole Indians*, by Bill Lund Gr. 3-7

Seminoles, by Irene Estep Gr. 3-8

Story of the Seminoles, by Marion Gridley Gr. 3-8

War Chief of the Seminoles, by May McNeer (Landmark) Gr. 3-9

Seminole Indians, by Sonia Bleeker Gr. 4-12

Osceola and the Seminole Wars, by Clifford Alderman (Messner) Gr. 7-12

**Osceola*, by Rachel Koestler-Grack Unknown

**Osceola*, by Anne Todd (Native American Biographies) Unknown

**Seminole Indians*, by Caryn Yacowitz Unknown

Fiction/Historical Fiction

Naha: Boy of the Seminoles, by Wendell Wright Gr. 1-4

**Seminole Diary*, by Dolores Johnson Gr. 3-8
I've not read this; it is based on the fact that the Seminoles harbored runaway slaves.

Wildcat, the Seminole, by Electa Clark (Aladdin's American Heritage) Gr. 3-9
This series from yesteryear is usually very good; I've not read this one.

Red War Pole, by Louis Capron Gr. 5-12
I've not read this story of white mistreatment of Seminoles in Florida.

Seminole Trail and *War Chant*, by Dee Dunsing Gr. 6-12
I've not read these two stories of the Seminole War.

12p Black Hawk War

A complicated situation gave rise to the Black Hawk War, the last major clash (1832) between Indians and settlers east of the Mississippi. Chief Keokuk of the Sauk &

Fox Indians sold all lands east of the Mississippi after decades of pressure and treaty disagreements between the tribe and the U.S. government. The sold lands included the village of Black Hawk, who was angry both with Keokuk and with the government. He gathered warriors to reclaim the lands by force, but there were many tragedies for him as one of his leaders was wrongfully shot, his surrender flag was ignored, etc. A Sioux war party joined the local militias and federal troops in hunting Black Hawk. All in all, it's quite a story.

Black Hawk: Indian Patriot, by LaVere Anderson (Garr. Am. Indian) Gr. 1-5

Black Hawk, by Cathrine Cleven (Childhood) Gr. 1-6

**Story of the Black Hawk War*, by Jim Hargrove (Cornerstones) Gr. 2-6

Chief Black Hawk, by Frank Beals (American Adventures) Gr. 3-8
There is a new Christian series and another series called *American Adventure*, but this book is in a great older series by that name! It's a favorite of my youngest son!

Country of the Hawk, by August Derleth (Aladdin's American Heritage) Gr. 3-8

Black Hawk, by Arthur Beckhard Gr. 6-12

Indian America: The Black Hawk War, by Miriam Gurko Gr. 9-12

Black Hawk, Sac Rebel, by Nancy Bonvillain (N. Am. Indians of Achievement) Unknown

Fiction/Historical Fiction

Sandy and the Indians, by Margaret Friskey Gr. 4-10
A boy gets involved in Black Hawk's war in this lovely, older book.

Feather in the Wind, by Beverly Butler Gr. 7-12
The life of a tomboyish young woman during the Black Hawk War.

12q Sequoyah

Sequoyah, of the Cherokee tribe, has long been respected for his amazing work in developing a written language for the Cherokee and in providing valuable leadership. You'll want to meet him!

Sequoyah, by Ruby Radford (See and Read) Gr. 1-3

**Sequoyah: Cherokee Hero*, by Joanne Oppenheim (Troll)	Gr. 1-5
Sequoyah: The Cherokee Who Captured Words, by Lillie Patterson (Gar. Am. Ind.)	Gr. 1-5
Talking Leaves: The Story of Sequoyah, by Bernice Kohn	Gr. 1-5
Sequoyah, by Dorothea Snow (Childhood)	Gr. 1-6
Sequoyah: Father of the Cherokee Alphabet, by David Peterson	Gr. 2-6
Sequoyah: Leader of the Cherokees, by Alice Marriott (Landmark)	Gr. 3-10
Captured Words, by Frances Browin (Aladdin's American Heritage)	Gr. 4-12
Sequoyah and the Cherokee Alphabet, by Robert Cwiklik	Gr. 5-10
**Sequoyah's Gift: A Portrait of the Cherokee Leader*, by Janet Klausner	Gr. 5-12
**Lame One: The Story of Sequoyah*, by Jill Wheeler	Unknown
**Sequoyah*, by Michelle Levine	Unknown
**Sequoyah*, by Anne Todd	Unknown
**Sequoyah: Inventor of the Cherokee Written Language*, by Diane Shaughnessy	Unknown
**Sequoyah: Native American Scholar*, by C. Ann Fitterer	Unknown

Fiction/Historical Fiction

**Ahyoka and the Talking Leaves*, by Peter & Connie Roop — Gr. 3-7

I've not read this new novel which shows the apparent role of Sequoyah's daughter in developing the written language of the Cherokee.

13 Famous Pioneers

You folks from other nations have your own frontier heroes, but for the Americans, I mention three of our notables. Let's start with the folk hero, Johnny Appleseed. Here's a trivia question: what was his real last name? Chapman! Your library may sort biographies about him under that name. So, did we stump you? But, there's another frontier character you'd better get to know—Davy Crockett! What can we say about him? He seems to have done just about everything, and ended up at the Alamo (which we'll discuss later). Lastly,

you'll want to meet a frontiersman whose exploits were different than you might expect: the ambition of John James Audubon was to discover unknown bird species and record them in gorgeous paintings! What he went through, including an earthquake (the famous New Madrid quake of 1811/1812) to accomplish that is an amazing story, and his wife had no easily life either. Then there's the great mystery surrounding his French birth—was it royal? Good reading, I tell you!

13a Johnny Appleseed

Johnny Appleseed, by Gertrude Norman (See and Read) Gr. 1-3

**Johnny Appleseed*, by Steven Kellogg Gr. 1-4

**Johnny Appleseed*, by Reeve Lindbergh Gr. 1-4
A poetic rendition from the daughter of Charles Lindbergh.

**Johnny Appleseed*, by Louis Sabin (Troll) Gr. 1-4

**Story of Johnny Appleseed*, by Aliki Gr. 1-4

**True Tale of Johnny Appleseed*, by Margaret Hodges Gr. 1-4
This book relates the actual facts of Chapman's life.

Value of Love: Johnny Appleseed, by Anne Johnson (ValueTales) Gr. 1-4

**Johnny Appleseed*, by Stephen Vincent Benét, illustrated by S.D. Schindler Gr. 1-5
Illustrated version of classic poem from yesteryear. Older students can read the full poem, if they'd like...or sneak and enjoy this rendition instead!

**Folks Call Me Appleseed John*, by Andrew Glass Gr. 2-5

**Little Brother of the Wilderness*, by Meridel LeSueur Gr. 2-5

Johnny Appleseed, by Eva Moore Gr. 2-6

**In Praise of Johnny Appleseed*, Vachel Lindsay Gr. 2-8
This fun poem can be found in many poetry collections.

Restless Johnny, by Ruth Holberg Gr. 3-10

**Johnny Appleseed: The Story of a Legend*, by Will Moses Gr. 4-6

Real Johnny Appleseed, by Laurie Lawlor Gr. 4-8

Trail of Apple Blossoms, by Irene Hunt — Gr. 4-12

Better Known as Johnny Appleseed, by Mabel Leigh Hunt — Gr. 5-12

**Johnny Appleseed*, by David Collins (Sower) — Gr. 5-12
This biography is in a distinctly Christian series.

13b Davy Crockett

There's another frontier character you had better know—Davy Crockett! He was involved in so many streams of American history that I don't quite know where to put him. So here he is, plunked right in the middle of all the pioneering! He did end up at the Alamo, so you'll see him again then, but right now is a good time to meet this man who paved the way for so many others.

**Picture Book of Davy Crockett*, by David Adler — Gr. K-2

Davy Crockett, by Anne Ford (See and Read) — Gr. 1-3

**Davy Crockett: Young Pioneer*, by Laurence Santrey (Troll) — Gr. 1-4

Davy Crockett: Hero of the Wild Frontier, by Elizabeth Mosely (Garr. Discovery) — Gr. 1-5

**Davy Crockett*, by Aileen Parks (Childhood) — Gr. 1-6

Quit Pulling My Leg: A Story of Davy Crockett, by Robert Quackenbush — Gr. 2-6
Another of Quackenbush's comical biographies.

Davy Crockett, by Frank Beals (American Adventures) — Gr. 3-7
There is a new Christian series and another series by the name *American Adventure*, but this book is in a great older series by the same name! A favorite of my son's!

Davy Crockett, by Sanford Tousey — Gr. 3-7
Boys love this book, but it's too rare to be sought. If you have it, though, enjoy!

Davy Crockett, by Stewart Holbrook (Landmark) — Gr. 3-8

Story of Davy Crockett, by Enid LaMonte Meadowcroft (Signature) — Gr. 3-8

**Story of Davy Crockett*, by Walter Retan — Gr. 3-8
I think this is a former "Dell Yearling" book.

**Davy Crockett*, by Carl Green & William Sanford — Gr. 4-8

Old Whirlwind, by Elizabeth Coatsworth — Gr. 4-8

Yankee Thunder, by Irwin Shapiro (Messner) — Gr. 4-12

**Adventures of Davy Crockett*, by Davy Crockett — Gr. 5-12
Actually, there are versions of Crockett's autobiography for various ages.

Chanticleer of Wilderness Road, by Meridel LeSueur — Gr. 5-12

Davy Crockett, by Constance Rourke — Gr. 6-12

**Life of David Crockett*, by David Crockett — Gr. 8-12
There are versions of Crockett's autobiography for various ages; this is another.

**Davy Crockett*, by George Sullivan (In Their Own Words) — Unknown
Sullivan uses Crockett's own autobiography to tell his story.

Fiction/Historical Fiction

**Davy Crockett Saves the World*, by Rosalyn Schanzer — Gr. 1-4
A whopping tall tale!

Narrow Escapes of Davy Crockett, by Ariane Dewey — Gr. 1-4
Crockett is telling the tall tales in this book.

**Sally Ann Thunder Ann Whirlwind Crockett*, by Steven Kellogg — Gr. 1-4
Meet the tall-tale wife of Davy Crockett; she was a character right from birth!

How Davy Crockett Got a Bearskin Coat, by Wyatt Blassingame — Gr. 1-5
Another fun tale tale.

Davy Crockett's Earthquake, by William O. Steele — Gr. 2-6
Fun tall tales!

Film

**Davy Crockett: King of the Wild Frontier*, starring Fess Parker — All ages
Many families enjoy this great series of films from the good, ol' days when Disney was making wholesome films about American heroes.

13c John James Audubon

Almost any American art book will feature Audubon's magnificent paintings!

Did I say we were done meeting famous frontier folk? If so, I messed up, because there is one more. And what an unusual story he has, for he did not go west to settle but to paint pictures of birds! Yet, that doesn't begin to tell the drama of his life...and that of his family. Let's see, there was his mysterious French origin, the earthquake....oh, I better let you discover it all on your own. But promise me you'll find one of the many books showcasing his famous paintings—and then bask in them!

Into the Woods: John James Audubon Lives His Dream, by Robert Burleigh — Gr. 1-5
Wonderful, beautiful and *reverent* picture-bio of Audubon. Lovely!

John James Audubon: Bird Artist, by James Ayars (Garrard Discovery) — Gr. 1-5

Young Audubon, by Miriam Mason (Childhood) — Gr. 1-6
This seems to have also been published as *John Audubon.*

Boy Who Drew Birds, by Jacqueline Davies — Gr. 2-4

Audubon: Painter of Birds in the Wild Frontier, by Jennifer Armstrong — Gr. 2-5

Boy of the Woods, by Maie Lounsbury Wells & Dorothy Fox — Gr. 3-8
Nicely-illustrated older book; rare.

Story of John J. Audubon, by Joan Howard (Signature) — Gr. 3-8

John James Audubon, by Margaret & John Kieran (Landmark) — Gr. 3-9

Capturing Nature, by Peter & Connie Roop — Gr. 3-12
This recent book highlights Audubon's writings and artwork.

Audubon and His Sons, by Amy Hogeboom — Gr. 5-12

John James Audubon: Wildlife Artist, by Peter Anderson — Unknown

13d Audubon's young apprentice, Joe Mason

Joe Mason: Apprentice to Audubon, by Charlie May Simon — Gr. 5-12
Fact-based, young man helps Audubon find birds.

On the Frontier with Mr. Audubon, by Barbara Brenner — Gr. 5-12
Fact-based, young man helps Audubon find birds.

14 Mountain Men

I hope you non-Americans aren't bored; admittedly, we have covered several American topics right in a row. It would help, though, if you could realize the difference. The European nations had been humming along for centuries. Yes, they'd just been through the Napoleonic Wars and the Industrial Revolution, but we've covered those major events already. Now life in Europe had settled into something of a groove during the 1820s and 1830s. Yes, we'll later look back on these years in Europe, but there is something more pressing at the moment: during the same two decades, America, like a young boy, was growing like a weed...and spreading just as quickly! There's simply a lot to cover as America goes through her rapid expansion and maturation. In short order, she would be more settled, like her European ancestors. So, please bear with us.

Right now, then, we can look at some American adventurers who simply weren't content with a log cabin beyond the Appalachians or Ohio River...risky as even those endeavors were! No, these "mountain men" charged into the vast wilderness of the Rocky Mountains and beyond...seeking new frontiers, trapping beaver pelts, building friendships with the Indians, and blazing trails used by later pioneers. What a brave lot!

14a General overview

We'll cover Kit Carson and John Frémont later because they were involved in the Oregon Trail and in the conflict for California, respectively.

Fur Trappers of the Old West, by A.M. Anderson (American Adventures) Gr. 2-7
There is a new Christian series and another series by the name *American Adventure*, but this book is in a great older series by the same name!

**Heroes of the Western Outposts* and **Hunters Blaze the Trails* (Frontiers of Am.) Gr. 3-7
by Edith McCall
These two entries are from another thrilling series which has just been reprinted!

Mountain Men: True Grit and Tall Tales, by Andrew Glass Gr. 3-7
Three true tales and some tall ones thrown in...all in this rollicking overview. It was recently in print, so is probably still in most public libraries.

Stories of the Early Times in the Great West, by Florence Bass Gr. 3-8
This antique is too rare to be sought, but if you have it, enjoy!

Trappers and Traders of the Far West, by James Daugherty (Landmark) Gr. 3-8
Daugherty's books are usually very well-written.

When Mountain Men Trapped Beaver, by R. Glendinning (Gar. How They Lived) Gr. 3-8

Mountain Men, by Don Berry — Gr. 4-12
I've not seen this, but it sounds interesting.

Mountain Men of the Early West, by Olive Burt — Gr. 4-12

Trails West and the Men Who Made Them, by E. Dorian & W. Wilson — Gr. 4-12

Westward with American Explorers, by Walter Buehr — Gr. 4-12

Mountain Men, by Wyatt Blassingame and Richard Glendinning — Gr. 5-10

Last Wilderness: The Saga of America's Mountain Men, by N. Gerson (Messner) — Gr. 7-12

Negroes in the Early West, by Olive Burt (Messner) — Gr. 7-12

**Jedediah Smith and the Mountain Men of the American West*, by John Allen — Unknown
This will also be cited in the specific section on Jedediah Smith below. It seems to give general coverage as well, though, so is also placed here.

Fiction/Historical Fiction

Git Along, Old Scudder, by Stephen Gammell — Gr. K-3
Don't miss this fun little book!

Beaver Water, by Rutherford Montgomery — Gr. 4-12
Two brothers face challenges as early furtrappers.

Jube: Story of a Trapper's Dog, by Thomas Hinkle — Gr. 4-12

Andy of Pirate Gorge, by H.R. Langdale — Gr. 5-12
Boy faces challenges when working on an Astor furtrapping crew.

Buckskin Brigade, by Jim Kjelgaard — Gr. 5-12
A novel about the wilderness men.

East of Astoria, by Merritt Parmelee Allen — Gr. 5-12
Early fur crew on intensely difficult journey from St. Louis to Oregon in 1810. Allen's books have been very, very highly recommended to me.

Saga of Andy Burnett, by Stewart Edward White — Gr. 5-12
Boy with heirloom rifle travels with mountain men.

Spirit of the Eagle, by Merritt Parmelee Allen — Gr. 5-12
A man, released by the Indians, helps Benjamin Bonneville explore.

Young Mac of Fort Vancouver, by Mary Jane Carr — Gr. 5-12
Boy works in the area around Northwest fort.

Buffalo and Beaver, by Stephen Meader — Gr. 7-12
Another adventurous tale from this beloved author.

**Hugh Glass, Mountain Man*, by Robert McClung — Gr. 7-12
Novelized version of real events; man survives vicious bear attack, then must crawl miles for help after cruel friends left him for dead. May be too intense for some.

14b Grizzly Adams

Adams seems more famous for his pet bears than his years in the mountains.

Grizzly Adams, by Harry James (Frontiers of America) — Gr. 2-7

True Adventures of Grizzly Adams, by Robert McClung — Unknown

14c John Jacob Astor

You may already know that Astor created a fur empire!

John Jacob Astor, by Dorothy Anderson (Childhood) — Gr. 1-6

**John Jacob Astor and the Fur Trade*, by Lewis Parker (American Tycoons) — Unknown

14d Jim Beckwourth

Beckwourth was an African-American trapper who became an Indian chief! How can you top that for excitement?

**Jim Beckwourth: Adventures of a Mountain Man*, by Louis Sabin (Troll) — Gr. 1-4

Jim Beckwourth, by Wyatt Blassingame (Garrard Discovery) — Gr. 1-5

Jim Beckwourth: Negro Mountain Man, by Harold Felton — Gr. 4-12

**James Beckwourth*, by Sean Dolan (Black Americans of Achievement) — Unknown

**James Beckwourth*, by Rick Burke (American Lives) — Unknown

14e Benjamin Bonneville

Ever heard of the Bonneville Salt Flats in Utah? Now you know where they got their name!

Benjamin Bonneville, by Helen Markley Miller — Gr. 6-12

14f Jim Bowie

Ah, another famous name! I bet all you boys have heard of the Bowie Knife.

Jim Bowie, by Gertrude Winders (Childhood) — Gr. 1-6

James Bowie and His Famous Knife, by Shannon Garst (Messner) — Gr. 4-12

**Jim Bowie: Frontier Legend, Alamo Hero*, by J.R. Edmondson — Gr. 5-12
This focuses heavily on Texas history and battle at the Alamo, in which Bowie fought, so you might want to read this later.

**Jim Bowie*, by Marianne Johnston (American Legends) — Unknown

14g Jim Bridger

Wow, Bridger did so much! I couldn't begin to list it all!

Jim Bridger: Man of the Mountains, by W. & C. Luce (Garrard Discovery) — Gr. 1-5

Jim Bridger, by Gertrude Winders (Childhood) — Gr. 1-6

Jim Bridger, by Sanford Tousey — Gr. 2-7
Boys love this book, but it's too rare to be sought. If you have it, enjoy it!

Jim Bridger: Greatest of the Mountain Men, by Shannon Garst — Gr. 4-12

Fiction/Historical Fiction

Moccasins through the Rye, by Elaine Egbert — Gr. 4-12?
I've never seen this story of Mary Anne Bridger, JimBridger's daughter, but one mother told me it is one of her favorite girlhood books, and she saved her copy for her children.

Western Star, by Merritt Parmelee Allen — Gr. 4-12

Novelized version of Bridger's life story from very good author. I know boys around the country who do special jobs just to earn money to buy more Allen books!

14h John Colter

Colter started his adventurous career as one of the men in the Lewis & Clark Expedition! That was only the beginning. No one believed his reports of the geological oddities in what is now Yellowstone Park!

Who'd Believe John Colter? by Mary Blount Christian — Gr. 3-7

This was recently in print, so it is probably still in most libraries.

Giant of the Rockies, by Elisa Bialk — Gr. 4-12

John Colter: Man Who Found Yellowstone, by Mark Boesch — Gr. 6-12

Colter's Run, by Judith Edwards (Highlights from American History) — Unknown

The Blackfeet Indians had captured Colter and for sport gave him a chance to escape by running through the desert for his life...without shoes or clothes. Did Colter outrun them with his allowed headstart? This was recently in-print, so is probably still in most libraries, but I've not seen it.

14i Broken-Hand Fitzpatrick

If you just heard of a man named "Broken-Hand," you'd probably guess that he was a mountain man! You would be right. He discovered the much-used South Pass into Oregon.

Adventures of Broken-Hand, by Frank Morriss — Gr. 4-9

Broken-Hand Fitzpatrick, by Shannon Garst (Messner) — Gr. 6-12

14j Joe Meek

Meek had a big role in the development of Oregon.

Joe Meek: Man of the West, by Shannon Garst (Messner) — Gr. 6-12

Mountain Man, by Rutherford Montgomery — Gr. 6-12

14k Edward Rose

Like Beckwourth, Rose was an African-American mountain man!

Edward Rose: Negro Trail Blazer, by Harold Felton — Gr. 4-12

14l Jedediah Smith

Smith was reportedly a very committed Christian!

Jed Smith: Trailblazer and Trapper, by Frank Latham (Garrard Discovery) — Gr. 1-5

(Young) Jed Smith, by Olive Burt (Childhood) — Gr. 1-6

Jed Smith: Trail Blazer, by Frank Latham (Aladdin's American Heritage) — Gr. 3-9

Jedediah Smith, by Hal Evarts — Gr. 4-12

Jedediah Smith: Fur Trapper of the Old West, by Olive Burt (Messner) — Gr. 7-12

**Jedediah Smith*, by Sharlene Nelson — Unknown

**Jedediah Smith and the Mountain Men of the American West*, by John Allen — Unknown

Fiction/Historical Fiction

Sun Trail, by Merritt Parmelee Allen — Gr. 5-12

This story was based on Smith's actual maps and journals, and many boys enjoy Allen's books exceedingly.

15 Santa Fe Trail

Before we leave America's Wild West, let's touch on one more topic. We've got to travel the famed Santa Fe Trail! The route was first used commercially in 1821 by William Becknell, and for several decades it served as a trade route between Kansas City and the outpost at Santa Fe. It also served as a pathway for many settlers and adventurers heading west. What adventures and heartbreaks that trail has seen!

15a General overview

**Right Fine Life: Kit Carson on the Santa Fe Trail*, by Andrew Glass Gr. 1-4
This is a fun book of young Kit you can enjoy now, but please note that we'll later study Kit Carson in greater detail because he served as a chief guide to the Oregon Territory.

**Where the Buffalo Roams*, by Jacqueline Geis Gr. 1-7
Though not specifically about the trail, this is a lovely picture-book tour of the land.

**Santa Fe Trail*, by Judy Alter (Cornerstones) Gr. 2-7

**Tree in the Trail*, by Holling Clancy Holling Gr. 2-7
This long-beloved book brings the entire Great Southwest area to life and includes mention of the Santa Fe trail. Beautiful Feet Books (www.bfbooks.com) offers a lovely companion study guide and fill-in map.

**Santa Fe Trail*, by Jean Blashfield (We the People) Gr. 3-6
An online reviewer claimed this was dry.

When Wagon Trains Rolled to Santa Fe, by Erick Berry (Gar. How They Lived) Gr. 3-8

Santa Fe Trail, by Samuel Adams (Landmark) Gr. 3-9

Wagons to the Wilderness, by Samuel Adams (Winston Adventure) Gr. 3-9
This excellent series highlights the little known contributions of young people.

Story of the Southwest, by May McNeer Gr. 4-10
This book offers a general, narrative history of the Great Southwest and therefore includes the impact of the Santa Fe Trail.

Trail to Santa Fe, by David Lavender (North Star) Gr. 4-12
It appears this book, originally in a great series, was reprinted in 1995 by Holiday House.

**Empires Lost and Won: The Spanish Heritage in the Southwest*, by Albert Marrin Gr. 8-12
You probably already know that Marrin provides wonderful narrative history books for older readers! This book covers the general history of the Great Southwest, and therefore includes material on the Santa Fe Trail.

**Santa Fe Trail*, by Ryan Randolph (Library of Westward Expansion) Unknown

Fiction/Historical Fiction

**Lewis & Papa: Adventure on the Santa Fe Trail*, by Barbara Joosse — Gr. 1-4
This is a touching book about a young boy and his gentle father.

**Meet Josefina*, by Valerie Tripp (and others in this *American Girl* series) — Gr. 1-6

**All the Stars in the Sky: The Santa Fe Trail Diary of....* (Dear America) — Gr. 3-8
by Megan McDonald
Tone and content of this series is uneven, I've found. Please check carefully.

We Were There on the Santa Fe Trail, by Ross Taylor (We Were There) — Gr. 3-8
This fun series places fictional children at real historical events.

Trails West, by George Franklin — Gr. 3-9
A teen gets a chance to head west.

Message from the Mountains, by Edith McCall — Gr. 4-10
Two teens, one of them young Kit Carson, dream of going on the Santa Fe Trail.

Silver Wolf, by Merritt Parmelee Allen — Gr. 5-12
High adventure on the Santa Fe Trail with Kit Carson; wonderful author!

**Wagons Westward*, by Armstrong Sperry — Gr. 5-12
Wonderful news: someone is reprinting Sperry's books!

15b Alec Majors

Majors was a trail boss on the Santa Fe Trail.

Alec Majors: Trail Boss, by A.M. Anderson (American Adventures) — Gr. 2-6
There is a new Christian series and another series by the name *American Adventure*, but this book is in a great older series by the same name!

15c Bent's Fort

Bent's Fort was an important stop along the Santa Fe Trail.

Bent's Fort: Crossroads of the West, by Wyatt Blassingame (Garr. How They...) — Gr. 3-8

Bent's Fort, by Melvin Bacon & Daniel Blegen Gr. 4-10

Covers the fort, the nature of the Santa Fe Trail, and travelers first-person accounts.

William Bent and His Adobe Empire, by Shannon Garst (Messner) Gr. 7-12

16 Erie Canal

With all this talk about the Great West, I hope you aren't forgetting that the people back east were tackling big projects too...like the Erie Canal! It really is amazing to think of New Yorkers digging in, *literally!* But, hey, it was the Era of Good Feelings, remember? People were excited about their nation, their future, and their power to make things better. It is excellent to see that folks were working hard to improve their towns and livelihoods; God does want us to take dominion and do our best. Our excitement and efforts, though, must be founded on Him, not ourselves, or else.... Well, you'll see later. Right now, then, we can applaud this feat of engineering and the fact that New Yorkers funded the project themselves![32]

16a Erie Canal

**Story of the Great Republic*, by H.A. Guerber, Ch. XVIII Gr. 3-7

**Erie Canal*, by Peter Spier Gr. K-4

Fun illustrations showcase words to famous folk song about the Erie Canal.

Story of the Erie Canal, by R. Conrad Stein (Cornerstones) Gr. 2-7

This has gone out-of-print, but most libraries have this whole series.

**Amazing Impossible Erie Canal*, by Cheryl Harness Gr. 2-8

A vivid new book.

**Erie Canal*, by Craig Doherty (Building America) Gr. 3-7

**Erie Canal*, by Andrew Santella (We the People) Gr. 3-8

**Erie Canal*, by R. Conrad Stein (Cornerstones II) Gr. 3-8

---

32 Carson 3:104.

Erie Canal, by Samuel Hopkins Adams (Landmark) Gr. 3-9

Erie Canal, by Nicholas Nirgiotis (First Book) Gr. 7-12

Waterway West: The Story of the Erie Canal, by Mary Kay Phelan Gr. 8-12

Fiction/Historical Fiction

**Erie Canal Pirates*, by Eric Kimmel Gr. 1-4
Pirates—"Terror of Buffalo"—attack an Erie Canal boat in this just-for-fun book!

Dick and the Canal Boat, by Sanford Tousey Gr. 1-5
A fictional boy helps on the Erie Canal; this book is too rare to be sought, though.

Molly's Hannibal, by Robert Willis Gr. 2-7
A girl and her mule help pull boats through the canal.

Timothy O'Dowd and the Big Ditch, by Len Hilts Gr. 3-7

We Were There at the Opening of the Erie Canal, by E. Meadowcroft (We Were...) Gr. 3-8
This fun series puts fictional kids at real historical events!

Brother of the Wind, by Jerry Wolfert Gr. 5-12
Keelboat boy has adventures near Niagara Falls and is part of conflict between Buffalo and Black Rock as end of Erie Canal.

Chingo Smith of the Erie Canal, by Samuel Hopkins Adams Gr. 5-12
Boy works on the canal in hopes of becoming a boat captain.

Watergate: Story of the Irish on the Erie Canal, by Herbert Best (Land of the Free) Gr. 5-12

16b Life on canals and barges

After the success of the Erie Canal, many other canals were built around the country. Many folks found their livelihoods on these busy waterways!

Life on a Barge, by Huck Scarry Gr. 3-12
Intricately illustrated book shows life on a canal barge.

River and Canal, by Edward Boyer Gr. 4-12
This nice book pictures the building of a fictional canal.

16c DeWitt Clinton

Mr. Clinton was a driving force behind the Erie Canal, and had political prominence.

DeWitt Clinton, by Mabel Widdemer (Childhood) Gr. 1-6

17 Simon Bolivar, James Monroe, and the Monroe Doctrine

Do you think America was the only New World colony to fight for freedom from European control? No! During the 1810s and 1820s, many Spanish colonies in South America waged their own wars of independence. Behind much of the action was Simon Bolivar, *El Libertador*. You may also have heard him called the "George Washington of South America," for he was founder and president of not just one, but of several new South American nations! In fact, Bolivia (formerly Upper Peru) was named in his honor! These were difficult uprisings as there was a different spiritual base in these lands, but we cannot cover that here. You already know that these South American nations have struggled even after achieving political freedom.

Anyway, at the time of the revolts, Spain was making noises—loud noises—about getting these wayward colonies back. Furthermore, they asked for the help of their European neighbors, who also had far-flung colonies, telling them that a concerted crackdown would subdue everyone's colonies. America had gained its freedom; and while Europe deemed us a shaky proposition, they didn't want other colonies getting ideas. Enter James Monroe! His storied contribution to this nation all through his days as a soldier in the Revolutionary War, his role in acquiring Louisiana, his governorship of Virginia, his years of foreign ambassadorship, and his stint as Secretary of State and Secretary of War during the War of 1812 is amazing...but he wasn't done fighting for freedom yet. While serving as America's fifth president from 1817-1825, he supported the South American freedom fight by declaring the *Monroe Doctrine* (1823) which said America would resist Old World domination anywhere in the New World. Much of the Doctrine was actually written by John Quincy Adams, then Secretary of State to Monroe, but the president's support of it was crucial.

17a Simon Bolivar and Latin American freedom

**Story of the World: Vol. 3*, by Susan Wise Bauer, Ch. 34 Gr. 3-6

Some families enjoy this book's scope, so ask us to cite it; others seek different worldview; so, parental decision.

**Picture Book of Simon Bolivar*, by David Adler Gr. K-2

Simon Bolivar, by Nina Brown Baker Gr. 3-8

Simon Bolivar, by Arnold Whitridge (Landmark) Gr. 3-8

Simon Bolivar, by Carol Greene (People of Distinction) Gr. 4-7

Bolivar the Liberator, by Ronald Syme Gr. 4-12
Syme writes powerful, adventurous biographies, though I've not read this one.

Against All Odds: Pioneers of South America, by Marion Lansing Gr. 5-12

Men of Power, by Albert Carr, Ch. 5 Gr. 5-12

Simon Bolivar, by Dennis Wepman (World Leaders Past & Present) Gr. 6-12

He Wouldn't Be King: The Story of Simon Bolivar, by Nina Brown Baker Gr. 7-12
Baker has produced many nice, narrative biographies.

Fiction/Historical Fiction

With Bolivar Over the Andes, by C.M. Nelson Gr. 5-12
A fictional boy helps Bolivar's freedom fight.

17b James Monroe and the Monroe Doctrine

Don't forget there are so many book series about the various presidents that I needn't cite them all.

**From Sea to Shining Sea for Children*, by Marshall & Manuel, Ch. 9 Gr. 1-5

**Story of the Great Republic*, by H.A. Guerber, Ch. XIXa Gr. 3-7

**This Country of Ours*, by H.E. Marshall, Ch. 71 Gr. 3-8

**From Sea to Shining Sea*, by Marshall & Manuel, Ch. 8 Gr. 6-12

**Basic History of the United States: Vol. 2*, by Clarence Carson, Ch. 10f Gr. 9-12

**James Monroe: Young Patriot*, by Rae Bains Gr. 1-3

**James Monroe*, by Mike Venezia (Getting to Know the U.S. Presidents) Gr. 1-5

James Monroe, by Mabel Widdemer (Childhood) Gr. 1-6

James Monroe, by Christine Fitzgerald (Encyclopedia of Presidents) Gr. 5-12

Defiance to the Old World: Story of the Monroe Doctrine, by George Dangerfield Gr. 7-12

Great Doctrine, by Henry Commager Gr. 7-12

In Defense of Freedom: Story of the Monroe Doctrine, by P. Rink (Messner/Milestone) Gr. 8-12

**James Monroe*, by Ann Gaines (Our Presidents) Unknown
I think this is for younger readers.

**James Monroe*, by Andrew Santella (Encyclopedia of Presidents II) Unknown

**Monroe Doctrine: An End to European Colonies in America*, by M. Alagna Unknown

18 Early American Literature

America was a "young thing" when it comes to nations, but she was producing her first national literature. (We'll cover international writers later.) I think you're now familiar enough with the spiritual temperature of the era—though we're about to launch into some new issues in upcoming sections—that you can bring some analysis to these literary works if you decide to probe them and/or their authors at this time.

18a General overview

**Basic History of the United States: Vol. 3*, by Clarence Carson, Ch. 5a, c Gr. 9-12

18b William Cullen Bryant

Bryant was one of America's earliest poets. His most famous works ares ****Thanatopsis*, ****To a Waterfowl*, ****Forest Hymn*, *etc.*, but he wrote several others, and was also an influential editor of New York's *Evening Post*.[33]

Famous American Authors, by Sarah Bolton Gr. 6-12
There is a chapter on Bryant in this nice book.

33 Morris 639.

18c James Fenimore Cooper

Cooper's father, a Congressman, contributed to the settlement of what is now Cooperstown, New York. After time at Yale, and in the navy, Cooper's wife challenged him to "make good on his boast that he could write a better novel than the one they were reading together."[34] Cooper's most famous works include: *_Last of the Mohicans_ and others in the _Leatherstocking Tales_ series. He later wrote essays critical of American culture and thus lost public popularity.[35]

James Fenimore Cooper, by Gertrude Winders (Childhood) — Gr. 1-6

James Fenimore Cooper, by Isabel Proudfit (Messner) — Gr. 5-12

18d Nathaniel Hawthorne

Hawthorne was interested in the themes of earlier America, especially the Puritan era. I've often wondered if he wanted to understand the Puritans but couldn't fully do so without accepting the new life in Christ which brought meaning and joy to Puritan life. Hawthorne was left to struggle with issues of sin, discipline, and determination without understanding the spirit that sustained them and instead with the growing secular ideas of his day. Hence his criticism of the Puritans. Please note, though, that I have not researched Hawthorne's life or work. You can go much father than I on this topic! His more famous works are: *_House of Seven Gables_, *_Scarlet Letter_, *_Twice-Told Tales_, *_Tanglewood Tales_, *_Wonder Book_, *_Grandfather's Chair_, *_Blithedale Romance_, and the *_Marble Faun_.

Famous American Authors, by Sarah Bolton — Gr. 6-12
There is a chapter on Hawthorne in this nice book.

Nathaniel Hawthorne: American Storyteller, by Nancy Whitelaw (World Writers) — Gr. 7-12

New England Men of Letters, by Wilson Sullivan — Gr. 7-12
There is a chapter on Hawthorne in this book also.

Romantic Rebel: Nathaniel Hawthorne, by Hildegarde Hawthorne — Gr. 7-12

**Invitation to the Classics*, edited by Cowan & Guinness, pp. 237-240 — Gr. 8-12
Christian analysis of famous authors and literature.

34 *Webster's Biographical Dictionary* (Springfield, MA: G. & C. Merriam Co., 1943) 347.
35 Morris 647.

18e Oliver Wendell Holmes

Holmes was a man of many talents: a doctor, a professor, as well as a poet, novelist, and biographer! (Don't confuse him with his famous son, though; Oliver Wendell Holmes, Jr., was a Supreme Court justice whom we will study in the next *TruthQuest History* guide.) His most famous works are: *_Autocrat of the Breakfast-Table_, *_Old Ironsides_, *_Chambered Nautilus_, and *_Lost Leaf_.[36]

18f Washington Irving

Mr. Irving had a fascinating life...at least in my opinion. He was a lawyer for a short time, but preferred writing.[37] **Working in the U.S. embassy in Spain and England gave Irving the opportunity for travel, and he wrote books while abroad. His more famous works are: *_Legend of Sleepy Hollow_, *_Rip Van Winkle_, *_Knickerbocker History of New York_, *_Alhambra_, *_Chronicle of the Conquest of Granada_, *_Sketch Book_, and *_Oliver Goldsmith_.**

Washington Irving, by Mabel Widdemer (Childhood) Gr. 1-6

Washington Irving: His Life, by Catherine Owens Peare Gr. 3-9

Washington Irving, by Anya Seton (North Star) Gr. 6-12

**Washington Irving: Storyteller for a New Nation* by David Collins (World Writers) Gr. 6-12

18g William McGuffey

Mr. McGuffey was a college professor[38] **who first published an immensely popular and influential series of reading primers in 1838. Generations of Americans grew up on the moral lessons in his *_Eclectic Readers_. In fact, they are _still_ being published and you might have read them yourself!**

William McGuffey, by Barbara Williams (Childhood) Gr. 1-6

36 Webster's Biographical Dictionary 723.
37 Webster's Biographical Dictionary 762.
38 Webster's Biographical Dictionary 943.

18h William Gilmore Simms

Simms, born in South Carolina, is sometimes seen as the James Fenimore Cooper of the American South.[39] His books capture Southern sensibilities and values. Sorry, I know of no youth books written about him in particular. His famous works include: *_Yemassee_ and *_Guy Rivers_.

18i Noah Webster

Not everyone can write the great American novel. Someone has to write the dictionaries and the educational primers. Well, Noah Webster was that man. Recognize the last name? Think of the dictionary that is probably sitting on your own family's bookshelf! You see, Webster had a passion that Americans develop their own distinct strain of English, one that reflected our unique nation. He was also concerned that American young people grow up with a great education...which naturally included Christian truth.

This gave rise to his history book and primers, one of which was so widely used for an entire century that it was called by its nickname, the *_Blue-Backed Speller_. Another great achiever, Webster was also a lawyer, newspaper editor, friend of Benjamin Franklin, legislator, historian, college founder (Amherst) and administrator; he even wrote an important book about epidemics and served as a soldier in the War for Independence![40] His *_American Dictionary of the English Language_ is still admired for its excellence and moral inclusions. Overall, Webster had a large impact on American English. I'm evening using a Webster book to write this very section!

Noah Webster, by Helen Higgins (Childhood)	Gr. 1-6
**What Do You Mean?* by Jeri Ferris (Carolrhoda's Creative Minds)	Gr. 2-7
**Noah Webster*, by David Collins (Sower) This biography series always includes the Christian faith of the subject.	Gr. 5-12
Noah Webster, by Isabel Proudfit (Messner)	Gr. 6-12
**Autobiographies of Noah Webster*	Gr. 10-12
**Noah Webster and the First American Dictionary*, by Luisanna Fodde	Unknown

39 Carson 3:81.
40 Webster's Biographical Dictionary 1553-1554.

19 Honeymoon is Over: The Era of Good Feelings Gives Way to Sectionalism

Well, we've had a long tour throughout the American continent; we've met many famous folk. What's more important, though, is what's happening in the heart of a nation...and the American heart was indeed changing, as we've been hinting. All the victories and growth had gone to some American heads. There wasn't the same earnest pursuit of godly principles and restraints which had characterized so many of the starving Pilgrims, founding fathers, and bloody-footed soldiers huddled at Valley Forge.

Do you remember at the beginning of this guide that we talked about America's wonderful limited government, and the resulting freedom and responsibility to be *self*-governing? Those who had paid the price knew the inestimable value of this restraint. They saw how different life was in Europe, where people still labored under heavy-handed despots. We have the advantage of retrospect and can see how right they were, for even when the power of the Industrial Revolution was let loose, the stodgy monarchies could not make as much of the opportunities.

Anyway, we were talking about the early American emphasis on limited government. As proof, I'll repeat a quote from Thomas Jefferson:

> *A wise and frugal Government, which shall restrain men from injuring one another, shall leave them otherwise free to regulate their own pursuits of industry and improvement, and shall not take from the mouth of the labor the bread it has earned. This is the sum of good government...*[41]

It all depended on the hearts of the people. Did they want to embrace the godly wisdom of restraint? If not, the American political system could be used quite selfishly for assuming their posterity would always be wise, they left it open-ended (in other words, *free*). So, Americans sat again at a fork in the road! Would the people push the government to fill a trough at which they could feed? Would politicians siphon everyone's taxes to pay for projects that made them popular, or would they realize they should be a *true* blessing, as God says? See? It's always a spiritual issue! If God was honored first (*Big Belief #1*), financial security would then be found in following His principles, not in the government sneaking money from the taxpayers, or the taxpayers sneaking money from the government! If His command to be a blessing, not a curse, to others, was followed (*Big Belief #2*), no one would try to get ahead at the expense of others. Let's see what happened. It's going to take a while to work through all this, but we need to give the time, for this is important stuff!

I'm sad to report that already by the 1820s, you'll see individual Americans moving away from thinking of government as limited (only keeping the most basic peace and protecting everyone's right to work), and instead thinking of how its power could be personally beneficial. The consequences of this increasing selfishness had an absolutely deadly outcome in the end, as you'll soon discover!

---

41 Carson 157.

How did it start? As usual, geography was affecting history. The poorer soil of the North (especially New England) made farming difficult, but her hilly terrain and many streams made watermill-driven industry successful; her natural seaports were thriving. The South, with few harbors and flat, fertile land, excelled in agriculture, especially in growing the cotton craved by the new textile mills of New England and Britain. The West (meaning the frontier areas newly penetrated by pioneers, even if they were still east of the Mississippi River) had access to that great river for shipping, and a bent toward agriculture as well, so there was a linkage between the South and the West.

These three *sections* (North, South, and West) could have worked together as a team, like parts of one body, but each section became increasingly self-oriented. This is called *sectionalism*. Each section saw that government could be finagled to give them a boost, not caring that it required a more involved government, was unconstitutional, and was unfair to the other sections.

Sectionalism

Yep, it's easy to dream up goodies for ourselves. It's hard to think of the consequences. Did these Americans wonder what would happen when government was less limited? Did they know that a government "vending machine" would also make government more controlling and expensive, and would pit one American against another? Did it occur to them that a government which could be manipulated *by* them could also be manipulated by others *against* them? Did they realize they were starting to replace Biblical principles of government with their own ideas? Here's the big question: how vibrant and strong were the churches if so many Americans were thinking selfishly?

The *Era of Good Feelings* fell apart when everyone started demanding their own way, I'll give you an example that raised a lot of controversy—tariffs. "Tariffs?" you're probably thinking. "Who's ever heard of those?" Everyone that lived during the 1820s, that's who! Tariffs are fees added to imported items, to discourage people from buying from foreign countries (and sending American money there) when someone in America is trying to make and sell the same thing.

Tariff

What does that have to do with anything? The Northerners were making lots of goods in their new factories. They didn't want Southerners and Westerners buying the same goods from Europe, so they asked the government to put tariffs on imported goods. That meant Joe Southerner had to cough up extra money if he wanted a British thing-a-ma-jig just to help a Northern factory owner make more money. Fair? It sure violated the principles of free enterprise!

Things got even hotter when South Carolina claimed the right to *nullify* and disobey any federal law which they believed hurt their state. This triggered a violent reaction, as people contemplated the impact of that position. How could the union function *or survive?* Senators Daniel Webster and Robert Hayne sparred in a famous debate on the topic.[42]

Nullify

42 Carson, Ch. 3.

I can give you a couple more examples of sectionalism too, neither of which make the North look very good. Many New Englanders were miffed when the government made it easy for people to move west by selling the land so cheaply. They urged their congressmen to stop it. This made Westerners soooo mad! Southerners—partial to the West and worried about "competing" with Northern industrial might—claimed New England was just trying to keep desperate people from moving west so they'd have to stay and work in miserable Northern factories. Ouch, that had to hurt!

> ***ThinkWrite 5: "The race is on!"***
>
> Why did many Americans feel they were in a race with other Americans, competing for dominance? Why didn't they work together as a good team?

That's not all, though I wish it were. Some New Englanders were getting panicky about all that cotton shipping down the Mississippi River through New Orleans. What if they lost their monopoly on American shipping? That'd shoot a hole in a Northern pocketbook or two. While there was a desire for better transportation, the projects Northerners supported were those like canals which led to New England seaports. I can still hear the Western and Southern howls![43] (Do *ThinkWrite 5* now.) **Someone else has described sectionalism in a lot fancier language:**

> *Political jockeying, the enactment of legislation for the supposed benefit of one region at the expense of another, can give rise to sectional jealousies and rivalries.*[44]

There *were* some still calling for the government to stop playing sectional games and get back to the limited business of protecting the most basic liberties. Their words are poignant! Let me share a few, rich quotes here:

> *...the people generally should control government so as to limit and restrain it from acting for the benefit of the few at their expense.*[45]

That quote came from Andrew Jackson, who believed federal spending should only be for Constitutionally instituted responsibilities which benefitted *all* Americans. That was a hallmark of the Democratic Party he founded; I wish more Americans held to these high principles today! Others were saying the same things, too. Just bask in these words:

> *As a general rule, the prosperity of rational men depends upon themselves. Their talents and virtues shape their fortunes. They are therefore the best judges of their own affairs and should be permitted to seek their own happiness in their own way, untrammeled by the capricious interference of legislative bungling, so long as they do not violate the equal rights of others.*
>
> *If government were restricted to the few and simple objects contemplated in the democratic creed, the mere protection of person, life, and property..., we should find reason to congratulate ourselves on the change in the improved tone of public morals as well as in the increased prosperity of trade.*[46]

---

43 Carson, Ch. 2. (Much material in this section has been taken from Carson's book.)

44 Carson 13.

45 Carson 28.

46 Carson 29, quoting William Leggett.

Maybe Walt Whitman, later a famous poet, said it best:

> *One point, however, must not be forgotten—ought to be put before the eyes of the people every day; and that is, although government can do little* positive *good to the people, it may do an* immense deal of harm. *Democracy would prevent all this harm. It would have no man's benefit achieved at the expense of his neighbors... While mere politicians, in their narrow minds, are sweating and fuming with their complicated statues, this one single rule...is enough to form the starting point of all that is necessary in government; to make no more laws than those useful for preventing a man or body of men from infringing on the rights of other men.*

Well, those of you following Mr. Carson's books will want to get his insight on this matter:

**Basic History of the United States: Vol. 2*, by C. Carson, Ch. 10g Gr. 9-12
**Basic History of the United States: Vol. 3*, by C. Carson, Ch. 1-2a, pp. 94-109 Gr. 9-12
Chapter 1 is actually an introduction to this third volume of Carson's. It opens by briefly discussing the Civil War and Reconstruction and so seems anachronistic to our study. But then Carson shows how these events grew from beliefs and attitudes of the 1820s through 1860s—the very era we're now studying—so reading this first brief chapter is still quite helpful to your deeper understanding.

20 Slavery!

There is a huge sectional controversy we haven't tackled yet because it needs our fullest attention—slavery! I wanted to mention the other sectional haggles first, though, so you wouldn't think slavery was the only sectional issue, as many of us adults were told.

It's quite difficult to talk about slavery because it has devastated so many people, first and foremost the slaves! While modern whites hope that blacks will not hold against them the sins of their fathers, some of the consequences of that sin are still being felt, both by blacks and whites, and that makes for a very sensitive issue. As fair as we will try to be here, our ethnic and geographical roots do color our outlook on this topic. The British can proudly say that banned slavery earlier than we Americans. We'll meet the Englishman behind that great accomplishment—William Wilberforce—later in this guide.

Why was slavery a sectional issue in America? Because slaves were desired mostly in the South, where huge plantations and the backbreaking work of raising their most profitable crop (cotton) in the intense heat made large amounts of cheap labor especially desirable.

This is where I'd like to be able to tell you that the North's opposition to slavery was due to an awareness of the full equality of Negro people (I'll use the word used at the time—*Negro* —so we're in historical context). With a few notable exceptions, the North (where it wasn't uncommon for free Negroes to be raided and violated, and to have their houses torn part,

and where people, such as Prudence Crandall, who tried to educate Negroes in her own home, were fiercely persecuted) was possibly as racist as the South! This gave the South much opportunity to cry *Hypocrite!* and suspect that the North's anti-slavery motives were not as noble as they might claim. The town fathers of one New England village sent for one hundred teams of oxen to pull a school for Negroes right off its foundation! Not only did few town constables punish the wrongdoers, they were often leading the pack! What had happened to *rule of law?*

Yes, amongst anti-slavery people, there was a mixed bag of motives. A small minority correctly saw Negroes as equals and knew that slavery was totally wrong. A much larger group deemed the Negroes an inferior race, but thought enslaving them was going too far. Some just didn't want the South to have the financial advantage (they thought they were "competing") of having cheap labor when they had to hire their workers, though there were some slaves in the North.

It might help to begin with the history of slavery. I hope you can find this compelling book: *All Times, All Peoples*, by Milton Meltzer. Students of most ages can read it. Meltzer, himself a black/African-American, reveals what few Americans are taught in the politically-correct atmosphere surrounding the issue of slavery: it is not just a white-black issue. Probably more whites have been enslaved since the beginning of time than have blacks, and most of the African slaves we're focusing on in this unit, who served in America and Europe, were first captured and sold into slavery by fellow blacks and handled by Muslim, North African traders. You can't imagine how shocked I was to first learn this, after all my years in school where it was subtly implied that the enslaving of others was a particularly white-skinned sin.

The question is often raised: how could the earlier founding fathers have held slaves when they wrote that "all men are created equal...[and] are endowed by their Creator with certain unalienable rights...among these are life, liberty, and the pursuit of happiness." Actually, these freedom lovers were wracked over the slavery issue at a time when few gave it a single thought! Many released their slaves on their deaths and were desperate to have slavery banned in the Constitution. The Deep South, though, refused to sign such a Constitution. These same founding fathers knew that without a Constitution, the thirteen loose states were at risk of a British re-invasion and a fallen America would dash the hopes of the watching world. The Deep South promised they'd soon phase out slavery anyway. So, the founding fathers yielded to Southern demands, in hopes that a new nation, united by the Constitution, could deal with this thorny problem. (If you like Peter Marshall's books, a review of the constitutional battle regarding slavery is provided in Chapter 1 of both **From Sea to Shining Sea* and **From Sea to Shining Sea for Children*.)

Truth is, after the Constitution was enacted and America began growing, slavery was dramatically *increasing* in the South, where some held that slavery made possible the highly sophisticated (and therefore *acceptable*) culture of the South. (One might suspect *utilitarianism* in that position.) Slavery, never as widespread in the North, was decreasing there since the Industrial Revolution was changing the economic landscape and consciences were gradually being pricked by people known as *abolitionists* (thus titled since

they worked to *abolish* slavery). We'll talk much more about abolition, the Underground Railroad, and many slavery topics later in this unit when things were even more stoked. The point here is that the North and South were moving further apart!

Even if the whole world was accustomed to slavery (which it was), slavery was still awful, though some church-goers claimed the Bible allowed enslaving Negroes since they were descendants of Noah's son, Ham, who angered God with his sin.

Think about this while exploring slavery:

> 1) Focus first on the slaves themselves, not just the issues. Real people suffered! Even where slaves were treated kindly, would you trade places?
>
> 2) How did slavery affect slave owners? Did they become "petty tyrants," as someone said?
>
> 3) Possible resolutions were *very* complex in a then-racist society (North and South) which deprived Negroes of full respect, political and legal rights, education, work, and opportunity. Was it best, then, to return them to Africa? The nation of Liberia (with Monrovia as its capital in honor of James Monroe who promoted the plan) was created as a home for returned slaves. Few wanted to go back, however, for they were Americans now. Should everyone pay taxes to reimburse slave owners for freed slaves? And here was a big issue—did the federal government have the political right to ban slavery in states that wanted it? This was the thorny *states' rights* issue! Of course that raised an even deeper question—was God's moral law higher than the law of the land? There was certainly disagreement over the essence of His moral law. Whew!

While the slaves were living and dying, while their families were torn apart at the auction block, and while southerners lived in fear of revolt (such as Nat Turner's in 1831), America kept putting off the decision. South Carolina's threat to nullify the federal tariff let everyone know what would happen if a slavery law they didn't like was passed. It truly tested American hearts to decide whether they'd be willing to split over slavery, especially since their fight to *become* a nation was still *very* fresh in their minds.

Though various states were moving against slavery, and in 1808 the federal government banned the importing of any more slaves on those dreadful slave ships, the issue was still only simmering. There were as many *slave* states as *free* states. That is, the issue was only simmering until the Missouri Territory asked for statehood as a pro-slavery state! The precarious balance was blown, and stormy debate ensued. In the end, the Missouri Compromise was enacted in 1820, and the issue was swept under the carpet for a few more years. Of course, it wasn't "under the carpet" for the slaves!

In fact, it wasn't under the carpet for free Americans either, as can be seen in the turmoil over the *Amistad* mutiny, which, though it didn't occur until 1839, we will mention now.

The mutiny is such a story, that I won't retell it here, but I will ask you to take note of the widespread uproar and the wonderful role played by seventy-three-year-old John Quincy Adams in defending the *Amistad* slaves.

Well, I've talked a lot longer than usual, but what a subject!

20a Sectionalism and the Missouri Compromise (1820)

**From Sea to Shining Sea for Children*, by Marshall & Manuel, Ch. 10-11 Gr. 1-5

**Story of the Great Republic*, by H.A. Guerber, Ch. XIXb Gr. 3-7

**From Sea to Shining Sea*, by Marshall & Manuel, Ch. 10-11 Gr. 6-12

Road to Fort Sumter, by Leroy Hayman Gr. 5-10

This book seeks to thoroughly explore the many causes of the Civil War, but I'll mention here as we are beginning our discussion of sectionalism, slavery, "compromises," etc. If you wish to dig to this depth, you may want to choose only certain portions.

Fight for Union, by Margaret Coit Gr. 7-12

This book seeks to thoroughly explore the many causes of the Civil War, but I'll mention here as we are beginning our discussion of sectionalism, slavery, "compromises," etc. If you wish to dig to this depth, you may want to choose only certain portions.

20b Slavery

We'll cover slavery again when the Underground Railroad is in full swing and the Civil War is looming large. For now, we'll concentrate on the lives of slaves.

**From Sea to Shining Sea for Children*, by Marshall & Manuel, Ch. 16 Gr. 1-5

**Story of the World: Volume 3*, by Susan Wise Bauer, Ch. 36 Gr. 3-6

Some families enjoy this book's scope, so ask us to cite it; others seek different worldview; so, parental decision.

**From Sea to Shining Sea*, by Marshall & Manuel, Ch. 16 Gr. 6-12

**With Open Hands: A Story about Biddy Mason*, by Jeri Ferris (Creative Minds) Gr. 3-6

The true story of a slave girl who traveled west with her masters, finally gained her freedom, and became both a generous nurse and a wealthy woman.

**Strength of These Arms*, by Raymond Bial — Gr. 3-7

Strong photos and text show daily life in the slave quarters.

**Daily Life on a Southern Plantation*, by Paul Erickson — Gr. 3-8

**Kidnapped Prince: The Life of Olaudah Equiano*, by Olaudah Equiano — Gr. 3-8

Stirring biography of a boy who went from royalty to slavery.

**Bound for America*, by James Haskins (From African Beginnings) — Gr. 3-10

If you need to go back and explore the beginnings of the slave trade, this is a good overview.

All Times, All Peoples, by Milton Meltzer — Gr. 3-12

**Amos Fortune, Free Man*, by Elizabeth Yates — Gr. 3-12

True, moving story of slave who worked hard to free himself.

**Many Thousand Gone*, by Virginia Hamilton — Gr. 4-9

A history of American slavery up to the 13th Amendment of 1865, so you may want to read only the first portion now. It will be cited again when we later discuss the final phase of slavery.

**My Family Shall Be Free! The Life of Peter Still*, by Dennis Fradin — Gr. 6-12

True story of a slave who works his way to freedom and then tries to free his family.

Outlaw Voyage, by Val Gendron — Gr. 6-12

Activity on a slave ship.

**Rebels Against Slavery*, by Patricia & Fred McKissack — Gr. 6-12

I've not seen this book, but know it's about various slave revolts.

**Black Americans: A History in Their Own Words*, edited by Milton Meltzer — Gr. 7-12

Accounts from real slaves. This was previously published as *In Their Own Words*.

Many Faces of Slavery, by I. E. Levine (Messner) — Gr. 7-12

**To Be a Slave*, by Julius Lester — Gr. 7-12

Accounts from real slaves.

Tears for a King, by Ron Rendleman — Gr. 7-12

Check your church library for this Christian testimony of an African king, captured and enslaved, who gave his life to Christ.

Full Hold and Splendid Passage, by Bill & Gene Bonyun, Ch. 8 Gr. 8-12
Describes "slavers" (awful slave-running ships).

**Slavery Time When I Was Children*, by Belinda Hurmence Gr. 8-12
Excerpts from the narratives of real slaves who look back on their experiences.

Then Was the Future, by Douglas Miller, Ch. 5 (Living History Library) Gr. 8-12
Discusses the racial prejudices of the North.

Rum, Slaves, and Molasses, by Clifford Alderman Gr. 9-12
Describes the triangular trade route.

**African Preachers*, by White Unknown
Highlights four African-American preachers of the early 1800s. I've not read this.

**Slave Family*, by Bobbie Kalman Unknown

**Solomon Northup's Twelve Years a Slave*, by Sue Eakin Unknown
True story of free black man from New York who was kidnapped and enslaved for twelve years in Louisiana. I've not seen this.

Fiction/Historical Fiction

Who Owns the Sun? by Stacy Chbosky Gr. 1-4
Many of you will recognize this Five-in-a-Row title.

**Nettie's Trip South*, by Ann Turner Gr. 2-6
Northern girl witnesses Southern feelings about slaves. Touching...

Ahipment for Susannah, by Eleanor Nolen Gr. 2-8
Very rare story of slave girl to Washington's granddaughter, Nelly Custis.

**Escape from Slavery;* **Cincinnati Epidemic;* **Riot in the Night;* **Fight for Freedom;* Gr. 3-8
**Enemy or Friend?* by various authors (American Adventure #16-20)
These volumes in a new Christian series by various authors are set in early Cincinnati and include topics such as an earthquake and a drought.

**I Thought My Soul Would Rise and Fly*, by Joyce Hansen (Dear America) Gr. 3-10
Story of slave girl in fictionalized diary. I've found this series to have uneven "tone," attitudes, outlook, etc., so parents please discern.

**Picture of Freedom: Diary of Clotee, a Slave Girl*, by P. McKissack (Dear America) Gr. 3-10
I've heard this shows good character, but includes "forced relationships." As noted above, I've found this series to vary a great deal in terms of its "tone."

**Seaward Born*, by Lea Wait Gr. 4-7

Slave boy working in Charleston harbor gets a unique opportunity to escape in 1805.

**School for Pompey Walker*, by Michael Rosen Gr. 4-8

I've not seen this book, but have read that it's based on the true story of a slave (Gussie West) who, with the help of his white friend, sells himself into slavery many times (and then escapes) to raise money for a school for African-American children.

**A Girl Called Boy*, by Belinda Hurmence Gr. 4-12

Modern black girl goes back in time to 1850s slavery.

**Jump Ship to Freedom*, by James & Christopher Collier Gr. 4-12

The tense story of a hunted fugitive slave boy who wants to use his father's old Revolutionary War money to buy mother's freedom. Collier's books can be gritty and have strong language, but I've not read this one.

**Slave Dancer*, by Paula Fox Gr. 4-12

I've not read this tense story of an indentured boy who is forced to play the fife for the slaves' daily exercise aboard a slave ship.

**Slave Girl*, also titled *Cowslip*, by Betsy Haynes Gr. 4-12

The life of one slave girl.

Bimby, by Peter Burchard Gr. 5-12

Moving story of slave boy who dreams of freedom.

Young Squire Morgan, by Manly Wade Wellman Gr. 7-12

This esteemed Southern author tells of a plantation-owner's son.

**Roots*, by Alex Haley Gr. 9-12

Check age-appropriateness of the book or film version for your students, parents!

20c Nat Turner's Revolt (1831)

**From Sea to Shining Sea for Children*, by Marshall & Manuel, Ch. 16 Gr. 1-5

This chapter was also cited earlier.

**Story of the World: Volume 3*, by Susan Wise Bauer, Ch. 38b Gr. 3-6

Some families enjoy this book's scope, so ask us to cite it; others seek different worldview; so, parental decision.

From Sea to Shining Sea, by Marshall & Manuel, Ch. 16 Gr. 6-12
This chapter was also cited earlier.

Nat Turner, by Judith Griffin Gr. 2-7

**Nat Turner and the Virginia Slave Revolt*, by Rivvy Neshama Gr. 3-6
I've not seen this book, but have read that it handles some details of the uprising a bit more gently.

**Nat Turner*, by Susan Gregson (Let Freedom Ring) Gr. 3-8

**All Times, All Peoples*, by Milton Meltzer, p. 47 Gr. 3-12

Our Blood and Tears, by Ruth Wilson, Section 2 Gr. 5-12

**Nat Turner's Slave Rebellion*, by Judith Edwards (In American History) Gr. 6-12

**Nat Turner*, by Terry Bisson (Black Americans of Achievement) Gr. 7-12

**Nat Turner and the Slave Revolt*, by Tracy Barrett Unknown
I've not seen this book, but have heard that it includes coverage of some of the violent aspects of the revolt; be cautious! I think it's for middle students.

Fiction/Historical Fiction

Uprising at Dawn, by Lee Roddy (Between Two Flags) Gr. 4-9
I believe this is about the Nat Turner uprising. There are others in this Christian series, so you can check your church library since the series is now out-of-print.

20d *Amistad* Revolt (1839)

What a dramatic story! Cinque led his fellow slaves in mutiny aboard a horrific Spanish slaver, but then the ship ended up on the shore of New England even though they'd told the crew to take them back to Africa...and Americans had to decide what to do. It was John Quincy Adams who defended the slaves all the way to the Supreme Court as brave freedom-fighters, not pirates or mutineers...and the case was watched closely by Americans. How did it end up? You'll have to find out!

**Story of the* Amistad, <u>also titled</u> *Slave Ship* and *Long Black Schooner*, by E. Sterne Gr. 3-12
This well-written (and twice-retitled) story is being reprinted from a wonderful older series. Highly readable narrative! (*Long Black Schooner* is the original work; it appeared in Aladdin's fine *American Heritage* series.)

*Amistad *Mutiny*, by Barbara Somervill (Journey to Freedom) Gr. 4-7
I've not seen this, but gather that it is for Gr. 4-7.

*Amistad *Slave Revolt and American Abolition*, by Karen Zeinert Gr. 5-12

**Freedom's Sons: True Story of the* Amistad *Mutiny*, by Suzanne Jurmain Gr. 5-12

*Amistad: *Long Road to Freedom*, by Walter Dean Myers Gr. 6-12

Amistad *Revolt*, by Helen Kromer (Focus Books) Gr. 9-12
True story of captives on Spanish slave ship who mutiny.

Fiction/Historical Fiction

*Amistad *Rising*, by Veronica Chambers Gr. 4-7

20e Prudence Crandall

**Prudence Crandall*, by Eileen Lucas (On My Own) Gr. 1-4

Prudence Crandall: Woman of Courage, by Elizabeth Yates Gr. 4-12
This has long been an admired book. Girls especially enjoy this biography.

21 John Quincy Adams & Andrew Jackson

We just mentioned seventy-three-year-old John Quincy Adams taking on case of the *Amistad* slaves, and we haven't yet talked about his earlier career...as President of the United States! We were on a roll with the slavery issues, and I didn't want to stop, but we can catch up a bit now, and then we'll move on to European issues again.

You might wonder if we're going to go into the details of each American president. We're not, but the election involving Adams and Jackson was very controversial, which allows me to tell you that the U.S. Constitution did not totally determine how presidents were to be elected! Why? Because of issues basic to America's foundation itself, and these were at stake during the political windstorms of the early 1800s.

You see, the founding fathers knew a pure democracy (where the majority totally rules because the common man votes directly on leaders and laws) would allow errors—due to lazy thinking, a rejection of Judeo-Christian truths, or selfish desires for government

handouts, for example—to easily lead to bad law and the election of bad officials. Good law and leadership are crucial for quality life and must be protected!

Instead, America was wisely established as a constitutional republic, which means we have representative government limited by a constitution. The voters would select (if they were wise and noble) the most committed, qualified, and thoughtful representatives to govern. Yet, the people were still rightfully involved and government was by their consent, *as it should be!* (We've talked about this deeply in previous *TruthQuest History* guides, so won't go further here.)

Because the election of the president is especially important, the founding fathers devised a special plan. Rather than a direct vote of the president by the people, they created an intermediary, a buffer: the Electoral College. This is a group of *electors* selected by each state (there's the issue we'll get to) who would actually elect the president *by state*. Thus the votes from a few large cities wouldn't offset the votes of several smaller states. The electors were charged with the responsibility of picking the very best candidates to represent the people who had in turn elected them. During the Early Republic era, the Electoral College members were traditionally selected by the state legislatures, since the Constitution did not specify.

The Electoral College vote of 1824 was so close that it took a further vote by the U.S. House of Representatives to choose the president—they elected John Quincy Adams over Andrew Jackson. This experience intensified the public demand for a more popularly controlled presidential election process. (*Popular* here means related to the *population*).

After what happened in the Bush-Gore presidential election of 2000, I want to make a big point right now though! Notice that the people of the 1800s did *not* disband the Electoral College; the weight it gives each state's presidential vote, as mentioned above, is so terribly important. Think carefully now! If the presidential election were *only* popular, the votes coming from a few large cities (where values and needs are different) could even more powerfully offset the votes of vast areas of more remote farmers and townsfolk than already occurs. An honest Electoral College brings some balance and buffer, as it was designed.

By 1828, the "common man" did have enough voting power to elect another "common man" as president—Andrew Jackson. Born in a log cabin—but later wealthy due to his hard work, bravery, and sacrifice—Jackson epitomized the American rags to riches dream. John Quincy Adams' presidency was over in just one term, and it marked the end of an era when most phases of America's government was handled only by highly educated men, who had deeply studied the highest principles of law, morality, history, and government (though not without error).

Electorate

The key here is that the common man *was* getting more voting power. Previously, most states had limited voting privileges to white men who met certain requirements, such as land ownership, etc., with a goal of ensuring a wise, sober, careful, more educated *electorate* (body of voters). But as U.S. citizens became less British and more American, and by that I mean less class-conscious and more

independent, rough-and-ready, and aware of their individual worth and contribution to society, they insisted that all white men be given the vote (it would be some time before all American adults could vote, women and non-whites). This time you were awake, right? You noticed that America was now facing another fork in the road, because more widespread voting had the capacity to bless America with more accountability and participation, or curse America with even more unwise or selfish voting.

Does it sound like I think only people with thirty-two college degrees should be allowed to vote? Hope not, because my point is only that everyone needs to carefully handle the awesome God-given right to participate in government!

Wondering how politics changed? I'll put it simply: it became more like it is now. The horn-tooting, banner-waving, marching band style of presidential campaign (designed to win the common man's votes) began. There's nothing wrong with horns, banners, marching bands, or TV ads, but there was something that *did* go wrong. The political parties gained an abnormal amount of influence, and—afraid to lose votes—they avoided talking about real issues and real problems, except to tickle ears by laying blame, whether justified or not. This quote explains:

> *The result was the development of new political tactics aimed at appealing to the common man. Political battles became sharply contested. Fiery, emotional rhetoric replaced rational deliberation as both parties bid for mass support.*[47]

Here's what Alexis de Tocqueville, a French observer, wrote. His words are shockingly intense. What would he say *now?*

> *In the whole world I do not see a more wretched and shameful sight than that presented by the different coteries (they do not deserve the name of parties) which now divide the Union. In broad daylight one sees all the petty, shameful passions disturbing them which generally one is careful to keep hidden at the bottom of the human heart. As for the interest of the country, no one thinks about it...*
>
> *It is pitiful to see what a deluge of coarse insults, what petty slander and what gross calumnies, fill the newspapers that serve as organs for the parties, and with what shameful disregard of social decencies they daily drag before the tribunal of public opinion the honour of families and the secrets of the domestic hearth.*[48]

Alexis de Tocqueville, a Frenchman, traveled around America during the 1800s and wrote a very famous book based on his observations. Older students may want to read it: **Democracy in America*. It receives Christian analysis in **Invitation to the Classics*, edited by Cowan & Guinness, pp. 225-228, Gr. 8-12 (some families will not appreciate artwork in this section).

It was now more tempting for presidents (and candidates) to put too much emphasis on their popular appeal. Listen carefully, for *you* may be President (or Prime Minister) one day, but if not, you'll *certainly* be voting for them! Here goes: presidents (and all elected

47 Miller 84.
48 Miller 100-101.

officials) must walk a very, very fine line; they *must* maintain government that is *of* the people, but they also must hold firmly to God's higher law when public opinion is wrong. Without that "higher law," anything unwisely desired by 51% of the population would not be challenged.

Note carefully this comment made by a writer who was actually praising Andrew Jackson's position on this very issue, but I think it should concern you:

> *He has collected and embodied the wishes of the people; he has seemed to lead public opinion, it has been because he is endowed with a penetration which has enabled him to see its* [popular opinion's] *current, and by throwing himself at its head, to bring its full force to sustain him. Guided by the fundamental principles, that the will of the majority should, in all cases, control, he has never attempted to defeat that will....Many a plain farmer or mechanic...feels that the breast of the President beats in unison with his own.*[49]

The best public servant, a *statesman*, is someone who serves the people (they are the true source of power because they are created in His image) by working toward what is truly right. A great statesman thinks about the long-term effects of decisions, not just re-election. Might you be America's next great statesman or Electoral College member?

I hope this talk didn't imply that politics is dirty business. On the contrary! God established human governments and they function best with the involvement of godly men and women! Also, I hope it didn't sound like Jackson was some kind of uneducated weasel. He had great strengths, and increasingly sought the Lord as he aged. Of course, he had great flaws as well, as you'll also discover. One thing is certain—he had one of the most eventful lives *ever!* In fact, just as John Marshall influenced the current role of the Supreme Court, Andrew Jackson first asserted (maybe rightly) that the Constitution gave power to presidents that current presidents *still* wield.[50]

Whew, that was a deep conversation, wasn't it? Few adults understand this, and it's exciting to think how much you're learning while still young. You'll be great citizens! Thanks go to all you non-American readers for allowing us time to work through this issue. (Do *ThinkWrite 6* now.)

> ***ThinkWrite 6: "How's'about you?!"***
>
> You'll be old enough to vote before you know it! Any thoughts on how you'll handle this precious and awesome responsibility?

21a John Quincy Adams

As always, please note that I won't cite all the books on Adams in the multitude of presidential book series. They are all easily "findable" on your library's shelves.

**Story of the Great Republic*, by H.A. Guerber, Ch. XXa — Gr. 3-7

49 Miller 87-88.
50 Miller 91.

**This Country of Ours*, by H.E. Marshall, Ch. 72 Gr. 3-8

**Basic History of the United States: Vol. 3*, by Clarence Carson, Ch. 2b-d Gr. 9-12

**Young John Quincy*, by Cheryl Harness Gr. 1-4
Very nicely illustrated picture-biography.

**John Quincy Adams*, by Mike Venezia (Getting to Know the U.S. Presidents) Gr. 1-5

John Quincy Adams, by Ann Weil (Childhood) Gr. 1-6

**First Son and President*, by Beverly Gherman (Creative Minds) Gr. 2-5

**Mothers of Famous Men*, by Archer Wallace, Ch. XIII (Lamplighter) Gr. 3-12
We met Abigail Adams in the last unit, but this is a special focus on her motherhood of John Quincy Adams.

John Quincy Adams, by Milton Lomask Gr. 7-12

Yankee in the White House, by Mary Hoehling (Messner) Gr. 7-12

Louisa: Life of Mrs. John Quincy Adams, by Laura Kerr Gr. 8-12
Girls will especially enjoy this biography of John Quincy's wife!

Fiction/Historical Fiction

**Dear Mr. President: John Quincy Adams: Letters from a Southern Planter's Son* Gr. 4-9
by Steven Kroll (Dear Mr. President)
I have not seen this new series, but it entails fictional letters to a real president about real issues. A key issue in this particular book is the boy's disagreement with his father over the forced removal of the Creek Indians. Parents, you'll have to decide. Because of the recent publication date, and the child-parent discord, I am concerned.

21b Activities

**How to Draw the Life and Times of John Quincy Adams*, by Betsy Dru Tecco Various
If you like this, there are others in the series about various presidents.

21c Andrew Jackson

As always, please note that I won't cite all the books on Jackson in the multitude of presidential book series. They are all easily "findable" on your library's shelves.

**From Sea to Shining Sea for Children*, by Marshall & Manuel, Ch.12 Gr. 1-5

**Story of the Great Republic*, by H.A. Guerber, Ch. XXb-XXI Gr. 3-7
You should also read Ch. XXII to learn about the presidents just after Jackson.

**This Country of Ours*, by H.E. Marshall, Ch. 73 Gr. 3-8
You should also read Ch. 74-75 which covers the presidents just after Jackson, including John Tyler, who was left with the Seminole conflict in Florida.

**From Sea to Shining Sea*, by Marshall & Manuel, Ch. 12 Gr. 6-12

**Basic History of the United States: Vol. 3*, by Clarence Carson, Ch. 2-3 Gr. 9-12

Meet Andrew Jackson, by Ormonde de Kay (Step-Up Books) Gr. K-3

**Andrew Jackson: Frontier Patriot*, by Louis Sabin Gr. 1-4

**Andrew Jackson*, by Mike Venezia (Getting to Know the U.S. Presidents) Gr. 1-5

Andrew Jackson: Pioneer and President, by John Parlin (Garrard Discovery) Gr. 1-5

Andy Jackson, by Augusta Stevenson (Childhood) Gr. 1-6
The new reissue is by George Stanley and is titled **Andrew Jackson: Young Patriot.*

Rachel Jackson, by Christine Govan (Childhood) Gr. 1-6
There is also a "Childhood" biography of Jackson's wife!

Andrew Jackson: An Initial Biography, by Genevieve Foster Gr. 2-7
One of Foster's rare, beloved biographies for young children.

**Andrew Jackson*, by Steve Potts (Photo-Illustrated Biographies) Gr. 3-7

Andy Jackson: Long Journey to the White House, by P. Angell (Alad. Am. Her) Gr. 3-8

Snowball Fight in the White House, by Louise Davis Gr. 3-8
True story of the children in the White House during Jackson's presidency.

Story of Andrew Jackson, by Enid LaMonte Meadowcroft (Signature) Gr. 3-8

***Who Let Muddy Boots into the White House?* by Robert Quackenbush Gr. 3-8
Another of Quackenbush's lighthearted biographies.

Andrew Jackson, by Clara Ingram Judson Gr. 4-12
Esteemed author.

Young Hickory, by Stanley Young Gr. 5-12

Andrew Jackson, by Jeannette Covert Nolan (Messner) Gr. 7-12

Jacksons of Tennessee, by Marguerite Vance Gr. 7-12
This focuses on the life of both Andrew & Rachel Jackson. Girls would enjoy this.

**Old Hickory: Andrew Jackson and the American People*, by Albert Marrin Gr. 7-12
Marrin's books are usually a wonderful choice!

Life of Andrew Jackson, by Marquis James Gr. 12+
Border Captain and *Portrait of a President* in one volume; this is too time-consuming for most students.

Fiction/Historical Fiction

Andy Jackson's Water Well, by William O. Steele Gr. 3-8
Another of Steele's fabulously funny tall tales. Boys love these!

President's Lady, by Irving Stone Gr. 9-12
This is more of an adult biographical novel of Rachel Jackson; content unknown.

21d Activities

**Andrew Jackson and His Family Paper Dolls*, by Tom Tierney (Dover) Various

22 Change...and Turmoil Come to Britain

Finally, we can get back to Europe! When we last saw Britain, it was in the great flush of its Industrial Revolution. Don't forget, this is where it all started. The Industrial Revolution blossomed out of British genius, fortitude, and beliefs. Stephenson's railway tracks were soon crisscrossing the countryside, Watt's steam engines were powering mills, and Wilkinson's iron smelters were churning out goods for the entire world! In fact, Britain

exported more goods than all other nations combined,[51] but the plight of the poor was still awful.

I hear you! You're saying: "Hey, what about all that opportunity you told us about? You said the Industrial Revolution helped the poor in some ways. So, what gives?" You're right. I did say that, and it is true...at least when we look back from two centuries later. There was great opportunity for enterprising individuals; some of the most important inventions came from poor, uneducated tinkerers. It is also true, though, that conditions had been dreadful for so long that even an improvement left most folks in a bad way yet.

We can't even say that the improvements—such as they were—came right away. In fact, with Britain still reeling from the Napoleonic Wars and the War of 1812, goods were scarce and prices were high. The new industrialization took jobs from some age-old occupations...and at a terrible time. Meanwhile, the new free-market ideas were changing pricing and business and labor, so there was great upheaval. As you know, economic change has a powerful effect! It didn't help that the earliest factory-produced goods were of poor quality and too many factory owners (smitten with the heady perfume of *progress*) were taking advantage of workers, as we discussed earlier. It was very messy, and, with only my human insight, I cannot really evaluate the total net impact of the subjective aspects of the cultural changes; I only know God is sovereign and has a plan for the nations.

Anyway, with what they could see in the present moment, some desperate workers banded together (c. 1811-1815) in what was called the Luddite Society to protest, and the British government eventually had to send thousands of soldiers to stop them since the Luddites sometimes broke into factories and smashed machines! The "Peterloo" episode was a sad example of a disturbance in 1819. We can see, then, that though there were going to be some eventual gains, there would be a very looooong road until improvements were significant. As *TruthQuest History* veterans could have guessed, the conditions were worst in countries which were most spiritually bankrupt. In fact, the old feudal system was still in place in many eastern European nations, which shows you that even the ability to choose one's own place of labor was something of an improvement!

Anyway, all this brings us to another fork in the road. Like America, Britain faced a decision: should the poor be assisted...and *how* could that really be accomplished, since poverty is caused by so many factors, some unalterable except by the poor themselves. You can bet this is a spiritual issue at its core. You'll see the *Big 2 Beliefs* at work...and the British beliefs would be sorely tested during the grievous event we'll study next—the Irish Potato Famine!

I'm getting ahead of myself, though. We hashed through this sticky topic in *TruthQuest History: Ancient Rome*, but it's been a while. You may need a refresher. I will briefly list four points made in Scripture about the poor. You can find *many* more, and I urge you to develop a keen understanding of this issue. Our reading on this topic will be the Bible itself!

---

51 R.J. Unstead, *The Story of Britain* (Camden, NY: Thomas Nelson, 1969, 1970) 288.

1) God is not a respecter of persons, meaning He doesn't respect a rich aristocrat more than a poor servant. Yeah! Our worth is not based on wealth, even if a class-conscious society thinks so.

Is he not the One who...shows no partiality to princes and does not favor the rich over the poor, for they are all the work of his hands? (Job 34:19)

He who mocks the poor shows contempt for their Maker... (Prov. 17:5)

2) The overarching financial principle is that God wants to be our source, and His principles, when obeyed both individually and nationally, are the best hope for adequate provision. His principles include tithing, appropriate investing and priorities, free enterprise, the necessity of work, private ownership of property, strong disapproval of those who could provide for their families but don't, etc.

The Lord is my shepherd, I shall not be in want. (Psalm 23:1)

Honor the Lord with your wealth, with the firstfruits of all your crops; then your barns will be filled to overflowing, and your vats will brim over with new wine. (Prov. 3:9-10)

"...Bring the whole tithe into the storehouse, that there may be food in my house. Test me in this," says the Lord Almighty, "and see if I will not throw open the floodgates of heaven and pour out so much blessing that you will not have room for it..." (Mal. 3:10)

3) When God taught Moses the ruling law for the Israelites, He directed *individuals*, not the government to care for the needy! In the New Testament, we see the gathered individuals of the church caring for others.

If one of your countrymen becomes poor and is unable to support himself among you, help him as you would an alien or a temporary resident, so he can continue to live among you....You must not lend him money at interest or sell him food at a profit. (Lev. 25:35-37)

If there is a poor man among your brothers in any of the towns of the land the Lord your God is giving you, do not be hardhearted or tightfisted toward your poor brothers. Rather be openhanded and freely lend him whatever he needs. (Deut. 15:7-8)

Selling their possessions and goods, they gave to anyone as he had need. (Acts 2:45)

For Macedonia and Achaia were pleased to make a contribution for the poor among the saints in Jerusalem. (Rom. 15:26)

4) Everyone must care about the poor, in a way that truly helps, not one that is enabling or disabling.

Now this was the sin of your sister Sodom: She and her daughters were arrogant, overfed and unconcerned; they did not help the poor and the needy. (Ezek. 16:49)

Defend the cause of the weak and fatherless; maintain the rights of the poor and oppressed. (Ps. 82:3)

There will always be poor people in the land. Therefore I command you to be openhanded toward your brothers and toward the poor and the needy in the land. (Deut. 15:11)

Ah, the beauty of God's Word and how it brings good to all! I won't list any other reading here, since we covered details of the British Industrial Revolution earlier in this guide and we have been focusing on the spiritual aspects here, except a handful of novels which can be mentioned. Dig in!

Adventures of Tom Leigh, by Phyllis Bentley — Gr. 5-12

This is set just prior to 1800, but it captures the enormous changes of the Industrial Revolution as the reader sees the adventures that befall a young weaver's apprentice.

Oath of Silence, by Phyllis Bentley — Gr. 5-12

Another story set during the Industrial Revolution.

Thread of Victory, by Helen Lobdell — Gr. 9-12

This story includes the "Peterloo" episode; I've not read it and do not know its tone. Do be aware that it heroicizes (I think) Robert Owen, who though well-meaning, was quite humanistic.

**North and South*, by Elizabeth Gaskell — Gr. 10-12

Noted novel showing life in newly industrialized northern city in England, with issues of family moved up from the picturesque south of England, the factory work, etc. Few would have time to read this, but there is also a nice film version (see below).

**Through the Fray*, by G.A. Henty — Unknown

I've not seen this, but have been told it's written for an older audience than usual.

Film

**North and South*, starring Daniela Deby-Ashe and Richard Armitage

Film version of Elizabeth Gaskell's book of the same name cited above, showing life in newly industrialized city, with issues of family, work, etc. Beautifully done.

23 Looking Deeper: Humanism and European Philosophers in the 1800s

We're about to face up to the horrific Irish Potato Famine, but to do that we must look deeper at the changing *Big 2 Beliefs* which shaped England's response to it (England ruled Ireland then). This will, of course, give us a glimpse of European beliefs generally, for the English and most other western Europeans had moved far into Enlightenment humanism, as we've said. They had already accepted the first wave during the Renaissance which said truth could be apprehended and applied using only human faculties. You know that was called *rationalism*, and the era of its later blossoming was called the *Age of Reason*. The sublimity of God's truth and His role in revealing truth to us at a spiritual level—as understood during the Reformation—were ignored. Under rationalism, then, God might still be acknowledged in a ritual or cultural way, but He was deemed as a distant grandfather at best.

Okay, you already know that, but are you remembering what was new to the 1800s? We mentioned two names in the very introduction to this guide—Immanuel Kant and Georg Hegel—because these two Germans were instrumental in changing the *Big 2 Beliefs* of western civilization at this time. That's a big statement, so let's explore!

Kant, who died in 1804, and Hegel, who died in 1831, built on the earlier work of Jean Jacques Rousseau, whom we got to know quite well in the last *TruthQuest History* guide since he was active in the mid-late 1700s, and whom we also mentioned in the introduction to this guide. Rousseau made a huge step away from rationalism, as described by Carson:

> *Rousseau celebrated feeling, sentiment, intuition, and the natural man...*[52]

Kant further shot a hole in rationalism in his book, *Critique of Pure Reason*. He showed the incompleteness of sensory input and the role of subjective thinking in the creation of our conclusions. Duh! While it may sound at first like Kant did Christianity a favor in confirming a Biblical understanding of mankind's limitations and his more-than-just-rational nature, don't get too excited. Kant went further. One walked away from his books with the idea that since great philosophical and spiritual issues could not be apprehended by human senses nor by one's mental sense of experiences (for various complex reasons), that they then couldn't really be understood authoritatively at all.

Then came Georg Hegel. He too said that rationalism was inadequate, and in that he was right. But he *also* went further. He said that one's rationality is used to state a fact, but that later, someone will, with their rationality, be able to dispute that fact...and the resulting discussion will lead to a newer and higher understanding since more facets are understood. Well, that new understanding then becomes a "fact," and causes someone to later dispute it, and..........you see that the whole process (which he called *dialectic*) spirals ever onward. So, for Hegel, the search for truth was a <u>progressive</u> journey as man's understanding <u>evolved</u> to greater and greater heights.

---

52 Carson 3:66.

Did you notice two key words in that last sentence? Yes! They were forms of the words *progress* and *evolution*. You already know these ideas were the heartbeat of the 1800s as folks considered the stunning changes wrought in science, invention, economics, and government, and then came to believe they had *progressed* to a point which allowed them to in turn manage the world and work in tandem with the power of nature! The churches were even teaching this *progressivism* as part of God's plan! Mankind was no longer infantile, and thus in need of a Father; mankind was full-grown, so God could now retire! Mankind didn't need to soak in the Bible to gain understanding of the universe. No. People would discover it through their Hegelian dialectic. In fact, they thought it was their duty to do so! This was mankind's high position in and contribution to nature. Once folks reached that conclusion, they soon declared that anyone "clinging" to religion was holding back progress!

Progressivism

Stop and recall right now the *Big 2 Beliefs* of most mainline churches at this time in Europe. Do you remember Jeremy Jackson saying that they no longer deemed God as Master, Creator, and Savior? Instead, the church had made Him merely the capital "N in Nature."[53] Well, now you know why men like Kant and Hegel were able to come to their conclusions...and why they spread so rapidly throughout Europe...and to her colonies, such as America, Canada, etc.

Yes, a new way of thinking was gaining sway; it is called Romanticism because it focuses on man's creative and intuitive side, the opposite of rationalism's focus on the intellectual side. The beauty and power of nature were also idealized. Is it any wonder that Charles Darwin (whom we'll meet in the next guide) would come out with his tale of biological evolution in nature? One thing's certain, when we do study Darwin, you'll know that he was not the first to attribute God-like power to nature; the church had been doing it for decades before him.

What I don't understand is this: these Europeans of the early-mid 1800s had been given a close-up view of the wipe-out of the humanistic French Revolution and Napoleon's quick slide into human tyranny. Doesn't it seem, then, that Enlightenment humanism would have been debunked? But, no. It was still spreading! Humanism *is* flattering, after all. Thus, many European churches hung on tenaciously to their natural religion, while the American version—Unitarianism—was gaining converts too. Thus, though I just bemoaned natural religion above, it still bears closer inspection, such as that of Jeremy Jackson:

> *...nineteenth century natural religion—religion cut down to human size—gushes forth into the post-Napoleonic world, often in sophisticated guises, but "natural" nonetheless. Being a religion made to human order, it is always the flexible matrix for current fashions in scholarship and philosophy. Indeed, marking the growing secularization of society, rather than the crucible in which men's ideas were formed, this natural religion was becoming a mere repository of ill-sorted, ill-defined problems within the crucible of contemporary thought. The day would come when, most of these problems having been catalogued under different headings, religion could be thrown aside as excess baggage.*[54]

---

53 Jackson 193.
54 Jackson 229.

Yes, many people and churches who carried the name *Christian* were not actually God-followers. These churches were salons for the discussion of trendy, progressive ideas or were social clubs; they did not truly prick the consciences of society's bullies or impact them if they were church members. Naturally, there were some God-honoring churches who yet understood that man's reason alone could never manage the world. They knew that in spite of industrial progress, mankind was still fallen and in need of a Savior and Lord. But too many were filled with believers (maybe like us?) who busy pursuing their own lives and missed many of the spiritual and physical needs around them. This gave the humanists—as well as the poor—a great opportunity to vilify the church, as we've said previously.

Let's ponder once more the words of Francis Schaeffer on this subject:

> *The churches could have changed things in that day if they had spoken with clarity and courage. The central reason the church should have spoken clearly and courageously on these issues is that the Bible commands it. Had the church been faithful to the Bible's teaching about the compassionate use of wealth, it would not later have lost so many of the workers. And if it had spoken clearly against the use of wealth as a weapon in a kind of "survival of the fittest," in all probability this concept as it came into secularized science* [later with Darwin and others] *would not have been so automatically accepted.*[55]

Why is Schaeffer talking about the *survival of the fittest* here, when we haven't come to Darwin yet? The answer to that question brings us closer to the Irish Potato Famine, believe it or not. Because, as I've already said, the humanistic emphasis on ration and nature—which sounded like rah-rah progress—had already bred a horrible idea: *utilitarianism*. Remember? Issues were to be evaluated only upon the *usefulness* of their results. Well, *useful to whom?* Yes, useful to those in power...and what is more dangerous than that? One thing the elite found *un*useful, or at least unfit, was the existence of so many poor people. Overpopulation became a theme of the new humanism...and it still is! Are you catching the clue bus here? As soon as God was no longer God, humans became expendable. There's a *Big Two Beliefs* lesson in a nutshell! Why can't folks see that they're safe is *in* God?

Hold on just a minute, though. While I am decrying rationalism, I'm absolutely *not* saying that Christianity and intellect don't mix. That could hardly be the case when God is the ultimate intelligence, and the very reason humans are so intelligent is because we're created in His intelligent image! Furthermore, Jeremy Jackson teaches us that great damage was done when Christians abandoned intellectual matters to the humanists. God created our minds and want us to use them excellently in His service. So, I'm *certainly* not suggesting you use your brain only for ballast! The difference is in approach. We can't be like Descartes (remember?) and say that mankind will eventually express all universal truths using *only* mathematical equations, thereby reducing great spiritual truths and powers only to the man-made mathematical symbols which can be understood by our brains.

***If* all the universe could fit into and be expressed by the human mind, wouldn't any god then be lesser than the human mind? Hmmm, I think we've just stumbled onto the heart of**

---

55 Schaeffer 117.

humanism, of our sin nature: the desire to minimize God and maximize ourselves. If we stop to think about it though, we wouldn't really want to live in a world which was only as big as our minds, especially since our brains are the first thing to rot when we die! I'm so happy my God and the universe He created are so much bigger than me...and my nation's progress. That's why He's fascinating and worth exploring! To know that God alone *is* all truth and that He wants to reveal those truths to me...well, that's just awesome!

Remember, then, it's not that intellect and God don't mix. It's that one has to have a humble *heart* to receive truth from a greater source than one's own mind. That's why the fear of the Lord is the beginning of wisdom![56] Without that humility, a man will spend his life bouncing from one leaking philosophy to another in the hope of finally figuring life out. That reminds me of a verse:

> *See to it that no one takes you captive through hollow and deceptive philosophy, which depends on human tradition and basic principles of this world rather than on Christ (Col. 2:8).*

Yes, it is hollow and deceptive to think the human mind can rule the universe. Truth is, it can't even control our own wills![57] What's at stake, then, is not the human mind, it's the human heart, which alone controls the human will. That's why our spiritual connection with God is not something off in la-la-land. It's more real that the grittiest realities; it can tackle the grimiest problems. That's why we can't forget the spiritual element of progress! It comes about when people follow His principles. So many great and beneficial discoveries were made precisely because folks had a Biblical worldview! That's the part we always forget: that we have God to thank for our abilities and blessings. He is the source, not us! (Begin *ThinkWrite 7* now.)

ThinkWrite 7: "What does it all mean?"

Please describe in your own words the beliefs of the *Romantic Movement.* And you better not come up with some lovey-dovey, "cupidy" answer! You know this is not about a bouquet of flowers or a box of chocolates, but it is about the feeling side of mankind, right? Tell us more, such as how romanticism compared with rationalism.

I'll close with this: it's Christ's own body, the church, which clings to His truths. That brings us to our theme verse (in the paraphrase we have used just for this one verse, to express the thought to the youngest students):

> *The church, you see, is not peripheral to the world; the world is peripheral to the church. The church is Christ's body, in which he speaks and acts, by which he fills everything with his presence. (Eph. 1:22-23, Message)*

Do you get a sense of your importance? We are to be the servant-leaders, which we can only do when intimately connected to Him. That's the high calling we carry! To that end, I've

56 Proverbs 1:7.

57 This point is made in various locations throughout Jeremy Jackson's book (*No Other Foundation*) and Ruth Beechick's book (*The Biblical Psychology of Education*).

listed further reading for you. Yes, some of these chapters were cited earlier, but it would be great to dig into them again here. These are topics that we usually must delve into more than once!

**Basic History of the United States: Vol. 3*, by Clarence Carson, Intro to Ch. 5 Gr. 9-12

**Seven Men Who Rule the World from the Grave*, by Dave Breese, Ch.6 Gr. 8-12
This is a *very* important book, I think.

**History through the Eyes of Faith*, by Ronald Wells, Ch. 13 Gr. 9-12
We'll read this chapter again in next *TruthQuest History* guide and develop it further.

**How Should We Then Live?* by Francis Schaeffer, Ch.7 & pp. 113-119, 160-163 Gr. 9-12
This resource is always *terribly* important! Please note that Video Episode #6 is the same as Ch. 7 of the book, so either will serve.

No Other Foundation: The Church Through Twenty Centuries, by J. Jackson, Ch. 18 Gr. 11-12
This is too difficult for most students, but is so profound that I always mention it...

24 Irish Potato Famine

Our last talk may have seemed ridiculously abstract, but those topics determine the very nature of *real* life. Want proof? You saw that Europe had embraced natural religion, as well as the humanist philosophies of utilitarianism and over-population. Well, those ideas helped kill one million Irish! How so? When, in 1846, the dreadful Potato Famine dealt massive starvation through the land, the English government decided to withhold meaningful help so the weak would be "eliminated" and only the "fit" would survive. Galbraith discusses this somewhat in his aforementioned book (pp. 33-37). Their humanistic, "progressed" minds told them this would make Ireland a stronger nation. But their action—or lack of it—is downright hard to comprehend, especially when you consider that most of these English decision-makers were probably church members who should have been taught the truth!

Now, you can't be surprised at their decision (right?), because you're not ignorant of what happens when people make humanistic, God-minimizing (*Big Belief #1*) decisions. The results are always both dreadful and ironic: in the end, humanism always devalues humans (*Big Belief #2*). Yes, a million Irish died horrible deaths, and almost a million more crossed the ocean in horrible conditions, hoping for a better life as immigrants in America, Canada, and elsewhere. It's a sad, sad story.

For a sweeping, Christian novel of Ireland's history, see: *Banks of the Boyne*, by Donna Crow (Gr. 9-12).

Shamrock Cargo, by Anne Colver (Winston Adventure) Gr. 3-9
Little known contribution of real teens are featured in this terrific series!

**How I Survived the Irish Famine*, by L. Wilson Gr. 5-12

Fiction/Historical Fiction

Under the Hawthorn Tree, by Marita Conlon-McKenna Gr. 5-12

**Escape from Home* and **Lord Kirkle's Money*, by Avi (*Beyond the Western Sea*) Gr. 7-12
I've not read these novels of Irish peasants fleeing poverty.

25 A Move toward Movements: Reform and Missions

Do you think God was silent during this slide into humanism and progressivism? Well, His enemy is *not* His equal, you know. He found people who yearned to participate in His great plan. He birthed a massive missionary movement that still affects the world, as He extended Christianity to the Orient, India, and Africa! Much of it sprang from the earlier revivals in England and America we've already discussed. Isn't it wonderful to see them continue to bear fruit? For example, John Wesley had visited the elders of Hudson Taylor! Other Christians worked with the poor (such as notable Lord Shaftesbury), with those in prison (such as Elizabeth Fry), with factory workers, and some even dealt with the shockingly horrible way the retarded and insane were kept. We must laud William Wilberforce for his vigorous fight against slavery in Great Britain. What a man! Louis Braille, while still a sight-impaired teen, improved the lot of the blind with his Braille alphabet. A temperance movement (against drunkenness) swelled in the US in the 1850s. There was also, however, a humanistic reform movement. As an extension of mankind's high opinion of his own ration, as a sign of his self-proclaimed progress, he set out to fix all the world's problems *on his own* and with his *own* wisdom. As you watch remaining history, you'll see the differing results. For now, just remember that *reform* was the hot word of the mid-1800s! So, let's meet these folks, remembering some worked with the Lord and some worked on their own. (Do *ThinkWrite 8* now.)

> ***ThinkWrite 8: "Select-a-Guy!"***
>
> Several amongst the list below are heroes and heroines of the faith. Would you like to select one for deeper study? We can learn much from these folks!

25a General overview

**Basic History of the United States: Vol. 3*, by Clarence Carson, Ch. 5e Gr. 9-12
Please note that we'll discuss the growth of public education in the next guide.

Fire Upon the Earth, by Norman Langford, Ch. 17b Gr. 4-12

**How Should We Then Live?* by Francis Schaeffer, Ch.7, and pp. 113-119 Gr. 9-12

No Other Foundation: The Church Through Twenty Centuries, by J. Jackson, Ch. 19 Gr. 11-12
I know this wisdom-packed book is too hard and time-consuming for most students, but I always mention it just in case...

Fiction/Historical Fiction

**Jessica's Mother Comes Home*, by Hesba Stretton & Mark Hamby (Lamplighter) Gr. 3-10
The sequel to the beloved *Jessica's First Prayer* finds Jessica and Mr. Dan'el in London reaching out to an unfit mother.

25b Charles Loring Brace

Mr. Brace founded the Children's Aid Society in 1853 which was largely responsible for the Orphan Trains.

Fiction/Historical Fiction

**Roundup of the Street Rovers* Gr. 3-8
by Dave & Neta Jackson (Trailblazer)
Fictional kids meet the real Charles Loring Brace. (We'll study the kids on the Orphan Trains in the next guide since most of them went to communities in the Great Plains, and we've not yet covered Plains pioneering.)

There was even concern for mistreatment of animals! In 1824, the Royal Society for the Prevention of Cruelty to Animals was founded. An American branch was opened by Henry Bergh. Both still function today. You may have read stories such as *Black Beauty* which reveal the sad way animals were previously treated. Be careful not to value animals more highly than or equal with humans though, as is sometimes done today.. Instead, remember that God commands humans to be stewards over the earth, His servants caring for and wisely using all that He has created. I don't know the worldview of Mr. Bergh.

Henry Bergh, by Harlow (Messner) Gr. 6-12

25c Louis Braille

Braille lost his sight as a young boy and perfected the Braille alphabet for the blind when we was just a teen!

**Louis Braille*, by Jayne Woodhouse (Lives and Times) Gr. K-2

**Picture Book of Louis Braille*, by David Adler Gr. K-2

Louis Braille, by Dennis Fradin (Remarkable Children) Gr. 1-4

*_Louis Braille_, by Margaret Davidson Gr. 3-8
This would likely be more narrative then newer "off-the-assembly-line" series.

*_World at His Fingertips_, by B. O'Connor (Creative Minds) Gr. 3-8

*_Louis Braille: Inventor_, by Jennifer Bryant (Great Achievers) Gr. 4-8

Seeing Fingers, by Etta DeGering Gr. 4-12
I've heard that this is excellent.

Touch of Light, by Anne Neimark Gr. 4-12
I think this is the version used in Beyond Five-in-a-Row.

Louis Braille, by Beverley Birch Gr. 5-8

*_Out of Darkness_, by Russell Freedman Gr. 6-12

25d William Carey

Carey, an Englishman, is credited as the first great modern missionary. He worked in India.

Young Man in a Hurry, by Iris Clinton Gr. 4-12

*_Trial and Triumph: Stories from Church History_, by Richard Hannula, Ch. 36 Gr. 5-12

*_William Carey_, by Janet Benge (Christian Heroes, Then and Now) Gr. 5-12
Some Benge books are being put into audio format also.

*_William Carey: Father of Modern Missions_, by Sam Wellman (Heroes of the F...) Gr. 5-12

*_Ambassadors for Christ_, edited by John Woodbridge, pp. 20-29 Gr. 7-12
This is a compendium of short biographies of Christian heroes.

*_William Carey_, by Basil Miller (Men of Faith) Gr. 8-12

Film

*_Candle in the Dark_
I've not seen this, but it is by Gateway/Vision, so is probably reliable.

25e Dorothea Dix

Dix was an American who worked with the insane in prisons, etc., and supervised Civil War nurses. I read online that she converted to Unitarianism, which could be called a religious outflow of the "Enlightenment," and which appealed to reformers at the time (when it seemed to be only about kindness and goodness, and when too many Christian churches were happy to let injustice go unchanged and may even have resisted improvements, alas), so be very discerning as to books about her.

Dorothea Dix, by Grace Melin (Childhood) Gr. 1-6

**Dorothea Dix*, by Barbara Witteman (Let Freedom Ring) Gr. 4-8

Angel of Mercy, by Rachel Baker (Messner) Gr. 4-12

Dorothea Lynde Dix, by Gertrude Norman Gr. 5-12

**Dorothea Dix: Crusader for the Mentally Ill*, by Amy Herstek (Hist. Am.) Gr. 7-12
An online reviewer said this was dry, but thorough.

Dorothea L. Dix: Hospital Founder, by Mary Malone Unknown

25f Elizabeth Fry

Fry took her Christianity to England's dreaded Newcastle Prison.

**Hero Tales: Vol. II*, by Dave & Neta Jackson, pp. 57-67 Gr. 3-6

Value of Kindness, by Spencer Johnson (ValueTale) Gr. 3-8

Young Elizabeth Fry, by Patrick Pringle Gr. 7-12

Fiction/Historical Fiction

**Thieves of Tyburn Square*, by Dave & Neta Jackson (Trailblazer) Gr. 3-8
Fictional kids meet the real Fry in this distinctively Christian series.

25g Adoniram Judson

Judson was the first great modern American missionary. He worked in Burma.

**Hero Tales: Vol. I*, by Dave & Neta Jackson Gr. 3-6
One of the chapters in this first volume covers Judson.

**Adoniram Judson: God's Man in Burma*, by Sharon Hambrick Gr. 3-7

Fire Upon the Earth, by Norman Langford, Ch. 17b Gr. 4-12

**Ambassadors for Christ*, edited by John Woodbridge, pp. 30-35 Gr. 7-12
This is a compendium of short biographies of Christian heroes.

Fiction/Historical Fiction

**Imprisoned in the Golden City*, by Dave & Neta Jackson (Trailblazer) Gr. 3-9
Fictional kids meet real heroes!

25h Philippe Pinel

Pinel was a French doctor who worked on behalf of the insane who were usually kept in abysmal conditions.

Philippe Pinel: Unchainer of the Insane, by Bernard Mackler (Immortals...) Gr. 6-12

25i Elizabeth Ann Seton

Seton, an American woman, founded an important Catholic charity group.

Mother Seton and the Sisters of Charity, by Alma Powers-Waters (Vision) Gr. 3-12

**Saint Elizabeth Ann Seton*, by Jeanne Grunwell (Encounter the Saints) Unknown
It looks like this is for upper-elementary, but I've not seen it in person.

25j Lord Shaftesbury

The list is long, indeed, of all the people Shaftesbury helped: child laborers, miners, street urchins, the insane, chimney sweeps, the impoverished, etc., and he did it all in the name of the Lord!

**More than Conquerors*, edited by John Woodbridge, pp. 245-251 Gr. 7-12
This is a compendium of short biographies of Christian heroes.

25k Hudson Taylor

The missionary work of Taylor, an Englishman, in China is still legendary!

**Hudson Taylor*, by Susan Miller (Young Reader's Christian Library) Gr. 1-3

*_Hero Tales: Vol. I_, by Dave & Neta Jackson — Gr. 3-6
One of the chapters in this first volume covers Taylor.

*_Hudson Taylor_, by Janet Benge (Christian Heroes, Then and Now) — Gr. 5-12
Some Benge books are being put into audio format also.

*_Hudson Taylor_, by Vance Christie (Heroes of the Faith) — Gr. 5-12

*_Ambassadors for Christ_, edited by John Woodbridge, pp. 157-162 — Gr. 7-12
*_More than Conquerors_, edited by John Woodbridge, pp. 50-55 — Gr. 7-12
These offer short biographies of Christian heroes.

*_Hudson Taylor_, by Hudson Taylor (Men of Faith) — Gr. 8-12
This is probably an abridged version of the two-volume masterwork below.

*_Hudson Taylor's Spiritual Secret_, by Howard Taylor — Gr. 8-12
Here, Taylor's son has written a more succinct, but powerful, biography of his amazing father (see below). I've heard that this book is life-changing.

*_Hudson Taylor: Vol. 1 and 2_, by Howard Taylor — Gr. 10-12
This two-volume series brings the full breadth and depth of Taylor's life courtesy of Taylor's son. I've heard these are some of the most inspiring books ever!

Hudson Taylor and Maria, by J.C. Pollock — Gr. 10-12

Fiction/Historical Fiction

*_Shanghaied to China_, by Dave & Neta Jackson (Trailblazer) — Gr. 3-9
Fictional kids meet real heroes!

251 William Wilberforce
Wilberforce's strenuous and unrelenting efforts led to British abolishment of slavery much earlier than was achieved in America. His strong Christian faith propelled him mightily. What an inspiration!

*_Island Story_, by H.E. Marshall, Ch. C — Gr. 3-8

----

*_Hero Tales: Vol. IV_, by Dave & Neta Jackson — Gr. 3-6
One of the chapters in this volume covers Wilberforce.

Freedom Fighter, by Betty Everett — Gr. 7-12

*_He Freed Britain's Slaves_, by Charles Ludwig — Gr. 7-12

More than Conquerors, edited by John Woodbridge, pp. 240-244 — Gr. 7-12
This is a compendium of short biographies of Christian heroes.

Real Christianity, by William Wilberforce — Gr. 9-12
Wilberforce's own call to a life of sold-out Christianity!

Film

Amazing Grace, starring Ioan Gruffudd — All ages
One of the most powerful films I've ever seen. Awesome! Excellent! Don't miss it!

William Wilberforce — Unknown
This film is produced by Gateway/Vision Video, a company specializing in religious productions; I've not seen it, but it is probably wonderful.

26 Romantic Movement in Art

We've talked about the emphasis on human rationality...but (are you surprised?) folks began to feel dissatisfied. Something was missing, but that was not daunting. Remember, the experts now felt it was actually their place to reinvent the world according to their own progressive insights. So, *voila!* They just whipped up a new realization...that mankind's more sensitive, creative nature was being ignored due to all this emphasis on intelligence. "Let's feel, let's create!" they said. "Let's not just do math. It's with our caring hearts, not with our rational minds, that we will make earth a perfect place, a utopia!" A new wave of culture was born; it's been called the *Romantic Movement* because it was so *feeling*.

Now, I'm not saying that the Romantic Movement was inherently wrong; God did make our emotional and creative sides too, and that's something to celebrate. In fact, some participants in the Romantic Movement were godly people who were glad to bring another aspect of God's creation of us into view.

The movement only became wrong when it implied that one's emotions alone were an adequate base for life, and that mankind could thus create utopia—not by each individual getting right with God, but by changing society. Many in the humanistic elite were now trying to convince the masses that their romantic plans for *progress* would certainly succeed. Sound familiar? Do you hear the same claims today? If not, listen more closely to political speeches, pleas for educational funding, promotions for self-help books, etc. "Now we're whole! Now we've got it all put together!" they claim.

This wearisome search for wholeness outside of God makes me think of a precious passage about Jesus Christ from God's Word:

From beginning to end he's there, towering far above everything, everyone. So spacious is he, so roomy, that everything of God finds its proper place in him without crowding. Not only that, but all the broken and dislocated pieces of the universe—people and things, animals and atoms—get properly fixed and fit together in vibrant harmonies, all because of his death, his blood that poured down from the Cross (Col. 1:19-20, Message, if you'll permit use of paraphrase which uniquely captures thought for young students).

This Romantic Movement bears closer inspection. It sure produced some incredibly beautiful music! It also spawned a lot of literature and art. I'm sure many considered these achievements to be "proof" of mankind's *progress.* When I think of Europe, either medieval castles come to mind *or* this busy time of beautiful music and art. You're going to enjoy this topic!

Older students should read the quote immediately below. It mentions a lot of people we'll study next (so don't feel ignorant), and it thoroughly describes the essence of the Romantic Movement. Younger students can skip to a briefer summary below.

The romantic composers sought to express emotion through music in a more direct way than had been thought desirable before. This development in music was mirrored by similar changes in painting and literature, and was also a reflection of the upheavals taking place in European thought and politics at the end of the eighteenth and the beginning of the nineteenth centuries. The "Age of Revolution," between 1789 and 1848, was closely identified with the active involvement of artists and intellectuals. In France, writers, painters and musicians—among them George Sand, Baudelaire, Flaubert, Hugo, Rimbaud, Delacroix and Berlioz, and the great impressionist painters of the latter half of the century—sought to shock contemporary society out of its complacency and materialism.

In the mood that pervaded Europe at this time, men found themselves in a social climate that led their nations out of the autocratic rule of the princely courts into the democratic participation of the new middle class. Everyone was imbued with the desire for participation, for liberation and for the brotherhood of man.

The creative consciousness of the romantic artist was inspired by many external forces: by the quest for national and personal liberty, by nature, poetry, the primitive, the childlike, and by oppressed peoples and their destinies. The new self-awareness was however coloured by a corresponding disillusion. Revolutionary idealism had proved abortive and equality had not banished oppression. When Napoleon, who had declared himself the enemy of oppression and had led the struggle for liberty, equality and fraternity, went on to declare himself emperor, Beethoven tore up the title-page dedication (to "General Bonaparte") of his Eroica symphony, and substituted the words "To the memory of a great man."

Failed idealism triggered off another strong element of romantic art: escapism. The novels of Scott and Dumas fils [Dumas, Jr., we'd say], *the music of Berlioz and Mendelssohn, the paintings of Turner and Delacroix and the poetry of Tennyson, Baudelaire and Rimbaud all share a longing for the exotic, for faraway lands and for experiences outside the tedium of everyday life. The past, particularly the Dark and Middle Ages, exerted a strong attraction for romantic artists. So did the strange, the macabre and the distorted, as the writings of Dostoevsky, Poe and Baudelaire show.*[58]

58 Rowley 40.

Said briefly, the Romantic Movement was about emotion, hope, patriotism, and idealism. Later, romanticists became disappointed with their movement's inability to change the world, and their emotions proved to be an inadequate basis for life and decisions. (Emotions are fickle, after all, and cannot fully apprehend truth, though our modern world tells us, "Do what feels right in your heart! Your feelings never lie!") Then romantic art became darker, more discouraged, and more interested in strange things and far away places.

> ### *ThinkWrite 9: "Select-another-Guy!"*
>
> Please select one of the Romantic Movement composers, painters, or authors and explain how their works showed the essence of Romanticism. Please keep in mind, though, that just because someone is considered a Romantic composer, for example, does not necessarily mean that they rejected a Biblical view of mankind. It might have been simply that they were relieved that rationalism was crumbling and they were glad to represent the facet of mankind's God-given creativity. Please probe these issues with your artist of choice. Enjoy!

Let's get to know some of these geniuses (and do *ThinkWrite 9, please*)**. Sadly, we haven't time to meet Berlioz, Franck, Mahler, Bruckner, Verdi, and Saint-Saëns (composers); Shelley, Byron, and Pushkin (writers); Bellini, Gericault, and Ingres (painters). You'll still see the great energy of the Romantic Movement! Six, quick housekeeping items first, though:**

1) Not all artists were completely aligned with the Romantic Movement, of course, but it was still the dominant culture of the time.

2) Some of these artists were mentioned in the previous *TruthQuest History* guide, but are mentioned again here because they also worked in the 1800s and we're more fully discussing the basis for their art in this guide.

3) Some are known by their last names only, some by their full names. I'll attempt to stick with convention when listing them.

4) Please don't try to study them all! Just pick a few and get to know them. Listen to their music. Gaze at their art. Read their poems and books. Now's the chance to absorb it all in context, not under the microscope of a textbook's analysis!

5) As the parent, you'll need to determine the suitability of the artworks and literary works your children will be viewing, reading, and hearing.

6) Specific biographies, written at youth level, will of course be listed here. Otherwise, you'll certainly find info in your favorite art/music/literature history books, such as: *Story of Painting for Young People*, by the Jansons, **Looking at Pictures*, by Joy Richardson, **Lives of the Artists*, by Kathleen Krull, *Famous Paintings*, by Chase, and *Sister Wendy's many art books; *The Book of Music*, edited by Gill Rowley (pp. 40-47), *Story-Lives of Great Composers* and *Story-Lives of American Composers*, both by Katherine Bakeless; *Famous Authors*, by Ramon Coffmann, and **Lives of the Writers*, by Kathleen Krull; etc.

26a Composers—Beethoven

Important! Beethoven's life shows how Christians (including us) can be influenced by the popular philosophies of the day. You see, Beethoven spoke of his love for God, and he wanted his music to glorify the Lord. Yet, gradually his life became overly based on emotion. Thus, Beethoven's music moved toward discouragement near the end of his life, and away from ending with a clear resolution as had earlier classical music—such as Bach's—which was based on the beliefs of the Reformation. Due to Beethoven's influential genius, this change affected subsequent music, as Francis Schaeffer insightfully explains (see below).

**Beethoven*, by Wendy Lynch (Lives and Times) Gr. 1-3

**Heroic Symphony*, by Anna Celenza Gr. 1-4
The story of Beethoven's symphony about Napoleon...includes a CD!

**Ludwig van Beethoven*, by Louis Sabin (Troll) Gr. 1-4

Ludwig van Beethoven, by Carol Greene (Rookie) Gr. 1-5

**Ludwig van Beethoven*, by Mike Venezia (Getting to Know the World's...) Gr. 1-6
Humorous pictures and interesting text.

Ludwig Beethoven and the Chiming Tower Bells, by Opal Wheeler Gr. 1-6
A delightful biography, with snatches of music.

**Beethoven*, by Greta Cencetti (World of Composers) Gr. 2-6

**Beethoven Lives Upstairs*, by Barbara Nichol (Classical Kids) Gr. 2-6
Also available in dramatized audio and video format.

**Beethoven*, by Ann Rachlin (Famous Children) Gr. 3-6
Shows episodes from Beethoven's childhood.

Story of Beethoven, by Helen Kaufmann (Signature) Gr. 3-9

Boyhoods of Famous Composers, Vol. 2, by Catherine Gough, Ch. 2 Gr. 4-9

**Ludwig van Beethoven*, by Dynise Balcavage (Great Achievers) Gr. 4-9

Beethoven: Master Musician, by Madeline Goss Gr. 4-10

**Beethoven and the Classical Age*, by A. Bergaamini (Masters of Music) Gr. 5-12

Beethoven, by Reba Paeff Mirsky Gr. 6-12

**Introducing Beethoven*, by Roland Vernon (Introducing Composers) Gr. 6-12
I've read that this book attempts to explain the cultural and political influences on the various composers.

**Spiritual Lives of Great Composers*, by Patrick Kavanaugh, Ch. 5 Gr. 6-12
This inspiring book has chapters on the spiritual walks of various composers.

Beethoven and the World of Music, by Manuel Komroff Gr. 9-12

**How Should We Then Live?* by Francis Schaeffer, pp. 158, 190-193 Gr. 9-12

**Ludwig van Beethoven: Musical Genius*, by Brendan January (Great Life) Unknown

Audio/Film

**Beethoven Lives Upstairs* (Classical Kids) Gr. 2-6
Available not only in book form (see above), but also as audio and video!

26b Composers—Brahms

Ah, could the second movement of his "Piano Concerto No. 1 in D-minor" be any lovelier?

**Johannes Brahms*, by Mike Venezia (Getting to Know the World's...) Gr. 1-6
Humorous pictures and text highlight this little biography.

Young Brahms, by Sybil Deucher Gr. 2-7
Another delightful biography, with snatches of music.

**Brahms*, by Ann Rachlin (Famous Children) Gr. 3-6
Shows episodes from Brahms' childhood.

Brahms, by Reba Paeff Mirsky Gr. 4-12
Mirsky's biographies are greatly enjoyed.

**Life & Times of Johannes Brahms*, by Jim Whiting (Masters of Music) Gr. 4-12

**Johannes Brahms and the Twilight of Romanticism* (Masters of Music) Gr. 5-12
by Donna Getzinger

26c Composers—Chopin

**Frederic Chopin*, by Mike Venezia (Getting to Know the World's...) Gr. 1-6
Humorous pictures and text highlight this little biography.

**Chopin*, by Greta Cencetti (World of Composers) Gr. 2-6

**Frederic Chopin*, by Jacqueline Dineen (Tell Me About) Gr. 2-6
I've not seen this so don't know how it handles Chopin's life for children of this age.

Frederic Chopin: Early Years* **and *Frederic Chopin: Later Years*, by Opal Wheeler Gr. 2-7
A precious older biography with snatches of music, now being reprinted!

**Chopin*, by Ann Rachlin (Famous Children) Gr. 3-6
Shows episodes from Chopin's childhood.

Boyhoods of Famous Composers, Vol. 2, by Catherine Gough, Ch. 3 Gr. 4-9

Chopin, by Antoni Gronowicz Gr. 4-12

**Life & Times of Frederic Chopin*, by Jim Whiting (Masters of Music) Gr. 4-12

**Introducing Chopin*, by Roland Vernon (Introducing Composers) Gr. 6-12

26d Composers—Liszt

**Life & Times of Franz Liszt*, by Jim Whiting (Masters of Music) Gr. 4-12

**Spiritual Lives of the Great Composers*, by Patrick Kavanaugh, Ch. 8 Gr. 6-12
This inspiring book has chapters on the spiritual walks of various composers.

Franz Liszt, by Victor Seroff Gr. 8-12

26e Composers—Mendelssohn

Boyhoods of Great Composers, Vol 1, by Catherine Gough, Ch. 4 Gr. 4-9

On Wings of Song, by Dena Humphreys Gr. 4-12

**Spiritual Lives of the Great Composers*, Patrick Kavanaugh, Ch. 7 Gr. 6-12
This inspiring book has chapters on the spiritual walks of various composers.

Mendelssohn, by Michael Hurd — Gr. 7-12

**Life & Times of Felix Mendelssohn*, by Susan Zannos — Unknown

26f Composers—Paganini

Paganini, by Lillian Day — Gr. 3-8

Paganini: Master of the Strings, by Opal Wheeler — Gr. 3-8
Another delightful biography, with snatches of music.

26g Composers—Rossini

Blithe Genius, by Gladys Malvern — Gr. 5-12

26h Composers—Schubert

A Little Schubert, by M.B. Goffstein — Gr. 1-4
I've not seen this, but get the feeling from description that it's for young children.

Franz Schubert and His Merry Friends, by Opal Wheeler & S. Deucher — Gr. 2-7
Another precious biography with snatches of music.

**Schubert*, by Ann Rachlin (Famous Children) — Gr. 3-6
Shows episodes from Schubert's childhood.

Boyhoods of Great Composers, Vol. 1, by Catherine Hough, Ch. 3 — Gr. 4-9

**Spiritual Lives of the Great Composers*, by Patrick Kavanaugh, Ch. 6 — Gr. 6-12
This inspiring book has chapters on the spiritual walks of various composers.

Schubert, by Peggy Woodford — Gr. 7-12
Just the facts.

**Franz Peter Schubert*, by Eric Summerer — Unknown

26i Composers—Robert & Clara Schumann

Robert Schumann and Mascot Ziff, by Opal Wheeler — Gr. 1-6
Another delightful biography, with snatches of music.

**Schumann*, by Ann Rachlin (Famous Children) — Gr. 3-6
Shows episodes from Schumann's childhood.

**Her Piano Sang*, by Barbara Allman (Creative Minds) — Gr. 3-9
Meet talented Clara Schumann.

**Clara Schumann: Piano Virtuoso*, by Susanna Reich — Gr. 5-10

Duet: The Story of Clara and Robert Schumann, by Elizabeth Kyle — Gr. 5-12

26j Composers—Johann Strauss II

Strauss was nicknamed the "Waltz King."

Tales from the Vienna Woods, by David Ewen — Gr. 5-12

Waltz King, by Kurt Pahlen — Gr. 7-12

26k Composers—Tchaikovsky

Tchaikovsky is my favorite....not that you asked. Ah,his "Piano Concerto No. 1 in B-flat minor," and the "1812 Overture" already mentioned, plus "Nutcracker" and "Romeo and Juliet Overture." I could go on...

**Peter Tchaikovsky*, by Mike Venezia (Getting to Know the...) — Gr. 1-6
Humorous pictures and interesting text.

**Tchaikovsky*, by Greta Cencetti (World of Composers) — Gr. 2-6

Peter Tchaikovsky and the Nutcracker Ballet, by Opal Wheeler — Gr. 2-7
Another delightful biography, with snatches of music.

**Tchaikovsky Discovers America*, by Esther Kalman (Classical Kids) — Gr. 2-7
Relates Tchaikovsky's trip to America and fictional children who traveled with him; the companion audio plays much of his music.

**Tchaikovsky*, by Ann Rachlin (Famous Children) — Gr. 3-6
Shows episodes from Tchaikovsky's childhood.

Boyhoods of Great Composers, Vol. 2, by Catherine Gough, Ch. 5 — Gr. 4-9

Stormy Victory: The Story of Tchaikovsky, by Claire Purdy (Messner) — Gr. 6-12

Audio

**Nutcracker* — Various

There are book, audio, and film versions of Tchaikovsky's *Nutcracker Suite*, which is often staged at Christmas time...hint, hint! You can check a ballet company near you. This beaming "Aunt Michelle" was privileged to watch her niece, Jenna, play the lead role of Clara in our town's performance!

**Tchaikovsky Discovers America* (Classical Kids) — Gr. 2-7

Another exciting, high-quality, educational intro to a great composer as fictional children meet the real Tchaikovsky.

26l Composers—Verdi

**Verdi*, by Greta Cencetti (World of Composers) — Gr. 2-6

**Life & Times of Giuseppe Verdi*, by Jim Whiting (Masters of Music) — Gr. 4-12

**Introducing Verdi*, by Roland Vernon (Introducing Composers) — Gr. 6-12

26m Composers—Wagner

**Wagner*, by Greta Cencetti (World of Composers) — Gr. 2-6

Adventures of Richard Wagner, by Opal Wheeler — Gr. 3-8

Another delightful biography, with snatches of music.

**Life & Times of Richard Wagner*, by Jim Whiting (Masters of Music) — Gr. 4-12

**Spiritual Lives of the Great Composers*, by Patrick Kavanaugh, Ch. 9 — Gr. 6-12

This inspiring book has chapters on the spiritual walks of various composers.

Richard Wagner: Titan of Music, by Monroe Stearns (Immortals?) — Gr. 8-12

**Richard Wagner and German Opera*, by Donna Getzinger — Unknown

26n Painters—Constable

Child's History of Art, by Hillyer & Huey (*Painting* section, Ch. 24) Gr. 2-8
OR *Young People's Story of Fine Art: Last Two Hundred Years*, pp. 30-41

Activities

**Constable*, by Emily Cottrill (Picture Study Portfolios) All ages

These insightful booklets, with good-sized reproductions and activities in a wonderful portfolio format, are written by a family friend and published by *Simply Charlotte Mason.*

26o Painters—Delacroix

**Eugene Delacroix*, by Mike Venezia (Getting to Know the World's Great...) Gr. 1-6

Child's History of Art, by Hillyer & Huey (*Painting* section, Ch. 22b) Gr. 2-8
OR *Young People's Story of Fine Art: Last Two Hundred Years*, pp. 12-13, 17-19

26p Painters—Goya

**Francisco Goya* by Mike Venezia (Getting to Know...) Gr. 1-6

Goya, by Elizabeth Ripley Gr. 8-12

Audio/Visual

**Goya: Awakened in a Dream* (Artists' Specials) Various

Activities

**Goya*, by Emily Cottrill (Picture Study Portfolios) All ages

These insightful booklets, with good-sized reproductions and activities in a wonderful portfolio format, are written by a family friend and published by *Simply Charlotte Mason.* She is working on Goya now, so by the time you read this, it will probably be ready. If not, keep checking back!

26q Painters—Turner

**Joseph Turner*, by Jayne Woodhouse (Life and Work of...) Gr. K-2

Child's History of Art, by Hillyer & Huey (*Painting* section, Ch. 24) Gr. 2-8
<u>OR</u> *Young People's Story of Fine Art: Last Two Hundred Years*, pp. 30-41

**J.M.W. Turner*, by Robert Kenner (First Impression) Gr. 5-12
Turner's life (unknown content) and work; you can at least enjoy the paintings.

Activities

**Turner*, by Emily Cottrill (Picture Study Portfolios) All ages
These insightful booklets, with good-sized reproductions and activities in a wonderful portfolio format, are written by a family friend and published by *Simply Charlotte Mason.*

> Are you making certain to enjoy the music, the art, the literature? Are you remembering to have fun? Are you cooking historic foods, drawing, putting on skits, writing fun diary entries, sewing historic costumes, publishing a newspaper with the issues of the day, or doing whatever activities are meaningful to you and your family? Are you continually asking God for His wisdom as you study? He promises His wisdom to those who ask! Now that's something to really enjoy since our goal is to know Him!

26r Authors—Jane Austen

Austen was not necessarily a Romantic writer, but her books show the great emphasis the culture put on material status in post-Industrial Revolution England. Her books are rightfully beloved. High-quality reads!

Famous works include: **Pride and Prejudice*, **Sense and Sensibility*, **Emma*, etc. It would actually be a great time for older girls (especially) to read these because they delightfully illuminate England's early nineteenth-century life...and its foibles!

**Lives of the Writers: Comedies, Tragedies (and What the Neighbors Thought)* Gr. 3-8
by Kathleen Krull, pp. 24-27

**Jane Austen*, by Deirdre Le Faye (British Writers' Lives) Gr. 7-12

**Jane Austen*, by Heather Wagner (Who Wrote That?) Gr. 7-12

Young Jane Austen, by Rosemary Sisson — Gr. 7-12

**Invitation to the Classics*, edited by Cowan & Guinness, pp. 203-206 — Gr. 8-12
Christian analysis of famous authors and literature.

Presenting Miss Jane Austen, by May Lamberton Becker — Gr. 9-12

Activities

**Pride and Prejudice Paper Dolls*, by Brenda Mattox — Various

Films

**Miss Austen Regrets*, starring Olivia Williams — Parental decision

26s Authors—William Blake

Did you know that Blake was also an artist?

Famous works include: **Songs of Innocence*, **Tyger*, etc.

**A Visit to William Blake's Inn*, by Nancy Willard — Gr. 1-8
Imaginary visit shows artistic style of poet.

Child's History of Art, by Hillyer & Huey (*Painting* section, Ch. 24) — Gr. 2-8
OR *Young People's Story of Fine Art: Last Two Hundred Years*, pp. 30-41

Famous Poets for Young People, by Laura Benét, pp. 14-16 — Gr. 5-12

William Blake, by James Daugherty — Gr. 7-12

**William Blake*, by Harold Bloom — Gr. 9-12
Offers serious literary analysis, but I've not seen it and do not know its worldview.

26t Authors—Dostoevksy

I've been told that Dostoevsky later held a Christian view.

Famous works include: **Crime and Punishment*, **Brothers Karamazov*, etc.

**More than Conquerors*, edited by John Woodbridge, pp. 104-107 — Gr. 7-12
This is a compendium of short biographies of Christian heroes.

**Invitation to the Classics*, edited by Cowan & Guinness, pp. 283-286 Gr. 8-12
Christian analysis of famous authors and literature.

**Fyodor Dostoevsky*, by Harold Bloom (Bloom's BioCritiques) Gr. 10-12
I'm not familiar with Bloom's worldview.

26u Authors—Goethe

Goethe has had a great deal of influence on western thought, much of it unbiblical, I think I can fairly say. Remember that Goethe lived at the same time as Hegel and just after Kant. Be careful to acquire top-notch Christian analysis of Goethe if you decide to study this extremely powerful figure.

Famous works include: **Faust*, **Sorrows of Young Werther*, **Wilhelm Meister's*.

**Mr. Goethe's Garden*, by Diana Cohn Parental decision
I cite this as relevant, but not recommended, for two reasons: Goethe's literature had a profound, humanistic impact on civilization. The idea of the book, however, is so nice that maybe it is surprisingly good: a German girl befriends Goethe and he shares his thoughts on plants (Goethe was very interested in natural sciences) and life. I've not read it myself.

**Mothers of Famous Men*, by Archer Wallace, Ch. IX Gr. 3-12

Goethe: Pattern of Genius, by Monroe Stearns (Immortals of Literature) Gr. 8-12

**Invitation to the Classics*, edited by Cowan & Guinness, pp. 207-210 Gr. 8-12
Christian analysis of famous authors and literature. Get this info, if studying Goethe!

26v Authors—Victor Hugo

As you saw during our study of Napoleon, I recommend reading (or viewing) Les Misérables as it well shows the horrors of life during and after the Napoleonic cataclysm in France.

Famous works include: **Les Misérables*, **Hunchback of Notre Dame*, **Ninety-Three*

**Invitation to the Classics*, edited by Cowan & Guinness, p. 256 (brief) Gr. 8-12
Christian analysis of famous authors and literature.

Audio/Film

**Les Misérables* Various
There are varying film and audio versions. Focus on the Family's audio is superb!

26w Authors—Keats

Keats was an English poet.

Famous works include: **Ode on a Grecian Urn, *Ode to a Nightingale*

Young Keats, by Jean Haynes — Gr. 7-12

**Invitation to the Classics*, edited by Cowan & Guinness, pp. 221-224 — Gr. 8-12
Christian analysis of famous authors and literature.

FYI, Biedermeier furniture was popular at this time in history.

26x Authors—Henry Wadsworth Longfellow

Famous works include: **Hiawatha, *Paul Revere's Ride, *Evangeline,* etc. Many are collected in two lovely youth books: **Henry Wadsworth Longfellow* in the "Poetry for Young People" series, and the *Children's Own Longfellow.*

Henry Wadsworth Longfellow, by Grace Melin (Childhood) — Gr. 1-6

American Bard, by Ruth Langland Holberg — Gr. 4-12

26y Authors—Edgar Allan Poe

Careful: many of Poe's writings are very dark; indeed, "macabre" is a word often applied to them. I have read that he was interested in codes, and that one man, who became a student of codes after reading Poe's "Gold Bug" as a boy, was able to crack a Japanese code during World War II.

Famous works: **The Raven, *Pit and the Pendulum, *Gold Bug, *Fall of the House of Usher, *Annabel Lee, etc. He is credited with founding "detective mysteries" as a genre.*

**Lives of the Writers: Comedies, Tragedies (and What the Neighbors Thought)* by Kathleen Krull, pp. 32-37 — Gr. 3-8

Young Edgar Allan Poe, by Laura Benét — Parental discretion

26z Authors—Sir Walter Scott

Scott is one of Scotland's favorite sons. His stories are much-beloved and I am unaware of any moral concerns. They are written in the "high" language of his day, so can challenge modern readers. But those who read his "Ivanhoe," for example, are always glad that they did. I was able to see the magnificent monument to him in Edinburgh.

Famous works include: *_Ivanhoe_, *_Waverly_, *_Marmion_, *_Lady of the Lake_, *_Rob Roy_, *_Heart of Midlothian_, *_Kenilworth_, *_Talisman_, *_Quentin Durward_, *_Tales of a Grandfather_, etc.

Young Walter Scott, by Elizabeth Jane Gray Gr. 7-12

Fiction/Historical Fiction

Lad with a Whistle, by Carol Ryrie Brink Gr. 5-12

Sounds great. Boy gets involved in an Edinburgh mystery with Sir Walter Scott!

26aa Authors—Alfred, Lord Tennyson

Tennyson was a beloved English poet. I've seen illustrated children's versions of his "Charge of the Light Brigade." My limited understanding is that you're likely to find the bulk of his work appropriate for youth.

Famous works: *_Charge of the Light Brigade_, *_Idylls of the King_, *_Lady of Shalott_, *_In Memoriam_, *_Maud_, etc. Tennyson was appointed Poet Laureate by Queen Victoria (whom we'll study in the next guide). Do you recall Anne of Green Gables quoting from _Lady of Shalott_ so glowingly? I found an interesting quote about him:

> *Tennyson in 1886 published a new volume of poetry, containing "Locksley Hall Sixty Years After" and consisting mainly of imprecations against decadence and liberalism and a retraction of the earlier poem's belief in inevitable human progress.*[59]

Hmmm... Some day I want to read his books!

Young Tennyson, by Charlotte Hope Gr. 7-12

**Alfred, Lord Tennyson*, by Harold Bloom (Bloom's Major Poets) Gr. 10-12

I do not know Bloom's worldview.

59 *Merriam Webster's Encyclopedia of Literature* (Springfield, MA: Merriam-Webster, Inc., 1995) 1099.

26bb Authors—Tolstoy

Tolstoy is an veryimportant Russian novelist.

Famous works include: ****War and Peace***, ****Anna Karenina*****, ****Resurrection.***

Count Who Wished He Were a Peasant, by Morris Philipson — Gr. 8-12
This looks very readable for older students.

**Invitation to the Classics*, edited by Cowan & Guinness, pp. 279-282 — Gr. 8-12
Christian analysis of famous authors and literature.

**Leo Tolstoy*, by Harold Bloom (Bloom's Modern Critical Views) — Gr. 10-12
I do not know Bloom's worldview.

**Classic Fables and Tales for Children*, by Leo Tolstoy — Unknown
This might be interesting. Stories Tolstoy told for the younger set! (I've not seen it.)

26cc Authors—William Wordsworth & Samuel Taylor Coleridge

One source said that Lyrical Ballads, *written by both Wordsworth and Coleridge, actually helped launch the English Romantic movement.*[60]

Famous works include: ****Lyrical Ballads* **(which contained Coleridge's** ***Rime of the Ancient Mariner*** **and Wordsworth's** ***Tintern Abbey*****).**

Young Wordsworth, by Trudy West — Gr. 7-12

**Invitation to the Classics*, edited by Cowan & Guinness, pp. 211-214 — Gr. 8-12
Christian analysis of famous authors and literature.

27 Karl Marx

Want to meet a man whose thoughts were clearly born of the 1800s, and whose ideas have possibly impacted more lives than anything but the Bible? Allow me to introduce Karl Marx. This atheistic, German Jew was the father of *communism*, which still holds millions in its grip. But Marx's thoughts waltz through the capitals and town councils of America, Canada, Australia, and most European countries as well! Better know 'em!

I hardly know where to begin. There's so much that could be said. I think I'll just give you thoughts rapid fire. Try to swallow them, then digest. You'll have many new thoughts of your own, too, as you prayerfully seek God for wisdom on this potent topic!

60 Merriam-Webster's Encyclopedia of Literature 1214.

■ Before I really start yakking, though, let me say this: try very hard to purchase Dave Breese's book, **Seven Men Who Rule the World from the Grave.* Read chapters 4-5. Breese exposes the spiritual roots of Marxism in an incredibly insightful and fascinating way. Many church libraries possess this book, and it's still in print, so it should be easy to find (Gr. 7+, parents too!)

■ Remember, in the 1800s, God was no longer seen as the *prime force* of the universe, thus Marx was taught by Hegel (whom we mentioned earlier) that all of history was the result of an *evolutionary* process. Waves of history (waves of dialectic human debate) were going to culminate in human perfection. Marx, seeing the horrendous plight of Europe's poor, concluded that the force that impelled history's onward progression was the fight for survival—for the means to obtain food, clothing, and shelter. The "means to obtain goods" is another way of defining the term *economics.* (I always thought *economics* was some word pulled out of the ether that related to boring textbooks about business; not so!) Anyway, to put it in fancy terms, Marx believed in *economic determinism*, meaning he believed the *fight* for work/money/basic needs was what determined all of history, not the plans of a loving God. He felt the rich (upper class) and the poor (lower class) were always locked in battle; he called this *class struggle.*

■ Let's be honest. What was Marx seeing around him? While there were some devoted reformers, most of the church was doing very little for the poor. Events like the *clearances* were occurring, where landlords who owned huge sections of Scotland, burned the peasants out of their houses, in an effort to *clear* them off their land! They wanted to instead raise sheep since the new textile mills made wool so profitable! These peasants knew nothing except farming the landlord's land and hoping for a share of the food, as their ancestors had done for centuries. They had nowhere to go. Did some of these landlords go to church? I bet so! These same churches (most of them Protestant) were teaching the peasants to accept their lot in life—to be good, contented Christians. What did Marx conclude? That religion was an "opiate" (an opium-based drug that lulled people into passivity). This statement, *religion is the opiate of the people*, is one of Marx's most famous, and communist nations are therefore stridently atheistic. I ask you, therefore, this question: what if Marx had seen a vibrant Christianity which truly exemplified the love, power, and provision of our God? What did he see in the Lutheran school he briefly attended?

Capital
Socialism

■ Marx reached another conclusion too. He saw in Europe that a tiny number of people, the aristocrats, owned most of the land. That's why they were so powerful. Land was *capital*—meaning it was something that produced wealth for its owner. Therefore, Marx insisted that all private ownership of land cease. Instead, he believed all land should be owned by society at large. This was the basic premise of the newly emerging philosophy of *socialism.*

■ Marx went further! He saw that the new middle class that had been birthed by the Industrial Revolution (he called them the *bourgeoisie*, pronounced, boo(r)-shwa-zee) now also owned capital—things that made money for them, such as factories, water mills, trains, farm tools, looms, coal, wood, etc. After seeing how badly most factory workers were treated (since all they had to sell was their labor), Marx declared that *all* capital should belong to the people as a whole, to society, and that this ownership should be managed by a temporary government, until the poor workers (Marx called them the *proletariat*) were accustomed to power and had fully developed the *communes* (group working associations, group farms) within which they would work. Hence the term, *communism.*

Communism

■ To accomplish these dramatic changes, Marx urged the poor—the proletariat—to form militant labor unions and overthrow their nations, even if violence was necessary. In fact, Marx greatly idealized the French Revolution (even though it was so bloodily chaotic), and Communist countries teach their citizens to do the same.

■ Of course, Marx's views are the total opposite of free enterprise, or *capitalism*, which encourages individuals to own their own capital (land, tools, and businesses) so they can pursue their own dreams and be motivated by their own goals and needs. Here's the amazing thing: while Marx felt certain that the longer capitalism existed the greater would be the gap between owners and laborers, the opposite is true! It's in communist nations that you see a tiny, wealthy elite, and masses of poverty-stricken workers, who are totally dominated by a tyrannical government. Even so, our evening newscasts make *capitalism* sound like a dirty word, though it means private ownership and individual freedom. Marx would be shocked to see that it's the nations based on capitalism/free enterprise which have *huge*, comfortable middle classes, with lots of fairness and opportunity for everyone. Yes, poverty still exists in capitalistic nations, but the reasons are more social than economic. Who knows where the next Bill Gates might pop up? Yet, we must again be honest. The potential and liberties of free enterprise/capitalism are so great that they can easily be abused. Marx *did* see abuse. He just concluded that capitalism itself was wrong, when it was actually the spiritual heart of the capitalist that was wrong! *Big difference!* As we discussed previously, the Bible strongly shows private ownership, but it also strictly demands employees be given a fair wage and be treated as the employer himself would want to be treated.

■ Want my opinion? I think Marx missed one of the most basic truths of life...and this is it: we're spiritual individuals, because we're created in God's image. This is *so* basic! It's *Big Belief #2!* It only makes sense, though, that if you deny the existence of our Creator God (*Big Belief #1*), you also have to deny the most intimate, God-reflecting aspects of humankind. Marx ignored this individuality, this spirituality, as well as the fact that all of history is really powered by God's drawing of mankind to Himself. Therefore, Marx's entire thought structure—which makes sense in a spiritual vacuum—fails miserably in the real, spiritually driven world.

■ Let's explore this individuality, this soul of mankind, more deeply. It's what makes us tick, after all. The way Marx outlined the deadly combat people must endure to live, makes me think he's describing animals! But, then, Marx was an atheist; he had to deny spirituality. He *had* to believe people were nothing more than highly coordinated animals.

■ We're not just animals, though! We have dreams and unique talents, and we want our life's work to reflect that! While Marx spoke of human fulfillment through work, everywhere his principles have been implemented, individuality matters less than diddly-squat. The people are told society will work best if they accept being a human cog in the economic machine. Is it any wonder that the people of communist lands are so empty? I've been there. I've seen them. They are hollow shells, for they've been told their total value as human beings is based on the work they can do for the "state." Work, work, work. Even communist artworks—sculpted tiles on buildings, the statues in the city square—glorify just one thing—work! Economics! They're not told they're eternal, unique, God-loved, spiritual individuals. Alas!

■ Yes, work is a big part of life...but it's not the essence of life! It's something we joyfully do for the benefit of our families. It's with love that a father provides food for his growing children. Yes, Marx spoke of the human aspects of work, but he was strongly opposed to the traditional family. Therefore, Marxism lacks true love and family teamwork. In fact, because we want the best for our families, there's a deep motivation within us to do our best, to think creatively, to build a better mouse trap, so that we might increase. All of this contributes to *real progress!* Maybe you won't be shocked to hear that Marx was an absolutely dreadful provider for his own family. Three of his children died of starvation and cold while he kept on writing, depending on his wealthy friend Engels to send money. I've been in that sad, despicable apartment; it shows a side of Marx much of the world does not see. All I could think while standing in that dreadful place (now an office building, I'm told) was that if the world had seen the conditions he put his family into, they would have said *no* to communism, and the entire mess would never have happened!

■ Marx's denial of the spiritual nature of individuality means he missed an important part of work as an enjoyable expression of our unique abilities, and as a way in which we could pleasantly contribute to the lives of others and serve God. Is it any wonder that every single communist-made brick seems to crumble? Every product is shoddy. Every road has potholes.

■ His views often seem so negative. On one hand he was concerned about personal alienation, but he also talked impersonally about "the masses." He didn't esteem one's years of employeehood, of contributing to a growing business as a team member; instead he saw the "selling of one's labor" as an impersonal, dreadful thing. (Yet, his elimination of private ownership of capital left everyone with only their labor to "sell.") He didn't talk about voluntary cooperation (a hallmark of free enterprise); he spoke of combat and competition.

■ Furthermore, he saw employers and employees as enemies, because he believed that if an employee's wages rose, the business would no longer be profitable. It would have to shut down, and the worker would lose his job. Thus, Marx thought capitalism left the poor with just two choices: low wages or no wages. Wrong! Truth is, motivated workers produce superior products, public demand for their products thus increases, and everyone makes more money. This is called the *trickle-down effect* and it is powerful! Factories and offices can be places of cooperation, not a war between labor and management, for God demands that employers give appropriate wages and respect, and that employees work as unto the Lord. That's the setting for fabulous teamwork! In fact, the "workers" can amass enough capital to purchase their own lands, tools, and businesses! They will then, in turn, hire their own employees, who will likewise have the opportunity to advance themselves. Everyone benefits.

■ Marx was wrong about something else. He was sure that capitalists would never relax their grip. Instead, more social reform has come to capitalistic nations that non-capitalistic nations!

■ A positive by-product of the individuality of free enterprise is that people are accustomed to independence and being responsible for one's self and family. They thus resist tyranny to a much greater degree!

■ I just thought of two other Marx-related beliefs that are commonly heard in *non-communist* conversations: one is that only the poor are considered to be "workers," but except for a few very wealthy people who inherit their wealth (meaning an ancestor probably worked effectively), people of *all* classes work! Secondly, Marx saw the universe's resources as quite limited, of course! His man-centered mindset forced everything to be smaller than man, who is admittedly quite limited. Truth is, more people generate more ideas which engender the creation of more wealth and more resources (or more efficient use of resources). Again, it's a win-win situation when handled God's way. This is true economic progress—the generation of wealth and goods that never before existed!

■ Remember, you're going to meet many people who see society's needs (I'm glad they care) but who also think socialism/communism is the answer. Haughtiness and hostility are the *last* thing needed. Instead, express the warmth, individuality, and love that are missing from Marxism. That's what everyone is really seeking!

Well, I said an awful lot...and I was trying to keep it brief. That's scary! Do let me credit Mr. Breese and Mr. Galbraith for many of the thoughts in this section. Books will be cited below, but be aware of anti-Judeo-Christian bias. (Begin *ThinkWrite 10* now.)

ThinkWrite 10: "What's the diff?"

Try not to get uptight about this, but do please explain some of the basic principles of Karl Marx in your own words. Focus on explaining how humanistic beliefs and atheism led to his conclusions. Where did his thinking go wrong?

**Seven Men Who Rule the World from the Grave*, by Dave Breese, Ch. 4-5 Gr. 7-12
I urged you to read this already, but will do so again!

Prophet of Revolution: Karl Marx, by Alfred Apsler (Messner) Gr. 8-12

**Understanding the Times*, by David Noebel Gr. 9-12
This Christian author thoroughly analyzes the basis and impact of Marxism.

Age of Uncertainty, by John Kenneth Galbraith, Ch. 3 Gr. 9-12
A well-written, humorous history of economic ideas. The author is liberal, but tries to be fair...usually (but not always!)

Challenge of Marxism: A Christian Response, by Klaus Bockmuehl Gr. 12+

28 Revolution of 1848

Remember, all this didn't happen in a void. Discontent in Europe was especially rampant because the churches had soaked up empty humanism, and thus old aristocratic ways could hold people in bondage still; the intended force for heart change—which also results in social change—wasn't playing its role! Yes, many of the liberties of capitalism *were* being abused, and humanism and natural religion were so barren. Renewal and transformation *were* needed! The question was...what kind of change would be initiated those who *did* act when the inert church left a void?

Here are some of Karl Marx's demands for change. Am I the only one thinking that many of these have already been implemented, or are being actively sought right now, in the west right now, in countries that supposedly deny Marxism?![61] (Of course, a couple of the changes were needed, but it is how, why, and who would control that differs with Marxism.)

- **Ending of private ownership of land**
  [High property taxes also hamper private ownership.]
- **Progressive income tax**
  [Taxes the wealthy at a higher rate since it is considered wrong for some to have more than others, no matter how much they worked to get it; the wealthy thus have less capital to start businesses which hire employees, purchase from producers seeking to sell their wares, or give to charitable causes, as Andrew Carnegie and J.C. Penney did. Most European wealth at the time, though, was in the aristocracy which controlled land and its laborers.]

61 This list is taken from: John Kenneth Galbraith, *The Age of Uncertainty* (Boston: Houghton Mifflin, 1977) 93. Comments in brackets are my own.

- Abolition of family inheritances
  [A high inheritance tax also nullify inheritance.]
- A national bank with a monopoly on banking operations
- Public ownership of railroads and communications
- Better soil management
- Free education
- Abolition of child labor
- Education along with work

Remember, the need for reform was real, and the church should always be the first to see needs and connect God's heart, power, and wisdom to them. Instead, Marx offered totally atheistic answers, and where *rightful* reform did *not* occur, revolution did! Yes, because hopeless poverty and mistreatment were left unattended in most of Europe, revolutions were popping up all over. So many occurred in 1848 that it's called the *Year of Revolution!* You see, people were getting quite fed up with aristocrats and having no potential for advancement even after hard work. Strong feelings of national patriotism were sweeping Europe, as people banded together to seek change! Let's take a look around.

France was a mess. Descendants of Napoleon and King Louis were taking turns on the throne. One minute there was a King Louis the Umpteenth, the next minute there was a new emperor, Napoleon the Who-Knows-What-th, ruling the Five Hundredth Empire, or so it seemed. Their 1848 revolution was awful!

Various German states were struggling for freedom, and Garibaldi was trying to reunite Italy. Kossuth led the charge in Hungary. Vienna had its October Days of revolt. Other Eastern European nations, some still trying to throw off medieval feudalism (can you believe that, poor things?), were fitfully mounting revolutions whenever they could, but with little success, sadly. Is it any wonder that they would later give all to emigrate to America, Canada, Australia, etc., unweighted by the past?

In Russia, some wise nobles had earlier (1825) tried to seek change on behalf of the people, just like we saw a few concerned souls in other lands, but their December activities, known as the *Decembrist Revolution*, were utterly crushed by the czar. Too bad, because conditions worsened until one of the most devastating revolutions in history would come to Russia, as you'll discover in the next *TruthQuest History* guide. Has the efforts of the early, positive reformers have been heeded.....the last czar and his family wouldn't have ended up full of bullets in a hole in the ground....and all of Russia and its conquered lands taken over by Marxism.... In other words, when will people learn that God's ways are *good* and are the *only* way to personal and national blessing? And when we will remember that we believers need to be the first to meet spiritual and earthly needs, before the world proposes its own horrific, dehumanizing solutions in the void?

Anyway, there was a lot of turmoil. We had better dig in!

28a General overview

**1848: Year of Revolution*, by R.G. Grant — Gr. 5-12

Fiction/Historical Fiction

**Letzenstein Chronicles* series, by Meriol Trevor (Bethlehem Books) — Gr. 4-12

Four books (*Crystal Snowstorm, Following the Phoenix, Angel & Dragon*, and *Rose & Crown*) together tell of young people living through Revolutions of 1848 in Europe. These come from a strongly moral publisher, but I have not read them.

House on Liberty Street, by Mary Ann Weik — Gr. 7-12

European family disappointed by results of 1848 uprisings emigrates to America. I'm not sure how much of the story is set in Europe, and how much is in America.

28b Garibaldi of Italy

Garibaldi: Father of Modern Italy, by Marcia Davenport (Landmark) — Gr. 4-12

Garibaldi: The Man Who Made a Nation, by Ronald Syme — Gr. 6-12

**Giuseppe Garibaldi*, by Herman & Susan Viola (World Leaders Past...) — Gr. 7-12

Fiction/Historical Fiction

Follow My Black Plume **and** *A Thousand for Sicily*, by Geoffrey Trease — Gr. 6-12

Trease's books are usually high adventure!

**Out with Garibaldi*, by G.A. Henty — Gr. 7-12

Another Henty!

28c Decembrist Revolution in Russia

Since I cannot find books which discuss this topic in particular, I'll remind you that any resources on Russian history will probably serve.

Princess of Siberia, by Christine Sutherland — Gr. 10-12

Tells the true story of a Russian princess and her husband whose efforts on behalf of the peasants condemned them to a Siberian prison.

29 Nationalist Movement in Art

Remember? I just said strong feelings of national patriotism were swirling through Europe, as people tried to bring changes to their nations and the people were basking in the rosy glow of *progress*. Can you blame them? The advent of city sewers *did* make life more pleasant!

Of course, these feelings would show up in the literature, drama, music, sculpture, and paintings of the era, since art expresses the worldview of the artist. Indeed, an entire art movement was birthed—*nationalism*. Composers began to incorporate their nation's folk music into their great symphonic works, while painters focused more on the beauty of their nation's countryside and common people, and writers delved more into the real life of their countrymen. See for yourself!

Nationalism

First, I'll concisely remind you of our art study notes:

1) Not all artists of the period were completely aligned with the Nationalist movement, of course, but it was still the dominant culture of the time.

2) Some are known by their last names only, some by their full names. I'll attempt to stick with convention when listing them.

3) *Don't* try to study them all. Pick an artist or country of interest. Listen to their music. Gaze at their art. Read their poems and books. Now's the chance to absorb it all in context, not under the microscope of a textbook's analysis!

4) Parents, you must decide suitability of topic and resources (such as art books) used. Some contain images you may not want your children to see and you'll not want to read all authors.

5) Not all artists have had youth books written about them, though where specific books are available, they will certainly be listed here. If you see nothing listed, just check your own favorite art/music/literature history books, such as *Story of Painting for Young People*, by the Jansons, **Looking at Pictures*, by Joy Richardson, **Lives of the Artists*, by Kathleen Krull, *Famous Paintings*, by Chase, and *Sister Wendy's many art books; *The Book of Music*, edited by Gill Rowley (pp. 48-49), *Story-Lives of Great Composers* and *Story-Lives of American Composers*, both by Katherine Bakeless; *Famous Authors*, by Ramon Coffmann, and **Lives of the Writers*, by Kathleen Krull; etc.

6) Since we're dealing with nationalism, I'll group them by nation, okay? That will help those exploring the music or literature of one country; you'll be able to hear/see the unique ethnic strains. Enjoy! Oh, some of the Romantic composers we discussed earlier, such as Chopin and Liszt, also incorporated ethnic themes. Sadly, there are many writers musicians, such as Puccini and Toscanini, we can't get to here, but feel free to study on your own. Please note that there was no real nationalist music movement in France, and nationalist music (Aaron Copland, Charles Ives) in America, came much later, so we'll meet them in the next guide. Try to tuck in Hans Christian Andersen, a Dane. Kids love his stories!

Ready, let's dive in!

29a Bohemian/Czech Composers—Dvořák, Janáček, Smetana

Sorry, I'm not aware of any books specifically about Smetana and Janáček, but there are several on Dvořák. I have always enjoyed his music very much too. I'd have to put him in my top five!

**Dvorak in America*, by Joseph Horowitz — Gr. 4-8

Slavonic Rhapsody, by Jan Van Straaten — Gr. 6-12

**Spiritual Lives of the Great Composers*, by Patrick Kavanaugh, Ch. 10 — Gr. 6-12
This inspiring book has chapters on the spiritual walks of various composers.

Antonín Dvořák: Composer from Bohemia, by Claire Purdy (Messner) — Gr. 7-12

Fiction/Historical Fiction

Two Scarlet Songbirds, by Carole Lexa Schaefer — Gr. 1-4
Hearing a bird sing, Dvořák finds inspiration in this fact-based story! It was recently in-print, so is probably still on your library's shelves.

29b English Composers—Edward Elgar and Ralph Vaughan Williams

These composers were active after 1900 but were nationalistic, so we'll cite them now and in the next unit.

Boyhoods of Great Composers, Vol. 1, by Catherine Gough, Ch. 6 — Gr. 4-9
This chapter covers Mr. Elgar.

Boyhoods of Great Composers, Vol. 2, by Catherine Gough, Ch. 6 — Gr. 4-9
This chapter covers Mr. Williams.

Vaughan Williams, by Michael Hurd — Gr. 7-12

29c Finnish Composer—Jean Sibelius

Finlandia: The Story of Sibelius, by Eliot Arnold — Gr. 7-12

29d Hungarian Composers: Bartók, Kodály

Sorry, I'm not aware of any books specifically on these composers; just check your general resources.

29e Norwegian Composer—Edvard Grieg

Edvard Grieg: Boy of the Northland, by Sybil Deucher Gr. 2-7

Boyhoods of Great Composers, Vol. 1, by Catherine Gough, Ch. 5 Gr. 4-9

Song of the North, by Claire Lee Purdy Gr. 7-12

29f Polish Composer—Paderewski

Paderewski: Pianist and Patriot, by Antoni Gronowicz Gr. 6-12

29g Russian Composers—Borodin, Glinka, Mussorgsky, Rimsky-Korsakov

Sorry, I'm not aware of any books specifically about these composers, but you can always check general resources such as the one listed below. My son and I were just at a concert where Mussorgsky's "Pictures at an Exhibition" composition was played by a small orchestra from St. Petersburg, Russia. Now, every time my son hears portions of it played (which is more often that I would have imagined), his head pops up with recognition! I missed it every time, but he caught it! Yup, sad, but true.

**Pictures at an Exhibition*, by Anna Celenza Gr. 1-4
Fact-based, colorful book shows Mussorgsky's visit to art museum which inspired music.

Book of Music, edited by Gill Rowley, p. 48 Gr. 7-12

29h Spanish Composers: Albéniz and de Falla

Sorry, I'm not aware of any books specifically on these composers; just check your general resources.

29i Painting

We're going to do things a little differently here too. Let's simply enjoy looking at the works of Millet and Corot, because these two French painters perfectly typify the nationalist movement in art. You'll probably recognize two of Millet's well-known paintings: *The Gleaners* and *The Sowers.* They warmly present rustic French peasants at their humble work. Maybe you've also seen Corot's works, which often display French country scenes. Together, these will give you a great feeling for the heart of nationalist painters.

Child's History of Art, by Hillyer & Huey (*Painting* section, Ch. 25) Gr. 2-8
<u>**OR**</u> *Young People's Story of Fine Art: Last Two Hundred Years*, pp. 42-51

Millet Tilled the Soil, by Sybil Deucher and Opal Wheeler Gr. 3-12
Lovely, lovely, lovey book, as are all by this duo of yesterday. Oh, if only all children's books could be like this.......

Corot from A to Z, by Caroline Larroche Unknown

29j Sculpture

We'll just cite one resource here, since sculpture was less involved.

Child's History of Art, by Hillyer & Huey (*Sculpture* sect., Ch. 21, 24) Gr. 2-8
<u>**OR**</u> *Young People's Story of Sculpture*, pp. 87-90, 96-101

29k French Author—Jules Verne

Jules Verne was excited by all the new breakthroughs in science and invention. What makes him especially amazing, though, is not just his highly imaginative tales of adventure, but that they include his astonishingly accurate forecasts of scientific advances yet to come! Famous works include: **20,000 Leagues Under the Sea*, **Around the World in Eighty Days*, **Journey to the Center of the Earth*, **From the Earth to the Moon*, **Michael Strogoff*, etc.

**Science Fiction Pioneer*, by Thomas Streissguth (Carolrhoda's Creative Minds) Gr. 2-6

Who Said There's No Man on the Moon? by Robert Quackenbush Gr. 2-7
Quackenbush's biographies are lots of fun!

Jules Verne: His Life, by Catherine Owens Peare — Gr. 4-10

Peare has written several nice biographies of yesteryear.

Jules Verne: The Man Who Invented the Future, by Franz Born — Gr. 8-12

Jules Verne: Portrait of a Prophet, by Russell Freedman — Gr. 9-12

291 English Authors—Brontës, Brownings, Charles Dickens, George Eliot, Gerard Manly Hopkins, Edward Lear, and Robert Louis Stevenson

The English nationalist authors are more frequently called Victorian writers because they wrote during the powerful reign of Queen Victoria, a time of great national pride, progress, reform, and expansion.....as you'll see in the very next section! It's said that the sun never set on her reign, for it spanned the globe.[62] Because Victoria reigned both before and after 1865 (the final year covered in this history guide), we'll discuss these writers and her reign now, and will offer them again in the next guide (*Age of Revolution III*), where we will also add in post-1865 events and persons. Anyway, let's meet the early "Victorian authors" now, and then the Queen herself!

i. Charlotte, Emily, and Anne Brontë

Famous works include: *_Jane Eyre_, by Charlotte Brontë (and is one of my lifetime favorites, such character!); *_Wuthering Heights_, by Emily Brontë (_this_ is sooo dark, in my opinion); *_Agnes Grey_ and *_Tenant of Wildfell Hall_, by Anne Brontë.

**Brontës*, by Catherine Brighton — Gr. 1-4

This author yields beautifully illustrated picture biographies, but parents should be sensitive that this book could sadden young children by revealing gloomier aspects of the Brontës' lives.

**Glass Town*, by Michael Bedard — Gr. 2-7

This book gives a glimpse into the unusual childhood of the Brontës.

**Charlotte Brontë and Jane Eyre*, by Stewart Ross — Gr. 3-7

**Lives of the Writers: Comedies, Tragedies (and What the Neighbors Thought)* by Kathleen Krull, pp. 42-47 — Gr. 3-8

62 Louise Cowan and Os Guinness, editors, *Invitation to the Classics* (Grand Rapids, MI: Baker, 1998) 275.

**Brontë Family: Passionate Literary Geniuses*, by Karen Kenyon Gr. 5-9

Gift with a Pen: Charlotte Brontë, by Elisabeth Kyle Gr. 7-12
This looks like a lovely older biography.

Young Brontës, by Phyllis Bentley Gr. 7-12
This series contains many enjoyable readable biographies.
**Emily Brontë*, by Robert Barnard (British Library Writers' Lives) Gr. 9-12

**Brontës*, by Harold Bloom (Bloom's Major Novelists) Gr. 10-12
I'm not familiar with Bloom's worldview.

ii. Robert & Elizabeth Barrett Browning

Famous works include: **Sonnets from the Portuguese*, and too many other poems to mention. The love story of Robert & Elizabeth is itself a great "poem!"

Silver Answer, by Constance Burnett Gr. 7-12
This looks like a lovely narrative "meeting" with the famous couple.

Young Elizabeth Barrett Browning, by Clare Abrahall Gr. 7-12
This series brings pleasant biographies to youth readers.

**Elizabeth Barrett Browning*, by Harold Bloom (Bloom's Modern Critical...) Gr. 10-12
I'm not familiar with Bloom's worldview.

**Robert Browning*, by Harold Bloom (Bloom's Major Poets) Gr. 10-12
I'm not familiar with Bloom's worldview.

Film

**Barretts of Wimpole Street*, starring Frederic March Parental decision
This older film tells the story of Elizabeth and Robert's wholesome, budding relationship,but under the shadow of a intensely, overly possessive father.

iii. Charles Dickens

Dickens claimed a strong Christian faith and even retold Christ's early life for his children in "The Life of our Lord." You can see throughout his books that Dickens was very, very concerned about the plight of the downtrodden in England. Yes, you might be thinking, reform was a common impulse during this Progressive Era, but Dickens had the additional motivation of his deep Christian concerns. It's a great time to read some Dickens because he really captures the many facets of his era, but he will also be cited in the next guide, because he overlapped that period.

Famous works include: **David Copperfield, **Great Expectations**, **A Christmas Carol**, **A Tale of Two Cities**, **Oliver Twist**, **Pickwick Papers**, **Our Mutual Friend**, **Nicholas Nickleby**, and too many more to mention! There are both book and film versions of many of these classics. Enjoy!**

Value of Imagination: Charles Dickens, by Spencer Johnson (ValueTales) Gr. 1-5

**Tales for Hard Times*, by David Collins (Carolrhoda's Creative Minds) Gr. 2-5

**Charles Dickens: The Man Who Had Great Expectations*, by Diane Stanley Gr. 3-7
This book contains the ever-wonderful illustrations which are Stanley's hallmark!

**Lives of the Writers: Comedies, Tragedies (and What the Neighbors Thought)* Gr. 3-8
by Kathleen Krull, pp. 38-41

Dogs of Destiny, by Fairfax Downey Gr. 3-12
Ready to meet Dickens's dog!

Great Ambitions, by Elisabeth Kyle Gr. 6-12
Another of this author's lovely, older biographies about authors!

**Charles Dickens*, by Donna Dailey (Who Wrote That?) Gr. 7-12

Charles Dickens: His Life, by Catherine Owens Peare Gr. 7-12
This is a nice, older biography.

Young Dickens, by Patrick Pringle Gr. 7-12
This series offers many nicely narrative biographies.

**Invitation to the Classics*, edited by Cowan & Guinness, pp. 259-262 Gr. 8-12
Christian analysis of famous authors and literature.

Charles Dickens, by Charles Haines (Immortals of Literature) Gr. 9-12

Life in Charles Dickens' England, by Diane Yancey (Way People Live) Gr. 9-12
The awful conditions for the English poor, and how they affected Dickens and appear in his works. I've not read this and do not know its worldview.

**Charles Dickens*, by Harold Bloom (Bloom's Major Novelists) Gr. 10-12
I'm not aware of Bloom's worldview.

Fiction/Historical Fiction

What the Dickens! by Jane Curry Gr. 4-6
American girl overhears plot to steal Dickens manuscript during his trip to the USA.

Films

**Ghosts of Dickens' Past: The Untold Story of a Simple Act of Charity* All ages
starring Christopher Heyerdahl (Feature Films for Families)
This is not actually about "ghosts," but about Dicken's concern for poor children.

iv. George Eliot

Famous works include: ****Silas Marner, *Middlemarch, *Mill on the Floss.* **Eliot seems to have given up on Christianity—the way it was shown to her, Mary Anne Evans was Eliot's real name—having the answers, but the books show that wrestling....**

**Invitation to the Classics*, edited by Cowan & Guinness, pp. 271-274 Gr. 8-12
Christian analysis of famous authors and literature. So good to have this insight if you're going to tackle one of Eliot's books...

**George Eliot*, by Harold Bloom (Bloom's Major Novelists) Gr. 10-12
I'm not familiar with Bloom's worldview.

v. Gerard Manley Hopkins

Famous works include many different poems.

**Invitation to the Classics*, edited by Cowan & Guinness, pp. 275-278 Gr. 8-12
Christian analysis of famous authors and literature.

vi. Robert Louis Stevenson
Don't miss some of these gems; several show spirit of sea-faring adventure which characterized Victorian life.

Famous works include: ****Treasure Island*, ****Kidnapped***, ****Black Arrow***, ****David Balfour***, ****Master of Ballantrae***, ****Strange Case of Dr. Jekyll and Mr. Hyde***, etc. His ****Child's Garden of Verse*** **features some beloved classics, such as** ***The Moon***, ***My Shadow***, ***Land of Counterpane***, ***From a Railway Carriage***, **etc. You know these already!**

**Voyage of the Ludgate Hill*, by Nancy Willard Gr. 1-3
Unusual picture book relates Stevenson's zany trip to America.

**Robert Louis Stevenson*, by Francene Sabin (Troll) Gr. 1-4

Robert Louis Stevenson, by Carol Greene (Rookie) Gr. 1-5

**Robert Louis Stevenson* (Poetry for Young People) Gr. 2-6
I just have to mention this nicely illustrated collection of Stevenson's poems!

Robert Louis Stevenson, by Katharine Wilkie (Piper) Gr. 2-7
This is from a rare, but delightful, series of biographies for elementary readers!

**Lives of the Writers: Comedies, Tragedies (and What the Neighbors Thought)* Gr. 3-8
by Kathleen Krull, pp. 66-69

Story of Robert Louis Stevenson, by Joan Howard (Signature) Gr. 3-8

Robert Louis Stevenson: His Life, by Catherine Owens Peare Gr. 5-12

Robert Louis Stevenson, by Eulalie Grover Gr. 6-12

Robert Louis Stevenson, by G.B. Stern Gr. 6-12

Treasure Hunter: Story of Robert Louis Stevenson, by Isabel Proudfit (Messner) Gr. 6-12

Young Robert Louis Stevenson, by Ian Finlay Gr. 7-12

30 Queen For a Day *plus* 23,000!—Victoria

Remember, we're studying a time when there was a great upheaval in people's beliefs. The Judeo-Christian roots were still there, but the new humanistic ideas—rationalism and romanticism—were lambasting them *at the same time in the same people!* So, you won't be able to calmly watch while one civilization follows a single set of beliefs and experiences a single set of effects, as in past units. Indeed, we can't even divide people clearly into two camps—the black hats and the white hats, *hee hee*—because most people believed some of *both* worldviews and were thus doing contradictory things. Even those who were fully committed to humanism, had to select from various versions, since no one humanistic "truth" stood up to reality, and new varieties of "truth" had to be cooked up to answer the failings of the last ones. Craziness!

So, instead of just "consuming" facts like a baby bird, you must instead juggle all the "stuff" coming at you and then prayerfully chew on it until you find truth and wisdom. Because our real goal—and don't forget it or I'll come lookin' for you! ☺—is to probe deeply for God's hand at work in this era, to understand how beliefs of the heart have people

in their grip, for better or worse. And, we're going to find out how God is leading *you* to bless this world with your life!

Well, you'll get plenty of practice doing just that as we tackle one of the hugest, if not *the* hugest world empire of all times! Do you think we're jumping back to Alexander the Great or Julius Caesar or Genghis Khan? Nope. At the center of it all was a young lady, a *very* young lady, *not much older than you!* Allow me to introduce her. Uh, er, well, it's not like I know her personally or anything. *Ta da!* Queen Victoria!

Crowned in 1837, she would have an entire age named after her, but you would too if you'd led your country from the turbulent onset of the Industrial Revolution to a time of enormous wealth, stability, and empire, as well as a subsequent flourishing of literature, learning, invention, and exploration. See, under Queen Victoria, England came to control about one-fourth of the world's population! Look at a map, or make one. See the vastness? See the hugeness of China, India, Southeast Asia, Africa, the East & West Indies, Canada, Australia, New Zealand, *and more!* Can you get a sense of this? With England having begun the Industrial Revolution, she first had the technological advantage to use mighty battleships and massive artillery to defeat natives wielding only wooden spears and arrows. While England had not recently fought with the other European powers to gain their land, she did quickly lead the race to control and colonize the rest of the world. Now this brings up *very complex* issues we covered in the last guide (*Age of Revolution I*) as to God's view on conquest and how even harmful human actions sometimes have the indirect effect of opening inroads for the gospel, but I dare not take time to repeat them here. The point right now is that Victorians soon began to feel a "sense of mission" in "bettering the world" with their rule. You can bet that the British people were feeling rather capable, even "special."

Well, they tried to live up to their billing. They worked hard on elegant manners, fancy clothes, ornate homes, and even charming gardens filled with plants from their many colonies. They formed all sorts of self-improvement clubs and reform movements. Everything was *so* civilized. Why, the aristocrats didn't even chop people's heads off any more! Queen Victoria had a very personal impact too, for as an upright wife and devoted mother of many children, she helped make honorable living popular. (That's saying *a lot* if you think of past monarchs!) You can certainly see, then, why the Victorian Era is famed for being very proper, mannerly, and reform-minded. Of course, properness is scorned by many today, so you may have heard the term *Victorian* used as a slur!

While much they did was good and wise, there is still some truth in the slur. Why? Because something had changed, remember? Most English churches (and the same was all too true in America) were filled with that natural religion, or Deism, or Unitarianism, or whatever brand of "elegant" and "distinguished" pushing-aside of God you want to name. Folks wanted to be good, but they wanted to be good on their own, without God—a religious species of humanism. So their goodness was just external, not internal, meaning it wasn't deep. This is the recipe for hypocrisy, which the world can sniff at fifty paces.

You'll see it in the way the Victorians ruled their colonies, in the way they launched their reform movements, the "survival-of-the-fittest" attitude they had toward the poor (all of which helped Karl Marx, who lived in England, convince the sufferers that communism was the answer). There often wasn't real humility or a real servant attitude. For many, there wasn't accountability to God; there was just devotion to one's pet theories on "remaking the world." With the thrum of *progress* pulsing in their hearts, Englishmen gallantly stepped forward to "relieve" God (that elderly Providence, who could now retire, having brought mankind to the point where he could manage things on his own) of His duties. Solving the world's problems was going to be easy, just a simple matter of applying the right psychology or sociology or education or some other means of improving the environment of a "noble savage," so he could be free to find his perfect self. It was ridiculously out-of-date to think of human problems as spiritual ones, for humanism had debunked the bothersome concept of human sin. (Since the great sin is wanting to be God, those who wanted to be God just denied the existence of sin. Easy!)

To be honest, most Victorian Englishmen probably didn't realize that a whole new set of beliefs were oozing into their churches, their culture, their colleges, etc., as romanticism was edging out rationalism and both were belittling Christianity. But that's no excuse, for we're all required to be vigilant, to be thinking. It's the easiest thing in the world to be passive—to just go with the flow, to live for the moment, worried only about "fitting in." But wake up, Bud! *You're* supposed to set the standards, because you're part of the Body of Christ! Better do a heart check right now—*are you trying to fit into others' standards, or set His?* Now you know the dilemma of Victorian England...and all other eras as well!

To be fair, England did have more on the ball than most European nations at the time. Her past foundation was helping to bring jobs, prosperity, and affordable goods to many impoverished people for the first time. Britain was even exerting some good influence in her colonies—suppressing horrific warlords, bringing better medical care, and even banning gruesome cultural practices such as burning women upon the death of their husbands. Furthermore, England's vast empire indirectly made possible massive missionary work around the globe, for there were God-followers in England who were completely sold out to Him, as you'll see. But there still was *so much* wrong believing and acting, as you'll also see!

So as you study Victorian England, you must remember what a mixed bag it was, for at the same time the English were proper enough to dust their knickknacks, one of their countrymen—Charles Darwin—was whipping up his own theory of evolution! (We'll cover him in the next guide: *Age of Revolution III.*) You see? Some good, some bad, all swirled in one pot. Okay, I'll shut up now, and you can dig into all these fascinating topics yourself!

Please remember that we will also begin *Age of Revolution III* with Queen Victoria, since her very long reign spanned both periods. So, you can explore more of the Victorian Era then also, which is when we will cite persons and events occurring in the post-1865 part of her rule, such as Mr. Stanley finding David Livingstone, Cecil Rhodes of South Africa, the writings of Rudyard Kipling, missionaries like Mary Slessor and reformers like William &

Catherine Booth, as well as Jewish-born Prime Minister Benjamin Disraeli, etc. My point? You needn't do it all now. But do dig in!

30a Queen Victoria

Remember, feel free to cover only the pre-1865 portion of her reign, since we will explore the second half in the next TruthQuest History guide. Most resources will cover all, from her youth and 1837 coronation onward, so decide how you want to handle it! You needn't worry about the timing exactly. Just have fun, and know that you have two chances to work through it all! Be at peace...

**Island Story*, by H.E. Marshall, Ch. CI-CX — Gr. 3-7

**Mothers of Famous Men*, Ch. VII, by Archer Wallace (Lamplighter) — Gr. 3-12

Queen Victoria, by Noel Streatfeild (Landmark) — Gr. 4-12

Seven Queens of England, by Geoffrey Trease, Ch. 6 — Gr. 5-12

Story of Britain, by R.J. Unstead, pp. 288-289 — Gr. 5-12

True Story of Queen Victoria, by Arthur Booth — Gr. 6-12

Defender of the Faith, by Charles Ludwig — Gr. 7-12
This Christian biography has been recommended to me.

Queen Victoria, by Molly Haycraft (Messner) — Gr. 7-12

Young Victoria, by Lettice Cooper — Gr. 7-12

**Victoria and Her Times*, by Jean-Loup Chiflet — Gr. 8-12
Typical modern book: not a readable, narrative biography, but pieced overview.

**Victoria*, by John Guy — Unknown

Fiction/Historical Fiction

**Victoria: May Blossom of Britannia*, by Anna Kirwan (Royal Diaries) — Gr. 3-8

Film

**Young Victoria*, starring Emily Blunt — Parental decision
I enjoyed this film very much. It treated the wedding night with great restraint, but parents should still decide at what age even that is appropriate. I don't recall particularly with this film, but dresses are often low-cut in period films.

30b Victorian Era (in England and dependencies)

**Story of the World: Vol. 4*, by Susan Wise Bauer, Ch. 1-3, 4b — Gr. 3-6

Some families enjoy this book's scope, so ask us to cite it; others seek different worldview; so, parental decision. Sections of Ch. 1-3 will also be listed below under specific topics.

Story of the Seashore, by John Goodall — Gr. K-3

Wordless book, with gorgeous illustrations, shows Victorian seashore holidays.

**Popcorn at the Palace*, by Emily McCully — Gr. 1-4

Fact-based, Queen Victoria is introduced to popcorn by an American farmer and his daughter in this colorful picture book. Sadly, their fellow church-goers are presented as extremely narrow and negative; you may want to "edit" as you read.

**Marigold Garden*, by Kate Greenaway — Gr. 2-8

Pictures and rhymes of Victorian children.

Looking at History, by R.J. Unstead, Book 4, Part 2 — Gr. 3-6

Daily Life in a Victorian House, by Laura Wilson — Various

I've been told this is for browsing, so student can see photos of Victorian home life.

Fiction/Historical Fiction

Time at the Top, **<u>and</u>**, *All in Good Time*, by Edward Ormondroyd — Gr. 5-12

In these fun books, a modern girl steps off an elevator into the Victorian era.

**Encounter the Light*, by Donna Fletcher Crow — Gr. 8-12

This sweeping Christian novel relates life during Victorian England, including the Industrial Revolution and the Crimean War.

30c Activities

Some of you may enjoy learning about Victorian clothing, furniture, architecture, etc. Feel free to launch into this explorations, as you desire.

**Victoria and Albert* paper dolls, by Tom Tierney — Various

**Victorian Days*, by David King (American Kids in History) — Various

Activities, recipes, games, projects, etc.

**Victorian Family Paper Dolls*, by Brenda Mattox — Various

**Victorian House Coloring Book* (Dover) — Various

30d Crimean War and wars in India

The Crimean War ran from 1853-1856, but the wars in India stretched over a much longer period...

**Story of the World: Vol. 4*, by Susan Wise Bauer, Ch. 2b — Gr. 3-6

Some families enjoy this book's scope, so ask us to cite it; others seek different worldview; so, parental decision.

Story of Britain, by R.J. Unstead, pp. 290-293 — Gr. 5-12

Crimean War, by James Barbary — Gr. 6-12

**Charge of the Light Brigade*, Alfred, Lord Tennyson — Various

One of Tennyson's most famous poems tells of an actual battle during the Crimean War. You'll find it in any compendium of English poetry, and there are even illustrated versions for children!

Fiction/Historical Fiction

Jack Archer, by G.A. Henty — Gr. 7-12

Fictional boys figure in these accurate historical novels.

Kevin O'Connor and the Light Brigade, by Leonard Wibberley — Gr. 7-12

Nicholas Carey, by Ronald Welch — Gr. 7-12

Another in fascinating series about one family over centuries of English history.

Film

**Charge of the Light Brigade*, starring Errol Flynn & Olivia de Haviland — Parental decision

Only at the end does it refer to the actual battle; its focus is more on the earlier involvement of that brigade in India, but this is also of historical value.

> Many of G.A. Henty's beloved novels tell of Britain's wars in India—*Tiger of Mysore, At the Point of the Bayonet, With Cochrane the Dauntless, On the Irrawaddy, Through the Sikh War, In Times of Peril, Rujub the* Juggler—and in other lesser known conflicts—*In Greek* Waters (Grecian fight for independence), *With the British Legion* (Carlist War in Spain), and *To Herat and Cabul* and *For Name and Fame* (in Afghanistan)—you probably haven't a scrap of time to learn about these events. We have *so* much to cover in this unit, and we're just getting started! Most of Henty's books are being reprinted. You could also read **Gunga Din*, one of Rudyard Kipling's poems about a British soldier and Indian water-carrier.

30e Florence Nightingale

Nightingale was a heroine of the Crimean War, admired for her strong Christian faith and her willingness to sacrifice for the care of others. I was very moved as a young girl when reading about her, and it probably accounts for my plan—from age five forward—to work in the medical field. (As you can see, that didn't happen!)

**Picture Book of Florence Nightingale*, by David Adler	Gr. 1-3
Value of Compassion: Florence Nightingale, by Johnson (ValueTales)	Gr. 1-4
Florence Nightingale, by Anne Colver (Garrard Discovery)	Gr. 1-5
**Florence Nightingale*, by Kristi Lorene (Young Reader's Christian Library)	Gr. 1-5
**Hero Tales—Vol. II*, by Dave & Neta Jackson, pp. 116-127	Gr. 3-7
Story of Florence Nightingale, by Margaret Leighton (Signature)	Gr. 3-8
Florence Nightingale, by Ruth Fox Hume (Landmark)	Gr. 3-9
**Lady with the Lamp*, by Lee Wyndham	Gr. 3-10
Faithful Friend: Florence Nightingale, by Beatrice Siegel	Gr. 4-8
**Florence Nightingale: Nurse to Soldiers*, by Sandy Dengler This is a Christian biography.	Gr. 4-12
Florence Nightingale's Nuns, by Emmeline Garnett (Vision) Distinctly Catholic biography.	Gr. 4-12
Florence Nightingale, by Jeannette Covert Nolan (Messner)	Gr. 5-12
**Florence Nightingale*, by Sam Wellman (Heroes of the Faith)	Gr. 5-12
**Florence Nightingale*, by David Collins (Sower) Distinctly Christian biography series.	Gr. 6-12
Young Florence Nightingale, by Lettice Cooper	Gr. 7-12
**Florence Nightingale*, by Basil Miller (Women of Faith)	Gr. 8-12
Lonely Crusader: Florence Nightingale, by Cecil Woodham-Smith There are two versions: abridged and unabridged.	Various

Fiction/Historical Fiction

**Drummer Boy's Battle*, by Dave & Neta Jackson (Trailblazer) Gr. 3-9
In his exciting Christian series, fictional kids meet the real Florence Nightingale.

We Were There with Florence Nightingale..., by Robert Webb (We Were There) Gr. 3-9
Fictional kids meet the real Florence Nightingale. Beloved series.

Audio

Your Story Hour (Volume 7) contains an audio presentation on Nightingale

30f British Commonwealth and colonialism—Canada, Australia, New Zealand, etc.

Britain had, for example, very strong involvement in Canada (a British colony after the French lost control), Australia (which began as a British penal colony at Botany Bay) and New Zealand, where the aborigines and Maori, respectively, fought hard to oust British control, as well as in China, India, and Africa (we'll cover the African aspect in *Age of Revolution III*.) These nations are still closely affiliated with the British Commonwealth. We've talked a bit about Canada's settlement in other units, but, if you have extra time or live in these beautiful lands, you may want to learn about the settlement of Australia and New Zealand which was in full swing at this time. China, India, etc., weren't settled in the same way; their populations remained mostly native, under British governors and bureaucracy.

It's hard to fathom one queen ruling one-fourth or one-fifth of the world's population, but it happened. The sun never set on the British Empire, the saying went. Why? Well, the European powers had been scooping up colonies for some time, but England's realm was huge, in large part, because she started the Industrial Revolution and first had "modern" weapons which easily defeated primitive natives. Too often, there was a belief that natives were not just trapped in paganism and poor conditions, but actually lesser human beings. To go from the cathedrals of Europe to the mud huts, and to have seen some of the horrors of pagan practices, must have come as quite a shock, yet human worth itself is unchanging.

I gladly leave it to God to judge this since all people, lands, and nations are really His, and only He knows when He calls one nation to rule another. We can at least point out that the British had *some* positive effects on the lands they ruled. They tried to stop widow-burning, twin-killing, etc., and they halted the ravages of many gruesome warlords. They also introduced better health practices, medical care, and education, as well as indirectly making a vast amount of missionary work possible by opening inroads into remote areas. But the wrongs must also be admitted...

***If, if, if* Britain was meant to have this vast colonial empire, one thing is certain: she didn't fulfill her calling as God would have mandated, for her pride and greed (spiritual problems) caused her to demean the people she ruled and take advantage of their natural resources, especially through the principle of *mercantilism*, which served to enrich the mother country at the expense of the colonial people. This built resentment that was later harnessed by communist agitators, and you'll see many colonies eventually become communistic. Wrong attitudes and actions *always* have consequences, and they aren't fun for anyone!**

Think about how different things would have been if Britain had been a servant instead—helping native people grow spiritually, politically, and economically. How much better would they have viewed Christianity, if it hadn't been the religion of their invading overlords? It's a lot to think about... Thankfully, there were some wonderful exceptions.

**Story of the World: Vol. 4*, by Susan Wise Bauer, Ch. 6b, 11a, 12a — Gr. 3-6

Some families enjoy this book's scope, so ask us to cite it; others seek different worldview; so, parental decision.

This is Australia, by Miroslav Sasek — Gr. 1-4

KIDS Discover magazine: *Australia* (January, 1996) — Gr. 1-6

**This Place is Lonely: Australia*, by Vicki Cobb — Gr. 2-7

**Hero Tales—Vol. III*, by Dave & Neta Jackson, pp. 56-67 — Gr. 3-7

Tells of Samuel Leigh, an early missionary to Australia.

Take a Trip to New Zealand, by Geoff Burns — Gr. 3-7

Story of Australia, by A. Grove Day (Landmark) — Gr. 3-9

**Australian Aborigines*, by Richard Nile — Gr. 4-10

Canadian Story, by May McNeer; illustrated by her husband, Lynd Ward — Gr. 4-10

Maori and Settler, by G.A. Henty — Gr. 8-12

This is an actual account of one family in the fray.

Age of Uncertainty, by John Kenneth Galbraith, Ch. 4 — Gr. 9-12

Admittedly, this writer does *not* have a biblical worldview, but he makes some excellent points. Read his works very cautiously, and enjoy his excellent wit!

Films

*_Five Mile Creek_ series — All ages

Fine, wholesome series about settlement of Australian frontier. May be set around 1870, but fits our discussion here.

30g Missions

Let's focus now on missions (the *real* missionaries, not those whose sole aim seemed to be making the natives act and dress like westerners), as we watch our ever-active God birth a massive missionary movement, extending Christianity around the world. Don't ever forget God's highest goal: drawing people to Himself!

We saw the William Carey working in India earlier in the 1800s. Well, by the mid-1800s, Hudson Taylor was on his way to China! Now, Britain's activities in China were *much* less than honorable (especially related to opium), but her presence there did allow men like Hudson Taylor to present Christ to that huge land. Mr. Taylor was mentioned earlier in this guide also, but if you didn't cover him before, you may wish to now. You could also use this as an opportunity to update your study of China; we haven't mentioned it much since Marco Polo's journey there in the Middle Ages. (We'll cover its Boxer Rebellion and communist revolution in the next guide.)

*_Hudson Taylor_, by Susan Miller (Young Reader's Christian Library) — Gr. 1-3

*_Hero Tales: Vol. I_, by Dave & Neta Jackson — Gr. 3-6

One of the chapters in this first volume covers Taylor.

*_Hudson Taylor_, by Janet Benge (Christian Heroes, Then and Now) — Gr. 5-12

Some Benge books are being put into audio format also.

*_Hudson Taylor_, by Vance Christie (Heroes of the Faith) — Gr. 5-12

*_Ambassadors for Christ_, edited by John Woodbridge, pp. 157-162 — Gr. 7-12

*_More than Conquerors_, edited by John Woodbridge, pp. 50-55 — Gr. 7-12

These offer short biographies of Christian heroes.

*_Hudson Taylor_, by Hudson Taylor (Men of Faith) — Gr. 8-12

This is probably an abridged version of the two-volume masterwork below.

*_Hudson Taylor's Spiritual Secret_, by Howard Taylor — Gr. 8-12

Here, Taylor's son has written a more succinct, but powerful, biography of his amazing father (see below). I've heard that this book is life-changing.

**Hudson Taylor: Vol. 1 and 2*, by Howard Taylor Gr. 10-12

This two-volume series brings the full breadth and depth of Taylor's life courtesy of Taylor's son. I've heard these are some of the most inspiring books ever!

Hudson Taylor and Maria, by J.C. Pollock Gr. 10-12

Fiction/Historical Fiction

**Shanghaied to China*, by Dave & Neta Jackson (Trailblazer) Gr. 3-9

Fictional kids meet real heroes!

31 "Heat" in the American Southwest

I hope you haven't forgotten that America has been sitting on the other side of the ocean this whole time, going about its business of growing, growing, growing. While America's history throughout this century was quite different from that of Europe's, you'll continuously see (especially in the sequel to this guide, *Age of Revolution III*) that many of the idea wars soon crossed the Atlantic!

> 1839 was a great year for kids! Baseball and bicycles were invented!!
>
> **Abner Doubleday* (Childhood/Young Patriot) by Montrew Dunham Gr. 1-6

First, though, let's get back to the uniqueness of America's mid-1800s history, so we must jump back a bit in time (compared to where we just were in Europe's history). It contrasts significantly from the same era in Europe, which was indeed experiencing some positive changes (especially in England), but was also shuddering under the Revolutions of 1848, the awful working conditions for many in agriculture and industry, and the continuing feudalism of eastern Europe and Russia. For free citizens of America, though, there was widespread excitement...from the eastern cities, through the midwestern farms, to the pioneers and adventurers sweeping west. In fact, Americans were beginning to believe in a concept called *manifest destiny:* "to overspread the continent allotted by Providence for the free development of our yearly multiplying millions," as the coiner of the phrase put it.[63]

All over the west, land claims were awhirl, as the Texas story will clearly show you...because the Spanish government gave Moses Austin and his son, Stephen, permission to settle in Texas in 1821. But then the Mexicans threw off Spanish control later in 1821, and Mexico claimed all the land once owned by Spain even though Spain didn't have settlers on those lands, and Mexico was so wracked by revolutions (it averaged one per year for many years)[64] that it couldn't control those lands. A short time later, General Santa Anna, who dreamed of

63 Richard Morris, *Encyclopedia of American History* (New York: Harper & Brothers, 1953) 193.
64 Carson 3: 114.

being a Mexican Napoleon,[65] seized the Mexican government, changed some policies in Texas, had Stephen F. Austin imprisoned when he went to Mexico City to make a plea, and eventually sent Mexican troops into Texas! I won't tell the whole story, but you know it included the siege of the Alamo (1836) and the Battle of San Jacinto (1836), which lasted just twenty minutes!

The Republic of Texas might have existed, after the fighting was over, in the minds of Texans after a few years of independence, but Mexico did not acknowledge it. When the Mexican government reneged on agreements to pay Americans for damages done during their many revolutions, President Polk asked Mexico to sell New Mexico and California as part of the debt repayment.[66] (America was hoping to get these lands, and many Americans already lived there, but other nations, such as Britain, hoped for California as well, just as Britain encouraged Texas to remain independent and side with it, rather than seeking American statehood.) The US negotiations with Mexico did not go well, and through a series of events, it came to war...the Mexican War in 1846. The war took place from Texas all the way into California, on land and on sea. A US force even attacked Mexico City itself. All in all, it went very quickly, but I won't tell more; you'll want to find out yourself. It wasn't until after the war, in 1853, that America was able to buy additional parts of what is now New Mexico and Arizona in the Gadsden Purchase. All in all, the American Southwest had been formed...and rather quickly! You'll recognize the names of most of the important players in this drama!

Don't forget that the Indians of these regions were enormously impacted by this influx, but we'll cover them in the next guide, when the West was more fully opened and the conflict was at its height. Also remember that once these new areas became American territories, the slavery issues boiled over again. The earnest goal in Washington was to keep an equal number of slave and free states. Anyway, for now, we'll look only at the military struggle which began in Texas and then became the Mexican War in Texas, California, the entire Southwest, and Mexico itself. It's a bit hard to lay resources out clearly, though, because most books about the Mexican War also cover the earlier action in Texas and its years as an independent republic. Regardless, after our spines, we'll first cite Texas-specific resources and then list Mexican War resources. Juggle them as you feel best!

Remember though, as you read secular books with a secular mindset, that while we cannot know the full will of God regarding to the Mexican War, we do know the spiritual makeup of the two nations was very different and we know that all land is the Lord's; He has the right to give it as He wills. You can ask Him if He did that, or if Americans or Mexicans were disobedient. He loves to reveal Himself to us and answer our questions!

---

65 Carson 3:116.

66 Carson 3:114.

31a General overview

We're listing only our spine resources here.

From Sea to Shining Sea for Children*, by Marshall & Manuel, Ch. 15 **and Gr. 1-5
**Sounding Forth the Trumpet for Children*, by Marshall & Manuel, Ch. 5-8

**Story of the World: Vol. 3*, by Susan Wise Bauer, Ch. 40 Gr. 3-6
Some families enjoy this book's scope, so ask us to cite it; others seek different worldview; so, parental decision.

**Story of the Great Republic*, by H.A. Guerber, Ch. XXVI Gr. 3-7

**This Country of Ours*, by H.E. Marshall, Ch. 76 Gr. 3-8

From Sea to Shining Sea*, by Marshall & Manuel, Ch. 15 **and Gr. 6-12
**Sounding Forth the Trumpet*, by Marshall & Manuel, Ch. 10-22

**Basic History of the United States: Vol. 3*, by Clarence Carson, Ch. 6c Gr. 9-12

31b Settlement of Texas, Alamo (1836), Battle of San Jacinto (1836), etc.

Most books about the Alamo tell the full story of Texan independence.

**Texas Jack at the Alamo*, by James Rice Gr. K-3
An illustrated account of the Alamo...told by a jackrabbit!

**Alamo*, by Kristin Nelson (Pull Ahead Books) Gr. 1-3
I believe this is for young students, but I've not seen it.

**Susanna of the Alamo*, by John Jakes Gr. 1-5
True story of a woman in the Alamo; picture-book format.

Story of the Alamo, by Norman Richards (Cornerstones) Gr. 2-7
This has gone out of print, but some libraries may still have this original version.

**Alamo*, by Michael Burgan (We the People) Gr. 3-6

Stalwart Men of Early Texas, by Edith McCall (Frontiers of America) Gr. 3-8

**Alamo!* by George Sullivan Middle students
I believe this is for middle students.

**Alamo*, by Tom McGowen (Cornerstones II) Gr. 4-8
An earlier version is called **Battle of the Alamo* and was written by Andrew Santella.

Remember the Alamo! by Robert Penn Warren (Landmark) Gr. 4-9
The Landmark series is a favorite with many.

Last Stand at the Alamo, by Alden Carter (First Books) Gr. 5-10

Birth of Texas, by William Johnson (North Star) Gr. 5-12
The North Star series contains many wonderfully narrative books.

Girl of the Alamo, by Rita Kerr Gr. 5-12
Another version of Susanna Dickinson's amazing story.

**Inside the Alamo*, by Jm Murphy Gr. 5-12
Many folks enjoy Murphy's newer history books.

**Alamo*, by Tim McNeese (Sieges that Changed the World) Gr. 6-9
I believe this contains info on the subsequent conflict at Goliad also.

After the Alamo, by Burt Hirschfeld (Messner/Milestones in History) Gr. 7-12

Alamo, by Leonard Everett Fisher Gr. 7-12
Fisher's books are distinguished by strong text and illustrations.

Their Shining Hour, by Ramona Mahler Gr. 7-12
Another book about the woman surviving the Alamo.

Valiant Few: Crisis at the Alamo, by Lon Tinkle (Macmillan Battle Books) Gr. 7-12

Bound for the Rio Grande, by Milton Meltzer (Living History Library) Gr. 9-12
This series includes many primary resources.

**Alamo*, by Mark Stewart (American Battlefields) Unknown
I believe this is for older students.

**Outnumbered: Davy Crockett's Final Battle at the Alamo*, by Eric Fein Unknown

Fiction/Historical Fiction

Johnny Texas* **and **Johnny Texas on the San Antonio Road*, both by Carol Hoff Gr. 2-9
Wonderful! German immigrant boy finds new life in early Texas.

*_Line in the Sand: Alamo Diary of Lucinda Lawrence_, by S. Garland (Dear Amer.) Gr. 3-8
Some families enjoy this series, others don't care for it.

We Were There at the Battle of the Alamo, by Margaret Cousins (We Were...) Gr. 3-8
(Currently being printed as, *_Boy in the Alamo._) Fictional kids at real historical events.

Ladd of the Lone Star, by Allan Bosworth (Aladdin's American Heritage) Gr. 3-9
This is an excellent older series.

Panther Lick Creek, by Nelma Haynes Gr. 3-9
Boys in Peters' Colony, which would become Dallas, have many adventures.

Passage to Texas, by Iris Vinton (Aladdin's American Heritage) Gr. 3-9
Settlers with Stephen Austin.

*_I Remember the Alamo_, by D. Anne Love Gr. 4-7
I've not seen this book, but have read that it is the story of a Kentucky family who moves to Texas and gets involved at the Alamo. The online description makes me wonder if the main character, a young girl, is disrespectful.

*_Victor Lopez at the Alamo_, by James Rice Gr. 5-8
I've not seen this story of a Mexican boy who observes the Battle of the Alamo.

*_Voices of the Alamo_, by Sherry Garland Gr. 5-12
Relates the lives of the many people who lived on the land where sits the Alamo.

*_Texan Scouts, Texan Star,_ **and** _Texan Triumph_, all by Joseph Altsheler Gr. 8-12
These stories are reputed to be of very high quality and are being reprinted/republished!

*_Promise at the Alamo_, by Dorothy Hoobler Unknown
A girl of San Antonio gets caught up in the action at the Alamo.

31c Heroes of Texas—Stephen F. Austin

Some of these characters were involved in the fuller Mexican War, so you may want to cover them later. Now you know what the capital of Texas is named Austin!

*_Stephen F. Austin and the Founding of Texas_, by James Haley Gr. 4-8

Wilderness Pioneer, by Carol Hoff Gr. 4-12

**Moses Austin and Stephen F. Austin*, by Betsy Warren Unknown

31d Heroes of Texas—Sam Houston

Hey! I'm on a trip to the city of Houston while I'm writing this, and as I flew in and saw this huge metropolis (America's fourth largest) laid out before me, I thought: "What on earth would Sam Houston think if he could see this place?!"

Sam Houston, by Paul Hollander (See and Read) Gr. 1-3
This is a precious, older biography series for the very young.

Sam Houston of Texas, by Matthew Grant Gr. 1-3

**Sam Houston*, by Lisa Trumbauer (First Biographies) Gr. 1-4
I've not seen this, but believe it's for early readers.

Sam Houston: Hero of Texas, by Jean Lee Latham (Garrard Discovery) Gr. 1-5
These Discovery biographies are a favorite of many families.

Sam Houston, by Augusta Stevenson (Childhood) Gr. 1-6
These are being reprinted as Young Patriot books, so this may be back in print!

**Sam Houston: American Hero*, by Anne Crawford Gr. 2-4

Sam Houston: Fighter and Leader, by Frances Wright (Makers of America) Gr. 2-7

Sam Houston: Friend of the Indians, by Joseph Olgin (Piper) Gr. 2-7

**Sam Houston: A Leader for Texas*, by Judy Alter Gr. 3-8
I'm not sure of this grade recommendation, but it appears to be for this age group.

**Sam Houston: Soldier and Statesman*, by Tracey Boraas (Let Freedom Ring) Gr. 3-8
I'm notl sure of this grade recommendation, but it appears to be for this age group.

Sam Houston: The Tallest Texan, by William Johnson (Landmark) Gr. 4-10
The Landmark series is a favorite for many.

Sam Houston: Texas Hero, by Carl Green & William Sanford Gr. 4-12

**An American in Texas: The Story of Sam Houston*, by Peggy Caravantes Gr. 5-8

Retreat to Glory: Sam Houston, by Jean Lee Latham — Gr. 5-12

We have enjoyed several of Latham's biographies.

Six Feet Six, by Bessie & Marquis James — Gr. 5-12

Older, classic biography.

**Make Way for Sam Houston*, by Jean Fritz — Gr. 7-12

(Lone Star Leader:) Sam Houston, by Curtis Bishop (Messner) — Gr. 7-12

Fiction/Historical Fiction

**Liberty, Justice, and F'Rall*, by Marjorie Kutchinski — Unknown

I've not seen this, but it sounds fun; Houston's three dogs tell of the Mexican War.

31e Heroes of Texas—Sam Houston

Taylor was not only a general, but was later the 12th president of the United States! Therefore, all of the presidential series have books on Taylor, so I needn't list those specifically.

Zachary Taylor, by Patricia Miles Martin (See and Read) — Gr. 1-3

**Zachary Taylor*, by Mike Venezia (Getting to Know the....) — Gr. 1-5

Zach Taylor, by Katharine Wilkie (Childhood) — Gr. 1-6

These are being reprinted as Young Patriot books, so this may be in-print now!

Old Rough and Ready, by Bob & Jan Young (Messner) — Gr. 7-12

31f Mexican War (1846)

Don't forget the spine resources cited at the beginning of this section.

Boy Heroes of Chapultepec, by Maria Chambers (Winston Adventure) — Gr. 3-9

This series highlights the exciting contribution of real young people!

Pirate Flag for Monterey, by Lester del Rey (Winston Adventure) — Gr. 3-9

This series highlights the exciting contribution of real young people!

First Book of the War with Mexico, by Henry Castor (First Books) — Gr. 4-9

**Mexican War*, by Marc Nobleman (We the People) — Gr. 4-9

**Mexican War*, by Alden Carter (First Books) Gr. 5-10
This is in the newer First Books series; I've heard this is a good choice.

**War with Mexico*, by William Jay Jacobs (Spotlight on American History) Gr. 5-10

**Mexican War*, by Charles Carey (American War) Gr. 5-12

Ride with the Eagle, by Julia Davis Gr. 6-12
Doniphan's incredible march.

War with Mexico, by Irving Werstein Gr. 7-12

Young Generals, by James Norman Gr. 7-12

**Mexican War*, by Bronwyn Mills (America at War) Unknown

Fiction/Historical Fiction

**Blood in the Water*, by Pamela Dell (Scrapbooks of America) Younger grades
I've not seen this "scrapbook" of a fictional family during the Mexican War, but it seems to be for younger students.

Summer is for Growing, by Ann Nolan Clark Gr. 5-12
I've not read this story of a New Mexico girl during the conflict.

Dunderhead War, by Betty Baker Gr. 7-12
I've not read this story of the army which takes Santa Fe from the Mexicans.

Stand to Horse, by André Norton Gr. 7-12
I've not read this tale of Santa Fe during the Mexican War, but Norton tends to write very exciting stories.

Adella Mary in Old Mexico, by Florence Means Gr. 8-12
I've not seen this old story of a girl's life in New Mexico during the Mexican War.

31g Battles for California

Any book on California history will thoroughly cover these events, which is good, because I can find few topic-specific books.

Remember that California came into American hands quite easily, so there is not a great deal to study here. Yes, the *rancheros*, the Mexican plantation owners, did naturally offer some resistance, but they had little support from the Mexican army

due to all the chaos in the Mexican government, much of it caused by one power-seeking general or another.

By the way, I've not seen it, but I've been told that the study guide, *_His California Story_, by Lesha Myers, in addition to relating the history of California, has very interesting information about the Indian issues and the impact of Christianity on the state's settlement. It might be a great tool for folks studying California in depth. There are other guides, also, such as the one by Rea Berg.

Other stories of California:

**Song of the Swallows*, by Leo Politi Gr. 1-3
**Three Stalks of Corn*, by Leo Politi Gr. 1-3
See also Politi's **Rosa* and **Juanita* to better understand the Hispanic culture.
Carmen of the Gold Coast, by Brandeis Gr. 3-7
Fictional girl sees real CA history.
Island of the Blue Dolphins* **and **Zia* Gr. 4-12
both by Scott O'Dell
**Saga of the Sierras* series, by B. Thoene Gr. 4-12

Flag of the Dreadful Bear, by Robert Howard Gr. 3-8

Story of California, by May McNeer Gr. 4-12
Illustrated history of California.

Battle of San Pasqual, by Jonreed Lauritzen Gr. 5-12

**To Fly with the Swallows*, by Debbie Heller Unknown
California's first native-born nun sees the battles raging between American and Mexico for California.

Fiction/Historical Fiction

**Valley of the Moon*, by Sherry Garland (Dear America) Gr. 3-8
I've not read this story of a Hispanic servant girl in California during the Mexican War. Some families enjoy this series; others do not.

We Were There with the California Rancheros, by Stephen Holt Gr. 3-8

**Anita of Rancho del Mar*, by Elaine O'Brien Gr. 4-8
I've not read this story of 1830s California, just before the Mexican War. It shows life on the Mexican ranches there.

**Rosalba of Santa Juanita*, by Clara Stites Gr. 4-8
I've not seen this story of Hispanic family adjusting to political changes just after the Mexican War, but it sounds from the description as if it's for the middle grades.

Susan Peck, Late of Boston, by Carmel Martinez Gr. 5-10
Boston girl sees fall of Mexican rule in California.

Silver Spurs to Monterey, by Page Cooper Gr. 6-12
Story based on activities of the real Thomas Larkin.

**Carlota*, by Scott O'Dell Gr. 7-12
Novel of girl who experiences the Battle of San Pasqual.

31h California Heroes—John & Jessie Frémont

**Story of the Great Republic*, by H.A. Guerber, Ch. XXVIIa Gr. 3-7

Jessie Frémont, by Jean Wagoner (Childhood) Gr. 1-6
This series is gradually being reprinted as Young Patriot books.

John C. Frémont, by Sanford Tousey Gr. 2-7
Too rare to seek, but if you have it, enjoy!

**John C. Frémont*, by Kristin Petrie Gr. 3-6
I've not seen this, but it sounds like it's for upper elementary students.

**John C. Frémont: Soldier and Pathfinder*, by Carl Green & William Sanford Gr. 4-7

**John Charles Frémont*, by Barbara Witteman (Let Freedom Ring) Gr. 4-8

Boys' Life of Frémont, by Flora Seymour Gr. 6-12
One in an antique series.

John Charles Fremont: Trail Marker..., by Olive Burt (Messner) Gr. 6-12

I, Jessie, by Ruth Painter Randall Gr. 7-12

Jessie Benton Frémont, by Marguerite Higgins (North Star) Gr. 7-12

Year of the Big Snow, by Steve Frazee Gr. 7-12
Story of Frémont's fourth expedition.

Immortal Wife, by Irving Stone Gr. 11-12
This is actually an adult novel, but I've not read it.

**John C. Frémont*, by Harold Faber (Great Explorations) Unknown

**John C. Frémont*, by Hal Marcovitz (Explorers of New Worlds) Unknown

**John C. Frémont*, by D.M. Souza (Watts Library) Unknown

**Under a Strong Wind*, by Dorothy Morrison Unknown
A biography of Jessie Frémont.

31i California Pioneers

Right around the time of the Mexican War (1846), many American settlers were attempting the extremely difficult overland route to California. You may have heard the agonizing ordeal suffered by the Donner Party, also in 1846. (Parents should preview books about the Donner Party due to its *extreme* gruesomeness.) The Donner Party was hoping to accomplish what the Stevens Party had done in 1844: they were the first covered wagon train to make it over the Sierras. Wow, it is hard for me to even imagine such an ordeal. I'll let you read all about it, but let me just pass on one tidbit read online...which is that almost four times as many pioneers took the overland route to California as took the more famous Oregon Trail (which we'll get to next)!

**Covered Wagon, Bumpy Trails*, by Verla Kay Gr. K-3
Kay's books are wonderfully lively...and poetic!

**Wagon Train*, by Sydelle Kramer (All Aboard) Gr. 1-3
A simple look at one family's trip to California.

**Along the Santa Fe Trail: Marion Russell's Own Story*, by Russell/Wadsworth Gr. 2-5
Read the real story of a California pioneer who used the Santa Fe Trail to get there.

**Pioneers Go* West, by George Stewart (Landmark) Gr. 3-9
Originally titled, *To California by Covered Wagon*
Incredible tale of Steven's Party's endurance and accomplishment, seen through eyes of 17-year-old boy who was really on the trip!

**Donner Party*, by Roger Wachtel (Cornerstones of Freedom II) Gr. 4-8
Remember, parents should decide the age appropriateness of books relating the gruesome ordeal of the Donner Party.

**Ransom's Mark*, by Wendy Lawton (Daughters of the Faith) Gr. 4-8
This series, from Moody Press, tells the dramatic tale of a Christian pioneer girl and her capture by Indians.

**Patty Reed's Doll*, by Rachel Laurgaard — Gr. 4-12

Story of young survivor of the Donner Party. This may have been edited sufficiently for children, but parent's should always determine the age-appropriateness of books on this heart-rending topic.

Palace Wagon Family: A True Story of the Donner Party, by Margaret Sutton — Gr. 5-12

Use discretion; this party faced gruesome difficulties.

Rolling Wheels, by Katharine Grey — Gr. 5-12

I've not seen this, but it is about the Lamberts' early trek to California from Indiana during the Mexican War and their meeting of the Donner Party.

**Snowbound: Tragic Story of the Donner Party*, by David Lavender — Gr. 5-12

Use discretion; this party faced gruesome difficulties.

**Across the Plains in the Donner Party*, by Virginia Reed Murphy, ed. K. Zeinert — Gr. 6-10

Reed was one of the Donner survivors, and this is an edited collection of her letters and other reminiscences. Remember, parents should decide the age appropriateness of books relating the gruesome ordeal of the Donner Party.

**Donner Party*, by Marian Calabro — Gr. 6-12

Use discretion; this party faced gruesome difficulties.

**Perilous Journey of the Donner Party*, by Marian Calabro — Gr. 6-12

This is probably the same as the listing above, published under a different title. Use discretion; this party faced gruesome difficulties.

**Expedition of the Donner Party and Its Tragic Fate* — Unknown

by Eliza Donner Houghton

Remember, parents should decide the age appropriateness of books relating the gruesome ordeal of the Donner Party.

Fiction/Historical Fiction

**Josefina Story Quilt* (I Can Read) Gr. K-3
by Eleanor Coerr

Earlier in the 1800s, the Mormon Church was founded by Joseph Smith, who said an angel sent him to some golden tablets containing new revelations. Mormons were greatly resisted, and decided to head west under the new leader, Brigham Young. (**Caution!** Mormon views differ from orthodox Christian views in ***key*** areas.)

**Story of the Great Republic*, Ch. XXIV — Gr. 3-7
by H.A. Guerber

**This Country of Ours*, Ch. 81 — Gr. 3-8
by H.E. Marshall

Brigham Young, by Jordan (Childhood) — Gr. 1-6

Over the Mormon Trail, by Jones (Frontiers of America) — Gr. 3-8

Coming of the Mormons, by Kjelgaard (Landmark) — Gr. 3-9

Brigham Young, by O. Burt (Messner) — Gr. 7-12

Fiction/Historical Fiction:

Law or the Gun, by Frank Latham (Aladdin's American Heritage) — Gr. 3-9

**Araminta's Paint Box*, by Karen Ackerman Gr. 1-4

Pioneer girl loses her paint box on way to California, but it has adventure of its own!

**Sunsets of the West*, by Tony Johnston Gr. 1-4

A New England man longs to see the snow-covered Sierra Nevada Mountains.

**Journal of Douglas Allen Deeds*, by Rodman Philbrick (My Name is America) Gr. 5-8

I've found the "tone" and "attitudes" of this series to vary widely, so be careful. This is a fictional diary of the Donner Party, so parents must decide the age appropriateness of any books relating their gruesome ordeal.

Nancy Kelsey, by Virginia Evansen Gr. 7-12

I've not seen this fact-based novel, but it sounds interesting since it is about the first pioneer woman to come by land to California...and she was carrying a baby!

Torrie, by Annabel Johnson Gr. 7-12

This story finds a 14-year-old girl heading west.

If you'd like to know more about President James K. Polk, I've been told this is a surprisingly interesting biography of him:

This Slender Reed, by Milton Lomask Gr. 6-12

32 Oregon Territory and the Oregon Trail

Hey, the Mexican War wasn't the only thing happening in the US during the pivotal year 1846. What else? Well, let me ask you a question first. Did you notice earlier that we said Britain was in the soup? Yes, after the Louisiana Purchase, we're so accustomed to thinking of Oregon as part of the USA, that we forget Britain, Russia, and a few other nations claimed it too! They all could see the great value of the natural harbor at the mouth of the Columbia River, the rich land, and the many beaver pelts in what was then the vast Oregon Territory; in the end, though, it boiled down to Britain and America, and the border was hotly debated.[67] Do you remember the US motto? *54 ° 40', or fight!* Yes, at one point things were very tense, but in 1846, it was settled peacefully and the border was set at the 49th parallel, where it still stands today. The Oregon Territory, which included most of the Great Northwest, had now officially became American just as was happening with the Great Southwest. What a year!

67 Carson 3:111-112.

Folks had already been pouring down the Oregon Trail throughout the early 1840s, many of them guided by none other than Kit Carson! We will watch their epic journey, but first we're privileged to meet the very first white couple to live there: Marcus and Narcissa Whitman, missionaries to the Indians. What a story it is....

32a Marcus & Narcissa Whitman

I can find little in-print about the Whitmans other than the one book from the good Trailblazer series, which does give a sense of their lives, even though it is technically historical fiction.

Narcissa Whitman, by Louis Sabin (Troll) Gr. 1-3

Marcus and Narcissa Whitman, by Marian Place (Garrard Discovery) Gr. 1-5
This book is in a beloved, older series; it would be wonderful if you can find it, for I greatly enjoyed reading this to my young daughter.

Narcissa Whitman, by Ann Warner (Childhood) Gr. 1-6
Series is being reprinted as Young Patriot books, so a copy may soon be in-print!

**Tragic Tale of Narcissa Whitman and a Faithful History of the Oregon Trail* Gr. 4-8
by Cheryl Harness
This is a new book; I am unaware if it respects the Whitman's great faith.

Narcissa Whitman, by Jeanette Eaton Gr. 4-12
Looks like a wonderful narrative, but I've not read it to know how she handles Mrs. Whitman's faith. Because it was written in an earlier age, it may be excellent.

Eliza and the Indian War Pony, by Paul & Beryl Scott Gr. 5-12
I've not seen this, and am guessing on the age recommendation, but it is based on the memoirs of a girl whose missionary parents helped the Whitmans and whose ability to speak the language of the Nez Percé Indians helped after the massacre.

Marcus and Narcissa Whitman, by James Daugherty Gr. 7-12

Fiction/Historical Fiction

**Attack in the Rye Grass*, by Dave & Neta Jackson (Trailblazer) Gr. 3-8
Fictional kids have adventures based on real events in the lives of the Whitmans.

32b Oregon Trail

Travel on the Oregon Trail actually peaked during 1842-1843, and led pioneers into such areas as Oregon, Washington, Idaho, northern California, etc. You'll find here books about the Oregon Trail, of course, and also some of the general pioneer books we've been citing throughout. Of the latter, you need read only the pertinent chapters.

**From Sea to Shining Sea for Children*, by Marshall & Manuel, Ch. 14 — Gr. 1-5

**Story of the Great Republic*, by H.A. Guerber, Ch. XXIII — Gr. 3-7

**From Sea to Shining Sea*, by Marshall & Manuel, Ch. 14 — Gr. 6-12

True Book of Pioneers, by Mabel Harmer (True Books) — Gr. K-3
We also cited this book when studying earlier waves of pioneers; you'll only need the section referring to the Oregon Trail now.

For Ma and Pa on the Oregon Trail, by Wilma Pitchford Hays — Gr. 1-4
True story of children orphaned on the Oregon Trail.

**Fourth of July on the Plains*, by Jean Van Leeuwen — Gr. 1-4
Van Leeuwen's books are always soooo poignant!

**If You Traveled West on a Covered Wagon*, by Ellen Levine — Gr. 1-4

**Kindle Me a Riddle*, by Roberta Karim — Gr. 1-4
Precious!

**Life on the Oregon Trail*, by Sally Isaacs (Picture the Past) — Gr. 1-4

Oregon Trail, by Laurence Santrey (Troll) — Gr. 2-6

**Story of the Oregon Trail*, by R. Conrad Stein (Cornerstones) — Gr. 2-6

**Way West*, by Amelia Knight — Gr. 2-6
Illustrated excerpts from a real pioneer woman's journal.

**Oregon Trail*, by Jean Blashfield (We the People) — Gr. 3-6

**Daily Life in a Covered Wagon*, by Paul Erickson — Gr. 3-8
Some families enjoy Erickson's series.

First Book of Pioneers, by Walter Havighurst (First Books) Gr. 3-8

We also cited this book when studying earlier waves of pioneers; you'll only need the section referring to the Oregon Trail now.

First Book of the Oregon Trail, by Walter Havighurst (First Books) Gr. 3-8

**Prairie Schooners*, by Glen Rounds Gr. 3-8

Rounds has sprightly info on Conestoga wagons and drawings that boys love!

**(Taking) Wagons Over the Mountains*, by Edith McCall (Frontiers of America) Gr. 3-8

The original was titled *Wagons...*; the reprint is titled *Taking Wagons....*

When Pioneers Pushed West to Oregon, by Elizabeth Montgomery (Garr. How...) Gr. 3-8

**Oregon Trail*, by Sally Isaacs (American Adventure) Gr. 4-7

Here is another series named *American Adventure*, but this is a new, non-fiction series.

**Oregon Trail*, by Elizabeth Jaffe (Let Freedom Ring) Gr. 4-8

**Frontier Fort on the Oregon Trail*, by Scott Steedman (Inside Story) Gr. 4-10

Heroines of the Early West, by Nancy Wilson Ross (Landmark) Gr. 4-12

We also cited this book when studying earlier waves of pioneers; you'll only need the section referring to the Oregon Trail now.

**Life on the Oregon Trail*, by Gary Blackwood (Way People Live) Gr. 5-12

**On to Oregon!* by Honoré Morrow Gr. 5-12

True story of Sager children, orphaned on the trail. Also issued as *Seven Alone.*

Wheels West, by Evelyn Lampman Gr. 5-12

I've not seen this true story of a imaginative, lame, 66-year old woman who made the arduous trek to Oregon, but it sounds fascinating.

**Oregon Trail*, by Leonard Everett Fisher Gr. 6-12

Fisher's books are known for their strong, spare illustrations and text.

**Stout-Hearted Seven*, by Neta Frazier Gr. 6-12

True story of Sager children, orphaned on the Oregon Trail. This book is for a slightly older audience than *On to Oregon!* It covers not only their trip and arrival, but their stay with the Whitmans, and is now being reprinted (Flying Point Press?)

54°-40' or Fight! by Bob & Jan Young (Messner/Milestones) Gr. 7-12

Frontier Living, by Edwin Tunis Gr. 7-12

Detailed survey with meticulous drawings in his usual amazing style! Please save the portion on plains pioneers for later.

Oregon Trail, by Francis Parkman (also titled, *California and Oregon Trail*) Various

Well-known, highly esteemed narrative, written by a devoted historian who traveled the trail himself shortly after the big rush. There are many adapted versions at different levels because it is sooo famous. You may wish to experience it!

Across the Plains in 1844 **and** *Whitman Massacre of 1847*, by Catherine Sager Unknown

Catherine Sager herself wrote two books about their experiences. The first covers their journey and the second covers the massacre. I've not seen them.

Our Journey West, by Gare Thompson (National Geographic) Unknown

Fiction/Historical Fiction

When Pioneer Wagons Rumbled West, by Christine Graham Gr. 1-3

Apples to Oregon, by Deborah Hopkinson Gr. 1-4

Based on real Iowa pioneer, a man carts his beloved fruit trees across the country!

Bound for Oregon, by Jean Van Leeuwen Gr. 1-4

Van Leeuwen's books are very warm and wonderful, though I've not read this one.

Mississippi Mud, by Ann Turner (caution!) Gr. 1-4

I haven't been able to put this into my library; there is something that I just do not care for. I otherwise have many Ann Turner books in my collection!

Wagons West, by Roy Gerrard Gr. 1-4

Gerrard has an almost eccentric sense of humor in both his writing and drawing. Make sure it is something your family enjoys; I've not read this one.

I'm Sorry, Almira Ann, by Jane Kurtz Gr. 2-4

A girl sees how her "hasty spirit" gets her in trouble on the way to Oregon.

Roughing It on the Oregon Trail, by Diane Stanley Gr. 2-5

Time-traveling twins find themselves on the Oregon Trail!

Trouble for Lucy, by Carla Stevens Gr. 2-5

Facing West, by Kathleen Kudlinski (Once Upon America) Gr. 2-6

Young Mr. Meeker and His Exciting Journey to Oregon, by Miriam Mason Gr. 2-8

**Wagons Ho!* by Cynthia Mercati (Cover-to-Cover) Gr. 3-5
I've heard this is a streamlined story for reluctant readers.

**We Were There on the Oregon Trail*, by William Steele (We Were There) Gr. 3-8
Kids love this older series featuring fiction kids with real historic characters, and someone (American Home School Publishers?) is reprinting it!

**Across the Wide and Lonesome Prairie*, by Kristiana Gregory (Dear America) Gr. 3-9
I've found this series to vary widely in "tone," so please use caution. Fictional diary.

Challengers, by Jo Lundy (Aladdin's American Heritage) Gr. 3-9
This is from an admired, older series.

**Children of the Covered Wagon*, by Mary Jane Carr Gr. 3-9
This can be considered a ***don't-miss*** story about children on the Oregon Trail! Everyone who reads this—including my husband, aloud to our children—rave!

**Journal of Jedediah Barstow*, by Ellen Levine (My Name is America) Gr. 4-7
I've found this series to vary widely in "tone," so please use caution; there are some much-preferred books in this section, anyway.

**Daniel Colton* series, by Elaine Schulte Gr. 4-8
This is a distinctly Christian series.

One Long Picnic, by Neta Frazier Gr. 4-8
A boy meets Indians on the way to Oregon.

**Plain Prairie Princess*, by Stephen Bly (1st in *Retta Barre's Oregon Trail* series) Gr. 4-8
This is a distinctly Christian series.

**Brave Buffalo Fighter*, by John Fitzgerald (Bethlehem Books) Gr. 4-10
I've been told this is very exciting. Though it's set a bit later, we'll tuck it in here with the other books about westward journeys.

Caravan to Oregon **and** *River Boy*, by Herbert Arntson Gr. 4-12
Solid, older fiction.

A Head on Her Shoulders, by G. Bond Gr. 4-12
Girl and family try to make it to Idaho Territory.

Keep 'Em Rolling, by Stephen Meader Gr. 4-12
Meader's books are always adventurous; in this one, a teen boy guides pioneers along the Trail.

Treasure in the Covered Wagon, by Vera Graham Gr. 4-12
Solid, older fiction.

Nine Lives of Moses on the Oregon Trail, by Marion Archer Gr. 5-10
Adventures of the cat accompanying a pioneer family on the Oregon Trail.

Poor Felicity, by Sally Watson Gr. 5-12
Virginia girl struggles to adjust to new life in the Washington area.

Make Way for the Brave: The Oregon Quest, by Merritt Parmelee Allen Gr. 6-12
I know of one boy who does extra work just to earn money for Allen books because they are *so* adventurous!

Courage in Her Hands, by Iris Noble (Messner) Gr. 7-12
Real life of American lady in Northwest slightly earlier, when Russia had more control.

Keelboat Journey, by Zachary Ball Gr. 7-12

Keep the Wagons Moving! by West Lathrop Gr. 7-12

**Moccasin Trail*, by Eloise Jarvis McGraw Gr. 7-12

Tree Wagon, by Evelyn Lampman Gr. 7-12
Family carefully takes valuable tree on Oregon Trail to begin orchard.

Runaway Voyage, by Betty Cavanah Gr. 8-12
A group of women travel to Seattle quite early on; I've not read this.

Audio/Film

**History Alive Through Music: Westward Ho!* by Diana Waring
This audio features real songs sung by the pioneers!

**Seven Alone*, a film depicting the true story of the Sager children

32c Activities

**Make This Model American Fort* (Usborne) Various

**Pioneer Days*, by David C. King Various
An activity book with projects, games, and recipes.

**Pioneer Recipes*, by Bobbie Kalman Various

**Skillet Bread, Sourdough, and Vinegar Pie*, by Loretta Frances Ichord Various

32d Kit Carson

As we mentioned, Kit Carson was one of the key guides on the Oregon Trail. Do you remember briefly meeting him earlier when he was a young man on the Santa Fe Trail? This guy got around!

**Kit Carson*, by Jan Gleiter (First Biographies) Gr. 1-3

Kit Carson: Pathfinder of the West, by Nardi Campion (Garrard Discovery) Gr. 1-5
This is from a beloved series.

Kit Carson, by Augusta Stevenson (Childhood) Gr. 1-6
Series is being reprinted as Young Patriot books, so this title may be in-print now!

Kit Carson, by Sanford Tousey Gr. 2-7
Rare, but precious. Boys love the drawings

Kit Carson: Mountain Scout, by Donald Worcester (Piper) Gr. 2-7
I love this older series!

Life of Kit Carson, by C. Richard Schaare (included in his *Pioneer Stories* too) Gr. 2-8
Another very rare, older book, but its unusual illustrations are great for boys.

Kit Carson, by Frank Beals (American Adventures) Gr. 3-8
There is a new Christian series and another series by the name *American Adventure*, but this book is in a great older series using that title!

Story of Kit Carson, by Edmund Collier (Signature) Gr. 3-8

Kit Carson and the Wild Frontier, by Ralph Moody (Landmark) Gr. 3-9
Books in the Landmark series are a favorite with many families.

**Kit Carson: Frontier Scout*, by Carl Green & William Sanford — Gr. 4-8

**Kit Carson: Mountain Man*, by Tracey Boraas (Let Freedom Ring) — Gr. 4-8

Kit Carson of the Old West, by Mark Boesch (Vision) — Gr. 4-12
This is from a distinctly Catholic series.

**Life of Kit Carson*, by Edward Ellis (Lost Classics) — Gr. 5-12
This antique book has just been reprinted, and I've heard it's exciting! It may be for older students, though. I'm not quite sure of the age range.

Kit Carson: Trailblazer and Scout, by Shannon Garst (Messner) — Gr. 6-12

**Kit Carson*, by Rick Burke — Unknown

**Kit Carson's Autobiography*, by Kit Carson — Unknown

Audio/Film

**Historical Devotionals: Volume XII*, by Mantle Ministries — Various
Kit Carson is covered in one of these audio devotionals.

**Kit Carson*, by Richard "Little Bear" Wheeler — Various
Wheeler dresses as Carson and teaches a historical/spiritual lesson in this video.

32e Other ministers and contributors

**Exiled to the Red River*, by Dave & Neta Jackson (Trailblazer) — Gr. 3-8
Fictional kids "meet" Chief Spokane Garry, a brave evangelist to fellow native Americans.

Cross in the West, by Mark Boesch (Vision) — Gr. 4-10
Focuses on Catholic missionaries.

**Jason Lee: Winner of the Northwest*, by Charles Ludwig (Sower) — Gr. 5-12
This biography is from a distinctly Christian series.

They Rode the Frontier, by Wyatt Blassingame — Gr. 6-12
Preachers and priests spread the gospel on the frontier.

Frontier Doctors, by Wyatt Blassingame and Richard Glendinning — Gr. 7-12

33 Gold Fever—California Gold Rush!

When gold was found at Sutter's Mill in California in 1848, well, I bet you can guess what happened! By 1849, word had leaked out. People—nicknamed *forty-niners*—streamed to the California Gold Rush on foot, on mules, and on the newly designed clipper ships, which speedily rounded the southern horn of South America, and brought anxious gold panners up the entire west coast of the Americas to California. Now, America was smitten with both Oregon Fever *and* Gold Fever! Another tidal wave of settlers headed west!

33a General overview

**Sounding Forth the Trumpet for Children*, by Marshall & Manuel, Ch. 9 — Gr. 1-5

**Story of the World: Vol. 3*, by Susan Wise Bauer, Ch. 42 — Gr. 3-6
Some families enjoy this book's scope, so ask us to cite it; others seek different worldview; so, parental decision.

**Story of the Great Republic*, by H.A. Guerber, Ch. XXX-XXXII — Gr. 3-7
Ch. XXX gives a quick overview of California's earlier history, as well.

**This Country of Ours*, by H.E. Marshall, Ch. 77 — Gr. 3-8

**Sounding Forth the Trumpet*, by Marshall & Manuel, Ch. 23 — Gr. 6-12

**Gold Fever*, by Verla Kay — Gr. K-3
Powerful, fun poem expresses the essence of the Gold Rush! ***Don't miss it!***

**Striking it Rich!* by Stephen Krensky (Ready-to-Read 3) — Gr. 2-3

**California Gold Rush*, by Peter & Connie Roop (Scholastic History Reader) — Gr. 2-4
Looks like this is for younger students.

**Gold Fever!* by Catherine McMorrow (Step Into Reading 4) — Gr. 2-4

Story of the Gold at Sutter's Mill, by R. Conrad Stein (Cornerstones) — Gr. 2-6
This has been reissued (and maybe rewritten) as **California Gold Rush.*

**Gold Rush Adventures*, by Edith McCall (Frontiers of America) — Gr. 2-8
This precious series was just reprinted! Thank you!

**Forty-Niners,* by Cynthia Mercati (Cover-to-Cover) Gr. 3-5

I've heard that this is streamlined for reluctant readers (I've not seen it in person), but a well-written book (as Edith McCall's usually are, as cited above) may work just as well, and have the great content of yesteryear!

**Diary of David R. Leeper,* by David Leeper, ed. by the Roops (In My Own...) Gr. 3-6

Actual biography of an Indian youth who makes the long trek to California and then begins the search for gold. The Roops have edited this only slightly, and I've heard it's very good reading!

**Gold Fever!* by Rosalyn Schanzer Gr. 3-6

Schanzer's books are snappy-looking. I've not read one yet.

Rush for Gold, by Frank Beals (American Adventures) Gr. 3-8

There is a new Christian series and another series by the name *American Adventure,* but this book is in a great older series by the same name! It is one of my son's favorite series of all time!

**California Gold Rush,* by May McNeer (Landmark) Gr. 3-9

This is one of the few Landmarks that has been in print in paperback. Usually a solid choice.

Sutter's Fort: Empire on the Sacramento, by W. & C. Luce (Garrard How They...) Gr. 3-9

**California Gold Rush,* by Judy Monroe (Let Freedom Ring) Gr. 4-8

First Book of the California Gold Rush, by Walter Havighurst (First Books) Gr. 4-12

John Sutter, Californian, by Edwin Booth Gr. 5-12

**Lost in Death Valley,* by Connie Goldsmith Gr. 5-12

True, harrowing story of four families hurrying to the Gold Rush who must struggle through Death Valley and the Mojave Desert.

Gold in California, by Paul Wellman (North Star) Gr. 6-12

The North Star series features many wonderful books.

Gold Rush of 1849, by Arthur Blake Gr. 6-12

Sorry, but this one looks dry. Maybe it's not.

Great American Gold Rush, by Rhoda Blumberg Gr. 6-12

*_Hurry Freedom_, by Jerry Stanley Gr. 6-12

Stanley reveals the lives of African-American slaves who gained freedom in California (where slavery was illegal), and how they apprehended opportunity when possible! I've not read this, but it is an interesting topic.

Fiction/Historical Fiction

*_Chang's Paper Pony_, by Eleanor Coerr (I Can Read) Gr. 1-3

Chinese boy who works feeding miners longs for a real pony.

*_Legend of Freedom Hill_, by Linda Altman Gr. 1-4

Can a freed slave girl and her Jewish friend—mining community outsiders—save the slave girl's mother in time?

*_Nine for California_, by Sonia Levitin Gr. 1-4

This book and its sequels relate the adventures of a fun Gold Rush family. Nice!

*_Red Flower Goes West_, by Ann Turner Gr. 1-4

Another of Turner's lovely books; family headed to gold fields tries to bring flower.

Malachy's Gold, by Anico Surany Gr. 1-5

Prospector is helped by Indian boy.

Secret Valley, by Clyde Robert Bulla Gr. 1-5

A Missouri family heads for the California gold fields.

Jack Finds Gold, by Sanford Tousey Gr. 2-6

Very rare, but precious.

Prairie Schooners West, by Mildred Comfort Gr. 2-6

Becky and the Bandit, by Doris Gates Gr. 2-7

Girl must be brave for her Gold Rush family.

*_Gold Rush Days_, by Ellen Weiss Gr. 3-8

Ms. Weiss has picked up the story of the beloved doll in _Hitty, Her First Hundred Years_ (by Rachel Field) and now has Hitty headed west for the Gold Rush!

*_Seeds of Hope_, by Kristiana Gregory (Dear America) Gr. 3-8

Some families like this series; others do not.

We Were There with the California Forty-Niners, by Stephen Holt (We Were....) Gr. 3-8

Fictional kids experience real historical events. Series is usually very good.

River of Gold, by Gifford Cheshire (Aladdin's American Heritage) Gr. 3-9
This is from a very good series.

**Ballad of Lucy Whipple*, by Karen Cushman Gr. 4-12
I have *not* read this book, but know that Cushman's books can sometimes sport "attitude." Others have said they enjoyed this story of a mining camp girl who wanted to be elsewhere.

By the Great Horn Spoon Gr. 4-12
by Sid Fleischman
This *very* funny story of a boy—and his butler—trying to rescue the family fortune during the Gold Rush is also titled, **Bullwhip Griffin*. We loved it! There is also a film version (I've not seen.)

Bret Harte, an American author, gained fame by writing stories of the California Gold Rush:

Bret Harte, by J. Branham (Childhood) Gr. 1-6
Western Stories of Bret Harte (adapted) Gr. 5-12
Bret Harte of..., by Harlow (Messner) Gr. 7-12
**Luck of Roaring Camp & Other Stories* Gr. ?
Unknown content.

Lost Wharf, by Howard Pease Gr. 5-10
A San Francisco boy is busy during the Gold Rush.

Hank of Lost Nugget Canyon, by H.R. Langdale Gr. 5-12
A boy en route to the gold fields is captured by outlaws!

West to Danger, by Isabelle Lawrence Gr. 5-12
A family faces danger on steamship going to Gold Rush.

**Giants on the Hill* trilogy, by Lee Roddy Gr. 7-12
Three Christian novels set in the California Gold Rush.

Boy Emigrants, by Noah Brooks Gr. 8-12
Older boys head west alone in this old, rare book.

33b Activities

**California Gold Rush Cooking*, by Lisa Schroeder Various

**Gold Rush: Hands-On Projects About Mining the Riches of California*, by J. Quasha Various
I've heard that both projects and instructions are rather sparse.

**Gold Rush! Young Prospector's Guide...*, by James Klein Various
How to pan for gold yourself!

**Story of the California Gold Rush Coloring Book* (Dover) Various

33c People of the California Gold Rush

You have already met many forty-niners, but here are some folks of special note.

i. Lotta Crabtree

Lotta Crabtree, by Marian Place (Childhood) Gr. 1-6

This series is being reprinted as *Young Patriot* books, so this may soon be in print.

ii. Sylvia Stark

**Sylvia Stark*, by Victoria Scott Gr. 4-10

I've not seen this book, but have read that it relates the very full life of a young slave girl who traveled the Oregon Trail to a California Gold Rush town and who attempted to flee to Canada! I do *not* know about the tone or content.

iii. Levi Strauss

Mr. Strauss thought he could do better selling durable pants to miners than he could be panning for gold himself. I think he was right!

**Levi Strauss*, by Tiffany Peterson (Lives and Times) Gr. 1-3

**Mr. Blue Jeans: Levi Strauss*, by M. Weidt (Carolrhoda's Creative Minds) Gr. 2-7

First Blue Jeans, by Ricki Dru Gr. 3-8

**Everyone Wears His Name*, by Sondra Henry & Emily Taitz Gr. 5-12

**Levi Strauss: The Blue Jean Man*, by Elizabeth Van Steenwyk Gr. 5-12

I've heard this is a little dry, but that is quite subjective.

**Levi Strauss: The Man Behind Blue Jeans*, by Carin Ford (Famous Inventors) Unknown

iv. Snowshoe Thompson

Mr. Thompson was much appreciated by the folks in remote mining camps for he delivered the mail deep into the mountains in the most extreme weather on skis! He is also considered the "Father of Skiing" in the United States!

Snowshoe Thompson, by Nancy Levinson (I Can Read) Gr. 1-3

Legend of Snowshoe Thompson, by Cory La Bianca Gr. 3-8

Snowshoe Thompson, by Adrien Stoutenberg & L. Baker Gr. 7-12

33d Music of the '49ers

Clementine, by Ann Owen (editor) Various

Clementine, by Robert Quackenbush Various
Fun, illustrated lyrics.

Sweet Betsy from Pike, by Glen Rounds Various
Fun, illustrated lyrics.

34 Big Business on the High Seas

We mentioned that the newly designed clipper ships were used to cart *forty-niners* 'round the horn and off to the California gold fields. When the first one, the *Sea Witch* made it to San Francisco in stunningly record time, people on both American coasts were stunned. The entire ship-building world was abuzz! But did you think that's all the clippers did? No. They were used by many nations and greatly expanded the speed of world-wide trade. For example, many clipper ships were built in Aberdeen, Scotland and were used to transport China's tea back to Great Britain...especially after the Opium War ended in 1842, giving England control of Hong Kong![68] Anyway, you'll wan to check out these fleet and graceful beauties.

There were other endeavors upon the high seas, though. Whaling was big business in many nations: America, England, and (to some extent) Holland, for example. Whale oil and ivory had so many uses, from lighting to corset stays!

There was a great drive to open trade with the Far East. England had vast colonies there, and had been involved in the Opium War, as we mentioned earlier. The British also had vast tea colonies in several different lands, especially India, which you know was one of England's largest acquisitions. Well, the United States hoped to get in on some of this Asian trade. That's what impelled Matthew Perry into Japan!

68 This information was gleaned from a website: www.eraoftheclipperships.com, written by Donald Ross III.

34a Clipper ships and trade at sea

**Clipper Ship*, by Thomas Lewis (I Can Read History) Gr. K-2

**Mary Patten's Voyage*, by Richard Berleth Gr. 2-6
The don't-miss true story, especially for girls, of an admirable young wife who must captain a clipper around the horn when her husband sickens.

**Story of the Clipper Ships*, by R. Conrad Stein (Cornerstones) Gr. 2-7

King of the Clippers, by Edmund Collier (Aladdin's American Heritage) Gr. 3-8

River of the West, by Armstrong Sperry (Winston Adventure) Gr. 3-9
Boston sailors were doing business in Oregon! This book, like the rest in the series, brings out the true, little-known contributions of real young people!

When Clipper Ships Ruled the Seas, by James McCague (Garr. How They Lived) Gr. 3-9

Clipper Ship Days, by John Jennings (Landmark) Gr. 3-10

First Book of the China Clippers, by Louise Dickinson Rich (First Books) Gr. 5-12

Yankee Clippers: The Story of Donald McKay, by Clara Ingram Judson Gr. 5-12
Life of important clipper ship designer.

Sailing the Seven Seas, by Mary Ellen Chase (North Star) Gr. 6-12

Donald McKay and the Clipper Ships, by Mary Ellen Chase (North Star) Gr. 7-12

China Clipper, by Peter Guttmacher (Those Daring Machines) Gr. 7-12

Full Hold and Splendid Passage, by B. & G. Bonyun, Ch. 7 (Living Hist. Lib) Gr. 9-12

**Two Years Before the Mast*, by Richard Dana Gr. 9-12
This long-admired work tells of real sea voyages made in the 1830s. There are also abridged versions for younger readers.

Clippers and Whaling Ships, by Tim McNeese (Americans on the Move) Unknown

Fiction/Historical Fiction

Where is Papa Now? by Celeste Conway Gr. 1-4

White Sails to China, by Clyde Robert Bulla Gr. 1-5

**Bluewater Journal*, by Loretta Krupinski Gr. 1-6
Beautifully illustrated!

Wonderful Voyage, by Ruth Langland Holberg Gr. 3-9
Kids have adventure on the Pacific.

**Voyage of the Javelin*, by Stephen Meader Gr. 4-12
This great author tells story of boy who has adventures working on a clipper ship crew. Bethlehem Books is reprinting four Meader books (including this one) in a combo titled *Cleared for Action!*

**All Sail Set*, by Armstrong Sperry Gr. 5-12
Gripping, high adventure! Recently reprinted!

Adam Gray, Stowaway: Story of the China Trade, by Herbert Arntson Gr. 6-12

Fire in the Night, by Robert Carse Unknown
Boys on New York waterfront discover attempt to steal design for new clipper ship.

34b Whaling

America's whaling capitals were New Bedford, Cape Cod, and Nantucket.

**Life in a Whaling Town*, by Sally Isaacs (Picture the Past) Gr. 2-4

**Good-bye for Today*, by Peter & Connie Roop Gr. 2-5
This diary-type book is based on the life of real a whaling family's children.

**Story of the New England Whalers*, by R. Conrad Stein (Cornerstones) Gr. 2-6

**True Adventure of Daniel Hall*, by Diane Stanley Gr. 3-8
True story; teen boy goes through great ordeal on whaling ship and his subsequent escape. Maybe too intense for some children. (Picture book format with more text.)

**Seabird*, by Holling Clancy Holling Gr. 3-9
Don't miss this! Gull shares his bird's-eye view of whaling, shipping, etc..

**Whaling Days*, by Carol Carrick Gr. 3-9
A sweeping, illustrated history of whaling.

When Nantucket Men Went Whaling, by Enid Meadowcroft (Gar. How They...) Gr. 3-9

Harvest of the Sea, by Walter Buehr — Gr. 3-12

Includes a chapter on whaling.

**Whalers*, by Peter Chrisp (Remarkable World) — Gr. 4-8

A history of whaling in many times and places.

**Hunting Neptune's Giants*, by Catherine Gourley — Gr. 4-9

A history of American whaling based on real letters from whalers and their wives.

Sailors, Whalers, and Steamers, by Edith Thacher Hurd — Gr. 4-10

Whale Hunters, by Joseph Phelan — Gr. 5-12

**Black Hands, White Sails*, by Patricia McKissack — Gr. 6-12

Reveals the little-known role of black sailors in the whaling industry.

Fishing Fleets of New England, by Mary Ellen Chase (North Star) — Gr. 6-12

**Gone A-Whaling*, by Jim Murphy — Gr. 6-12

Blow Ye Winds Westerly, by Elizabeth Gemming — Gr. 7-12

Great Days of Whaling, by Henry Hough (North Star) — Gr. 7-12

Full Hold and Splendid Passage, by B. & G. Bonyun (Living History Library) — Gr. 9-12

Fiction/Historical Fiction

**John Tabor's Ride*, by Edward Day — Gr. 1-3

A new whaling boat sailor learns the hard way not to complain in this tall tale!

**Loud Emily*, by Alexis O'Neill — Gr. 1-3

In this romp, a girl born with a booming voice comes in handy on a whaling ship!

Thy Friend, Obadiah*, **Obadiah the Bold*, **Adventures of Obadiah*, **and **Rachel and Obadiah*, all by Brinton Turkle — Gr. 1-3

These long-beloved picture books tell of a dear Nantucket boy and his adventures; I would call these "don't-miss" books!

**Thar She Blows!* by Susan Kessirer (Smithsonian Odyssey) — Gr. 1-4

A boy goes back into whaling days!

**Journal of Brian Doyle*, by Jim Murphy (My Name is America) — Gr. 4-9

"Tone" varies widely in this series, so please be careful.

**Downright Dencey*, by Caroline Dale Snedeker Gr. 4-12

Warm, wonderful, character-filled story of Quaker girl from Nantucket. Really fine!

**Voyage of Patience Goodspeed*, by Heather Frederick Gr. 5-10

I've not read this, but have seen that it is the story of a girl and her brother suddenly finding themselves with their whaling father when their mother dies. It has the usual modern theme wherein the girl chafes against domestic duties, so be cautious.

**Whaler 'Round the Horn*, by Stephen Meader Gr. 5-12

Bethlehem Books is reprinting four Meader books (including this one) in a combo titled *Cleared for Action!* Meader writes such exciting novels for boys especially!

Lost Harpooner, by Leonard Wibberley Gr. 7-12

Secret Sea, by Richard Armstrong Gr. 7-12

This is definitely a gritty guy story!

**Meet the Allens in Whaling Days*, by John Loeper Unknown

I believe this is actually set during colonial times, but could still pertain here.

**Moby Dick*, by Herman Melville Various

This is considered an epic piece of American literature, the story of a bout with a great whale. It is a difficult and time-consuming reading for most students. Edited versions exist for various reading levels. If you decide to tackle it, I would recommend also reading the commentary in: *Invitation to the Classics*, edited by Cowan & Guinness, pp. 245-248. A book about Melville's life is: *Melville in the South Pacific*, by Henry Hough, in the North Star series. (Gr. 7-12)

**Stefan Derksen's Polar Adventure*, by Piet Prins Unknown

This comes from a distinctly Christian publisher.

34c Activities

**Cooking on Nineteenth-Century Whaling Ships*, by Charla Draper Various

Info and recipes.

**Story of Whaling Coloring Book*, by Peter Copeland (Dover) Various

34d England's eastern holdings and the Opium War

Sorry, at this time, I cannot find many books for youth on these topics in particular. Feel free, if you wish, to check any general resources on English, Chinese, or Indian history, depending on your area of interest. These topics will be discussed a bit more when we explore Queen Victoria's reign in the subsequent guide: 'TruthQuest History: Age of Revolution III: 1865-2000.)

**Story of the World: Vol. 4*, by Susan Wise Bauer, Ch. 1, 3a, 4b — Gr. 3-6
Some families enjoy this book's scope, so ask us to cite it; others seek different worldview; so, parental decision.

34e Matthew Perry and Japan

**Child's History of the World*, by V.M. Hillyer, Ch. 75b — Gr. 1-4

**Story of the World: Vol. 4*, by Susan Wise Bauer, Ch. 2a — Gr. 3-6
Some families enjoy this book's scope, so ask us to cite it; others seek different worldview; so, parental decision.

Matthew Calbraith Perry, by Alexander Scharbach (Childhood) — Gr. 1-6
Series is now being reprinted as Young Patriot books, so this may come into print!

Commodore Perry and the Opening of Japan, by Ferdinand Kuhn (Landmark) — Gr. 4-12
Landmark series is beloved by many families.

**Commodore Perry in the Land of the Shogun*, by Rhoda Blumberg — Gr. 5-12

Indestructible Commodore Matthew Perry, by Arthur Orrmont (Messner) — Gr. 7-12

35 American Cross-Country: Pony Express and Butterfield 8

After being at sea in the last section, we'll now be landlubbers. You see, America's new western residents wanted mail and news from back east. Train and telegraph service was only in its infancy, so...the Pony Express! The risks and rigors faced by the Pony Express riders are hard for us to even imagine now. Other overland mail service, such as the *Butterfield 8*, started also. Indeed, entrepreneurs were trying to connect America's East and West through its mostly empty middle. Let's jump in the saddle!

**Buffalo Bill and the Pony Express*, by Eleanor Coerr (History I Can Read) Gr. K-2
"Buffalo" Bill Cody was just a 15-year-old boy when he rode for the Pony Express. We'll talk more about Buffalo Bill in the next guide!

**Bronco Charlie and the Pony Express*, by Marlene Brill (On My Own) Gr. 1-4
The true story of the youngest rider (1861)!

**Ride Like the Wind*, by Bernie Fuchs Gr. 1-4

**Special Delivery*, by Betty Brandt (On My Own) Gr. 1-4
A history of the US mail service, but the emphasis is on the Pony Express.

**Camel Express*, by Ann Shaffer (It Really Happened) Gr. 1-5
A camel fills in on the Pony Express!

**First Ride: Blazing the Trail for the Pony Express*, by Jacqueline Geis Gr. 1-6
Newer book; shouldn't be difficult to find.

**Sweetwater Run: Story of Buffalo Bill and the Pony Express*, by Andrew Glass Gr. 2-6

**Pony Express!* by Steven Kroll Gr. 2-7

Story of the Pony Express, by R. Conrad Stein (Cornerstones) Gr. 2-7

**They're Off! The Story of the Pony Express*, by Cheryl Harness Gr. 2-7
As always, fabulously illustrated picture-book history.

**Pony Express*, by Cynthia Mercati (Cover-to-Cover) Gr. 3-5

**Pony Express*, by Jean Williams (We the People) Gr. 3-6

**Adventures of the Mail Riders*, by Edith McCall (Frontiers of America) Gr. 3-8
This series is usually excellent! Originally titled: *Mail Riders, from Paul Revere to the Pony Express.*

Mail Riders, from Paul Revere to the Pony Express, by Edith McCall (Frontiers...) Gr. 3-8

**Pony Express*, by Peter Anderson Gr. 3-8
I believe this is in the Cornerstones II series.

First Overland Mail, by Robert Pinkerton (Landmark) Gr. 3-9
An entry in the beloved Landmark series.

Pony Express, by Samuel Adams (Landmark) Gr. 3-9

Another entry in the beloved Landmark series.

**Young Pony Express Rider*, by Charles Coombs Gr. 3-9

This older book is wonderful...and is being reprinted! My son loved it!

**Stagecoaches and the Pony Express*, by Sally Isaacs (American Adventure) Gr. 4-7

Here's yet another series by the name *American Adventure*. This is a non-fiction series.

Do Not Annoy the Indians, by Betty Baker Gr. 5-10

I've not seen this story of three easterners trying to run a relay station in Arizona, but it includes some real instructions from the Butterfield, such as that in the book's title.

Pony Express Goes Through, by Howard Driggs Gr. 5-12

Actual Pony Express riders tell their own stories!

Riders of the Pony Express, by Ralph Moody (North Star) Gr. 6-12

Moody is a good writer, and this book is in a good series.

**Pony Bob's Daring Ride*, by Joe Bensen Unknown

Story of the longest run ever made by one rider (across Nevada); looks like it's for young-to-middle readers.

**Pony Express*, by Edward Dolan Unknown

Fiction/Historical Fiction

Jerry and the Pony Express, by Sanford Tousey Gr. 1-4

As always, Tousey's books are rare, but precious.

Riding the Pony Express, by Clyde Robert Bulla Gr. 1-5

Fictional story from beloved writer of historical fiction for young children.

**We Were There with the Pony Express*, by William O. Steele (We Were There) Gr. 3-8

Fictional kids experience real historical events. Series is usually terrific!

Honor Bound, by Frank Bonham Gr. 9-12

I've not read this story of the Great Overland Mail, but I've heard it's gripping.

Audio

**Wanted: A Few Bold Riders*, by Darice Bailer (Smithsonian Odyssey) Various

This book and companion audio tell of a boy viewing a museum exhibit about the Pony Express who suddenly finds he's back in time as a rider himself!

36 Underground Railroad, Abolition, and Battles over Slavery

We've had some adventure out in the new territories of the American West, but we must get back to the big issues casting their dark shadow over the United States as a whole, for the nation was about to be enmeshed in a horrific Civil War. We hope you non-Americans will be patient as we work through this subject, just as together we all tackled England's Civil War and other great upheavals amongst the European nations. What we're now facing, then, is *still* a delicate subject for many Americans and emotions are yet strong, but I ask you to step away from your current feelings and training about the war—whether Northern or Southern, black or white—and attempt to grasp how God saw the war. I'll be honest; I don't know exactly what His viewpoint is. I only know that Christians on both sides felt they were justified in their causes. Notice that I said causes. There is no *one* reason why the Civil War was fought. There was racism on both sides, sectionalism on both sides, sin on both sides, a different view of government and economics on both sides, and even validity of outlook on both sides. So we can either extend the unpleasant debate into our children's generation, or humbly step back and seek God's viewpoint, not the one handed us by our teachers and relatives.

Clearly, a huge issue in the coming Civil War *was* slavery. But it wasn't just an "issue" for many. It was "real life" for thousands and thousands of slaves! I say this because I don't want to lose the personal side. North and South may still debate the nature of an average slave's life, but God knows the truth. He also knows how few of us would have chosen to switch places with even the best-treated Negro, for slavery is more than just risk of maltreatment; its binding impact and painful sorrow are much deeper. He also knows that there were strong attempts by the South to extend slavery in the new territories, even though they had said at the Constitutional Convention that they'd eliminate it gradually on their own. More lives would be (and already had been) affected, though what He wanted done about that, I surely cannot say.

Before we dig in, though, please remember what we hashed through in an earlier section: entanglement with slavery was more widespread than you might think. Many Americans—*beside* the southern plantation owners—made a living off slaves, for in the North were slave shippers and factory-owners who gobbled up slave-raised cotton and sold poorly made goods back to slave owners for slave use.[69] Few, today, can be righteously indignant.

There was another huge issue in the coming Civil War also: *states' rights*. It was a doozie too! Did the federal government have the Constitutional power to ban slavery in states that wanted it? If so, what kind of federal government did we really have? An unbiblically powerful one? On the other hand, did states have the right to condone unbiblical positions? Of course, few slaveholders saw slavery as unbiblical, so that wasn't an issue in their mind, but I'm asking you to ponder these issues from God's point of view—even if I'm not sure what it is!

I say again, it amazes me that Christians on both sides could take such opposing positions, but we've seen throughout this unit that Christians often buy into the prevailing

69 Carson 3:128.

philosophies and conditions of the day, without carefully filtering them through God's Biblical standards. We do the same! The fact that a Christian, no matter how devout, takes a certain position, hardly makes that position right. It's right *only* if it's Biblical. That's an absolute. Let me say, though, that many Christians did speak up for what they felt was right.

Let's be honest. Both sides could point fingers. The Southerners could say that many Northerners were terrible racists without any real concern for slaves. Sadly, that's true, as you'll see in your readings for this unit. In fact, many northern soldiers in the coming Civil War did *not* fight to free the slaves, contrary to what I was taught as a young girl. The goal for many, if not most, was simply to keep the Union together. Yet, there *were* those—both soldiers and civilians—who were deeply concerned about living in a country where some members (such as slave owners) decided who did or did not have rights.

Most southern soldiers could rightfully say they were fighting for *states's rights* and to limit the power of the federal government. These are extremely valid concerns, ones that still haunt us today. Yet, many Northerners could wonder why the Southerners got that same federal government to pass a law in 1850—the *Fugitive Slave Act*—which overrode some of the anti-slavery laws in northern states. (All northern states had outlawed slavery well before the onset of the Civil War, several doing so as soon as they became states.)[70] This federal Act forbade Northerners from assisting escaping slaves *in their own states* and gave severe punishments to any *state* or *local* lawmen who did not work to return escapees. Yet, it's incorrect to think that all Southerners were fighting to keep their slaves. There were fewer slaveholders than you might think, and many poor southern whites resented the economic competition created by slave labor.

In this tense climate, Congressional leaders worried that a direct address of the issues would split the country in two. While President James Buchanan said, "...above all, the Christian pulpit [has] been persistently employed in denouncing slavery as sin,"[71] he must have been referring to individual pastors, for my understanding is that many Christian church denominations, as a whole, avoided making a clear-cut statement against slavery because they feared splitting their membership.[72] Not the Quakers, though! They did much to organize and staff a secret escape route for slaves, which was nicknamed the *Underground Railroad*. An amazingly brave former slave, Harriet Tubman, helped many slaves escape through this network of homes, barns, and hideouts, as did many others.

Abolition

Very, very slowly, an *abolition* movement (a push to *abolish* slavery) was growing in the North. It was helped, to some degree, by the revivals occurring there,[73] since many felt that fighting slavery (which they deemed to be a great sin of selfishness) was putting their gospel into action. Charles Finney, the most famed northern revivalist, spoke forcefully against slavery![74] I'm forced to admit, though, that the

70 Carson 3:9.
71 James Buchanan, quoted by Carson 3:134.
72 Sorry, I cannot recall now where I read this.
73 Carson 3:86, 87, 91.
74 Carson 3:91.

number of church-attendees concerned about slavery seems disappointingly small. Were they too absorbed in their own lives? Were they too passive to analyze the rightness of an institution that was already well-established? Did they simply not notice it because it had always existed? Did they deem the fight to end slavery as impossible and therefore pointless? (I raise the question, in part, because we face the same issues with the current horror of abortion and other moral emergencies!)

Even amongst those who *did* work to abolish slavery, there was controversy. Some of these abolitionists, as they were called, were so harsh that they may have created a deeper divide and may have shamed the movement; yet we must at least give them credit for feeling an urgent burden for the plight of others. Abolitionists didn't even agree on how slavery should be abolished and what would become of the slaves! This was, though, a difficult question (for abolitionists *and* slave owners) because everyone knew that few whites would hire Negroes, especially since they had been kept uneducated. If freed, would ex-slaves—frustrated by their treatment both before and after emancipation—have greater capacity to seek violent revenge?

Yet, the South was in an increasingly difficult situation.[75] Their dependency on slaves was actually growing, for their slave-based economy had virtually extinguished free enterprise and any industry that might have arisen. Virtually all southern income was invested in one thing—more slaves—not the bridges, railroads, libraries, businesses, inventions, mills, and other tools which had prospered and diversified the North. Since *cotton was king*, as the saying went, the land was quickly worn out with the intense production of just one crop. What was happening? The entire South was becoming poor! Even many plantation owners! Why? When the originally high profits induced many to grow cotton, the greater supply made prices plummet. How could they endure the ending of slavery?

It seems that awful philosophy of utilitarianism seeped across both sides of the Mason-Dixon line (which happened to divide the slave and free states). Northerners might have criticized Southerners for justifying slavery on the grounds that it made possible their wholesome, agrarian, gracious, and elegant way of life, but was not that same principle justifying terrible, but lucrative, factory conditions?

Well, the deadlock could not go on forever. It didn't. Henry Clay worked hard on the Compromise of 1850 (including the *Fugitive Slave Act* mentioned above, as well as the entrance of California as a free state), but it didn't satisfy anyone for very long. Then, in the famous case of Dred Scott, a slave taken into free Illinois and Wisconsin, the Supreme Court denied him legal standing, since they didn't consider him an American. That stoked the fires of conflict even more. Ex-slaves, such as Frederick Douglass and Sojourner Truth, became significant leaders in the abolition movement. They spoke powerfully of their experiences as slaves and the desperate need for freedom. Then, in 1852, Lyman Beecher's daughter, Harriet Beecher Stowe, wrote *Uncle Tom's Cabin*, about the dreadful conditions of a southern slave. It greatly aroused anti-slavery feelings in the North. (Not many books can be described as helping start a war, but this is one of them!) John Greenleaf Whittier, a great Quaker poet, wrote many poems that helped the anti-slavery cause as well.

75 Carson 3:127-128, for the material in this paragraph.

Meanwhile, the South was eloquently defending its position and decrying *Uncle Tom's Cabin* for having presented an unusually bad situation. Senator John C. Calhoun, of South Carolina, was already talking about leaving the Union, and Senator Daniel Webster, a Northerner, was speaking powerfully in favor of Union!

Wow, it seems to me that only God can reveal His completely correct view of this very complex conflict. I pray you seek Him on this issue. (Begin *ThinkWrite 11* now.)

> ***ThinkWrite 11: "Shining Example"***
>
> Harriet Tubman, Frederick Douglass, and Sojourner Truth are shining examples of someone who doesn't just look out for themselves, but goes back to help others....at great risk. What does this show you? What does it make you think about what you can do with your own life?

36a General overview

**Story of the Great Republic*, by H.A. Guerber, Ch. XXVIIb-XXIX — Gr. 3-7

**This Country of Ours*, by H.E. Marshall, Ch. 78 — Gr. 3-8

**Basic History of the United States: Vol. 3*, by Clarence Carson, Ch. 7a-c — Gr. 9-12

Road to Fort Sumter, by Leroy Hayman — Gr. 5-10
This book was mentioned earlier, because it seeks to thoroughly explore the many causes of the Civil War, but I'll also mention here it here again.

**Nation Torn*, by Delia Ray, Ch. 2-3 (Young Readers' History of the Civil...) — Gr. 5-12

**Prelude to War*, by Carter Smith — Gr. 6-12

Fight for Union, by Margaret Coit — Gr. 7-12
This book was mentioned earlier, because it seeks to thoroughly explore the many causes of the Civil War, but I'll also mention it here again.

**Divided in Two*, by James Arnold — Unknown

36b Dred Scott decision

**Dred Scott Decision*, by Brendan January (Cornerstones of Freedom) — Gr. 3-6

36c Underground Railroad and slave escapes

I'll list different books than those cited the first time we discussed this issue. Then we looked more at the lives of slaves, and this time we'll focus more on the Underground Railroad, slave escapes, etc.

**Sounding Forth the Trumpet for Children*, by Marshall & Manuel, Ch. 1-4, 10-21 Gr. 1-5

**Story of the Great Republic*, by H.A. Guerber, Ch. XXXIII Gr. 3-7

**This Country of Ours*, by H.E. Marshall, Ch. 79 Gr. 3-8

From Sea to Shining Sea*, by Marshall & Manuel, Ch. 16 **and Gr. 6-12
**Sounding Forth the Trumpet*, by Marshall & Manuel, Ch. 1-9, 24-48

**Follow the Drinking Gourd*, by Jeanette Winter Gr. K-2
The *Drinking Gourd* is what the slaves called the *Big Dipper* that guided them north.

**Daring Escape of Ellen Craft*, by Cathy Moore (Carolrhoda On My Own) Gr. 1-3

**Liberty Street*, by Candice Ransom Gr. 1-4
Fredericksburg slave mother encourages her own daughter to escape to Canada.

**Drinking Gourd*, by F.N. Monjo (I Can Read book) Gr. 1-5

Freedom Ship of Robert Smalls, by Louise Meriwether Gr. 1-5

**If You Traveled on the Underground Railroad*, by Ellen Levine Gr. 1-6

**Story of the Underground Railroad*, by R. Conrad Stein (Cornerstones) Gr. 1-7
Now issued as: **The Underground Railroad.*

Escape, by Richard Boning Gr. 2-5
The daring escape of William and Ellen Craft.

**Freedom River*, by Doreen Rappaport Gr. 2-5
John Parker worked to buy his own freedom, and then tried to help others cross the Ohio River to freedom.

**President of the Underground Railroad: A Story about Levi Coffin* (Creative Minds) Gr. 2-7
by Gwenyth Swain

**Escape from Slavery*, by Doreen Rappaport Gr. 3-8
Five true stories of attempted slave escapes. What these people endured!

Escape by Night, by Helen Wells (Winston Adventure) Gr. 3-9
True story, involving young people.

**Two Tickets to Freedom*, by Florence Freedman Gr. 3-12
The amazing escape of William & Ellen Craft.

**Underground Railroad*, by R. Conrad Stein (Cornerstones) Gr. 4-7
The newly released Cornerstones usually have a little higher reading level.

**Get On Board: The Story of the Underground Railroad*, by Jim Haskins Gr. 4-9

**Many Thousand Gone*, by Virginia Hamilton Gr. 4-9
History of American slavery up to the 13th Amendment of 1865. You may have read the first portion when it was cited earlier.

**Send 'em South*, by Alan Kay (Young Heroes of History 1) Gr. 4-9
I've not read this, but see that it is about an escaping slave girl and the aid of a Boston boy who faces his own trials as son of an Irish immigrant.

**Underground Railroad*, by Raymond Bial Gr. 4-9
Strong photos and strong text give a good overview.

**Following Freedom's Star: Story of the Underground Railroad*, by James Haskins Gr. 4-12
I've not seen this, so can only guess the reading level based on his other books.

**Anthony Burns: The Defeat and Triumph of a Fugitive Slave*, by Virginia Hamilton Gr. 5-12
Very powerful, true story of legal battle over escaped slave. Shows the many forces at work, and how much the legal system denigrated the rights of Negroes.

**Bound for the North Star: True Stories of Fugitive Slaves*, by Dennis Fradin Gr. 5-12
I believe this includes several primary resources.

**Freedom Roads*, by Joyce Hansen & Gary McGowan Gr. 6-12
Using technology, experts try to locate real sites used by the Underground Railroad.

**North Star to Freedom*, by Gena Gorrell Gr. 6-12
This book is from the Canadian point of view, and relates that country's rich history in helping escaped American slaves and offering them a new life.

**Rebels Against Slavery*, by Patricia & Fred McKissack Gr. 6-12
I've not seen this book, but know it's about various slave revolts.

*_Slave Narratives: Journey to Freedom_, by Elaine Landau (In Their Own Voices) Gr. 6-12
The true stories of four slaves show unique attempts to escape slavery.

Flight to Freedom: The Story of the Underground Railroad, by Henrietta Buckmaster Gr. 7-12

Then Was the Future, by Douglas Miller (Living History Library), Ch. 6-7 Gr. 8-12
Fascinating account, since it contains many first-person narratives.

Captain of the "Planter," by Dorothy Sterling Gr. 9-12
Another version of the shipboard escape of Robert Small.

*_Fleeing for Freedom: Stories of the Underground Railroad as Told by Levi Coffin and William Still_ Gr. 10-12
edited by George & Willene Hendrick
Actual works of Coffin and Still (a free Philadelphia black gentleman) condensed; both of these gentleman were significant participants in the Underground Railroad.

Fiction/Historical Fiction

*_Good Night for Freedom_, by Barbara Morrow Gr. 1-3

*_Allen Jay and the Underground Railroad_, by Marlene Brill (On My Own) Gr. 1-4

*_Almost to Freedom_, by Vaunda Nelson Gr. 1-4
A slave girl's rag doll "tells" of their escape attempt.

*_Journey to Freedom_, by Courtni Wright Gr. 1-4
Escaping slaves call on God for help.

*_Secret to Freedom_, by Marcia Vaughan Gr. 1-4
Slave girl later finds out fate of her escaped brother and the role of a quilt pattern in showing the escape route.

*_Sweet Clara and the Freedom Quilt_, by Deborah Hopkinson Gr. 1-5
Slave girl makes quilt design that serves as map for the Underground Railroad.

*_Under the Quilt of Night_, by Deborah Hopkinson Gr. 1-6
Hopkinson's books are always poignant.

*_Nettie's Trip South_, by Ann Turner Gr. 2-6
Northern girl witnesses Southern slavery firsthand. This is a powerful book.

*_Meet Addy_, by Connie Porter (American Girls) Gr. 2-7
This is the first in the popular series.

*_Thee, Hannah_, by Marguerite de Angeli Gr. 2-7
Quaker girl appreciates values when she helps a runaway slave. Precious book!

Freedom Star, by Marcia Mathews Gr. 2-8
Slave boy must make his run for freedom alone!

*_Dear Austin: Letters from the Underground Railroad_, by Elvira Woodruff Gr. 3-7
Young boy, the son of freed slaves, tries to rescue sister stolen by slave traders.

*_Freedom's Wings_, by Sharon Wyeth (My America) Gr. 3-7
There are actually sequels which follow the same slave boy. I've not read this, but do know that some families like this series, while others do not.

*_Danger on the Railroad_; *_Time for Battle_ (American Adventure #21-22) Gr. 3-8
by Susan Martins Miller
These volumes are in a distinctly Christian series.

*_Personal Correspondence of Hannah Brown and Sarah Smith_ (Liberty Letters) Gr. 3-8
by Nancy LeSourd
Another in the series (a Christian alternative to the Dear America series) which uses fictional letters to show adventure on the Underground Railroad.

By Secret Railway, by Enid Meadowcroft Gr. 3-10
A white boy tries to rescue a free black boy who has been captured by slavers. Even Chicago is not safe for them in this suspenseful story.

Stranger in the Storm, by Charles May Gr. 3-10
I've not seen this, and we've not yet discussed settlement in Iowa, but in this story two girls face the Great Blizzard of 1850 _and_ strangers hunting for fugitive slaves.

*_Come Morning_, by Leslie Guccione Gr. 4-7
The son of a freed slave must step in to help runaways when his father disappears.

*_Caleb's Choice_, by G. Clifton Wisler Gr. 4-8
Boy in Texas is torn between the law against helping runaway slaves and his grandmother's work in helping them get to the Kansas Territory. I've not read this.

*_Escape into the Night_, by Lois Walfrid Johnson (Riverboat Adventures) Gr. 4-8
The first in a series; a girl helps runaway slaves on her father's steamboat.

Boy with a Pack, by Stephen Meader Gr. 4-12

Seventeen-year-old peddler gets involved in the Underground Railroad. Boys especially love Meader's books for their great adventure and tone!

**Brady*, by Jean Fritz Gr. 4-12

A boy's family becomes involved in the Underground Railroad.

**Bright Freedom's Song*, by Gloria Houston Gr. 5-10

I've not read this new novel, but see that a former indentured servant's daughter discovers that her father and an escaped slave friend use their North Carolina farm as a stop on the Underground Railroad.

**Cezanne Pinto*, by Mary Stolz Gr. 5-10

I've not read this, but it sounds interesting. It gives a glimpse of an escaping slave's life...as the hero makes it to Canada and then begins a vivid life. At age 90, he looks back on all.

Escape to Freedom, by Ruth Fosdick Jones Gr. 5-12

A boy helps escaping slaves.

**Freedom Crossing*, by Margaret Goff Clark Gr. 5-12

A girl struggles with her family's role in the Underground Railroad.

North Winds Blow Free, by Elizabeth Howard (two authors bear this name) Gr. 5-12

Michigan teen girl debates involvement in Underground Railroad.

Susanna and Tristam, by Marjorie Allee Gr. 5-12

Teen girl is asked to help on Underground Railroad; too rare to be actively sought.

Freedom River: Florida, 1845, by M. Douglas Gr. 6-12

This story reveals the impact of slavery on a white, a Negro, and an Indian.

Hannah Herself, by Ruth Franchere Gr. 6-12

Illinois families wrestle with the slavery question in this youth novel.

**Stealing Freedom*, by Elisa Carbone Gr. 6-12

I've not read this, but see that it is heavily based on the life of a real Maryland slave girl who attempted escape when the rest of her loving family was suddenly sold elsewhere.

Looking for Orlando, by Frances Browin Gr. 7-12

A southern teen becomes involved with the Pennsylvania Underground Railroad.

Silver Key, by Beverly Butler — Gr. 7-12
A Wisconsin family helps escaped slaves.

Rebellion at Christiana, by Margaret Bacon — Gr. 8-12
Fact-based story of former slaves who help others escape.

**Aquila's Drinking Gourd*, by Pamela Dell (Scrapbooks of America) — Unknown
I've not seen this book.

**Escape to Freedom: Underground Railroad Adventures of Callie and William* — Unknown
by Barbara Brooks-Simon
I've not seen this book published by National Geographic.

**Freedom's Tremendous Cost*, by Raelene Phillips — Unknown
Book, published by a Christian publisher, tells of an 85-year-old Ohio woman who helps escaping slaves.

**Underground Man*, by Milton Meltzer — Unknown
An Ohio River logger helps slaves trying to cross it to freedom.

**Winding Road to Freedom*, by Randall Wisehart — Unknown
Levi Coffin helps an escaped slave woman go back for her son.

Audio

**Escape*, by Sharon Gayle (Smithsonian Odyssey) — Various
In book/cassette combo, a modern girl visiting a Smithsonian display about the Underground Railroad is suddenly transported to it herself!

36d Activities

**Underground Railroad for Kids: From Slavery to Freedom with 21 Activities* — Various
by Mary Kay Carson

36e Harriet Tubman

This amazing woman, a former slave herself, led many others to freedom on the Underground Railroad at enormous risk. No wonder she is called the "Moses" of her people. You'll find oodles of books on Harriet Tubman, so I've tried to list ones that seem more interesting or available.

**Picture Book of Harriet Tubman*, by David Adler — Gr. K-2

**Young Harriet Tubman*, by Anne Benjamin (Troll First-Start) — Gr. K-2
This is a book/cassette tape combo.

**Escape North! Story of Harriet Tubman*, by M. Kulling (Step Into Reading 3) — Gr. 1-3

**Wanted Dead or Alive: The Story of Harriet Tubman*, by Ann McGovern — Gr. 1-3

**Harriet Tubman*, by Wil Mara (Rookie Biographies) — Gr. 1-4

Harriet Tubman: The Road to Freedom, by Ray Baines (Troll) — Gr. 1-4

**Minty: Young Harriet Tubman*, by Alan Schroder — Gr. 1-4
Nicely illustrated picture-book biography.

Value of Helping: Harriet Tubman, by Anne Johnson (ValueTales) — Gr. 1-4

Harriet Tubman, by Gertrude Winders (Childhood) — Gr. 1-6
Also has been rewritten by Kathleen Kudlinski and reissued as **Harriet Tubman*. I don't know how much it has changed from the solid original.

Harriet Tubman: Flame of Freedom, by F. Humphreville (Piper) — Gr. 2-7
The Piper series is a favorite of mine, though I've not read this particular book.

**Go Free or Die*, by Jeri Ferris (Carolrhoda Creative Minds) — Gr. 2-8

**Hero Tales: Vol. I*, by Dave & Neta Jackson — Gr. 3-6
One of the chapters in this first volume covers Tubman.

**Story of Harriet Tubman*, by Kate McMullan — Gr. 3-7

Harriet Tubman: Guide to Freedom, by Sam & Beryl Epstein (Garr. Am. All) — Gr. 3-9

**Freedom Train: The Story of Harriet Tubman*, by Dorothy Sterling — Gr. 3-12

**Courage to Run*, by Wendy Lawton (Daughters of the Faith) — Gr. 4-8
This series, from Moody Press, tells the dramatic tale of Ms. Tubman.

Harriet Tubman, by Norma Jean Lutz (Famous Figures of the Civil War) Gr. 4-8
I've seen this author writing for Christian publishers.

Harriet Tubman: Conductor on the Underground Railroad, by Ann Petry Gr. 5-12

**Harriet Tubman: Freedombound*, by Janet & Geoff Benge (Christian Heroes) Gr. 5-12
This is in a distinctly Christian biography series.

Audio

**Young Harriet Tubman*, by Anne Benjamin (book/tape combo) Gr. K-2

Fiction/Historical Fiction

**Listen for the Whippoorwill*, by Dave & Neta Jackson (Trailblazer) Gr. 2-9
In this Christian series, fictional kids have adventures with this real heroine!

Railroad to Freedom, by Hildegarde Swift Gr. 4-12

36f Sojourner Truth

This ex-slave seems notably brave and godly; she traveled long miles speaking out against slavery. Be careful of books which are too politically correct.

**Picture Book of Sojourner Truth*, by David Adler Gr. K-2

Sojourner Truth: Freedom-Fighter, by Julian May Gr. 2-6

**Walking the Road to Freedom*, by Jeri Ferris (Creative Minds) Gr. 2-8

**Only Passing Through: Story of Sojourner Truth*, by Anne Rockwell Gr. 3-7
I've not read this biography; it has modern, impressionistic illustrations.

**Sojourner Truth*, by Peter & Connie Roop Gr. 3-7
I've not read this biography either, but it supposedly draws from many resources.

Sojourner Truth: Fearless Crusader, by Helen Peterson (Garrard Americans All) Gr. 3-9

**Sojourner Truth: Abolitionist, Suffragist, and Preacher*, by Norma Jean Lutz Gr. 6-12
I've not seen this, but Lutz has written for Christian publishers.

Sojourner Truth: Slave, Abolitionist, Fighter for Women's Rights (Messner) Gr. 7-12
by Aletha Lindstrom

36g Frederick Douglass

You'll find oodles of books on Frederick Douglass, since he was a crucial and tireless leader in the abolition movement and an ex-slave himself. I've tried to select ones that seem more interesting or available. Beware of books which are too politically correct.

Frederick Douglass, by Charles Graves (See and Read) Gr. K-2

**Picture Book of Frederick Douglass*, by David Adler Gr. K-2

**Young Frederick Douglass: Fight for Freedom*, by Laurence Santrey (Troll) Gr. K-2

**Frederick Douglass: The Last Day of Slavery*, by William Miller Gr. 1-3
I've not seen this, but it sounds interesting.

Frederick Douglass: Freedom Fighter, by Lillie Patterson (Garrard) Gr. 1-4

Frederick Douglass, by Elisabeth Myers (Childhood) Gr. 1-6
Series is being reprinted as Young Patriot books, so this may come back in print!

**Frederick Douglass Fights for Freedom*, by Margaret Davidson Gr. 2-7

**Voice of Freedom: Story about Frederick Douglass*, by M. Weidt (Creative Minds) Gr. 2-7

**Escape from Slavery: Boyhood of Frederick Douglass*, by Douglass & McCurdy Gr. 2-10
Highly abridged excerpts from Douglass's own autobiography.

**Frederick Douglass You Never Knew*, by James Collier Gr. 3-7

**Story of Frederick Douglass*, by Eric Weiner Gr. 3-7

**Frederick Douglass*, by Norma Jean Lutz (Famous Figures of the Civil War...) Gr. 4-8

Frederick Douglass: Slave-Fighter-Freeman, by Arna Bontemps Gr. 5-10

**Frederick Douglass: In His Own Words*, edited by Milton Meltzer Gr. 6-12
Excerpts from Douglass's life story, speeches, and writings.

**Narrative of the Life of Frederick Douglass*, by Frederick Douglass — Gr. 7-12
His own powerful life story.

Our Blood and Tears, by Ruth Wilson — Gr. 7-12
Contains a section on Frederick Douglass.

**Invitation to the Classics*, edited by Cowan & Guinness, pp. 233-236 — Gr. 8-12
Christian analysis of famous authors and literature.

Fiction/Historical Fiction

**Caught in the Rebel Camp*, by Dave & Neta Jackson (Trailblazer) — Gr. 3-9
Fictional boy (who is handicapped) meets Frederick Douglass.

36h Other noteworthy ex-slaves and abolitionists

Once out of slavery herself, Clara Brown worked extremely hard to build a new life in Colorado, became a leading citizen there, and was able to help many other slaves. Lucretia Mott was a Quaker woman who became deeply concerned about the plight of slaves; she then noticed that women were under some of the same prohibitions (such as on owning property) and began working in both fields...as happened with several other abolitionists, by the way. This means books about Mott can be especially politically correct; be careful. As a strong Quaker, Mott may have had a scriptural perspective on these issues, but modern books may not relate that. (We'll tackle woman's suffrage in the next guide.) William Lloyd Garrison was the chief editor of a leading abolition newspaper.

**Alec's Primer*, by Mildred Walter — Gr. 1-3
True story of Alec Turner, a slave boy who learns to read and then....

**Aunt Clara Brown*, by Linda Lowery (On My Own) — Gr. 1-5

Lucretia Mott: Foe of Slavery, by Doris Faber (Garrard Discovery) — Gr. 1-5

Lucretia Mott, by Constance Burnett (Childhood) — Gr. 1-6

**Lucretia Mott*, by Lucile Davis (Photo-Illustrated Biography) — Gr. 2-5

Lives of Poor Boys Who Became Famous, by Sarah Bolton, Ch. 7 — Gr. 4-12
Chapter covers William Lloyd Garrison, who edited a strong abolitionist newspaper.

Charlotte Forten, by Peter Burchard — Gr. 6-12
Black teacher worked hard to educate black children during Civil War era.

**One More Valley, One More Hill: Story of Aunt Clara Brown*, by Linda Lowery — Gr. 6-12

I Will Be Heard, by Doris Faber — Gr. 7-12
Biography of William Lloyd Garrison

Road to Freedom: 1815-1900, by James McCague — Gr. 7-12

Angry Abolitionist: William Lloyd Garrison, by Jules Archer (Messner) — Gr. 8-12

Lucretia Mott: Gentle Warrior, by Dorothy Sterling — Gr. 8-12

Thaddeus Stevens and the Fight for Negro Rights, by Milton Meltzer — Gr. 9-12

Fiction/Historical Fiction

**If You Please, President Lincoln*, by Harriette Robinet — Gr. 5-12
Though this book is slightly ahead of this time period, it is based on a real attempt to send ex-slaves to a colony in the Caribbean, a topic much debated by abolitionists.

36i Harriet Beecher Stowe and her book, *Uncle Tom's Cabin*

**Picture Book of Harriet Beecher Stowe*, by David Adler — Gr. K-2

Harriet Beecher Stowe, by Mabel Widdemer (Childhood) — Gr. 1-6

Harriet and the Runaway Book, by Johanna Johnston — Gr. 2-7
Very nice biography of Stowe which reveals the impact of her book.

Harriet Beecher Stowe, by Winifred Wise (Lives to Remember) — Gr. 6-12

**Harriet Beecher Stowe and the Beecher Preachers*, by Jean Fritz — Gr. 6-12
Caution! Mrs. Fritz is consistently anti-Christian, so she probably takes a negative view of the Beecher family. I list this book as relevant, but not recommended.

**More than Conquerors*, edited by John Woodbridge, pp. 100-103 — Gr. 7-12
This is a compendium of short biographies of Christian heroes.

Truth about the Man Behind the Book, by Frances Cavanah — Gr. 7-12
This reveals the real slave, Josiah Henson, upon which Mrs. Stowe built her story.

**Uncle Tom's Cabin*, by Harriet Beecher Stowe — Parental decision

Unfortunately, though this book was read by untold numbers of Americans, it is very difficult for modern readers, because it is uses lengthy sentences and dialogue. There are abridged versions. Those who have read the original do speak very highly of it!

Film

**Uncle Tom's Cabin*

Film version, starring Phylicia Rashad. Presents good values of Tom. Some scenes, such as when Tom is being beaten, may be too intense for some viewers.

36j John Greenleaf Whittier

John Greenleaf Whittier: Fighting Quaker, by Ruth Holberg — Gr. 5-12

36k Henry Clay

Henry Clay: Leader in Congress, by Helen Peterson (Garrard Discovery) — Gr. 1-5

Henry Clay, by Helen Monsell (Childhood) — Gr. 1-6

This series is being reprinted as Young Patriot books, so this may come into print!

Henry Clay: Statesman and Patriot, by Regina Kelly (Piper) — Gr. 3-9

Henry Clay, by Booth Mooney — Gr. 5-12

Man Who Wouldn't Give Up: Henry Clay, by Katharine Wilkie (Messner) — Gr. 7-12

**Henry Clay*, by Alison Tibbitts (Historical American Biographies) — Unknown

**Henry Clay: The Great Compromiser*, by Michael Burgan (Our People) — Unknown

36l John Calhoun

Patriotic Rebel: John Calhoun, by William Crane (Messner) — Gr. 5-12

**John C. Calhoun and the Roots of War*, by Thomas Durwood — Unknown

36m Daniel Webster

Dan Webster, by Bradford Smith (Childhood) Gr. 1-6

**Daniel Webster*, by Robert Allen (Sower) Gr. 5-12
Distinctly Christian biography.

**Daniel Webster: Liberty and Union, Now and Forever*, by Bonnie Harvey Gr. 5-12

Daniel Webster, by Alfred Steinberg Gr. 6-12

**Patriot's Handbook*, by George Grant Gr. 9-12
Some of Webster's speeches have been recorded in Grant's book.

Fiction/Historical Fiction

**Devil and Daniel Webster*, by Stephen Vincent Benét Gr. 6-12
Classic, witty piece of American lit! It's not dark, as you might think by the title.

37 Bleeding Kansas

America was aboil with sectionalism and argument. It wasn't long, though, before more than hot words were flying. Hot *lead* was flying! One of the first breakouts was in Kansas. Why there? Well, you just learned that Stephen Douglas's Kansas-Nebraska Act, which was to help determine the course of a future transcontinental railroad, carved out a new territory, with Kansas having slavery....if the residents so chose.[76] Immediately, folks of both stripes (slave and free) rushed in, many for no other reason than to get a majority, elect leaders from their party, and get the Kansas constitution to line up with their point of view. You can understand why, certainly, but all sorts of fraud, maneuvering, and strong-arming also went on. Some "border ruffians" from pro-slavery Missouri weren't afraid to get rough, but the anti-slavery settlers were having none of it...and dished out their own! They sent armed parties around the territory and into Missouri, and pulled some shady dealings themselves. For a while, there were actually two rival governments (1856), though neither was legal or effective.[77] President Pierce had to get make a decision, and he came down on the pro-slavery side.[78] A *super* intense abolitionist from back east, named John Brown, rushed into the Kansas fray. (Believe me, you'll be hearing more about Mr. Brown, because he felt slavery was *so* wrong that just about anything could rightfully be done to stop it.) Let me give you a taste of all that was happening in Kansas:

76 Carson 3:126.
77 Carson 3:136.
78 Morris 220.

Actual civil war broke out in Kansas in the late spring of 1856, by which time the Free State party had received from the East fresh shipments of arms (the Sharps rifles, popularly known as "Beecher's Bibles"). On 21 May, Lawrence [a leading city in Kansas] *was taken and sacked, as "Border Ruffians" joined Kansas proslavery men in burning down the Free State Hotel, pillaging many homes, and destroying the offices and presses of* [anti-slavery newspapers]. *Two lives were lost. Exaggerated accounts of the Lawrence affair inflamed Northern antislavery sentiment.*

In retaliation..., the fanatical John Brown, with seven companions, carried out the Pottawatomie massacre...with midnight executions of five proslavery colonists. Free State men disavowed this act of terrorism, but the incident raised feeling to a pitch and caused both parties to alert their military forces.[79]

Indeed, even back in Washington—in the very Capitol—it came to blows! When a northern senator delivered a loaded speech about the Kansas situation and insulted a southern senator, his son-in-law, a South Carolina representative, beat him with his cane to the point of unconsciousness![80] **The northerners nursed a new grudge and the southerners cheered a new hero!**

You need to see too, though, that even the anti-slavery Kansans passed a law barring Negroes from entering the territory;[81] **Negroes were between a rock and a hard place. Anyway, the territory earned the nickname *Bleeding Kansas*, and Americans were now putting weapons...or walking instruments...behind their words. Whew-ee!**

**Story of the Great Republic*, by H.A. Guerber, Ch. XXXIV — Gr. 3-7
The main portion of this chapter, despite its title, refers to our topic here.

**This Country of Ours*, by H.E. Marshall, Ch. 80 — Gr. 3-8

**Rangers, Jayhawkers, and Bushwhackers in the Civil War* (Untold History of...) by Douglas Savage — Gr. 4-8

Border Hawk: August Bondi, by Lloyd Alexander (Covenant) — Gr. 4-12
A Jewish immigrant works with John Brown in the border conflict.

**Nation Torn*, by Delia Ray, Ch. 4 (Young Readers' History of the Civil War) Gr. 5-12

Fiction/Historical Fiction

Sod House, by Elizabeth Coatsworth — Gr. 3-8
An immigrant family in Kansas wants slaves to be freed.

79 Morris 220.
80 Morris 221.
81 Morris 219.

Island on the Border, by Trella Dick — Gr. 4-12

An anti-slavery family must hide on an island.

Posse of Two, by Gertrude Bell — Gr. 5-12

Boys go after raiders.

**Jayhawkers*, by Patricia Beatty — Gr. 6-12

An intense and exciting story, from what I've heard, of the Kansas conflict which does, alas, include some instances of taking the Lord's name in vain.

38 John Brown's Raid

You already met John Brown out in Kansas. Well, now he was in Maryland...collecting arms...and getting ready to launch a slave revolt. What happened...and what did he raid in 1859? And who led the federal forces that captured him? You better learn the story of John Brown's Raid! But let me first quote Mr. Carson:

> *The raid stirred up feeling in the South, where Brown's activities were not only blamed on abolitionists but also on Republicans* [the party against slavery]. *On the other hand, John Brown was hailed as a martyr by abolitionists and eventually became a symbol of an undying spirit to put down slavery in the North. Feeling was outrunning reason.*[82]

Ready! Set! Find out!

**Story of the Great Republic*, by H.A. Guerber, Ch. XXXV — Gr. 3-7

John Brown: One Man Against Slavery, by Gwen Everett — Gr. 2-4

Powerful prose.

**John Brown*, by Thomas Streissguth (Carolrhoda) — Gr. 2-5

Story of John Brown's Raid, by Zachary Kent (Cornerstones) — Gr. 3-8

**John Brown: Abolitionist*, by Virginia Brackett (Famous Figures of the...) — Gr. 4-8

**John Brown's Raid on Harpers Ferry*, by Brendan January (Cornerstones II) — Gr. 4-10

New Cornerstones series is usually written for slightly older readers.

---

82 Carson 140.

**Harpers Ferry: The Story of John Brown's Raid*, by Tracy Barrett Gr. 5-10

**John Brown's Raid on Harpers Ferry*, by R. Conrad Stein (In American History) Gr. 6-12

John Brown, by Jeannette Covert Nolan (Messner) Gr. 7-12

John Brown: A Cry for Freedom, by Lorenz Graham Gr. 8-12

Fiction/Historical Fiction

**On the Trail of John Brown's Body*, by Alan Kay (Young Heroes of History 1) Gr. 4-9
I've not read this, but see it is the story of two boys who get involved with Brown.

**Lightning Time*, by Douglas Rees Gr. 5-10
I have not read this story, but see that it's the tale of a Quaker boy joining Brown for the Harpers Ferry raid; unknown content.

Benjie Ream, by C. G. Hodges Gr. 7-12
Kansas boy works with John Brown.

**John Brown's Body*, by Stephen Vincent Benét Gr. 10-12
You're probably already familiar with this famous work of American literature.

39 Presidential Election of 1860...and Abraham Lincoln

Now that you've met John Brown, maybe you can better understand something my son's history professor said: southerners began assuming *many* northerners were like John Brown: hotheaded, destructive, and overpowering. They already saw the federal government (especially after some of the intense speeches in Congress) as being the same. To again paraphrase my son's professor, the South seemed to feel the North wanted to overwhelm even its way of life—which happened to rely significantly on slavery. The idea of sharing a nation with millions of John Browns wasn't at all attractive. Indeed, southerners were weary of being made to feel unChristian for their stand on slavery.[83] I will admit that I do not understand this, because they were asking the federal government to reopen ports to foreign slave-selling ships[84] (these slaves had been captured against their will), and were otherwise seeking not only federal protection of slavery, but its *expansion* into new American territories,[85] in spite of what the South had promised during the original Constitutional convention. Of course, this is a lesson to us all, for we tend to assume—North and South—that whatever we grew up thinking is automatically right...but 't'ain't always so! We all have to submit our thinking to the plumb-line of God's thinking.

83 Carson 133-134.

84 Morris 225-226.

85 Carson 131.

As we've been saying, though, slavery was not the only—or really even the main—reason for the war. Yet, it was closely linked. What really was at stake was how the two regions had become so different, and especially how differently they had come to see the United States itself!

Maybe the Confederate Vice President, Alexander Stephens, said it best:

> *Slavery, so called, was but the* question *on which these two antagonistic principles, which had been in conflict, from the beginning on...were finally brought into actual and active collision with each other on the field of battle.*[86]

I'll try to describe what some of those "antagonistic principles" were. You older students should be able to follow along. You see, the South viewed the individual state as the key component of political power because the states existed *before* the United States of America. (Remember the old individual colonies and the way the independent states worked together under the Articles of Confederation?) So, southerners felt that the United States existed only because the states agreed to let it play a certain, limited, and beneficial role. Any time a state decided the United States (federal government) no longer had a beneficial role, that state could withdraw its support and its membership. Northerners saw things differently. They felt the United States government got its role from individual people, and since a majority of the people in the United States wanted the United States to continue its existence, then any particular state that backed out because it wanted to go its own way was rebellious; it was going against the will of most Americans.

Do you see the difference? Northerners saw themselves as Americans first (especially the many immigrants, who settled mostly in the north).[87] Southerners saw themselves as Virginians or South Carolinians or Georgians first, and Americans second.

So...when Lincoln was elected and it became obvious that the northern view of government had prevailed, the southern states did secede...they declared they were no longer part of the United States of America.[88] Mr. Carson comments:

> *The South did not secede from the Union simply because opponents in the North labeled slavery a sin, of course. Those Southern states which seceded did so after it became clear that those who were determined to stop slavery and undermine it had gained power over much of the government. Above all, the states which led in secession did so when all doubt had been removed that they had no hope of using the government effectively for expanding and maintaining slavery.*[89]

That northern commitment to keeping the union together (and—for some—resisting slavery) revealed, in the southern mind, the role northerners felt government should play because it elevated the opinions of the nation's people over the opinions of each state. Indeed, when Lincoln was campaigning for the Senate back in Illinois, when engaged in the famous Lincoln-Douglas debates (1858), and when running for president, Lincoln had made

86 Stephens, quoted in Carson 3:146.
87 Carson 3:127, 146-147.
88 Carson 3:141.
89 Carson 3:136.

it clear that he didn't believe a state could secede. He felt that the states (representing all the people) had agreed together to be a nation, and that only *together* could they agree to disband that nation.[90] Unlike the southerners, he felt he was doing the right thing to hold the Union together. He spoke to both issues in his inaugural address:

> *I have no purpose directly or indirectly to interfere with the institution of slavery in the States where it exists..... No State, upon its own mere action, can lawfully get out of the Union.*[91]

I'll say no more, but do know that Lincoln's beliefs were soon put to the test, for gunfire followed quickly after his election! It's no surprise, then, that folks in the North and South still feel differently about Abraham Lincoln. They interpret his beliefs, words, and actions in quite divergent ways.

What would happen at this stormy moment in American history? You'll have to find out! We'll first see Lincoln's rise to power, and will then go back and learn about his life, family, and more. You'll even learn about his harrowing inaugural journey into Washington, D.C. What a story it is!

39a Election of 1860 and the North

**Story of the Great Republic*, by H.A. Guerber, Ch. XXXVI — Gr. 3-7

**This Country of Ours*, by H.E. Marshall, Ch. 82 — Gr. 3-8
This chapter covers the last of Buchanan's term and the beginning of Lincoln's.

**Story of the Election of 1860*, by R. Conrad Stein (Cornerstones) — Gr. 2-6

Fight for Union, by Margaret Coit — Gr. 7-12
Select pertinent portions.

39b Northern overview

Because the election of 1860 is said to have revealed the Northern mindset, we'll tuck here a quick overview for anyone desiring it.

**Northerners*, by John Dunn (Voices from the Civil War) — Unknown

Activities

**Civil War Cooking: The Union*, by Susan Dosier — Various

90 Carson 3:147.
91 Morris 229.

39c Lincoln-Douglas debates

**Lincoln-Douglas Debates*, by Michael Burgan (We the People) Gr. 3-5

Lincoln and Douglas: The Years of Decision, by Regina Kelly (Landmark) Gr. 3-8

**Lincoln-Douglas Debates*, by Brendan January (Cornerstones II) Gr. 4-8

**Stephen Douglas: Champion of the Union*, by Mike Bonner (Famous Figures...) Gr. 4-8

Little Giant: Stephen A. Douglas, by Jeannette Covert Nolan (Messner) Gr. 6-12

Fiction/Historical Fiction

Henry's Lincoln, by Louise Neyhart Gr. 1-6
Fictional boy witnesses the Lincoln-Douglas debates.

39d Abraham Lincoln

There are so many books on Lincoln! I'll try to focus this list on the more noteworthy or available titles.

**Young Abraham Lincoln*, by Woods (Troll First-Start) Gr. K-1

**Picture Book of Abraham Lincoln*, by David Adler Gr. K-2

**Abraham Lincoln: A Man for All the People*, by Myra Cohn Livingston Gr. K-4
A high-toned ballad for the young.

**Abe Lincoln and the Muddy Pig*, by Stephen Krensky (Ready-to-Read 2) Gr. 1-2

Abraham Lincoln, by Patricia Miles Martin (See and Read) Gr. 1-2

**Abe Lincoln Remembers*, by Ann Turner Gr. 1-3
A very poignant picture-book biography. It's current and should be easy to find!

**Abe Lincoln: The Boy Who Loved Books*, by Kay Winter Gr. 1-3

**Abe Lincoln's Hat*, by Martha Brenner (Step into Reading 2) Gr. 1-3

**Abraham Lincoln*, by Ingri & Edgar d'Aulaire Gr. 1-3
The d'Aulaire picture biographies are much beloved. Don't miss this one!

**Abraham Lincoln*, by Carol Greene (Rookie Biography) Gr. 1-3

Indy and Mr. Lincoln, by Natalia Belting Gr. 1-3
A pig gets to know young Lincoln while he lived in Indiana.

**If You Grew Up with Abraham Lincoln*, by Ann McGovern Gr. 1-4
See what life was like in America during the time of Lincoln's boyhood.

**Meet Abraham Lincoln*, by Barbara Cary (Step-Up Books) Gr. 1-4

**Mr. Lincoln's Whiskers*, by Karen Winnick Gr. 1-4
The interesting story of the real girl who suggested to Lincoln that he grow a beard!

Value of Respect: Abraham Lincoln, by Johnson (ValueTales) Gr. 1-4

Young Abe Lincoln: The Frontier Days, 1809-1837*, **and, Gr. 1-4
**Abe Lincoln Goes to Washington*, both by Cheryl Harness
These two richly illustrated books together show Lincoln's life.

Abe Lincoln's Hobby, by Helen Kay Gr. 1-5
Relates Lincoln's love of cats; unfortunately, this is an older, hard-to-find book.

**Abraham Lincoln: For the People*, by Anne Colver (Discovery) Gr. 1-5

**Abraham Lincoln*, by Augusta Stevenson (Childhood) Gr. 1-6

Lincoln's Birthday, by Clyde Robert Bulla Gr. 1-6

Abe Lincoln's Beard, by Jan Wahl Gr. 1-8
Though this relates the beard story, it's laid out more like a scrapbook of Lincoln's own childhood. This is a very creative book!

**Abraham Lincoln*, by Amy Cohn & Suzy Schmidt Gr. 2-5

**Grace's Letter to Lincoln*, by Peter & Connie Roop Gr. 2-5
This is the most recent book on the topic of the girl who wrote to Lincoln suggesting he grow a beard, so should be the easiest to find.

**When Abraham Lincoln Talked to the Trees*, by Elizabeth Van Steenwyk Gr. 2-5
Lincoln practices oration by repeating sermons out in the woods.

Lincoln's Little Correspondent, by Hertha Pauli Gr. 2-6
Another story of the girl who wrote to Lincoln suggesting he grow a beard.

Abraham Lincoln: Man of Courage, by Bernadine Bailey (Piper) Gr. 2-7

Abraham Lincoln: An Initial Biography, by Genevieve Foster Gr. 2-7

Mr. Lincoln's Whiskers, by Burke Davis Gr. 2-8
One more story of the girl who wrote to Lincoln suggesting he grow a beard.

**Where Lincoln Walked*, by Raymond Bial Gr. 2-12
All ages would enjoy seeing vivid photos of Lincoln's boyhood homes, farms, etc.

1861: Year of Lincoln, by Genevieve Foster Gr. 3-7
This relates other events around the world, as well as the deeds of Lincoln.

Abe Lincoln Gets His Chance, by Frances Cavanah Gr. 3-8

**Abe Lincoln: Log Cabin to White House*, by Sterling North (Landmark) Gr. 3-8

Abraham Lincoln: Courageous Leader, by L. Bragdon (Makers of America) Gr. 3-8

Story of Abraham Lincoln, by Nina Brown Baker (Signature) Gr. 3-8

**Abraham Lincoln's World*, by Genevieve Foster Gr. 3-10

**Lincoln: A Photobiography*, by Russell Freedman Gr. 3-10
The first non-fiction book to win the Newbery Medal.

**River Road: A Story of Abraham Lincoln*, by Meridel LeSueur Gr. 3-10
Relates Lincoln's adventures when as a young man he rafted down the Mississippi.

**Abraham Lincoln*, by James Daugherty Gr. 3-12

**Abraham Lincoln: Friend of the People* Gr. 4-9
by Clara Ingram Judson
I've been told this is *very* good!

America's Abraham Lincoln, by M. McNeer Gr. 4-9

**Abe Lincoln Grows Up*, by Carl Sandburg Gr. 4-10

Just for fun....

Abraham Lincoln Joke Book Gr. 3-8
by Beatrice DeRegniers
Collection of funny stories told by, and about, Lincoln!

Abraham Lincoln, by Enid Lamonte Meadowcroft Gr. 5-9

**Abraham Lincoln*, by Janet & Geoff Benge (Christian Heroes) Gr. 5-12

Life in Lincoln's America, by Helen Reeder Cross (Landmark Giant) Gr. 5-12
See what American life was like during the years of Lincoln.

Lincoln Stories, by Honoré Morrow Gr. 5-12

**Nation Torn*, by Delia Ray, Ch. 5 (Young Readers' History of the Civil War) Gr. 5-12

**Abraham Lincoln*, by David Collins (Sower) Gr. 6-12
Distinctly Christian biography.

Abraham Lincoln, by Jeannette Covert Nolan (Messner) Gr. 7-12

**Abraham Lincoln: The Writer*, by Abraham Lincoln, edited by Harold Holzer Gr. 7-12
Holzer has collected and commented upon many of Lincoln's writings, from rhymes in the margins of his school books all the way to famous speeches, poems, and letters.

**More than Conquerors*, edited by John Woodbridge, pp. 14-21 Gr. 7-12
This is a compendium of short biographies of Christian heroes.

**Commander in Chief: Abraham Lincoln and the Civil War*, by Albert Marrin Gr. 8-12

Film

**Abraham Lincoln*, a very, very old film starring Walter Huston All ages

**Young Mr. Lincoln*, starring Henry Fonda All ages
Great film about Lincoln as a young country lawyer!

Audio

**Your Story Hour: Volume 6* audio All ages

Fiction/Historical Fiction

Martin and Abraham Lincoln, by Catherine Coblentz Gr. K-3
True story in picture-book format; son of Union prisoner-of-war meets Lincoln; this is rare, older, and lovely!

**A. Lincoln and Me*, by Louise Borden Gr. 1-3
Very nice book: a modern boy shares both a birthday and traits with Lincoln.

We Were There with Lincoln in the White House, by Earl Miers (We Were There) Gr. 3-8
I've heard this book (though part of a beloved series) was not well-written, although I've enjoyed books by this author; it's very rare and expensive to purchase used, so don't feel pressure to locate a copy.

Elizabeth for Lincoln, by Jacqueline McNicol Gr. 3-12
Fact-based story of a young girl (babysitter?) in Lincoln's home who helps out!

More than Halfway There, by Janet Ervin Gr. 3-12
Young Lincoln encourages a boy to get educated.

Abe Lincoln's Birthday, by Wilma Pitchford Hays Gr. 4-8
Story pictures Lincoln's twelfth birthday.

Longshanks, by Stephen Meader Gr. 4-12
Another exciting tale! Boy robbed by river pirates escapes to young Abe's raft.

Mary Florence: Little Girl Who Knew Lincoln, by Kathleen Tiffany Gr. 4-12

Great Captain, by Honoré Morrow Gr. 9-12
Novel of Lincoln's life.

39e Activities

**Abraham Lincoln and His Family Paper Dolls* (Dover) Various

**Abraham Lincoln Coloring Book*, by A.G. Smith (Dover) Various

**What Was Cooking in Mary Todd Lincoln's White House*, by Tanya Larkin Various

39f Lincoln's dangerous inaugural journey

A key role was played by Allan Pinkerton, the great detective, who saw the need to found the Secret Service.

Allan Pinkerton: First Private Eye, by LaVere Anderson (Garrard Am. All) Gr. 1-5

Allan Pinkerton, by Borland & Speicher (Childhood) Gr. 1-6

Detective Pinkerton and Mr. Lincoln, by William Wise Gr. 2-6

Allan Pinkerton, by Carl Green & William Sanford Gr. 4-7

Mr. Lincoln's Inaugural Journey, by Mary Kay Phelan — Gr. 4-12

Allan Pinkerton: America's First Private Eye, by Sigmund Lavine — Gr. 5-12

Pinkerton: America's First Private Eye, by Richard Wormser — Gr. 6-12

Master Detective: Allan Pinkerton, by Arthur Orrmont (Messner) — Gr. 7-12

39g Lincoln's family

Because there are so many books about Lincoln's family we'll put them in a section of their own. You know that Mary Todd Lincoln was his wife, Robert, Tad, and Willie were his sons, Nancy Hanks was his mother, and Sarah Bush Lincoln was his step-mother, marrying his father after Nancy died. Lincoln was extremely fond of women. There are many book series about the First Ladies, so we've listed just one example. You'll easily find many choices.

Mary Todd Lincoln: President's Wife, by LaVere Anderson (Garrard Discovery) — Gr. 1-5

Nancy Hanks of Wilderness Road, by Meridel LeSueur — Gr. 1-5
Nancy was Lincoln's dear mother.

Tad Lincoln: Abe's Son, by LaVere Anderson (Garrard Discovery) — Gr. 1-5

**Mary Todd Lincoln*, by Katharine Wilkie (Childhood) — Gr. 1-6

Nancy Hanks, by Augusta Stevenson (Childhood) — Gr. 1-6

Robert Todd Lincoln, by LaVere Anderson (Childhood) — Gr. 1-6

Tad Lincoln: White House Wildcat, by David Collins — Gr. 1-6

Me and Willie and Pa, by F.N. Monjo — Gr. 2-6
A happy family story from Tad's point of view. Don't miss this one!

Tad Lincoln and the Green Umbrella, by Margaret Friskey — Gr. 3-10
I have to admit that I don't know if this is a true story or not, but it's sure to be fun!

**Mothers of Famous Men*, by Archer Wallace, Ch. III-IV (Lamplighter) — Gr. 3-12
There is a chapter on both Nancy and Sarah!

Abe Lincoln's Other Mother, by Bernadine Bailey (Messner) — Gr. 4-12
Sarah actually had more time with Lincoln and was much loved by him.

Buffalo Trace: A Story of Abraham Lincoln's Ancestors, by Virginia Eifert — Gr. 6-12
Lincoln's grandfather pioneers in Kentucky.

**Mary Todd Lincoln*, by Dan Santow (Encyclopedia of First Ladies) — Unknown

Film

**Last of Mrs. Lincoln*
Video of Broadway play showing final years of Mary Todd Lincoln. — Unknown

Fiction/Historical Fiction

**Thanksgiving in the White House*, by Gary Hines — Gr. 1-3
Will Tad's pet turkey end up on the Thanksgiving table?

40 Confederate States of America

As you know, several states left the Union when Lincoln was made president. They formed the Confederate States of America (CSA). Their first, and only, president was Jefferson Davis. It wasn't long before the CSA called on Washington to give up all federal territory in the South, such as forts. To comply would mean Washington (the Union) was agreeing to secession.

The Confederacy must have known it would be tough going, for their population was 9 million (3.5 million of that number being slaves), while the population of the remaining Union was 23 million. Besides, the northern economy was very strong and diverse, factories rapidly churned out mechanical items, immigrants were still pouring in (400,000 would serve in the Union army), and the railroad system thoroughly united all parts. The South, basically, had one industry: agriculture. It had always relied on the North for banking, shipping, industrial products, etc. The Confederates doggedly moved ahead, though![92]

If you're going to be "in the know," you must be made aware of two important facts. First, there were four slave states which never did secede—Missouri, Kentucky, Maryland, and Delaware. Don't get me wrong, though. It was *very* tense in these Border States. Secondly, Virginia was one of the states which did later secede—after fierce deliberation—but a large group of counties in the western part of the state disagreed. They eventually became a state of their own—West Virginia—and adopted a constitution which gradually freed the slaves.[93]

92 Morris 230, and Delia Ray, *A Nation Torn* (New York: Lodestar Books/Dutton) 1990, Ch.2.
93 Morris 230.

40a General overview

First Book of the Confederacy, by Dorothy Levenson (First Books) Gr. 5-9

**Confederate Ladies of Richmond*, by Susan Beller Gr. 6-12
Through letters and diary excerpts, see the life of the women of the Confederate capital, especially when under siege later in the war.

**Illustrated Confederate Reader*, edited by Rod Gragg Gr. 7-12
Letters, journal entries, etc.

**Story of the Confederate States*, by Joseph Derry Gr. 7-12
A complete overview of the Civil War from the perspective of the South.

**Facts the Historians Leave Out: A Confederate Primer*, by John Tilley Gr. 8-12
Brief book answers common questions from Southern point of view. This was also listed in the above section on the Confederacy.

**Confederacy and the Civil War*, by Ann Gaines (In American History) Unknown

**Confederate Flag*, by Hal Marcovitz (American Symbols & Their Meaning) Unknown
I do not know the stand taken by this book which covers the various forms of the Confederate flag and the controversy surrounding it today.

**Jefferson Davis*, by Scott Ingram Unknown

**Secession: The Southern States Leave the Union*, by Judith Peacock Unknown

**Southerners*, by John Dunn (Voices from the Civil War) Unknown

Fiction/Historical Fiction

Jane Hope, by Elizabeth Janet Gray Gr. 8-12
A spunky North Carolina girl matures as the War Between the States nears.

40b Activities

**Civil War Cooking: The Confederacy*, by Susan Dosier Various

**Cut and Assemble a Southern Plantation* (Dover) Various

**Fashions of the Old South Paper Dolls* (Dover) Various

**Southern Belles Paper Dolls* (Dover) Various

40c Jefferson Davis

Mr. Davis was the first and only president of the Confederate States of America.

Jefferson Davis, by Patricia Miles (See and Read)	Gr. K-3
**Jefferson Davis*, by Susan Lee (Heroes of the Civil War)	Gr. 1-3
Jeff Davis, by Lena DeGrummond (Childhood)	Gr. 1-6
Jefferson Davis, by Zachary Kent (Cornerstones)	Gr. 2-7
**Jefferson Davis*, by Joey Frazier (Famous Figures of the Civil War Era)	Gr. 4-8
**Jefferson Davis*, by Perry Scott King (World Leaders Past & Present)	Gr. 6-12
President of the Confederacy: Jefferson Davis, by Margaret Green (Messner)	Gr. 6-12
I, Varina, by Ruth Randall This is the story of Mrs. Davis.	Gr. 7-12
* *Messages and Papers of Jefferson Davis and the Confederacy*	Gr. 11-12
**Jefferson Davis*, by E.J. Carter	Unknown

41 War Between the States

Lincoln's attempts to hold the United States together were not able to overcome the passionate issues that tore at America. The southern states began seceding (withdrawing from the union). Bullets first flew between the federal troops and those of South Carolina at Fort Sumter in the harbor of Charleston. The Civil War had begun, though both sides don't necessarily agree about who started it. In fact, there are *still* such differing perspectives on the war that it has various names! *The War of Northern Aggression? The War of Southern Rebellion? The War Between the States?* For the sake of brevity, I'll usually stick with *Civil War*. Anyway, the southern states formed their own nation: the *Confederate States of America*, with Jefferson Davis as president and their capital at Richmond, Virginia.

So, hang on! You're about to study the war that spilled more American blood than any other, before or since.[94] And this was not only because both sides could be called Americans; there were more reasons beside...as you'll see.[95] The War Between the States stretched over four long years, though everyone had first thought it would go quickly. It didn't.

94 Carson 3:144.
95 Carson 3:144-145.

To do justice to such an epic event, we'll need to look at many elements of the war. Let the *Table of Contents* help as you maneuver your way through the various topics. We'll begin by offering you resources which cover the breadth of the war in its entirety; some families may enjoy that glimpse, others may feel it steals the thunder. It's up to you. We'll then look more carefully at events in chronological order. Next, we'll meet significant persons and delve into unique side topics, such as spies, naval battles, and first-person journals. Finally, we'll close with a listing of fiction and historical fiction books which bring events to life. As you've probably guessed, there are too many wonderful books from which to choose, so select carefully. Hey, maybe your family has a unique geographic perspective to accent or maybe you had an ancestor involved. Well, just know that I've tried to include books from both the southern and northern perspective. Ready? Let's dive in!

41a General overview

As you can imagine, there are oodles of general resources; I'll list a few as samples. Remember, these books cover the war in its entirety, so you may want to use them judiciously so as not to "steal the thunder" of individual topics. On the other hand, you may feel they provide good continuity! We'll cover key figures of the War Between the States in a later section, as well as many special topics.

**Child's History of the World*, by V.M. Hillyer, Ch. 75c — Gr. 1-4

**Story of the World: Vol. 4*, by Susan Wise Bauer, Ch. 5a — Gr. 3-6
Some families enjoy this book's scope, so ask us to cite it; others seek different worldview; so, parental decision.

**Basic History of the United States: Vol. 3*, by Clarence Carson, Ch. 8 — Ch. 9-12

**If You Lived at the Time of the Civil War*, by Kay Moore — Gr. 1-5

**Kids During the American Civil War*, by Lisa Wroble — Gr. 2-4
I've not seen this, but know it uses a fictional family in the border state of Kentucky to teach kids about the real differences between northern culture and southern culture.

**Ghosts of the Civil War*, by Cheryl Harness — Gr. 2-5
Entire panorama of Civil War plays out before a modern girl using plot device of Willie Lincoln's ghost (who appears as a boy participating in the re-enactment the girl is observing) being the guide. Many families will not appreciate this plot device, though the book is filled with info, illustrations, etc. I've not seen it.

Civil War, by Fletcher Pratt — Gr. 2-8
Highly illustrated.

Two Flags Flying, by Donald Sobol Gr. 2-8
Fascinating collection of fifty, brief, true events that took place during the war.

War Between the States, by Eric Barnes Gr. 4-8

Billy Yank and Johnny Reb, by Earl Schenck Miers Gr. 4-10
Narrative telling of the Civil War.

**Civil War*, by John Stanchak (Eyewitness) Gr. 4-12
A museum in a book.

Strike the Tent, by Jeffrey Baker Gr. 4-12
A photo journal of Confederate battle sites.

**Billy Yank and Johnny Reb*, by Susan Beller Gr. 5-8
This book shows the everyday life of Union and Confederate soldiers.

First Book of the Civil War, by Dorothy Levenson (First Books) Gr. 5-9

**Civil War*, by Alden Carter Gr. 5-12

Civil War Sampler, by Donald Sobol Gr. 5-12
A collection of letters, articles, documents, etc.

**Fields of Fury: The American Civil War*, by James McPherson Gr. 5-12
I've not seen this, but have read that it provides a quick overview.

**Visual Dictionary of the Civil War*, by John Stanchak (DK) Gr. 5-12
Like a museum in a book.

This Hallowed Ground, by Bruce Catton Gr. 6-10

**Best Little Stories from the Civil War*, by C. Brian Kelly Gr. 6-12

**Civil War Battles and Leaders*, edited by Aaron Murray (DK) Gr. 6-12

Golden Book of the Civil War, by Charles Flato Gr. 7-12

Many Faces of the Civil War, by Irving Werstein (Messner) Gr. 7-12

Story of the Civil War, by Colonel Red Reeder Gr. 7-12

Civil War, by Don Nardo Gr. 8-12

Facts the Historians Leave Out: A Confederate Primer, by John Tilley Gr. 8-12
Brief book answers common questions from Southern point of view. This was also listed in the above section on the Confederacy.

Commander in Chief: Abraham Lincoln and the Civil War, by Albert Marrin Gr. 8-12
This covers Lincoln's role throughout the war.

Drum-Beat of the Nation, Marching to Victory, Redeeming the Republic, and *Freedom Triumphant* Gr. 10-12
all by Charles Coffin
If you enjoyed **The Story of Liberty*, by Charles Coffin, you may want to undertake the task of locating his very rare, very old, four-volume history of the Civil War. Coffin, because he was a war correspondent, had an eyewitness view of many events. He was also a personal friend of Lincoln's. Coffin writes from the Union point-of-view.

Legacy of the Civil War, by Robert Penn Warren Gr. 10-12
Warren contemplated the impact of the war at its centennial.

Reflections on the Civil War, by Bruce Catton Gr. 12+
This eminent historian reflects on the entire war.

Film

Civil War Diary
Based on children's novel, *Across Five Aprils*, a young boy sees war's effect on family.

Friendly Persuasion, starring Gary Cooper
A sincere Quaker family in Indiana faces issues during the Civil War.

41b Activities

This list contains many coloring books, many designed for older students, and paper soldier books, in addition to traditional activity books.

American Family of the Civil War Era Paper Dolls (Dover) Various

Billy the Union Soldier: With 24 Stickers, by A.G. Smith (Dover) Various
Sticker/activity book.

**Billy Yank* (Bellerophon) Various
Detailed coloring book.

**Civil War*, by Susan Spellman (Draw History) Various

**Civil War: A Fact-Filled Coloring Book*, by Blake Magner Various

**Civil War Days*, by David King Various
Lots of activities!

**Civil War for Kids*, by Janis Herbert Various
I've now been told that this provides more of an overview of the war than I first realized, with short articles on many topics chronologically. I guess it can, then, be used both as an overview *and* as an activity/map resource.

**Civil War Heroes* (Bellerophon) Various
Detailed coloring book.

**Civil War Paper Soldiers* (Dover) Various

**(Coloring Book of) Civil War Heroines* (Bellerophon) Various

**Confederate Army Paper Soldiers* (Dover) Various

**Food and Recipes of the Civil War*, by George Erdosh Various

**Johnny Reb* (Bellerophon) Various
Detailed coloring book.

**Johnny the Confederate Soldier: With 27 Stickers*, by A.G. Smith (Dover) Various

**Soldier's Life in the Civil War* (Dover) Various

**Songs and Stories of the Civil War*, by Jerry Silverman Gr. 5-12
Actual piano/guitar music, along with pertinent anecdotes, for Civil War era music.

**Story of the Civil War Coloring Book* (Dover) Various

**Union Army Paper Soldiers* (Dover) Various

42 Events of 1861

You sure don't want to hear me rattle on about each event in the war since we've already talked so much about the issues which fostered the war. I'll just send you right to the books! They'll do a bang-up job (ooh, bad pun) of taking you back to the war. Don't forget: we'll cover key figures and special topics in later sections.

42a Battle of Fort Sumter

It all began in the harbor of Charleston—the pulsing center of southern ideas.

**Story of the Great Republic*, by H.A. Guerber, Ch. XXXVII-XXXIX Gr. 3-7
The first of these chapters discusses Sumter; the other two cover early preparations once conflict had actually begun at Sumter.

**Story of Fort Sumter*, by Eugenia Burney (Cornerstones) Gr. 2-7

**Fort Sumter*, by Brendan January (Cornerstones II) Gr. 3-8

**Nation Torn*, by Delia Ray, Ch. 1, 6 (Young Readers' History of the Civil...) Gr. 5-12

**Firing on Fort Sumter: A Splintered Nation Goes to War*, by Nancy Colbert Gr. 6-12

**Fort Sumter: The Civil War Begins*, by Michael Uschan (Landmark Events) Unknown

**Shots Fired at Fort Sumter*, by Wendy Vierow (Headlines from History) Unknown

Fiction/Historical Fiction

**Yankee Girl at Fort Sumter*, by Alice Desmond Curtis Gr. 4-12

**Before the Creeks Ran Red*, by Carolyn Reeder Gr. 6-12
I've not seen this collection of three short stories about three different youths in different sections on the eve of the Civil War, but the first begins in Charleston.

42b First Battle of Bull Run

It was the northern press and politicians who were chomping for an attack toward the Confederate capital at Richmond, Virginia; General Scott felt forced to move before he was ready.[96] What happened? And what did the picnickers—no, I'm not kidding—who tramped out from Washington to view the action end up seeing? And how did General Thomas Jackson rightfully earn his nickname *Stonewall?*

96 Morris 232.

**This Country of Ours*, by H.E. Marshall, Ch. 83 — Gr. 3-8

Story of the Battle of Bull Run, by Zachary Kent (Cornerstones) — Gr. 3-7

**Battle of Bull Run*, by Deborah Kops — Gr. 5-10

First Bull Run, by Bruce Palmer (Battle Books) — Gr. 7-12

Sunday in Centreville: The Battle of Bull Run, by G. Allen Foster — Gr. 7-12

**Battle of Bull Run*, by Wendy Vierow — Unknown

Fiction/Historical Fiction

**Looking for Pa*, by Geraldine Susi — Gr. 4-8

I've not seen this story of Virginia children who try to join their father in Manassas when their mother dies...leading them to arrive in time for the Battle of Bull Run.

**Bull Run*, by Paul Fleischman — Gr. 4-12

Brings various fictional individuals together at the battle everyone thought would just be a "little show." Unusual, powerful book.

**Guns of Bull Run*, by Joseph Altsheler — Gr. 9-12

This is the first in an eight-book series of classic, long-beloved books being reprinted by Zeezok Publishing. If you want to work through the set as we come to each topic, enjoy!

43 Events of 1862

Don't forget: we'll cover key figures and special topics in later sections. The famous duel between the two ironclad ships—the Monitor *and the* Merrimac*—occurred during 1862, but we'll cover it in the upcoming section devoted to naval battles.*

43a Battle of Shiloh

**Story of the Great Republic*, by H.A. Guerber, Ch. XL — Gr. 3-7

This chapter covers Shiloh and other key events of the time.

**This Country of Ours*, by H.E. Marshall, Ch. 85 — Gr. 3-8

Battle of Shiloh, by Zachary Kent (Cornerstones) — Gr. 3-7

Shiloh, by Richard Steins Gr. 4-7

Fiction/Historical Fiction

**Guns of Shiloh*, by Joseph Altsheler Gr. 7-12
This classic adventure tale of yesteryear has been reprinted.

43b Andrews Raid

A handful of Union soldiers tried to push deep into Confederate territory and sneak back out...with a train!

**Stolen Train*, by Robert Ashley (Winston Adventure) Gr. 3-10
True story; Union soldiers attempt to get train from behind enemy lines. Thankfully, someone is reprinting this treasure.

Andrews Raid, or the Great Locomotive Chase, by Sam & Beryl Epstein Gr. 4-12

Film

**Great Locomotive Chase*, starring Fess Parker Parental decision
Wow....what a noble, inspiring, but sad, film....

43c Stonewall Jackson's Valley Campaign

**Story of the Great Republic*, by H.A. Guerber, Ch. XLII Gr. 3-7

**Stonewall's Courier: Story of Charles Randolph and General Jackson*, by V. Hinkins Gr. 5-12
I've not seen this true story of a 16-year-old courier for Jackson, but it sounds good. Since he was involved in many engagements, I'm not sure where to tuck this book in, but here it is!

Fiction/Historical Fiction

**Scouts of Stonewall*, by Joseph Altsheler Gr. 7-12
This classic adventure tale of yesteryear has been reprinted.

43d Battle of Antietam

Standing on this battlefield, I was overcome with emotion...

**Story of the Great Republic*, by H.A. Guerber, Ch. XLIII — Gr. 3-7

**Battle of Antietam*, by Zachary Kent (Cornerstones) — Gr. 3-9
Also titled, **The Story of Antietam.*

**Battle of Antietam*, by Chris Hughes — Gr. 5-10

**Battle of Antietam*, by James Reger — Gr. 6-12

Fiction/Historical Fiction

**Barbara Frietchie*, by John Greenleaf Whittier — Gr. K-3
Whittier wrote a poem about a brave elderly woman who supposedly spoke out against the incoming troops. Cute illustrations by Nancy Winslow Parker.

**Nowhere to Turn*, by Alan Kay (Young Heroes of History) — Gr. 4-9
I've not read this, but see that it tells of a boy who witnesses Antietam.

Lost Dispatch: Story of Antietam, by Donald Sobol — Gr. 7-12

**The Sword of Antietam*, by Joseph Altsheler — Gr. 9-12

43e Battle of Fredericksburg

**Robert Henry Hendershot*, by Susan Goodman (Ready-for-Chapter Books) — Gr. 1-5
True story: a boy captures a Confederate soldier at Fredericksburg.

**Battle of Fredericksburg*, by Scott Ingram — Unknown

Fiction/Historical Fiction

**Journal of Rufus Rowe*, by Sid Hite (My Name is America) — Gr. 4-9
Some families like this series; others do not. I've not read this.

Don't forget: we'll cover special figures and special topics in later sections!

44 Events of 1863

44a Emancipation Proclamation

On January 1, 1863, President Lincoln declared that all slaves in the territory still under the control of the Confederate States of America were "then, thenceforward, and forever free!" That is wonderful, and some people see it as a great step on the path toward liberty. Others, though, see it more as a political tool used by Lincoln. Depending on what books you choose to read, you may find either of these opinions. Why the discord?

Well, the Proclamation freed *only* the slaves on land under Confederate control. Some say this makes Lincoln a hypocrite, but he didn't think a president had Constitutional authority to free slaves. He simply couldn't declare freedom for slaves in Union states (they were bound by the US Constitution) or in CSA territory which had been reclaimed by the Union army (it was back in the Union and under the Constitution.) As you know, the only Union states that had slavery were the four Border States which had long been committed to it. The northern states had banned slavery earlier; in fact, some did so as soon as they became states under the Constitution. Additionally, Congress had recently abolished slavery in the territories,[97] since they weren't under the Constitution.

There was a new wrinkle, too, which pushed Lincoln toward the Proclamation. Some southern slaves were often being used to help the Confederate army, and that brought in a whole new set of principles, some of which allowed armies authority over enemy resources being used against them!

> *For more than a year after the outbreak of war, Lincoln had cautiously refrained from meddling with Southern slavery. He did not believe either the President or Congress had the authority to interfere with the institution in states where it existed. However, the power of the military to confiscate slaves was quite another thing, since by using them as teamsters, personal servants, or diggers of entrenchments, Confederates could free a larger proportion of their troops for actual fighting than was possible within the Union army....*
>
> *The grimmer the war became, the stronger grew Northern feeling against the slave-labor system of the South, quite simply because it maintained the rebellion.*[98]

Besides, there was another factor. Many slaves had attached themselves to the Union army when they had escaped in the turmoil of war, or when their plantations were overrun by Union troops. Was the Union army supposed to return them to their owners (according to the Fugitive Slave Act)? These same returned slaves might later be used against them! What could be done? What was the status of these

---

97 Olivia Coolidge, *The Statesmanship of Abraham Lincoln* (New York: Charles Scribner's Sons, 1976) 115-116. The point about Constitutionality was also made in: Irving Werstein, *Storming of Fort Wagner* (Scholastic, 1970) 20.
98 Coolidge 116.

slaves? Were they slaves? Were they free? Where should they go? What could they do?

Lincoln could see the complicated problems...so what did he do? Three things. He tried to establish colonies (such as in the Caribbean) where slaves could begin a new life;[99] he urged the Border States to phase out slavery;[100] and, he signed the Emancipation Proclamation we have just been discussing.

Interestingly, the Emancipation Proclamation was not all that popular in the north. The abolitionists had wanted to see every slave freed; they said it didn't go far enough. On the other side, some "looked back nostalgically to the good old days [of peace] and did not like to be told they were fighting for what amounted to a revolution."[101]

Lincoln responded with a letter to the *New York Tribune:*

> *My paramount object in this struggle is to save the Union, and is not either to save or destroy slavery. If I could save the Union without freeing any slave, I would do it; and if I could save it by freeing all the slaves, I would do it; and if I could save it be freeing some and leaving others alone, I would also do that....*
>
> *I have here stated my purpose according to my view of my official duty; and I intend no modification of my oft-expressed personal wish that all men everywhere should be free."*[102]

One thing can be said, though:

> *...nothing in the course of the war seemed to give Lincoln more personal satisfaction than this proclamation which he made as part of his duty to achieve something else. Over and over again when Negroes cheered him, he seemed to remind himself that here at least were people to whom he had given something positive and lasting. As a realist, he understood that he had not given much, for which reason he spent energy on colonization schemes which were doomed to disappointment. He also took an interest in Negro education, which he might have assisted more had he lived longer. He did not, like some idealists, assume that freedom would solve all the problems.*[103]

Well, let's dig in here!

**Story of the Great Republic*, by H.A. Guerber, Ch. XLIV — Gr. 3-7

**This Country of Ours*, by H.E. Marshall, Ch. 86 — Gr. 3-8

----

99 Coolidge 120.
100 Morris 238.
101 Coolidge 121-122.
102 Coolidge 119-120.
103 Coolidge 120.

Emancipation Proclamation, by Brendan January (Cornerstones) Gr. 3-8

Forever Free: The Story of the Emancipation Proclamation, by Dorothy Sterling Gr. 4-12
This book is written in a nicely narrative tone, it appears.

Emancipation Proclamation, by Ann Heinrichs (We the People) Gr. 5-10

Days of Jubilee, by Patricia McKissack Gr. 5-12

Great Proclamation, by Henry Steele Commager Gr. 7-12

Emancipation Proclamation, by Michael Martin Unknown

Lincoln and the Emancipation Proclamation in American History, by D. Holford Unknown

Lincoln, Slavery, and the Emancipation Proclamation, by Carin Ford Unknown

Fiction/Historical Fiction

Abraham Lincoln: Letters from a Slave Girl, by Andrea Pinkney Gr. 4-8
I've not read this book which presents fictional correspondence regarding the proclamation. Sounds good, though!

44b Battle of Chancellorsville

This battle saw the death of Stonewall Jackson, accidentally shot by his own men; we'll talk about Jackson specifically in a later section.

This Country of Ours, by H.E. Marshall, Ch. 87 Gr. 3-8

Battle of Chancellorsville, by Zachary Kent (Cornerstones) Gr. 3-8

Chancellorsville: Disaster in Victory, by Bruce Palmer (Macmillan Battle Books) Gr. 8-12

44c Battle of Gettysburg

As you probably already know, this battle was extremely impactful on the outcome of the war.

Story of the Great Republic, by H.A. Guerber, Ch. XLV Gr. 3-7

This Country of Ours, by H.E. Marshall, Ch. 88 Gr. 3-8

**Billy and the Rebel*, by Deborah Hopkinson (Ready-to-Read 3) Gr. 1-4
Based on true incident, a Gettysburg mother and son harbor a Confederate deserter.

Gettysburg, by F.N. Monjo Gr. 2-8
See the battle through Tad Lincoln's eyes. Don't miss this book!

**A Day that Changed America: Gettysburg*, by Shelley Tanaka Gr. 3-7

**Gettysburg*, by MacKinlay Kantor (Landmark) Gr. 3-9

**Charley Waters Goes to Gettysburg*, by Susan Sinnott Gr. 4-8
I've not seen this, but hear that this is a good view of Gettysburg through the eyes of a modern boy who visits with his family to re-enact.

**Thunder at Gettysburg*, by Patricia Gauch Gr. 4-8
Poignant view, as girl watches the battle.

Battle of Gettysburg, by Neil Johnson Gr. 5-9
This book was born at the 125th anniversary of the battle when many photographs were taken of the 14,000 re-enactors playing out the epic battle. I've heard great things about both the photos and the text.

**Gettysburg*, by Chris Hughes (Battlefields Across America) Gr. 5-10

**Battle of Gettysburg*, by Alden Carter Gr. 5-12

**Battle of Gettysburg*, by David C. King Gr. 6-12

To Hold This Ground, by Susan Beller Gr. 6-12
Info on Joshua Chamberlain, Confederate brigade, and common soldiers at Gettysburg.

**Long Road to Gettysburg*, by Jim Murphy Gr. 7-12

**Battle of Gettysburg*, by Gina DeAngelis (Let Freedom Ring) Unknown

**Gettysburg*, by Ruth Ashby Unknown

Fiction/Historical Fiction

**My Brother's Keeper*, by Mary Pope Osborne (My America, Civil War) Gr. 3-5
This is the first in a series of diaries kept by a girl in Gettysburg.

We Were There at the Battle of Gettysburg, by Alida Malkus (We Were There) Gr. 3-8
Fictional kids at real historical events. Usually an outstanding series!

**Kathleen: Yankee Girl at Gettysburg*, by Alice Desmond Curtis Gr. 3-12

**Abraham's Battle*, by Sara Banks Gr. 4-8
I'm not familiar with this story of an ex-slave from Gettysburg who meets with a young Confederate soldier...and then someone else who is very important!

**Moon Over Tennessee*, by Craig Crist-Evans Gr. 4-8
I've not seen this, and am not sure of the grade recommendation, but it seems to be the story of a Tennessee boy who loves his home deeply and has much to think about when his father dies at Gettysburg.

Boy at Gettysburg, by Elsie Singmaster Gr. 4-12
An older author brings a nice story.

Drummer Boy, by Larry Weinberg Gr. 4-12
I've not seen this and am guessing at the age recommendation, but it sounds interesting. A boy is horrified by rumors that his brother has deserted, and setting out to search for him, ends up in Gettysburg, among other places.

Sewing Susie, by Elsie Singmaster Gr. 4-12
Boy who wants badly to help the Union is teased for helping to sew uniforms.

**1863: A House Divided*, by Elizabeth Massie Gr. 6-12
I've not read this new novel which finds Gettysburg twins in the thick of events.

Three Days with Robert E. Lee at Gettysburg, by Paxton Davis Gr. 7-12

**Star of Gettysburg*, by Joseph Altsheler Gr. 9-12
Another in outstanding series, now being reprinted!

**Killer Angels*, by Michael Shaara Gr. 10-12
Very powerful, very factual novel of Battle of Gettysburg.

44d Siege of Vicksburg

The siege had begun a while before, but news of the fall came just on the heels of Gettysburg.

**Story of the Great Republic*, by H.A. Guerber, Ch. XLVI Gr. 3-7

**This Country of Ours*, by H.E. Marshall, Ch. 89 Gr. 3-8

Vicksburg Veteran, by F.N Monjo — Gr. K-4

See the battle through the eyes of Fred Grant, General Grant's son. Excellent!

**Vicksburg*, by Mary Ann Fraser — Gr. 5-12

**Battle of Vicksburg*, by David C. King — Unknown

Fiction/Historical Fiction

**Night Journey to Vicksburg*, by Susan Masters (American Adventures) — Gr. 3-6

Slaves attempting to escape run into the Battle of Vicksburg. This is in yet another series by the name *American Adventures* which I've not seen personally.

**Drummer Boy of Vicksburg*, by G. Clifton Wisler — Gr. 5-12

Story reveals real aspects of life of drummer boys.

Guns of Vicksburg, by Earl Schenck Miers — Gr. 5-12

Iowa soldier is at the Battle of Vicksburg with Fred Grant.

**Tamarack Tree*, by Patricia Clapp — Gr. 5-12

Nice novel of English girl living through siege of Vicksburg.

Mosquito Fleet, by Gordon Shirreffs — Gr. 7-12

High adventure for boys caught up in the battles of Vicksburg.

44e Attack on Fort Wagner

The African-American troops of the 54th Massachusetts regiment were extraordinarily brave!

**Undying Glory*, by Clinton Cox — Gr. 5-12

Storming of Fort Wagner, by Irving Werstein — Gr. 7-12

True story of courageous black soliders' attack.

One Gallant Rush, by Peter Burchard — Gr. 10-12

**Assault on Fort Wagner*, by Wendy Vierow — Unknown

**Massachusetts 54th*, by Gina DeAngelis (Let Freedom Ring) — Unknown

Fiction/Historical Fiction

North by Night, by Peter Burchard — Gr. 5-12
Fictional youth gets involved in the battle at Ft. Wagner.

44f Battle of Chickamauga

**Story of the Great Republic*, by H.A. Guerber, Ch. XLVII — Gr. 3-7
Chickamauga is one of many battles mentioned in this chapter.

Fiction/Historical Fiction

**Rock of Chickamauga*, by Joseph Altsheler — Gr. 7-12
Another in a series of long-beloved tales.

44g Battle of Chattanooga

**Battle of Chattanooga*, by David C. King — Unknown

Fiction/Historical Fiction

**Perilous Road*, by William O. Steele — Gr. 4-12
Acclaimed novel of the Civil War, with some action set at Signal Mountain.

44h Gettysburg Address

It would be wonderful if you Americans would memorize this, as students have been doing for decades.

**Gettysburg Address*, by Abraham Lincoln, illustrated by Michael McCurdy — All ages!
Strongly illustrated text of the Gettysburg address. Don't miss this!

**Just a Few Words, Mr. Lincoln*, by Jean Fritz — Gr. K-3

**Story of the Gettysburg Address*, by Kenneth Richards (Cornerstones) — Gr. 2-8

When Lincoln Went to Gettysburg, by Adele Nathan Gr. 2-8

**Gettysburg Address*, by Kenneth Richards (Cornerstones) Gr. 3-7

Mr. Lincoln Speaks at Gettysburg, by Mary Kay Phelan Gr. 6-12

Fiction/Historical Fiction

Mary Elizabeth and Mr. Lincoln, by Margaret Seyler Gr. 3-7
A girl has the chance to encounter Lincoln at Gettysburg.

Audio

**We Hold These Truths to be Self-Evident*, narrated by Max McLean Various
I've heard parts of these dramatic readings (Gettysburg Address, Lincoln's Second Inaugural Address, Declaration of Independence, and Preamble to Constitution) on Christian radio. Very good!

45 Events of 1864

45a Battle of the Wilderness & Spotsylvania

**Lost Cause*, by James Arnold & Roberta Wiener Gr. 5-10
You can focus on the chapters pertinent to this specific time period. I believe Wilderness and Spotsylvania are covered, but I've not yet seen a copy of this book.

**Road to Appomattox*, by Carter Smith (Sourcebook) Gr. 7-12
This book actually covers the entire closing phase of the war. Read now only the chapters pertinent to this event.

Fiction/Historical Fiction

**Shades of the Wilderness*, by Joseph Altsheler Gr. 7-12
Another in a series of long-beloved tales.

45b Battle of New Market

**Cadets at War*, by Susan Beller Gr. 7-12
Cadets from nearby Virginia Military Institute helped at the New Market conflict.

Fiction/Historical Fiction

Battle of New Market: A Story of V.M.I., by Paxton Davis — Gr. 7-12
This is a novelized tale of the real battle.

45c Siege of Petersburg

The battle for Petersburg began on June 14, 1864, but when the city didn't fall quickly to Union soldiers, something of a siege was begun.

**Lost Cause*, by James Arnold & Roberta Wiener — Gr. 5-10
You can focus on the chapters pertinent to this specific time period.

**Road to Appomattox*, by Carter Smith (Sourcebook) — Gr. 7-12
This book actually covers the entire closing phase of the war. Read now only the chapters pertinent to this event.

Fiction/Historical Fiction

**Across the Lines*, by Carolyn Reeder — Gr. 5-9
I've not read this story of a plantation owner's son who seeks refuge in Petersburg only to arrive in time for the siege...and his escaped slave boy.

45d Sheridan vs. Early

**Story of the Great Republic*, by H.A. Guerber, Ch. L — Gr. 3-7

45e Burning of Atlanta and Sherman's March

**Story of the Great Republic*, by H.A. Guerber, Ch. XLVIII-XLIX — Gr. 3-7

**This Country of Ours*, by H.E. Marshall, Ch. 90 — Gr. 3-8

**Story of Sherman's March to the Sea*, by Zachary Kent (Cornerstones) — Gr. 2-7

**Confederate Girl: The Diary of Carrie Berry, 1864*, by Carrie Berry Gr. 4-8

I've not seen this, but it is apparently the real diary of a girl who lived through the tumult of Sherman's march.

**Lost Cause*, by James Arnold & Roberta Wiener Gr. 5-10

You can focus on the chapters pertinent to this specific time period.

**Road to Appomattox*, by Carter Smith (Sourcebook) Gr. 7-12

This book actually covers the entire closing phase of the war. Read now only the chapters pertinent to this event.

Fiction/Historical Fiction

Mary Montgomery, Rebel, by Helen Daringer Gr. 3-12

Fact-based story of girl living through Sherman's march.

Yankee Traitor, Rebel Spy, by Elinor Case Gr. 4-12

Fact-based story of the burning of Atlanta.

46 Events of 1865

46a Lee surrenders to Grant at Appomattox Courthouse (April 9)

You can still visit the McLean House where the surrender actually occurred. It is extremely poignant...at least, I found it to be so.

**Story of the Great Republic*, by H.A. Guerber, Ch. LIIa Gr. 3-7

**Willie McLean and the Civil War Surrender*, by Candice Ransom (On My Own) Gr. 1-3

True story, I think, about boy who lived in house where the surrender was signed.

Story of the Surrender at Appomattox Courthouse, by Z. Kent (Cornerstones) Gr. 2-7

**Lee and Grant at Appomattox*, by M. Kantor (Landmark) Gr. 3-9

This is being reprinted!

**Surrender at Appomattox*, by Tom McGowen (Cornerstones II) Gr. 3-9

**Lost Cause*, by James Arnold & Roberta Wiener — Gr. 5-10
You can focus on the chapters pertinent to this specific time period.

Appomattox: Closing Struggle of the Civil War, by Burke Davis (Breakthrough) — Gr. 6-12

**Road to Appomattox*, by Carter Smith (Sourcebook) — Gr. 7-12
This book actually covers the entire closing phase of the war.

**Atillness at Appomattox*, by Bruce Catton — Gr. 10-12
This book actually covers the last year of the war.

Fiction/Historical Fiction

We Were There when Grant Met Lee at Appomattox, by Earl Miers (We Were...) — Gr. 3-8
Fictional kids at real historical events.

**Tree of Appomattox*, by Joseph Altsheler — Gr. 9-12

46b Re-election and assassination of President Lincoln

On March 4, Lincoln delivered a revered address for his second inauguration. But just five days after Lee's surrender at Appomattox, Lincoln's life was tragically taken by an angry assassin—John Wilkes Booth. Much had ended...

**Story of the World: Vol. 4*, by Susan Wise Bauer, Ch. 5b — Gr. 3-6
Some families enjoy this book's scope, so ask us to cite it; others seek different worldview; so, parental decision.

**Story of the Great Republic*, by H.A. Guerber, Ch. LIIb, LIV-LVI — Gr. 3-7
Guerber closes this section with a chapter on Lincoln's death, and then remembrances from his life.

**This Country of Ours*, by H.E. Marshall, Ch. 91 — Gr. 3-8

Story of Ford's Theater and the Death of Lincoln, by Zachary Kent (Cornerstones) — Gr. 2-6

**Assassination of Abraham Lincoln*, by Brendan January (Cornerstones II) — Gr. 4-8
I think this new version of Cornerstones series is written for slightly older students.

Death of Lincoln, by Leroy Hayman — Gr. 5-12

**John Wilkes Booth and the Civil War*, by Steven Otfinoski Gr. 7-12

Man Who Killed Lincoln, by Philip Stern Gr. 7-12
John Wilkes Booth and the events of the assassination.

Day Lincoln was Shot, by Jim Bishop Gr. 9-12

**Assassination of Abraham Lincoln*, by Michael Burgan Unknown

**Assassination of Abraham Lincoln*, by Robert Jakoubek Unknown

Fiction/Historical Fiction

**War's End*, by Norma Jean Lutz (American Adventure # 24) Gr. 3-8
Cincinnati kids face final stage of war and Lincoln's assassination in this book from a distinctly Christian series.

Audio

**We Hold These Truths to be Self-Evident*, narrated by Max McLean Various
I've heard parts of these dramatic readings (Gettysburg Address, Lincoln's Second Inaugural Address, Declaration of Independence, and Preamble to Constitution) on Christian radio. Very good!

46c Final phase of war

**Story of the Great Republic*, by H.A. Guerber, Ch. LIII Gr. 3-7

**Lost Cause*, by James Arnold & Roberta Wiener Gr. 5-10
You can focus on the chapters pertinent to this specific time period.

Fiction/Historical Fiction

**Emma and the Civil Warrior*, by Candy Dahl Gr. 4-10
I've not seen this and am not sure of the grade recommendation, but it is supposedly about the little-covered post-Appomattox days in Raleigh, NC.

47 Naval Battles and Naval Heroes

Now that you've seen the main flow of the war, we can go back and focus on issues of naval significance...and there were several!

47a General overview

**Story of the Great Republic*, by H.A. Guerber, Ch. XLI and LI — Gr. 3-7

First Book of Civil War Naval Actions, by Trevor Dupuy (First Books) — Gr. 4-12

**Civil War at Sea*, by George Sullivan — Gr. 6-12

Alabama Raider, by B.B. Anderson — Gr. 7-12
The story of the Confederate navy.

**Ships Versus Shore: Civil War Engagements Along Southern Shores and Rivers* by Dave Page — Unknown

Fiction/Historical Fiction

**Naming the Stones*, by Clara Stites — Gr. 3-7
I've not seen this book about a Massachusetts boy who must gather stones which will be used to sink old whaling ships as blockade of Charleston harbor; the reading recommendation is only an educated guess.

Powder Monkey, by B.B. Anderson — Gr. 4-9
A boy participates in battles on the Mississippi River.

**Phantom of the Blockade*, by Stephen Meader — Gr. 4-12
Exciting author tells of boy working on a Confederate blockade runner. Bethlehem Books is reprinting four Meader books (including this one) in a combo titled *Cleared for Action!*

Orphans of the Wind, by Eric Haugaard — Gr. 4-12
English boy ends up on ship headed to help the Confederacy.

**The 290*, by Scott O'Dell — Gr. 5-12

**Run the Blockade*, by G. Clifton Wisler — Gr. 5-12
I've not read this story of an Irish orphan boy who gets work on a ship headed for the Confederate States.

Day of the Arkansas, by Robert Alter Gr. 7-12
Story of boy on Confederate ironclad.

47b Ironclad Ships

**This Country of Ours*, by H.E. Marshall, Ch. 84 Gr. 3-8

**Monitor: The Iron Warship that Changed the World* (All Aboard 3) by Gare Thompson Gr. 2-4

**Duel of the Ironclads: The Monitor vs. the Virginia*, by Patrick O'Brien Gr. 3-8
I've heard that this is a dramatic book, but I've not seen it.

Monitor and the Merrimac, by Fletcher Pratt (Landmark) Gr. 3-9
This series is usually very solid....

John Ericsson and the Inventions of War, by Ann Brophy Gr. 3-10

Man of the Monitor, by Jean Lee Latham Gr. 3-12
This is the much-beloved story of John Ericsson, who helped design the *Monitor* and who pushed use of the screw propeller.

**Ironclads and Blockades in the Civil War*, by Douglas Savage (Untold History...) Gr. 4-8

Ironclad! by Seymour Reit Gr. 4-9

Battle of the Ironclads, by Alden Carter (First Book) Gr. 6-12

**Monitor vs. the Merrimack*, by Bruce Brager (Great Battles Through the Ages) Gr. 6-12

**Thank You Very Much, Captain Ericsson*, by Connie Wooldridge Unknown
Title makes it sound like this book about designer of *Monitor* is for younger children.

Fiction/Historical Fiction

Civil War Sailor, by Irving Werstein (Signal) Gr. 3-10
Non-stop adventure for a boy serving on the *Monitor.*

**Eben Tyne, Powdermonkey*, by Patricia Beatty & Phillip Robbins Gr. 5-12
Confederate boy works on the *Merrimac.*

Powder Boy of the Monitor, by Gordon Shirreffs Gr. 7-12

**Powder Monkey*, by Carole Campbell (Young American) Unknown
I have not seen this story about a boy on the *Virginia* (southern ironclad).

47c *CSS Hunley*

The CSS Hunley was the first submarine in history to sink an enemy ship! Some friends of mine (Hello, Cox family!) were participants in the ceremonies staged upon the honored raising of the Hunley.

**Civil War Sub: Mystery of the Hunley*, by Kate Jerome (All Aboard Reading 3) Gr. 2-5

**Story of the H.L. Hunley and Queenie's Coin*, by Fran Hawk Gr. 3-6

**Secrets of a Civil War Submarine*, by Sally Walker Gr. 4-10

Fiction/Historical Fiction

**Make it Three: Story of the CSS H.L. Hunley Civil War Submarine*, by M. Clary Unknown
I've not seen this; modern boy's curiosity about the *Hunley* causes him to learn much.

47d Naval heroes—Franklin Buchanan (Confederate)

Sorry, I can't find many books about Buchanan. Surely, though, he is included in the general resources listed earlier in this section.

Daring Sea Warrior: Franklin Buchanan, by G. Eliot (Messner) Gr. 9-12

47e Naval heroes—David Farragut (Union)

David Glasgow Farragut: Our First Admiral, by Jean Lee Latham (Garr. Disc.) Gr. 1-5
Great series, and great author!

David Farragut, by Laura Long (Childhood) Gr. 1-6

**Take Command, David Farragut!* by Peter & Connie Roop Gr. 3-6
Real story of Farragut's amazing career told through fictional letters from Farragut to his father.

**David Farragut, Union Admiral*, by Bruce Adelson (Famous Figures of the...) Gr. 4-8

Anchor's Aweigh, by Jean Lee Latham Gr. 4-12
This is an admired biography.

David Farragut: Sea Fighter, by Marie Mudra (Messner) Gr. 6-12

David Farragut and the Great Naval Blockade, by Russell Shorto Unknown

47f Naval heroes—Raphael Semmes (Confederate)

Raphael Semmes, by Dorothea Snow (Childhood) Gr. 1-6

Raphael Semmes: Confederate Admiral, by Robert Daly (American Background) Gr. 5-12

Rebel Raider: Admiral Semmes, by E. & B. Davis Gr. 6-12

48 Famous Folk of the War Between the States

In this section, we will meet important people who were involved so broadly or so uniquely that they couldn't be categorized in earlier sections. Enjoy getting to know some of these folks! Certainly, you don't need to study each one, but you can surely enjoy the many choices. The individual listings are alphabetical, after the first listing of general resources.

48a General overview

**Generals of the Civil War*, by William Davis Gr. 4-12
Large photo spreads show actual belongings of various generals.

Swords, Stars and Bars, by Lee McGiffin Gr. 6-12
Chapter bios of many great Confederate soldiers.

**Joseph E. Johnston, Confederate General*, by Christin Ditchfield Gr. 7-12

Military Life of Abraham Lincoln, by Trevor Dupuy Gr. 8-12

Northern Generals, by Red Reeder — Gr. 8-12

Southern Generals, by Red Reeder — Gr. 8-12

**Civil War Generals of the Confederacy*, by James Reger — Unknown

**Confederate Generals*, by Tom Head (Voices from the Civil War) — Unknown

48b Anna Carroll (Union)

Carroll was a female advisor to Lincoln at a time when that was very unusual!

Lincoln's Secret Weapon, by W. Wise — Gr. 7-12

Woman with a Sword, by Hollister Noble — Gr. 8-12

48c Bedford Forrest (Confederate)

Bedford Forrest, by Aileen Parks (Childhood) — Gr. 1-6

48d Ulysses S. Grant (Union)

Because Grant later became president, there are many books on him in the various presidential series, but he was not president until after the era covered in this guide. The books below tend to focus more on his role in the War Between the States.

Ulysses S. Grant: Horseman and Fighter, by Col. Red Reeder (Garr. Discovery) — Gr. 1-5

U.S. Grant, by Augusta Stevenson (Childhood) — Gr. 1-6

Story of Ulysses S. Grant, by Jeannette Nolan (Signature) — Gr. 3-9

**Ulysses S. Grant*, by Tim O'Shei (Famous Figures of the Civil War Era) — Gr. 4-8

**Ulysses S. Grant*, by Zachary Kent — Gr. 4-12

Ulysses S. Grant, by Henry Thomas — Gr. 5-9

**Ulysses S. Grant*, by Steven O'Brien Gr. 6-12

Reluctant Warrior: Ulysses S. Grant, by Bob & Jan Young (Messner) Gr. 7-12

Ulysses S. Grant, by Bill Bentley (First Books) Gr. 7-12

**Ulysses S. Grant*, by David C. King Gr. 7-12

**Unconditional Surrender*, by Albert Marrin Gr. 7-12
Marrin's books are usually a wonderful choice! I hope you can find this one!

Activities

**Ulysses S. Grant and His Family Paper Dolls* (Dover) Various

Fiction/Historical Fiction

Steve Marches with the General, by Marion Renick Gr. 3-8
Modern children learn about Grant while writing a play about his life.

48e Thomas "Stonewall" Jackson (Confederate)

Jackson is known for being a very strong Christian.

Young Stonewall, by Helen Monsell (Childhood) Gr. 1-6

Stonewall Jackson, by Jonathan Daniels (Landmark) Gr. 3-10

**Stonewall Jackson*, by Martha Hewson (Famous Figures of the Civil War Era) Gr. 4-8

**Stonewall Jackson*, by Chris Hughes Gr. 5-10

**Standing Like a Stone Wall*, by James Robertson Gr. 5-12

**Stonewall*, by Jean Fritz Gr. 5-12

**Stonewall Jackson*, by Charles Ludwig (Sower) Gr. 5-12
A distinctly Christian biography.

Valiant Virginian: Stonewall Jackson, by Felix Sutton (Messner) Gr. 6-12

**Confederate Trilogy for Young Readers*, by Mrs. M. L. Williamson — Gr. 7-12
One portion provides a biography of Jackson.

**More than Conquerors*, edited by John Woodbridge, pp. 22-25 — Gr. 7-12
This is a compendium of short biographies of Christian heroes.

Gallant Mrs. Stonewall, by Harnett Kane — Gr. 8-12
This book is about Jackson's wife!

**Jackson and Lee: Legends in Gray*, by James Robertson — Unknown
This book features the artwork of Mort Kuntsler.

48f Robert E. Lee (Confederate)

Wow, what an admirable man! I just can't say enough about his faith, virtue, etc. Make sure you meet ...not only because his life was so noteworthy, but also because he was the top military man of the Confederacy! Do know that he did not keep slaves himself and was very grieved about the breakup of the Union. His ancestor (a grandfather, if I recall) had assisted George Washington in the founding of America!

**Story of the Great Republic*, by H.A. Guerber, Ch. LVII — Gr. 3-7

**Picture Book of Robert E. Lee*, by David Adler — Gr. K-2

Robert E. Lee: The South's Great General, by Matthew Grant — Gr. K-3

Meet Robert E. Lee, by George Trow (Step-Up Books) — Gr. K-4

**Robert E. Lee: Brave Leader*, by Rae Bains (Troll) — Gr. 1-5

Robert E. Lee: Hero of the South, by Charles Graves (Garrard Discovery) — Gr. 1-5

**Robert E. Lee*, by Helen Monsell (Childhood) — Gr. 1-6

**Robert E. Lee: Leader in War and Peace*, by Carol Greene (Rookie) — Gr. 2-4

Lee: The Gallant General, by Jeanette Eaton — Gr. 3-6

Robert E. Lee and the Road of Honor, by Hodding Carter (Landmark) — Gr. 3-9

Story of Robert E. Lee, by Iris Vinton (Signature) — Gr. 3-9

America's Robert E. Lee, by Henry Steele Commager Gr. 4-8

**Robert E. Lee*, by Grabowski (Famous Figures of the Civil War Era) Gr. 4-8

Horses of Destiny, by Fairfax Downey Gr. 4-12
Contains a chapter on Lee's famous horse, Traveller.

Robert E. Lee, by Jonathan Daniels (North Star) Gr. 4-12

Lees of Arlington, by Marguerite Vance Gr. 5-12
Also shows the wonderful person of Mrs. Lee, a relative of Martha Washington.

**Robert E. Lee*, by Lee Roddy (Sower) Gr. 5-12
Distinctly Christian biography.

**Confederate Trilogy for Young Readers*, by Mrs. M.L. Williamson Gr. 7-12
One portion provides a biography of Lee.

**More than Conquerors*, edited by John Woodbridge, pp. 26-31 Gr. 7-12
This is a compendium of short biographies of Christian heroes.

Robert E. Lee, by Guy Emery (Messner) Gr. 7-12

**Robert E. Lee*, by David C. King (Triangle) Gr. 7-12

**Virginia's General: Robert E. Lee*, by Albert Marrin Gr. 8-12
Marrin's books are usually a wonderful choice! I hope you can find this!

**Call of Duty: The Sterling Nobility of Robert E. Lee*, by J. Steven Wilkins Gr. 9-12
High-level, Christian biography.

**Lee of Virginia*, by Douglas Southall Freeman Gr. 10-12
One-volume work based on Freeman's Pulitzer Prize-winning four-volume work.

**Mrs. Robert E. Lee*, by Rose MacDonald Gr. 10-12
Here is a biography of Lee's wife!

**Jackson and Lee: Legends in Gray*, by James Robertson Unknown
This book features the artwork of Mort Kuntsler.

**Robert E. Lee: Virginia Soldier, American Citizen*, by James Robertson Unknown
Robertson is historian at Virginia Tech, I believe. This was recommended to me, but I am not familiar with it.

Activities

**Robert E. Lee and His Family Paper Dolls* (Dover) Various

Fiction/Historical Fiction

Annie Lee and the Wooden Skates, by Margaret Friskey Gr. 3-7

I've not seen this and am guessing on the age recommendation, but it is a story about Lee's eight-year-old daughter Annie.

48g James Longstreet (Confederate)

**James Longstreet*, by Melanie Le Tourneau Unknown

48h Thaddeus Lowe (Union)

Thaddeus Lowe: America's One Man Air Corps, by Mary Hoehling (Messner) Gr. 6-12

Thaddeus Lowe: Uncle Sam's First Airman, by Lydel Sims Gr. 7-12

Inventor uses hot-air balloon during the Civil War.

48i George McClellan (Union)

**George McClellan, Union General*, by Brent Kelley (Famous Figures of...) Gr. 4-8

48j George Meade (Union)

**George Gordon Meade, Union General*, by Bruce Adelson (Famous Figures of...) Gr. 4-8

48k Thomas Meagher (Union)

Meagher was an Irish exile who ended up in America!

Rebel on Two Continents, by David Abodaher (Messner) Gr. 6-12

Thundermaker: General Thomas Meagher, by William Lamers Gr. 6-12

48l John Mosby (Confederate)

Mosby: Gray Ghost of the Confederacy, by Jonathan Daniels — Gr. 4-12
Exploits of elusive Confederate raider (hence the word "ghost" in the title).

**Mosby and His Rangers: Adventures of the Gray Ghost*, by Susan Beller — Unknown

48m Philip Sheridan (Union)

**Sheridan's Ride*, by Thomas Read — Gr. K-3
Fun story of the amazing horse ride of Sheridan.

**Philip Sheridan: Union General*, by Dynise Balcavage (Famous Figures of...) — Gr. 4-8

General Phil Sheridan and the United States Cavalry (American Background) by Milton Lomask — Gr. 5-10

Forked Lightning: The Story of General Philip H. Sheridan, by Albert Orbaan — Gr. 6-12

Sheridan: The General Who Wasn't Afraid to Take a Chance, by Red Reeder — Gr. 7-12

48n William Tecumseh Sherman (Union)

William Tecumseh Sherman, by Charles Graves — Gr. 3-12

**William Sherman, Union General*, by Henna Remstein (Famous Fig...) — Gr. 4-8

William Tecumseh Sherman, by Wyatt Blassingame (Hall of Fame) — Gr. 6-12

**William T. Sherman*, by David C. King — Gr. 7-12

William T. Sherman, by Marsha Landreth (Great American Generals) — Gr. 7-12

**William Tecumseh Sherman: Union General*, by Zachary Kent (Historical Amer.) Unknown

48o J.E.B. Stuart (Confederate)

Stuart was affectionately known as "Jeb" even though the component letters were really his first initials.

Jeb Stuart, by Gertrude Winders (Childhood) Gr. 1-6

This series is being reprinted as Young Patriot books, so this may be in print soon!

**James Ewell Brown Stuart, Confederate General*, by Meg Greene (Famous Figures) Gr. 4-8

Jeb Stuart, by Lena DeGrummond Gr. 5-12

**Life of J.E.B. Stuart*, by Mrs. M.L. Williamson Gr. 6-12

Very old biography, which has been reprinted by Christian Liberty; is also available in one bound volume entitled, **Confederate Trilogy for Young Readers.*

Fiction/Historical Fiction

Gray Riders, by Manly Wade Wellman (Aladdin's American Heritage) Gr. 3-10

Boy has adventures with Jeb Stuart.

Ride, Rebels! by Manly Wade Wellman Gr. 5-12

Adventures of Stuart's cavalry scouts; this is the second in a trilogy which is also cited in the *General Fiction* section.

49 Special Topics of the Civil War

Let's learn about some interesting topics of unique note. There are several, as you'll see. And what's not to love? You can meet spies, artists, African-American soldiers, field nurses, famous animals, and more. You can check Civil War uniforms, weapons, and prison camps. You can read real journals. You can even get the low-down on conflict out west. You can pick just a couple topics of interest, or you can dive into them all! Ready?

49a African-American soldiers

A total of about 180,000 African-American soldiers fought for the two sides, but they faced extra difficulties, as you'll see. Well, if you studied the attack of Ft. Wagner (cited earlier in this guide) and the special role of the 54th Massachusetts Regiment, you've already discovered some of the obstacles before these men.

**Pink and Say*, by Patricia Polacco Gr. 1-5

Don't miss this powerful, true story of a young ex-slave-turned-soldier helping wounded Union boy...and their facing of Andersonville prison together. Will also be cited in the section on prisons.

*_Between Two Fires: Black Soldiers and the Civil War_, by Joyce Hansen Gr. 5-12

*_Till Victory is Won: Black Soldiers in the Civil War_, by Zak Mettger (Young...) Gr. 5-12

*_Black, Blue & Gray_, by Jim Haskins Gr. 6-12
Covers the African-American soliders fighting on both sides of the war.

*_Slaves to Soldiers: African-American Fighting Men in the Civil War_ (First Book) Gr. 7-12
by Wallace Black

Activities

*_Black Soldiers in the Civil War_ (Dover) Various

Fiction/Historical Fiction

*_Which Way Freedom?_ by Joyce Hansen Gr. 4-12
Fact-based story of a runaway slave boy who fights for the Union.

*_Dog Jack_, by Florence Biros Gr. 5-12
Runaway slave boy and his dog enter the action.

49b First-person accounts

*_Diary of a Drummer Boy_, by Marlene Brill Gr. 3-6
I'm not sure where to place this because the journal entries are fictional, but they're based on the real life of an Illinois boy who won the Congressional Medal of Honor!

*_Mr. Lincoln's Drummer_, by G. Clifton Wisler Gr. 3-12
Relates life of real Union drummer boy.

*_Behind the Blue and the Gray_, by Delia Ray (Young Readers' History of the...) Gr. 5-12
See real life for the soldiers on both sides.

*_When Johnny Went Marching Home: Young Americans Fight the Civil War_ Gr. 5-12
by G. Clifton Wisler
I've not read this, but see that it contains the stories, letters, diaries, and pictures of many young Civil War soldiers.

*_Children of the Civil War_, by Candice Ransom Gr. 6-12
True stories: black and white, slave and free.

***Boys' War*, by Jim Murphy — Gr. 7-12
Very young Confederate and Union soldiers share their own stories.

Mount Up, by Julia Davis — Gr. 9-12
A confederate cavalry officer tells his story.

**Voices from the Civil War*, edited by Milton Meltzer — Gr. 9-12
A collection of personal letters, etc.

**Co. Aytch*, by Sam Watkins — Gr. 10-12
Tennessee man remembers his years in the Confederate army.

**Blockaded Family*, by Parthenia Hague — Unknown
Read of daily life for a real southern family during the blockade.

**Christ in the Camp*, by J. William Jones — Unknown
Actual chaplain of the Army of North Virginia shares about the revivals which took place in southern army camps.

**Confederate Soldiers*, by John Dunn (Civil War Voices) — Unknown
Based on excerpts from real diaries, letters, speeches, etc.

**Diary of a Southern Refugee During the War*, by Judith McGuire — Unknown

**Diary of Sam Watkins, A Confederate Soldier* (In My Own Words) — Unknown
by Samuel Watkins, edited by Ruth Ashby
I've not seen this.

**Union Soldiers*, by John Dunn (Civil War Voices) — Unknown
Excerpts from real letters, diaries, and speeches.

49c Civil War art and photography

Mathew Brady is famous for his numerous photographs of the Civil War. Any library should have a book of his works; you will be powerfully moved when viewing them.

**Civil War Artist*, by Taylor Morrison — Gr. 1-5
Very nice picture book shows the life of a northern newspaper artist.

**Mathew Brady: His Life and Photographs*, by George Sullivan — Gr. 6-12

**Mathew Brady: Civil War Photographer*, by Elizabeth Van Steenwyk (First Bk) Gr. 7-12

Mathew Brady: Historian with a Camera, by James Horan Gr. 8-12

**Mathew Brady: Photographer of the Civil War*, by Lynda Pflueger (Historical...) Unknown

Fiction/Historical Fiction

Mr. Brady's Camera Boy, by Frances Rogers Gr. 7-12

49d Civil War medics and nurses

There are more books about Clara Barton that I can even list, since she played such a key role and helped found the American Red Cross, but here are some samples...along with books about other war nurses. Your library should have plenty from which to choose.

**Clara Barton*, by Patricia Lakin (Ready-to-Read 3) Gr. 1-3

Clara Barton: Angel of the Battlefield, by Rae Bains (Troll) Gr. 1-4

Clara Barton: Soldier of Mercy, by Mary Rose (Garrard Discovery) Gr. 1-5

**Clara Barton*, by Augusta Stevenson (Childhood) Gr. 1-6

Clara Barton and Her Victory Over Fear, by Robert Quackenbush Gr. 1-6

**Clara Barton*, by David R. Collins (Young Reader's Christian Library) Gr. 2-4
This is one of those chunky books some kids like.

**Clara Barton*, by Wil Mara (Rookie) Gr. 2-6

Clara Barton, by Alberta Graham (Makers of America) Gr. 3-8

Clara Barton, by Helen Boylston (Landmark) Gr. 3-9

**Gentle Annie: The True Story of a Civil War Nurse*, by Mary Shura Gr. 3-9
Story of Anne Etheridge, a Civil War nurse from Michigan.

Story of Clara Barton, by Olive Price (Signature) Gr. 3-9

Civil War Medicine, by Douglas Savage (Untold History of the Civil War) Gr. 4-8
I've not seen this, and thus do not know if it is too gruesome.

Clara Barton: Courage Under Fire, by Janet & Geoff Benge (Heroes of History) Gr. 4-10
This is a distinctly Christian biography series.

Charity Goes to War, by Anne Heagney Gr. 5-12
The story of Catholic nurses in the Civil War.

Cornelia: Story of a Civil War Nurse, by Jane McConnell Gr. 5-12
The story of Cornelia Hancock.

Susie King Taylor: Civil War Nurse, by Simeon Booker Gr. 5-12
Story of Negro nurse.

Clara Barton, by Mildred Pace Gr. 6-12

(Story of) Clara Barton of the Red Cross, by Jeannette Covert Nolan (Messner) Gr. 6-12

Civil War Nurse: Mary Ann Bickerdyke, by Adele de Leeuw (Messner) Gr. 7-12

Hospital Sketches, by Louisa May Alcott Gr. 7-12
Famous author relates her experiences as a Civil War nurse.

Cyclone in Calico, by Nina Brown Baker Gr. 8-12
Relates the work of Mary Ann Bickerdyke, who did much for the wounded.

Clara Barton, by Kathleen Deady (Photo-Illustrated Biographies) Unknown

Clara Barton: Civil War Nurse, by Nancy Whitelaw (Historical American) Unknown

Diary of Susie King Taylor, Civil War Nurse, by Susie King Taylor *et al* Unknown

Susie King Taylor: Destined to be Free, by Denise Jordan and Higgins Bond Unknown

Audio

Your Story Hour: Volume 7, section on Clara Barton

49e Civil War spies

**Behind Rebel Lines*, by Seymour Reit Gr. 3-12

Story of Emma Edmonds, a Canadian woman who had lived in Michigan, and who so badly wanted to help the fight against slavery that she dressed as a man to be able to work for the Union as a spy. This has been an appreciated version, from what I hear.

**Spies in the Civil War*, by Victor Brooks (Untold History of the Civil War) Gr. 4-8

Rose Greenhow: Spy for the Confederacy, by Doris Faber Gr. 4-12

Yankee Spy: Elizabeth Van Lew, by Jeannette Nolan (Messner) Gr. 4-12

**Dear Ellen Bee*, by Mary Lyons & Muriel Branch Gr. 5-10

I've not see this, but it sounds interesting. A scrapbook format has been used to tell of the real exploits of a wealthy Richmond woman, Elizabeth van Lew, and Liza, the daughter of her freed slaves, and how they spied for the Union right in the Confederate capital!

Frank Thompson: Her Civil War Story, by Bryna Stevens Gr. 5-10

I've not read this story of Emma Edmonds who paraded as a man to spy, fight, etc.

Belle Boyd: Secret Agent, by Jeannette Nolan (Messner) Gr. 5-12

Confederate Spy Stories, by Katherine & John Bakeless Gr. 5-12

Girl Soldier and Spy: Sarah Emma Edmundson, by Mary Hoehling (Messner) Gr. 5-12

This book spells Emma's name differently.

**Petticoat Spies: Six Women Spies of the Civil War*, by Peggy Caravantes Gr. 5-12

Rose Greenhow: Confederate Secret Agent, by Dorothy Grant (Amer. Background) Gr. 5-12

Mr. Lincoln's Master Spy, by Arthur Orrmont (Messner) Gr. 6-12

Life of Lafayette Baker.

Spy for the Confederacy: Rose Greenhow, by Jeannette Covert Nolan (Messner) Gr. 6-12

Spies for the Blue and the Gray, by Harnett Kane Gr. 7-12

Eyes and Ears of the Civil War, by G. Allen Foster Gr. 8-12

Spies of both sides.

***Women Civil War Spies of the Confederacy*, by Larissa Phillips — Unknown
I do not know if there is feminism in this book.

Fiction/Historical Fiction

***Personal Correspondence of Emma Edmonds and Mollie Turner* (Liberty Letters) — Gr. 3-8
by Nancy LeSourd
This book is in a distinctly Christian series.

***Rebel Spy*, by Norma Jean Lutz (American Adventure # 23) — Gr. 3-8
Cincinnati kids find southern spy in this book from a distinctly Christian series.

Deserter, by Peter Burchard — Gr. 5-12

49f Civil War uniforms and weaponry

In Scarlet and Blue: The Story of Military Uniforms in America, by Dirk Gringhuis — Gr. 3-7

Runaway Balloon, by Burke Davis — Gr. 3-7
True story of flight of Confederate hot-air balloon.

***Secret Weapons in the Civil War*, by Victor Brooks (Untold History of the...) — Gr. 4-8

Activities

***Civil War Uniforms* (Dover) — Various

49g Civil War prisons

***Pink and Say*, by Patricia Polacco — Gr. 1-5
Don't miss this powerful, true story of ex-slave boy (whose family is shown to be very godly) and white boy facing Andersonville prison together. Also cited earlier.

Great Civil War Escapes, by A.I. Schutzer — Gr. 6-12

***Prison Camps of the Civil War*, by Linda Wade — Unknown
I've not seen this.

Fiction/Historical Fiction

Rat Hell, by Peter Burchard — Gr. 5-12
Union soldiers try to escape a Confederate prison.

Yankees on the Run, by John Brick — Gr. 5-12
Union prisoners try to escape from the notorious Andersonville prison.

49h Civil War in the West

**Civil War in the West*, by Douglas Savage (Untold History of the Civil War) — Gr. 4-8

**Civil War in the West*, by Jim Corrigan — Unknown

Fiction/Historical Fiction

Ride for Texas, by Lee McGiffin — Gr. 5-12
I've not seen this book, but I believe it is about Civil War matters in Texas.

**Rifles for Watie*, by Harold Keith — Gr. 6-12

Rebel Trumpet, by Gordon Shirreffs — Gr. 7-12
I believe this is about Union soldiers in the New Mexico Territory!

49i Union sympathizers in the South

**Southern Yankees*, by H. Speicher & K. Borland — Gr. 3-8

Man Who Said No, by Sally Edwards — Gr. 8-12
The life of James Petigru of South Carolina who strongly opposed secession.

49j Vinnie Ream, sculptor of Lincoln

At a time when it was quite unusual, a young woman was asked to make the sculpture of Lincoln which now stands in the Capitol Rotunda!

**Vinnie and Abraham*, by Dawn FitzGerald and Catherine Stock — Gr. 1-4

Vinnie Ream, by Gordon Hall — Gr. 5-12

Fiction/Historical Fiction

**Saving the President*, by Barbara Brenner (What If Mystery) Gr. 3-8
Fictional tale of Vinnie Ream helping Lincoln while at the White House sculpting.

**Letters from Vinnie*, by Maureen Sappey Gr. 6-12
Fictional letters reveal real life of Vinnie; I've heard this does have some romance, but I cannot comment since I've not read it.

49k Civil War animals

**Old Abe*, by Patrick Young Gr. 1-4
Wonderful, amazing story! I hope you can find it!

War Eagle: Civil War Mascot, by Edmund Lindop Gr. 1-6
True story of a bald eagle that was mascot for Wisconsin troops; very rare, but also very good, so I hope you can find it, or "Old Abe" listed above.

Famous Horses of the Civil War, by Fairfax Downey Gr. 4-12

Horse for General Lee, by Fairfax Downey Gr. 5-12
Tells of Lee's various horses and their keepers.

Fiction/Historical Fiction

Horse that Won the Civil War, by Bern Keating Gr. 6-12
Indian wins a mustang that later has an impact on the war.

50 Fiction/Historical Fiction—Civil War

These books are not tied to a particular person or event, but are good reading!

**Drummer Boy*, by Ann Turner Gr. 1-4
This fabulous picture book is quite recent.

**Li'l Dan the Drummer Boy*, by Romare Bearden Gr. 1-4
I've not seen this book, but have read that it tells the story of a slave boy who loves to drum, and uses his talent to help the Union soldiers who tell him he's free. It is written and illustrated by a now-deceased African-American artist, and I guess the images are quite bold.

*_Blue and Gray_, by Eve Bunting Gr. 1-5

Poignant picture book, as later black and white boys remember history of site.

*_Promise Quilt_, by Candice Ransom Gr. 1-5

Southern girl is torn by loss of her father, but the family pulls together beautifully. I've not read this, but it sounds like a wonderful tale of family love and sacrifice!

*_Red Legs_, by Ted Lewin Gr. 2-5

Modern boy is moved during Civil War re-enactment, and relates story of a real Union drummer boy. I've heard that it's a tearjerker.

*_Ballad of the Civil War_, by Mary Stolz Gr. 2-6

Union teen remembers his twin brother, who is fighting for the Confederacy.

*_Who Comes with Cannons?_ by Patricia Beatty Gr. 2-10

Quaker girl gets involved in the war.

Pony for Jeremiah, by Robert Miller Gr. 3-6

A family escaping from slavery makes a new home on the Nebraska prairie, but then Father goes back to fight in the Civil War.

Lucinda, a Little Girl of 1860, by Mabel Leigh Hunt Gr. 3-7

When Rebels Rode, by Grace Huffard Gr. 3-7

Older book about life of 12-year-old girl of southern Indiana during Morgan's raids. This looks precious...

*_Light in the Storm_, by Karen Hesse (Dear America) Gr. 3-9

The "tone" of this series varies widely, so please be discerning.

*_Among the Camps_, by Thomas Page Gr. 3-10

Southern family life during the war.

*_Two Little Confederates_, by Thomas Page Gr. 3-10

Beloved story of two southern brothers.

*_When Will This Cruel War Be Over?_ by Barry Denenberg (Dear America) Gr. 3-10

Warning: this fictionalized diary subtly pokes at Christianity of some slave holders.

*_Lottie's Courage: A Contraband Slave's Story_, by Phyllis Haislip Gr. 4-6

I've not seen this, but it's about the ex-slaves camped around Union soldiers.

Fifer for the Union, by Lorenzo Allen Gr. 4-7

**Island Far from Home*, by John Donahue Gr. 4-7

I've not read this story of a Union boy who begins exchanging letters with a Confederate prisoner near his own age.

**Three Against the Tide*, by D. Anne Love Gr. 4-7

I've not read this book about a 12-year-old Charleston girl who must protect her two younger brothers and their home during war.

Cyrus Holt and the Civil War, by Ann Holt Gr. 4-8

See how Civil War affects a New York family (based on the author's grandfather).

**Journal of James Edmond Pease*, by Jim Murphy (My Name is America) Gr. 4-9

The "tone" of this series varies widely, so please be discerning. This is story of a 16-year-old New York boy serving in Virginia during 1863.

Cadmus Henry, by Walter Edmonds Gr. 4-12

Boy in hot-air balloon drifts over the fronts, sees much action from both sides.

**Charley Skedaddle*, by Patricia Beatty Gr. 4-12

Boy who loves baseball faces his fears when he deserts.

Jed, by Peter Burchard Gr. 4-12

Union soldier is surprised to discover that Confederate family he meets is so nice.

**Shades of Gray*, by Carolyn Reeder Gr. 4-12

Boy is ashamed his guardian-uncle is not fighting, but then begins to see complexity.

**Wait for Me, Watch for Me, Eula Bee*, by Patricia Beatty Gr. 4-12

Brother tries to rescue sister held by Comanche Indians during the war.

**Pitch in Time*, by Robert Lytle Gr. 5-8

A boy raved about this story of a modern boy who "goes back in time" to 1864 in Michigan long enough to experience the Civil War's impact on locals and see the early stage of his beloved hobby, baseball.

Baxie Randall and the Blue Raiders, by Carl Hodges Gr. 5-9

I've not seen this book, but it is about a 12-year-old boy who is left to care for family when raiders strike his farm.

**No Man's Land*, by Susan Bartoletti Gr. 5-9

I've not read this story of a 14-year-old Georgia boy who joins up to prove his manhood, but ends up being surprised at the drudgery and pain of war.

Sycamore Tree, by Marion Havighurst Gr. 5-10
I've not read this adventure-romance with Morgan in Ohio and West Virginia.

**Across Five Aprils*, by Irene Hunt Gr. 5-12
Boy watches the deep effect of the war over its course in this long-beloved story.

Brother Against Brother, by Phyllis Fenner Gr. 5-12
Collected short stories; her collections are highly sought after.

Ghost Battalion, *Ride, Rebels!* and *Appomattox Road*, all by Manly Wade Wellman Gr. 5-12
A trilogy bringing adventure with the Iron Scouts of the Confederacy.

Johnny Reb, *The White Feather*, **and** *Blow, Bugles, Blow* Gr. 5-12
all three by Merritt Parmelee Allen
As mentioned before, I know boys who earn money just to buy Allen's books!

Muddy Road to Glory, by Stephen Meader Gr. 5-12

Rebel Mail Runner, by Manly Wade Wellman Gr. 5-12
Confederates risk their lives to get mail through enemy lines.

Rebel Rider, by Lee McGiffin Gr. 5-12
I'm not aware of the particular subject of this book, but since many boys enjoy McGiffin's books, I wanted to plug it in here somewhere!

Ride for Old Glory, by Jacqueline McNicol Gr. 5-12
Boy has amazing adventures; the last chapter reveals that much of the story is true!

**With Every Drop of Blood*, by James & Christopher Collier Gr. 5-12
I've not read this story of southern boy captured by black Union soldier his age...and the friendship that ensues. Collier books can be gritty and have strong language.

**Drummer Boy at Bull Run*, by Gilbert Morris (Bonnets and Bugles) Gr. 6-12
This is the first in a Christian series of historical fiction.

**Iron Scouts of the Confederacy*, by Lee McGiffin Gr. 6-12
Two brothers face the cost of defending their belief in states' rights.

Action Front! by Gordon Shirreffs Gr. 7-12
I believe this relates to horse artillery units.

Beneath Another Sun, by Marjory Hall Gr. 7-12
I've not read this story about a northern family living in Richmond during the war.

Coat for Private Patrick, by Lee McGiffin Gr. 7-12
Teen works on Civil War telegraph.

**Confederate Fiddle*, by Jeanne Williams Gr. 7-12

Ride Proud, Rebel, by André Norton Gr. 7-12

Confederate soldier perseveres through ordeals to make way to Bedford Forrest.

Roanoke Raiders, by Gordon Shirreffs Gr. 7-12

Adventure in Virginia!

**Sound the Jubilee*, by Sandra Forrester Gr. 7-12

I've not seen this story of North Carolina slaves who end up in "contraband" slave colony on Roanoke Island, but it seems to includes many of the very real difficulties.

Taken by the Enemy*, **Within the Enemy Lines*, **and,* *On the Blockade* Gr. 7-12

all by Oliver Optic

**Turn Homeward, Hannalee*, by Patricia Beatty Gr. 7-12

Experienced mill girl forced to work in the North; includes soldiers forcing attentions, I'm told, but I'm not sure how far. She tries to return home with brother.

**With Lee in Virginia*, by G.A. Henty Gr. 7-12

Cudjo's Cave, by J.T. Trowbridge Gr. 9-12

Quaker schoolteacher struggles with war issues in Tennessee.

**Guns of Bull Run*, **Guns of Shiloh*, **Rock of Chickamauga*, **Scouts of Stonewall* Gr. 9-12
Shades of the Wilderness, **Star of Gettysburg*, **Sword of Antietam*, **Tree of Appomattox*

by Joseph Altsheler

Wonderful fiction of yesteryear that is being reprinted!

**Little Shepherd of Kingdom Come*, by John Fox, Jr. Gr. 9-12

**Red Badge of Courage*, by Stephen Crane Gr. 9-12

This has long been considered a classic on the Civil War.

**Friendly Persuasion*, and, **Except for Me and Thee*, by Jessamyn West Gr. 10-12

Two books about Indiana Quaker family during the Civil War, and the issues the war raises for these pacifists. *Friendly Persuasion* was made into a film starring Gary Cooper.

Gods and Generals* **and **Last Full Measure*, by Jeff Shaara Gr. 10-12

These novels, companions to **Killer Angels*, by the author's father, delve deep into the hearts, character, and relationships of the leaders on both sides of the Civil War. I do not know if they contain inappropriate asides.

**Broken Drum*, by Edith Hemingway Unknown

I've not read this story of a Union drummer boy.

51 Closing Words

Looking back, we can be sure of one thing: when it comes to the Civil War, we can't be sure of much...not even what to call it! My sense is that both sides were right about some things (and they trumpeted those) and wrong about some things (and they overlooked those). That may be why the devastation—the terrible and long-lasting toll on our nation—has been so great. To this very day, tension often creeps into northern and southern voices when the war is discussed...even when amongst fellow Christian believers who serve the same God! The irony is that God, in His Heaven, looked down and saw the entire drama enacted. I wonder what He thinks, because that's what I want to think too. And that goes for all the topics we've discussed in this guide, the ones shaping life on both sides of the pond!

With that, we'll close this unit. I had hoped to cover the full century, but we've already gone so far and have explored so deep. In the next unit, we'll have to catch up on some of the people and events we just didn't get time for in this unit—Louis Pasteur, the Crimean War, the budding "women's movement," the Transcendental writers, and so much more! What's important, though, is that you grasp the subterranean issues that were the undercurrent of the tumultuous sixty-five years we've just studied.

Remember, the worldview of Europe and America was up for grabs. The most important post-Enlightenment thinkers (some of whom we'll meet in the next unit) threw out the Judeo-Christian base and began telling everyone that the most profound forces at work in individual people and in whole civilizations were not spiritual, but were economic (Marx), biological (Darwin), or psychological (Freud). That is *revolution* at the deepest point. That's why you saw so much change.

More change is coming, though! In *TruthQuest History: Age of Revolution III (1865-2000)* you'll see England achieve one of the largest empires in all of history under Queen Victoria. As America struggles to rebuild after the Civil War, her great plains will fill with people, immigrants will pour into her cities, and her energy will know no bounds. What will she do with her wealth and health, and what about those who are neither wealthy or healthy? Inventiveness and industry will send a man to the moon, but here's the big question...will you see the *progress* promised by humanism? Where will mankind's "evolution" lead him in the 1900s?

Two titanic world wars will be fought, and you'll see the godless worldviews of Marx, Darwin, and Freud propel communism to direct control over one-third of the world's population, while their ideas indirectly affect virtually every developed nation, bringing about big government, public education, and marginalization of Christianity and its moral standards. Where, in all this, will be the Body of Christ, charged with the awesome mission of being salt and light? For the first time, you'll be studying a history you've lived through, and that you'll effect! Can't wait to see you there!

Appendix 1: *ThinkWrite* Responses

You may with to keep these notes inaccessible to your students so that their thoughts are not colored by the author's. They can help you, the parent, guide discussion on these topics *before* they are assigned to the students, in addition helping you analyze their responses.

ThinkWrite 1:

> ***ThinkWrite 1: "Gimme the crown!"***
>
> As you sort through Napoleon's life, look for his *Big 2 Beliefs*. Remember, the last French king before their revolution said: *I am the state.* Was Napoleon's outlook any different? Why did he believe that he had the right to so much power, and to take so many lives?

Though only God knows the heart, Napoleon's actions make it seem clear he did not hold himself accountable to a higher law. His word, his whim, *was* law, in his mind. This reveals his *Big Belief #1*. His authority was higher than God's. He probably did not say so directly, and he may even have attended church, but when it was decision time.... In this, Napoleon's beliefs appear identical to the king overthrown during the French Revolution, when he said, "I am the state." It thus follows that he would not have the respect for others which God requires since people are made in His image and are beloved by Him. (*Big Belief #2*) With small value on the lives of others, Napoleon showed little hesitation to lay down the lives of millions of French soldiers to achieve his military goals. While his first battles *may* have been considered necessary to protect France during the European reaction to the French Revolution, we can easily see that his later battles were designed to create an empire for him that satisfied his ego. Again, this shows a preeminence on himself and a devaluing of those he used to achieve his goals. Very dangerous!

ThinkWrite 2:

> ***ThinkWrite 2: "Free?"***
>
> Find a good definition of free enterprise, but then go beyond to give a quick explanation for the basis of that freedom as we've discussed. Can you see how it contributes to scientific and industrial creativity?

Webster's Dictionary defines free enterprise as:

> *Freedom of private business to organize and operate for profit in a competitive system without interference by government beyond regulation necessary to protect public interest and keep the national economy in balance.*

What free enterprise protects is the God-given responsibility each individual has for making his way in this world. At no time does God's Word require governments to care for citizens. The Biblical emphasis is always on individual work, creativity, property ownership, and freedom.

This is a great freedom, because "working for the big guy, and in turn expecting the big guy to look after me" is nothing more than modern-day feudalism. Never forget: government support always comes with government control! There's no such thing as a free lunch!

Additionally, free enterprise helps nations experience true economic progress because free enterprise allows individuals to pursue their own goals and dreams, using their unique, individual talents. The inborn motivations of people to increase, to care for their own needs and those of their families, to succeed, to contribute to others, to accomplish work...all these lead toward great productivity when unhampered by governmental interference.

This emphasis on the individual comes from Christianity, as Clarence Carson explains so well:

> *The emphasis of Christianity is focused primarily on the individual. Only the individual survives eternally, according to Christian doctrine, not groups, not organizations, not governments—all of which are temporary and temporal. The individual is responsible for his deeds, both good and bad, and will be held to account for them. Within the Judeo-Christian framework, man is held to be free to choose his course, but he is therefore responsible for what he does with that freedom.*[104]

The liberties of free enterprise can be abused (as can *any* liberties), so enterprise is only *free* when it takes place within God's moral boundaries. Otherwise, free enterprise quickly becomes greed, corruption, and materialism.

ThinkWrite 3:

ThinkWrite 3: "Moolah!" What does God say about wealth? Don't stop when you've found a few Bible verses that support your preconceived notions! Instead, look for the full counsel of God!

104 Carson 47.

Here are just a few of the many Scripture verses (NKJV, except where noted) that could be found. Note, as my father points out, that God does not *give* us wealth, He gives us the *power to get* wealth. In other words, we cannot sit back idly and expect God to lavish financial gifts upon us; our obedience to His principles and priorities, as well as our work ethic and how we give and otherwise handle money are crucial. Money is *certainly* not to become our god or source of security, yet it is not the evil the church has sometimes claimed. It's how money is obtained, used, and considered that is key, in my opinion. The Bible says it best, of course:

> *But seek first his kingdom and his righteousness, and all these things shall be given to you as well.* (Mt. 6:33, NIV)

> *And you shall remember the Lord your God, for it is He who gives you power to get wealth.* (Deut. 8:18a)

> *Humility and the fear of the Lord bring wealth and honor and life.* (Prov. 22:4, NIV)

> *He who deals with a slack hand becomes poor, but the hand of the diligent makes one rich.* (Prov. 10:4)

> *The blessing of the Lord makes one rich, and He adds no sorrow with it.* (Prov. 10:22)

> *Wealth gained by dishonesty will be diminished, but he who gathers by labor will increase.* (Prov. 13:11)

> *Do not overwork to be rich; because of your own understanding, cease.* (Prov. 23:4)

> *The rich man is wise in his own eyes, but the poor who has understanding searches him out.* (Prov. 28:11)

> *A man with an evil eye hastens after riches, and does not consider that poverty will come upon him.* (Pr. 28:22)

> *As for every man to whom God has given riches and wealth, and given him power to eat of it, to receive his heritage and rejoice in his labors, this is the gift of God.* (Eccl. 5:19)

> *Thus says the Lord: "Let not the wise man glory in his wisdom; let not the mighty man glory in his might; nor let the rich man glory in his riches; but let him who glories glory in this, that he understands and knows Me."* (Jer. 9:23-24)

> *But said to him, "You fool! This night your soul will be required of you; then whose will those things be which you have provided?" So is he who lays up treasures for himself, and is not rich towards God.* (Luke 12:20-21)

> *Command those who are rich in this present age not to be haughty, nor to trust in uncertain riches, but in the living God, who gives us richly all things to enjoy.* (I Tim. 6:17)

A good man leaves an inheritance for his children's children, but a sinner's wealth is stored up for the righteous. (Prov. 13:22, NIV)

Better a little with the fear of the Lord than great wealth with turmoil. (Prov. 15:16, NIV)

When you ask you do not receive, because you ask with wrong motives, that you may spend what you get on your pleasures. (James 4:3, NIV)

ThinkWrite 4:

> ***ThinkWrite 4: "What does the 'Big Boss' say about being a boss?"***
>
> What does the Bible say to employers...*and* employees too? (Isn't it neat that God cares about people's jobs?!)

The Bible has quite a bit to say about employers (called *masters* in many versions) and employees (called *servants* in many versions). Even if your Bible uses the words *master* and *servant*, we can know that's Biblical terminology for *employers* and *employees* because wages are discussed. (Slavery doesn't involve wages, though some of these verses also address the slavery that existed at the time of the Bible's writing.) So, just exchange the more modern terms in your mind, and you'll grasp what God has to say about life on the job. You can find many more verses than those listed here; these are just a sample!

God's Word for Employers:

Masters, provide your slaves with what is right and fair, because you know that you also have a Master in heaven. (Col. 4:1)

For the Scripture says, "Do not muzzle the ox while it is treading out the grain," and "The worker deserves his wages." (I Tim. 5:18)

Look! The wages you failed to pay the workmen who mowed your fields are crying out against you. The cries of the harvesters have reached the ears of the Lord Almighty. You have lived on earth in luxury and self-indulgence. (James 5:4-5a)

As the eyes of slaves look to the hand of their master, as the eyes of a maid look to the hand of her mistress, so our eyes look to the Lord our God, till he shows us his mercy. (Psalm 123:2; how important it is for employers to respond to the vulnerability of their employees as God responds to our vulnerability.)

Do not withhold good from those who deserve it, when it is in your power to act. (Prov. 3:27)

A kind man benefits himself, but a cruel man brings trouble on himself. (Prov. 11:17; we saw clearly in this unit that employers who violated God's principles eventually suffered more restrictive and more damaging controls—from government, labor unions, etc. —than if they had been self-governing according to God's standards.)

One man gives freely, yet gains even more; another withholds unduly, but comes to poverty. A generous man will prosper... (Prov. 11:24-25a)

A righteous man cares for the needs of his animal... (Prov. 12:10; he should take even better care of his human workers, though, sadly, some were treated worse than animals)

He who oppresses the poor shows contempt for their Maker, but whoever is kind to the needy honors God. (Prov. 14:31; this includes being kind to those who *need* a job.)

He who oppresses the poor to increase his wealth...[will] *come to poverty.* (Prov. 22:16)

He who is kind to the poor lends to the Lord, and he [the Lord] *will reward him for what he has done.* (Prov. 19:17; it's best not to scrimp on those who have less, such as employees, whether or not they're technically poor.)

Do not rob the poor because he is poor...For the Lord will plead their cause, and plunder the soul of those who plunder them. (Prov. 22:22-23)

He who pampers his servant from childhood will have him as a son in the end. (Prov. 29:21)

And you, masters, [give] *up threatening, knowing that your own Master also is in heaven, and there is no partiality with him.* (Eph. 6:9)

<u>God's Word for Employees</u>:

Do you see a man skilled in his work? He will serve before kings... (Prov. 22:29)

The sluggard says, "There is a lion in the road, a fierce lion roaming the streets!" (Prov. 26:13; instead be the type of employee who sees why it *can* be done, not why it *can't* be done.)

A student is not above his teacher, nor a servant above his master. (Matt. 10:24)

Slaves, obey your earthly masters with respect and fear, and with sincerity of heart, just as you would obey Christ. Obey them not only to win their favor when their eye is on you, but like slaves of Christ, doing the will of God from your heart. Serve wholeheartedly, as if you were serving the Lord, not men, because you know that the Lord will reward everyone for whatever good he does, whether he is slave or free. (Eph. 6:5-8)

All who are under the yoke of slavery should consider their masters worthy of full respect, so that God's name and our teaching may not be slandered. Those who have believing masters are not to show less respect for them because they are brothers. Instead, they are to serve them even better, because those who benefit from their service are believers, and dear to them. These are the things you are to teach and urge on them. (I Tim. 6:1-2)

Teach slaves to be subject to their masters in everything, to try to please them, not to talk back to them, and not to steal from them, but to show that they can be fully trusted, so that in every way they will make the teaching about God our Savior attractive. (Titus 2:9-10)

<u>God's Word regarding *work*, in general</u>:

All hard work brings a profit, but mere talk leads to poverty. (Prov. 14:23)

I went past the field of the sluggard, past the vineyard of the man who lacks judgment; thorns had come up everywhere, the ground was covered with weeds, and the stone wall was in ruins. I applied my heart to what I observed and learned a lesson from what I saw: A little sleep, a little slumber, a little folding of the hands to rest—and poverty will come on you like a bandit and scarcity like an armed man. (Prov. 24:30-34)

Be sure you know the condition of your flocks, give careful attention to your herds; for riches do not endure forever... (Prov. 27:23-24a, NIV; this reminds us to be savvy and diligent, never taking things for granted, or assuming the future will be like the present.)

If you argue your case with a neighbor, do not betray another man's confidence, or he who hears it may shame you and you will never lose your bad reputation. (Prov. 25:9-10; this verse urges us to avoid gossiping about disputes, such as those that might occur on the job; it's always good to deal directly, not bringing in other people who may talk about the dispute with others.)

Rich and poor have this in common: The Lord is maker of them all. (Prov. 22:2; employers and employees should remember they're *all* accountable to the same God.)

ThinkWrite 5:

ThinkWrite 5: "The race is on!"

Why did many Americans feel they were in a race with other Americans, competing for dominance? Why didn't they work together as a good team?

To prefer others over ourselves, as the Bible requires, is indeed difficult. Our sin nature instead urges selfishness, which can be seen in the desire get the biggest piece for one's self. Also, the Bible commands that we have a servant heart toward others, but that certainly doesn't come naturally! A *me-first* attitude was becoming increasingly prevalent in America when the spiritual fires—necessary to live a Christ-like life—were cool. We *must* stay in tune with God in order to rightfully handle the great potentials of our political and economic freedoms.

ThinkWrite 6:

> ***ThinkWrite 6: "How's'bout you?!"***
>
> You'll be old enough to vote before you know it! Any thoughts on how you'll handle this precious and awesome responsibility?

This topic is completely personal, so no "correct answer" can be listed here. I hope it engenders interesting discussion around your dinner table!

ThinkWrite 7:

> ***ThinkWrite 7: "What does it all mean?"***
>
> Please describe in your own words the beliefs of the *Romantic Movement.* And you better not come up with some lovey-dovey, "cupidy" answer! You know this is not about a bouquet of flowers or a box of chocolates, but it is about the feeling side of mankind, right? Tell us more, such as how romanticism compared with rationalism.

I'll let Clarence Carson definite romanticism concisely:

> *The romantic mood was a revolt against the excessive claims of reason as well as emphasizing the imagination, feeling, emotion, intuition, inspiration, the inner light within the individual and an outward zeal for reform. ...Romanticism tended to exalt the heart over the head. In that especially, the romantic outlook differed from the preceding age of reason.*[105]

Influential thinkers, such as Jean Jacques Rousseau, Immanuel Kant, and Georg Hegel, all contributed to the demise of rationalism because they rightfully pointed out the limitations

105 Carson 3:66.

of human reason. However, they did *not* bring philosophy back to a Biblically whole view of mankind as created in God's multi-faceted and integrated image. Instead, they swung the pendulum to the opposite side of humanism with typically human shortsightedness and incompleteness. They emphasized human emotion, intuition, experience, creativity, innateness, judgment, etc.

Please keep in mind, though, that just because someone is considered a Romantic composer, for example, does not necessarily mean that they rejected a Biblical view of mankind. It might have been simply that they were relieved that rationalism was crumbling and they were glad to represent the facet of mankind's God-given creativity.

ThinkWrite 8:

> ***ThinkWrite 8: "Select-a-Guy!"***
>
> Several amongst the list below are heroes and heroines of the faith. Would you like to select one for deeper study? We can learn much from these folks!

Students will select various heroes of the faith, so we can provide no sample response here.

ThinkWrite 9:

> ***ThinkWrite 9: "Select-another-Guy!"***
>
> Please select one of the Romantic Movement composers, painters, or authors and explain how their works showed the essence of Romanticism. Please keep in mind, though, that just because someone is considered a Romantic composer, for example, does not necessarily mean that they rejected a Biblical view of mankind. It might have been simply that they were relieved that rationalism was crumbling and they were glad to represent the facet of mankind's God-given creativity. Please probe these issues with your artist of choice. Enjoy!

Students will select various artists, composers, or authors, so we can provide no sample response here.

ThinkWrite 10:

> ***ThinkWrite 10: "What's the diff?"***
>
> Try not to get uptight about this, but do please explain some of the basic principles of Karl Marx in your own words. Focus on explaining how humanistic beliefs and atheism led to his conclusions. Where did his thinking go wrong?

All the issues explored in this *ThinkWrite* were *very* thoroughly discussed in the main commentary of this guide (Section 27 on Marx). It would be redundant to restate them here. Parents, if you'll simply read that commentary, you'll be completely able to lead thought-provoking discussions and analyze your students' answers.

ThinkWrite 11:

> ***ThinkWrite 11: "Shining Example"***
>
> Harriet Tubman, Frederick Douglass, and Sojourner Truth are shining examples of someone who doesn't just look out for themselves, but goes back to help others....at great risk. What does this show you? What does it make you think about what you can do with your own life?

Answers will be completely personal. Enjoy good discussion!

Appendix 2: List of Cited Resources

✦ *Opportunity, not Obligation!* **Our *TruthQuest History* is completely different from curricula which depend on certain books, so users must think differently about it! Here, the goal is *not* to guide you through books, but through history...using books...whichever books are readily available. That's why so many are listed here—to give you the utmost opportunity to harness your public library (and inter-library loan), church library, neighborhood private school library, or the many free online books without missing a gem. When you (wisely!) decide to educate using real books, no matter what curriculum guide you choose, you're only able to use what's available. *Therefore*, this large booklist is *not* a burden, it's a benefit. It vastly increases the chances of finding the best available books on every topic. Relax! Enjoy!**

✦ **The size of this list proves that TruthQuest History does not require the use of any particular books, but only offers many suggestions (though a handful are highly recommended in the main text of this guide!)**

✦ **Not all of these sources are recommended; some are listed as only "relevant." Cautionary notes are in the main text of this guide. Many I've never even seen, but folks were asking for more listings of current books, so I've searched in-print lists for you.**

✦ **The books marked with an asterisk (*) are those deemed to be in-print at this time. It is not necessarily a preferred books, as new users sometimes assume.**

✦ **Please note that this resource list is copyrighted, and is only for use by purchasers of this guide. You may copy it only for your personal use.**

✦ **If a book is in a series, a brief version of the series named is in parentheses; e.g., *Childhood of Famous Americans* is noted as (Childhood). Short notes about books are in brackets [ ].**

✦ **The famous works of many authors are mentioned in this *TruthQuest History* guide. They will not be listed again here, because they are easily available and parental decisions must be made regarding which "classics" are appropriate reading and a beneficial use of valuable reading time. That can best take place when studying the authors "in context" as you will in this guide.**

**21 Great Scientists Who Believed the Bible*, by Ann Lamont	Gr. 7-12
54°-40' or Fight! by Bob & Jan Young (Messner/Milestones)	Gr. 7-12
**290*, by Scott O'Dell	Gr. 5-12
1812: The War and the World, by Walter Buehr	Gr. 4-10
**1812: The War Nobody Won*, by Albert Marrin	Gr. 7-12
**1848: Year of Revolution*, by R.G. Grant	Gr. 5-12
1861: Year of Lincoln, by Genevieve Foster	Gr. 3-7
**1863: A House Divided*, by Elizabeth Massie	Gr. 6-12
**A. Lincoln and Me*, by Louise Borden	Gr. 1-3
Aaron Burr, by William Wise	Gr. 7-12
**Aaron Burr and the Young Nation*, by Scott Ingram (Notorious Americans)	Gr. 7-12
**Abandoned on the Wild Frontier*, by Dave & Neta Jackson (Trailblazer)	Gr. 3-9

*_Abe Lincoln and the Muddy Pig_, by Stephen Krensky (Ready-to-Read 2) Gr. 1-2

Abe Lincoln Gets His Chance, by Frances Cavanah Gr. 3-8

*_Abe Lincoln Goes to Washington_, by Cheryl Harness Gr. 1-4

*_Abe Lincoln Grows Up_, by Carl Sandburg Gr. 4-10

*_Abe Lincoln: Log Cabin to White House_, by Sterling North (Landmark) Gr. 3-8

*_Abe Lincoln Remembers_, by Ann Turner Gr. 1-3

*_Abe Lincoln: The Boy Who Loved Books_, by Kay Winter Gr. 1-3

Abe Lincoln's Beard, by Jan Wahl Gr. 1-8

Abe Lincoln's Birthday, by Wilma Pitchford Hays Gr. 4-8

*_Abe Lincoln's Hat_, by Martha Brenner (Step into Reading 2) Gr. 1-3

Abe Lincoln's Hobby, by Helen Kay Gr. 1-5

Abe Lincoln's Other Mother, by Bernadine Bailey (Messner) Gr. 4-12

*_Abigail_, by Portia Sperry Gr. 2-8

*_Abigail's Drum_, by John Minahan Gr. 2-5

*_Abner Doubleday_, by Montrew Dunham (Childhood) Gr. 1-6

Above All a Physician, by Jeanne Carbonnier Gr. 9-12

*_Abraham Lincoln_, by Janet & Geoff Benge (Christian Heroes) Gr. 5-12

*_Abraham Lincoln_, by Amy Cohn & Suzy Schmidt Gr. 2-5

*_Abraham Lincoln_, by David Collins (Sower) Gr. 6-12

*_Abraham Lincoln_, by James Daugherty Gr. 3-12

*_Abraham Lincoln_, by Ingri & Edgar d'Aulaire Gr. 1-3

*_Abraham Lincoln_, by Carol Greene (Rookie Biography) Gr. 1-3

Abraham Lincoln, by Patricia Miles Martin (See and Read) Gr. 1-2

Abraham Lincoln, by Enid Meadowcroft Gr. 5-9

Abraham Lincoln, by Jeannette Covert Nolan (Messner) Gr. 7-12

*_Abraham Lincoln_, by Augusta Stevenson (Childhood) Gr. 1-6

*_Abraham Lincoln: A Man for All the People_, by Myra Cohn Livingston Gr. K-4

Abraham Lincoln: An Initial Biography, by Genevieve Foster Gr. 2-7

*_Abraham Lincoln and His Family Paper Dolls_ (Dover) Various

*_Abraham Lincoln Coloring Book_, by A.G. Smith (Dover) Various

Abraham Lincoln: Courageous Leader, by L. Bragdon (Makers of America) Gr. 3-8

*_Abraham Lincoln: For the People_, by Anne Colver (Discovery) Gr. 1-5

*_Abraham Lincoln, Friend of the People_, by Clara Ingram Judson Gr. 4-9

Abraham Lincoln Joke Book, by Beatrice DeRegniers Gr. 3-8

*_Abraham Lincoln: Letters from a Slave Girl_, by Andrea Pinkney Gr. 4-8

Abraham Lincoln: Man of Courage, by Bernadine Bailey (Piper) Gr. 2-7

*_Abraham Lincoln: The Writer_, by Abraham Lincoln, edited by Harold Holzer Gr. 7-12

*_Abraham Lincoln's World_, by Genevieve Foster Gr. 3-10

*_Abraham's Battle_, by Sara Banks Gr. 4-8

*_Across Five Aprils_, by Irene Hunt Gr. 5-12

*_Across the Lines_, by Carolyn Reeder Gr. 5-9

*_Across the Plains in 1844_, by Catherine Sager Unknown

*_Across the Wide and Lonesome Prairie_, by Kristiana Gregory (Dear America) Gr. 3-9

Action Front! by Gordon Shirreffs Gr. 7-12

Ada Byron Lovelace: The Lady and the Computer, by Mary Dodson Wade Gr. 5-12

Adam Gray, Stowaway: Story of the China Trade, by Herbert Arntson Gr. 6-12

Adella Mary in Old Mexico, by Florence Means	Gr. 8-12
**Adoniram Judson: God's Man in Burma*, by Sharon Hambrick	Gr. 3-7
Adventure at the Mill, by Barbara & Heather Bramwell (Buckskin)	Gr. 2-8
Adventures of Broken-Hand, by Frank Morriss	Gr. 4-9
**Adventures of Davy Crockett*, by Davy Crockett	Gr. 5-12
Adventures of Lewis and Clark, by John Bakeless (North Star)	Gr. 6-12
Adventures of Lewis and Clark, by Ormonde de Kay (Step-Up Books)	Gr. 1-3
**Adventures of Obadiah*, by Brinton Turkle	Gr. 1-3
Adventures of Richard Wagner, by Opal Wheeler	Gr. 3-8
Adventures of Tom Leigh, by Phyllis Bentley	Gr. 5-12
**African Preachers*, by White	Unknown
After the Alamo, by Burt Hirschfeld (Messner/Milestones in History)	Gr. 7-12
Against All Odds: Pioneers of South America, by Marion Lansing	Gr. 5-12
**Age of Uncertainty*, by John Kenneth Galbraith [See cautionary note.]	Parental decision
**Age of Napoleon*, by Harry Henderson (World History)	Gr. 7-12
A-Going to the Westward, by Lois Lenski	Gr. 7-10
**Ahyoka and the Talking Leaves*, by Peter & Connie Roop	Gr. 3-7
Alabama Raider, by B.B. Anderson	Gr. 7-12
Alamo, by Leonard Everett Fisher	Gr. 7-12
**Alamo*, by Michael Burgan (We the People)	Gr. 3-6
**Alamo*, by Tim McNeese (Sieges that Changed the World)	Gr. 6-9
**Alamo*, by Kristin Nelson (Pull Ahead Books)	Gr. 1-3
**Alamo*, by Mark Stewart (American Battlefields)	Unknown
**Alamo!* by George Sullivan	Middle students
Alamo Cat, by Rita Kerr	Gr. 3-9
Alec Hamilton: The Little Lion, by H.B. Higgins (Childhood)	Gr. 1-6
Alec Majors, by A.M. Anderson (American Adventures, older series)	Gr. 2-6
**Alec's Primer*, by Mildred Walter	Gr. 1-3
Alessandro Volta and the Electric Battery, by Bern Dibner (Immortals of Science)	Gr. 7-12
Alexander Hamilton and Aaron Burr, by Anna & Russel Crouse (Landmark)	Gr. 3-12
**Alfred, Lord Tennyson*, by Harold Bloom (Bloom's Major Poets)	Gr. 10-12
**All Sail Set*, by Armstrong Sperry	Gr. 5-12
**All the Stars in the Sky: The Santa Fe Trail Diary of....* (Dear America) by Megan McDonald	Gr. 3-8
All Times, All Peoples, by Milton Meltzer	Gr. 3-12
Allan Pinkerton, by Borland & Speicher (Childhood)	Gr. 1-6
Allan Pinkerton, by Carl Green & William Sanford	Gr. 4-7
Allan Pinkerton: America's First Private Eye, by Sigmund Lavine	Gr. 5-12
Allan Pinkerton: First Private Eye, by LaVere Anderson (Garrard Am. All)	Gr. 1-5
**Allen Jay and the Underground Railroad*, by Marlene Brill (On My Own)	Gr. 1-4
**Almost to Freedom*, by Vaunda Nelson	Gr. 1-4
**Along the Santa Fe Trail: Marion Russell's Own Story*, by Russell/Wadsworth	Gr. 2-5
Amazing Alexander Hamilton, by Arthur Orrmont (Messner)	Gr. 7-12
**Amazing Impossible Erie Canal*, by Cheryl Harness	Gr. 2-8
Amazing Stethoscope, by Geoffrey Marks	Gr. 3-12
**Ambassadors for Christ*, edited by John Woodbridge	Gr. 7-12

American Adventure series, Volumes 13-24, by various authors | Gr. 3-8
American Adventures, by Morrie Greenberg | Gr. 3-10
American Army of Two, by Janet Greeson | Gr. 1-5
American Family of the Civil War Era Paper Dolls (Dover) | Various
American in Texas: The Story of Sam Houston, by Peggy Caravantes | Gr. 5-8
American Indian, by Sydney Fletcher | Gr. 4-12
American Indian, by Oliver LaFarge | Gr. 5-12
*American Indian Families; *American Indian Food; *American Indian Games*, etc. all by Jay Miller (True Books) | Gr. 2-6
American Indian Prayer Guide, by Danette Maloof | Various
American Indian Story, by May McNeer | Gr. 4-12
American Twins of 1812, by Lucy Fitch Perkins | Gr. 1-6
America's Abraham Lincoln, by May McNeer | Gr. 4-9
America's Robert E. Lee, by Henry Steele Commager | Gr. 4-8
Amistad *Revolt*, by Helen Kromer (Focus Books) | Gr. 9-12
*Amistad *Rising*, by Veronica Chambers | Gr. 4-7
*Amistad *Slave Revolt and American Abolition*, by Karen Zeinert | Gr. 5-12
Among the Camps, by Thomas Page | Gr. 3-10
Amos Fortune, Free Man, by Elizabeth Yates | Gr. 3-12
Anchor's Aweigh, by Jean Lee Latham | Gr. 4-12
Andrew Jackson, by Clara Ingram Judson | Gr. 4-12
Andrew Jackson, by Jeannette Covert Nolan (Messner) | Gr. 7-12
Andrew Jackson, by Steve Potts (Photo-Illustrated Biographies) | Gr. 3-7
Andrew Jackson, by Mike Venezia (Getting to Know the U.S. Presidents) | Gr. 1-5
Andrew Jackson: An Initial Biography, by Genevieve Foster | Gr. 2-7
Andrew Jackson and His Family Paper Dolls, by Tom Tierney (Dover) | Various
Andrew Jackson: Frontier Patriot, by Louis Sabin | Gr. 1-4
Andrew Jackson: Pioneer and President, by John Parlin (Garrard Discovery) | Gr. 1-5
Andrews Raid, or the Great Locomotive Chase, by Sam & Beryl Epstein | Gr. 4-12
Andrews' Raiders, by Robert Feuerlicht (America in the Making) | Gr. 8-12
Andy Jackson, by Augusta Stevenson (Childhood) | Gr. 1-6
[The new reissue is by George Stanley and is titled **Andrew Jackson: Young Patriot*.]
Andy Jackson: Long Journey to the White House, by P. Angell (Alad. Am. Her) | Gr. 3-8
Andy Jackson's Water Well, by William O. Steele | Gr. 3-8
Andy of Pirate Gorge, by H.R. Langdale | Gr. 5-12
Angel of Mercy, by Rachel Baker (Messner) | Gr. 4-12
Angry Abolitionist: William Lloyd Garrison, by Jules Archer (Messner) | Gr. 8-12
Anita of Rancho del Mar, by Elaine O'Brien | Gr. 4-8
Annie Lee and the Wooden Skates, by Margaret Frisby | Gr. 3-7
Anthony Burns: The Defeat and Triumph of a Fugitive Slave, by Virginia Hamilton | Gr. 5-12
Antonín Dvořák: Composer from Bohemia, by Claire Purdy (Messner) | Gr. 7-12
Apples to Oregon, by Deborah Hopkinson | Gr. 1-4
Appomattox: Closing Struggle of the Civil War, by Burke Davis (Breakthrough) | Gr. 6-12
Appomattox Road, by Manly Wade Wellman | Gr. 5-12
Araminta's Paint Box, by Karen Ackerman | Gr. 1-4
Army in Pigtails, by Harriet Evatt | Gr. 2-5

**Aquila's Drinking Gourd*, by Pamela Dell (Scrapbooks of America)	Unknown
Army of Two, by Polly Curren	Gr. 1-4
Art of the New American Nation, by Shirley Glubok	Gr. 3-12
As the Crow Flies, by Cornelia Meigs	Gr. 7-12
**Assassination of Abraham Lincoln*, by Michael Burgan	Unknown
**Assassination of Abraham Lincoln*, by Robert Jakoubek	Unknown
**Assassination of Abraham Lincoln*, by Brendan January (Cornerstones II)	Gr. 4-8
**Assault on Fort Wagner*, by Wendy Vierow	Unknown
**At Aboukir and Acre*, by G.A. Henty	Gr. 7-12
At the Sign of the Golden Anchor, by Ruth Langland Holberg	Gr. 4-10
Attack at Fort Lookout, by Red Reeder	Gr. 7-12
**Attack in the Rye Grass*, by Dave & Neta Jackson (Trailblazer)	Gr. 3-8
Audubon and His Sons, by Amy Hogeboom	Gr. 5-12
**Audubon: Painter of Birds in the Wild Frontier*, by Jennifer Armstrong	Gr. 2-5
**Aunt Clara Brown*, by Linda Lowery (On My Own)	Gr. 1-5
**Aurora Means Dawn*, by Scott Sanders	Gr. 1-3
**Autobiographies of Noah Webster*, by Noah Webster	Gr. 10-12
**Away Goes Sally*, by Elizabeth Coatsworth	Gr. 2-8
**Back of Beyond*, by Andy Bowen (Creative Minds)	Gr. 2-7
**Ballad of Lucy Whipple*, by Karen Cushman [See cautionary note.]	Gr. 4-12
**Ballad of the Civil War*, by Mary Stolz	Gr. 2-6
Banks of the Boyne, by Donna Fletcher Crow	Gr. 9-12
**Barbara Frietchie*, by John Greenleaf Whittier	Gr. K-3
**Barbary Pirates*, by C.S. Forester (Landmark)	Gr. 3-12
**Basic History of the United States: Vol. 2*, by Clarence Carson	Gr. 9-12
**Basic History of the United States: Vol. 3*, by Clarence Carson	Gr. 9-12
**Battle for St. Michaels*, by Emily McCully	Gr. 3-5
**Battle of Antietam*, by Chris Hughes	Gr. 5-10
**Battle of Antietam*, by Zachary Kent (Cornerstones) [also titled, *Story of...*]	Gr. 3-9
**Battle of Antietam*, by James Reger	Gr. 6-12
Battle of Austerlitz, by Trevor Dupuy (Macmillan Battle Books)	Gr. 7-12
**Battle of Bull Run*, by Deborah Kops	Gr. 5-10
**Battle of Bull Run*, by Wendy Vierow	Unknown
**Battle of Chancellorsville*, by Zachary Kent (Cornerstones)	Gr. 3-8
**Battle of Chattanooga*, by David C. King	Unknown
**Battle of Fredericksburg*, by Scott Ingram	Unknown
**Battle of Gettysburg*, by Alden Carter	Gr. 5-12
**Battle of Gettysburg*, by Gina DeAngelis (Let Freedom Ring)	Gr. 4-8
**Battle of Gettysburg*, by David C. King	Gr. 6-12
Battle of Gettysburg, by Neil Johnson	Gr. 5-9
Battle of Lake Erie, by F. Van Wyck Mason (North Star Books)	Gr. 4-12
Battle of New Market: A Story of V.M.I., by Paxton Davis	Gr. 7-12
Battle of New Orleans, by Donald Chidsey	Gr. 8-12
Battle of San Pasqual, by Jonreed Lauritzen	Gr. 5-12
Battle of Shiloh, by Zachary Kent (Cornerstones)	Gr. 3-7

**Battle of the Alamo*, by Andrew Santella (Cornerstones)	Gr. 3-7
Battle of the Ironclads, by Alden Carter (First Book)	Gr. 6-12
Battle of Trafalgar, by Alan Villiers (Macmillan Battle Books)	Gr. 7-12
**Battle of Vicksburg*, by David C. King	Unknown
Battle of Waterloo, by Manuel Komroff (Macmillan Battle Books)	Gr. 8-12
**Battle of Waterloo*, by David Pietrusza (Battles of the Nineteenth Century)	Gr. 7-12
Battles for New Orleans, by F. VanWyck Mason (North Star)	Gr. 5-12
**Battles of the War of 1812*, by Diane & Henry Smolinski	Unknown
Baxie Randall and the Blue Raiders, by Carl Hodges	Gr. 5-9
Beaver Water, by Rutherford Montgomery	Gr. 4-12
Becky and the Bandit, by Doris Gates	Gr. 2-7
Bedford Forrest, by Aileen Parks (Childhood)	Gr. 1-6
**Beethoven*, by Greta Cencetti (World of Composers)	Gr. 2-6
**Beethoven*, by Wendy Lynch (Lives and Times)	Gr. 1-3
Beethoven, by Reba Paeff Mirsky	Gr. 6-12
**Beethoven and the Classical Age*, by A. Bergaamini (Masters of Music)	Gr. 5-12
Beethoven and the World of Music, by Manuel Komroff	Gr. 9-12
**Beethoven Lives Upstairs* (Classical Kids) Dramatizations: all ages; Book:	Gr. 2-6
Beethoven: Master Musician, by Madeline Goss	Gr. 4-10
**Before the Creeks Ran Red*, by Carolyn Reeder	Gr. 6-12
**Behind Rebel Lines*, by Seymour Reit	Gr. 3-12
**Behind the Blue and the Gray*, by Delia Ray (Young Readers' History of the...)	Gr. 5-12
Belle Boyd: Secret Agent, by Jeannette Nolan (Messner)	Gr. 5-12
Beneath Another Sun, by Marjory Hall	Gr. 7-12
Benjamin Bonneville, by Helen Markley Miller	Gr. 6-12
Benjie Ream, by C. G. Hodges	Gr. 7-12
Bent's Fort, by Melvin Bacon & Daniel Blegen	Gr. 4-10
Bent's Fort: Crossroads of the West, by Wyatt Blassingame (Garr. How They...)	Gr. 3-8
**Best Little Stories from the Civil War*, by C. Brian Kelly	Gr. 6-12
Betsy's Napoleon, by Jeannette Covert Nolan	Gr. 7-12
Better Known as Johnny Appleseed, by Mabel Leigh Hunt	Gr. 5-12
**Between Two Fires: Black Soldiers and the Civil War*, by Joyce Hansen	Gr. 5-12
Bewitching Betsy Bonaparte, by Alice Curtis Desmond	Gr. 8-12
Biblical Economics in Comics, by Vic Lockman	Gr. 6-12
**Big Cheese for the White House*, by Candace Fleming	Gr. 1-4
Big Sky: An Edition for Younger Readers, by A.B. Guthrie	Gr. 9-12
Bill Clark: American Explorer, by Sanford Tousey	Gr. 2-5
**Billy and the Rebel*, by Deborah Hopkinson (Ready-to-Read 3)	Gr. 1-4
**Billy the Union Soldier: With 24 Stickers*, by A.G. Smith (Dover)	Various
**Billy Yank* (Bellerophon)	Various
**Billy Yank and Johnny Reb*, by Susan Beller	Gr. 5-8
Billy Yank and Johnny Reb, by Earl Schenck Miers	Gr. 4-10
Bimby, by Peter Burchard	Gr. 5-12
**Birchbark House*, by Louise Erdrich [See cautionary note.]	Gr. 3-8?
Birth of Texas, by William Johnson (North Star)	Gr. 5-12
**Black Americans: A History in Their Own Words*, edited by Milton Meltzer	Gr. 7-12

Black, Blue & Gray, by Jim Haskins | Gr. 6-12

**Black, Blue & Gray*, by Jim Haskins	Gr. 6-12
Black Falcon, by Armstrong Sperry	Gr. 4-12
**Black Hands, White Sails*, by Patricia McKissack	Gr. 6-12
Black Hawk, by Arthur Beckhard	Gr. 6-12
Black Hawk, by Cathrine Cleven (Childhood)	Gr. 1-6
Black Hawk: Indian Patriot, by LaVere Anderson (Garr. Am. Indian)	Gr. 1-5
Black Hawk, Sac Rebel, by Nancy Bonvillain (N. Am. Indians of Achievement)	Unknown
Black Patriot and Martyr, by Ann Griffiths (Messner)	Gr. 7-12
**Black Soldiers in the Civil War* (Dover)	Various
Blithe Genius, by Gladys Malvern	Gr. 5-12
**Blockaded Family*, by Parthenia Hague	Unknown
**Blood in the Water*, by Pamela Dell (Scrapbooks of America)	Younger grades
Blow, Bugles, Blow, by Merritt Parmelee Allen	Gr. 5-12
Blow Ye Winds Westerly, by Elizabeth Gemming	Gr. 7-12
**Blue and Gray*, by Eve Bunting	Gr. 1-5
Blueberry Corners, by Lois Lenski	Gr. 4-8
**Bluewater Journal*, by Loretta Krupinski	Gr. 1-6
Boat Builder, by Clara Ingram Judson	Gr. 3-8
Boatswain's Boy, by Robert DuSoe	Gr. 4-12
**Bobbin Girl*, by Emily McCully	Gr. 2-5
**Bold Journey*, by Charles Bohner	Gr. 4-12
Bolivar the Liberator, by Ronald Syme	Gr. 4-12
Book of Indians, by Holling Clancy Holling	Gr. 4-12
Book of Music, edited by Gill Rowley	Gr. 7-12
Border Hawk: August Bondi, by Lloyd Alexander (Covenant)	Gr. 4-12
**Bound for America*, by James Haskins (From African Beginnings)	Gr. 3-10
**Bound for Oregon*, by Jean Van Leeuwen	Gr. 1-4
**Bound for the North Star: True Stories of Fugitive Slaves*, by Dennis Fradin	Gr. 5-12
Bound for the Rio Grande, by Milton Meltzer (Living History Library)	Gr. 9-12
Boy Emigrants, by Noah Brooks	Gr. 8-12
Boy Heroes of Chapultepec, by Maria Chambers (Winston Adventure)	Gr. 3-9
Boy of Gettysburg, by Elsie Singmaster	Gr. 4-12
Boy of the Woods, by Maie Lounsbury Wells & Dorothy Fox	Gr. 3-8
**Boy Who Drew Birds*, by Jacqueline Davies	Gr. 2-4
Boy with a Pack, by Stephen Meader	Gr. 4-12
Boyhoods of Famous Composers, Vol. 1 and 2, by Catherine Gough	Gr. 4-9
Boys' Life of Frémont, by Flora Seymour	Gr. 6-12
**Boys' War*, by Jim Murphy	Gr. 7-12
**Brady*, by Jean Fritz	Gr. 4-12
Brahms, by Reba Paeff Mirsky	Gr. 4-12
**Brahms*, by Ann Rachlin (Famous Children)	Gr. 3-6
**Brave Buffalo Fighter*, by John D. Fitzgerald	Gr. 4-10
Brave Soldier Janosh, by Victor Ambrus	Gr. 1-3
Bret Harte, by J. Branham (Childhood)	Gr. 1-6
Bret Harte of..., by Alvin Harlow (Messner)	Gr. 7-12
Brigham Young, by Olive Burt (Messner) [See note in guide.]	Gr. 7-12

Brigham Young, by Jordan & Frisbee (Childhood) [See note in guide.] Gr. 1-6
Bright Design, by Katherine B. Shippen Gr. 5-12
**Bright Freedom's Song*, by Gloria Houston Gr. 5-10
**British Redcoat of the Napoleonic Wars*, by Martin Windrow (Soldiers...) Gr. 4-10
Broad Stripes and Bright Stars, by Marion Marsh Brown Gr. 4-12
**Broken Drum*, by Edith Hemingway Unknown
Broken-Hand Fitzpatrick, by Shannon Garst (Messner) Gr. 6-12
**Bronco Charlie and the Pony Express*, by Marlene Brill (On My Own) Gr. 1-4
**Brontë Family: Passionate Literary Geniuses*, by Karen Kenyon Gr. 5-9
**Brontës*, by Catherine Brighton [See note in guide.] Gr. 1-4?
Brother Against Brother, by Phyllis Fenner Gr. 5-12
Brother of the Wind, by Jerry Wolfert Gr. 5-12
**Brothers of the Heart*, by Joan Blos Gr. 4-10
Buckskin Brigade, by Jim Kjelgaard Gr. 5-12
Buffalo and Beaver, by Stephen Meader Gr. 7-12
**Buffalo Bill and the Pony Express*, by Eleanor Coerr (History I Can Read) Gr. K-2
Buffalo Knife, by William O. Steele Gr. 3-8
Buffalo Trace: A Story of Abraham Lincoln's Ancestors, by Virginia Eifert Gr. 6-12
**Building the Capital City*, by Marlene Brill (Cornerstones) Gr. 3-6
**Bull Run*, by Paul Fleischman Gr. 4-12
**Bullwhip Griffin*, by Sid Fleischman [Also titled, *By the Great Horn Spoon.*] Gr. 4-12
Burning of Washington, by Mary Kay Phelan Gr. 8-12
**By Conduct and Courage*, by G.A. Henty Gr. 7-12
By Secret Railway, by Enid Meadowcroft Gr. 3-10
**By the Dawn's Early Light*, by Steven Kroll Gr. 2-6
By the Great Horn Spoon , by Sid Fleischman [Also titled, **Bullwhip Griffin.*] Gr. 4-12
By Wagon and Flatboat, by Enid LaMonte Meadowcroft Gr. 3-9

**Cadets at War*, by Susan Beller Gr. 7-12
Cadmus Henry, by Walter Edmonds Gr. 4-12
**Caleb's Choice*, by G. Clifton Wisler Gr. 4-8
**California Gold Rush*, by May McNeer (Landmark) Gr. 3-9
**California Gold Rush*, by Judy Monroe (Let Freedom Ring) Gr. 4-8
**California Gold Rush*, by Peter & Connie Roop (Scholastic History Reader) Gr. 2-4
**California Gold Rush*, by R. Conrad Stein (Cornerstones) Gr. 3-8
**California Gold Rush Cooking*, by Lisa Schroeder Various
**Call of Duty: The Sterling Nobility of Robert E. Lee*, by J. Steven Wilkins Gr. 9-12
**Camel Express*, by Ann Shaffer (It Really Happened) Gr. 1-5
Candle in the Night, by Elizabeth Howard [There are two authors by this name.] Gr. 4-10
Cape May Packet, by Stephen Meader Gr. 5-12
**Capital*, by Lynn Curlee Gr. 3-7
Capital Capital City: 1790-1814, by Suzanne Hilton Gr. 7-12
Capital for the Nation, by Stan Hoig Gr. 8-12
**Capital! Washington, D.C., from A to Z*, by Laura Melmud Gr. K-3
**Capitol*, by Andrew Santella (Cornerstones) Gr. 3-7
**Captain Hornblower* series, by C.S. Forester [See cautionary note.] Parental decision

Captain of Foot, by Ronald Welch	Gr. 8-12
Captain of the Planter, by Dorothy Sterling	Gr. 9-12
**Captain's Dog*, by Roland Smith	Gr. 5-8
Captive Island, by August Derleth (Aladdin's American Heritage)	Gr. 3-8
Capture at Sea, by Audrey Beyer	Gr. 1-6
**Capture of Detroit*, by Pierre Berton	Gr. 4-12
Captured Words, by Frances Browin (Aladdin's American Heritage)	Gr. 4-12
**Capturing Nature*, by Peter & Connie Roop	Gr. 3-12
Caravan to Oregon, by Herbert Arntson	Gr. 4-12
Carl Friedrich Gauss: Prince of Mathematicians, by W. Schaaf (Immortals...)	Gr. 8-12
**Carlota*, by Scott O'Dell	Gr. 7-12
Caroline and Her Kettle Named Maud **and** *Caroline and the Seven...*, by M. Mason	Gr. 1-5
Carmen of the Gold Coast, by Brandies	Gr. 3-7
Carry On, Mr. Bowditch, by Jean Lee Latham	Gr. 4-12
Castors Away! by Hester Burton	Gr. 5-12
**Caught in the Rebel Camp*, by Dave & Neta Jackson (Trailblazer)	Gr. 3-9
**Cezanne Pinto*, by Mary Stolz	Gr. 5-9
Challenge of Marxism: A Christian Response, by Klaus Bockmuehl	Gr. 12+
Challengers, by Jo Lundy (Aladdin's American Heritage)	Gr. 3-9
**Champions of Invention; *Champions of Mathematics;* and **Champions of Invention* all by John Hudson Tiner	Gr. 3-7
Chancellorsville: Disaster in Victory, by Bruce Palmer (Macmillan Battle Books)	Gr. 8-12
**Chang's Paper Pony*, by Eleanor Coerr (I Can Read)	Gr. 1-3
Chanticleer of Wilderness Road, by Meridel LeSueur	Gr. 5-12
Charity Goes to War, by Anne Heagney	Gr. 5-12
**Charles Dickens*, by Harold Bloom (Bloom's Major Novelists)	Gr. 10-12
**Charles Dickens*, by Donna Dailey (Who Wrote That?)	Gr. 7-12
Charles Dickens, by Charles Haines (Immortals of Literature)	Gr. 9-12
Charles Dickens: His Life, by Catherine Owens Peare	Gr. 7-12
**Charles Dickens: The Man Who Had Great Expectations*, by Diane Stanley *et al*	Gr. 3-7
**Charles Finney*, by Bonnie Harvey (Heroes of the Faith)	Gr. 6-12
**Charles Finney*, by Basil Miller (Men of the Faith)	Gr. 9-12
**Charley Skedaddle*, by Patricia Beatty	Gr. 4-12
**Charley Waters Goes to Gettysburg*, by Susan Sinnott	Gr. 4-8
**Charlotte Brontë and Jane Eyre*, by Stewart Ross	Gr. 3-7
Charlotte Forten, by Peter Burchard	Gr. 6-12
**Charlotte Years* series, by Melissa Wiley	Gr. 3-6
**Cherokee*, by Richard Gaines (Native Americans)	Gr. 2-5
Cherokee, by Emilie Lepthien (New True Books)	Gr. 2-5
Cherokee Boy, by Alexander Key	Gr. 7-12
Cherokee Indians, by Sonia Bleeker	Gr. 3-12
**Cherokee Indians*, by Bill Lund	Gr. 3-7
Chicago: Big-Shouldered City, by Regina Kelly	Gr. 7-12
Chief Black Hawk, by Frank Beals (American Adventures, older series)	Gr. 3-8
**Chief Justice*, by Charles Wetterer	Unknown
**Children of the Civil War*, by Candice Ransom	Gr. 6-12

*_Children of the Covered Wagon_, by Mary Jane Carr Gr. 3-9
*_Children of the Frontier_, by Sylvia Whitman Unknown
Child's History of Art, by Hillyer & Huey [or retitled version, _Young People's..._] Gr. 2-8
*_Child's History of the World_, by V.M. Hillyer (1924 original, pub. by Cent.-App.) Gr. 1-4
China Clipper, by Peter Guttmacher (Those Daring Machines) Gr. 7-12
Chingo Smith of the Erie Canal, by Samuel Hopkins Adams Gr. 5-12
Chippewa, by Alice Osinski (New True Books) Gr. 2-5
Chippewa Indians, by Sonia Bleeker Gr. 4-12
Choctaw, by Emilie Lepthien (New True Books) Gr. 2-5
*_Chopin_, by Greta Cencetti (World of Composers) Gr. 2-6
Chopin, by Antoni Gronowicz Gr. 4-12
*_Chopin_, by Ann Rachlin (Famous Children) Gr. 3-6
*_Christ in the Camp_, by J. William Jones Unknown
Chula: Son of the Mound Builders, by William Bunce [See cautionary note in guide.] Parent...
*_City! Washington, D.C._, by Shirley Climo Gr. 3-6
*_Civil War_, by Alden Carter Gr. 5-12
*_Civil War_, by Don Nardo Gr. 8-12
Civil War, by Fletcher Pratt Gr. 2-8
*_Civil War_, by Susan Spellman (Draw History) Various
*_Civil War_, by John Stanchak (Eyewitness) Gr. 4-12
*_Civil War: A Fact-Filled Coloring Book_, by Blake Magner Various
*_Civil War Artist_, by Taylor Morrison Gr. 1-5
*_Civil War at Sea_, by George Sullivan Gr. 6-12
*_Civil War Cooking: The Confederacy_, by Susan Dosier Various
*_Civil War Cooking: The Union_, by Susan Dosier Various
*_Civil War Days_, by David King Various
*_Civil War for Kids_, by Janis Herbert Various
*_Civil War Generals of the Confederacy_, by James Reger Unknown
*_Civil War Heroes_ (Bellerophon) Various
*_Civil War Heroines_ (Bellerophon) Various
*_Civil War in the West_, by Jim Corrigan Unknown
*_Civil War in the West_, by Douglas Savage (Untold History of the Civil War) Gr. 4-8
*_Civil War Medicine_, by Douglas Savage (Untold History of the Civil War) Gr. 4-8
Civil War Nurse: Mary Ann Bickerdyke, by Adele de Leeuw (Messner) Gr. 7-12
*_Civil War Paper Soldiers_ (Dover) Various
Civil War Sailor, by Irving Werstein (Signal) Gr. 3-10
Civil War Sampler, by Donald Sobol Gr. 5-12
*_Civil War Sub: Mystery of the Hunley_, by Kate Jerome (All Aboard Reading 3) Gr. 2-5
*_Civil War Uniforms_ (Dover) Various
Clara Barton, by Helen Boylston (Landmark) Gr. 3-9
Clara Barton, by Alberta Graham (Makers of America) Gr. 3-8
Clara Barton, by Mildred Pace Gr. 6-12
*_Clara Barton_, by Augusta Stevenson (Childhood) Gr. 1-6
Clara Barton and Her Victory Over Fear, by Robert Quackenbush Gr. 1-6
Clara Barton: Angel of the Battlefield, by Rae Bains (Troll) Gr. 1-4
*_Clara Barton: Courage Under Fire_, by Janet & Geoff Benge (Heroes of History)Gr. 4-10

Clara Barton: Soldier of Mercy, by Mary Rose (Garrard Discovery)	Gr. 1-5
**Clara Schumann: Piano Virtuoso*, by Susanna Reich	Gr. 5-10
**Classic Fables and Tales for Children*, by Leo Tolstoy	Unknown
**Clear(ed) for Action!* by Stephen Meader	Gr. 5-12
**Clementine*, by Ann Owen	Various
Clementine, by Robert Quackenbush	Various
Cliff Dwellers of Walnut Canyon, by Carroll Fenton & Alice Epstein	Parental decision
**Clipper Ship*, by Thomas Lewis (I Can Read History)	Gr. K-2
Clipper Ship Days, by John Jennings (Landmark)	Gr. 3-10
Clippers and Whaling Ships, by Tim McNeese (Americans on the Move)	Unknown
**Co. Aytch*, by Sam Watkins	Gr. 10-12
Coat for Private Patrick, by Lee McGiffin	Gr. 7-12
Coils, Magnets and Rings: Michael Faraday's World, by Nancy Veglahn	Gr. 3-8
**(Coloring Book of) Civil War Heroines* (Bellerophon)	Various
**Come Morning*, by Leslie Guccione	Gr. 4-7
Coming of the Mormons, by Kjelgaard (Landmark) [See note in guide.]	Gr. 3-9
**Commander in Chief: Abraham Lincoln and the Civil War*, by Albert Marrin	Gr. 8-12
Commodore Bainbridge, by James Barnes	Gr. 5-12
Commodore Perry and the Opening of Japan, by Ferdinand Kuhn (Landmark)	Gr. 4-12
**Commodore Perry in the Land of the Shogun*, by Rhoda Blumberg	Gr. 5-12
**Complete Brigadier Gerard*, by Sir Arthur Conan Doyle [*aka* Glorious Hussar]	Gr. 7-12
**Confederacy and the Civil War*, by Ann Gaines (In American History)	Unknown
**Confederate Army Paper Soldiers* (Dover)	Various
**Confederate Fiddle*, by Jeanne Williams	Gr. 7-12
**Confederate Flag*, by Hal Marcovitz (American Symbols & Their Meaning)	Unknown
**Confederate Generals*, by Tom Head (Voices from the Civil War)	Unknown
**Confederate Girl: The Diary of Carrie Berry, 1864*, by Carrie Berry	Gr. 4-8
**Confederate Soldiers*, by John Dunn (Civil War Voices)	Unknown
**Confederate Ladies of Richmond*, by Susan Beller	Gr. 6-12
Confederate Spy Stories, by Katherine & John Bakeless	Gr. 5-12
**Confederate Trilogy for Young Readers*, by Mrs. M. L. Williamson	Gr. 7-12
**Constable*, by Emily Cottrill (Picture Study Portfolios)	All ages
Consul's Daughter, by Ann Schlee	Gr. 7-12
Continent for Sale, by Arthur Groom (Winston Adventure)	Gr. 3-9
**Cooking on Nineteenth-Century Whaling Ships*, by Charla Draper	Various
Cornelia: Story of a Civil War Nurse, by Jane McConnell	Gr. 5-12
**Cornstalks and Cannonballs*, by Barbara Mitchell	Gr. 1-4
**Corot from A to Z*, by Caroline Larroche	Unknown
**Count of Monte Cristo*, by Alexandre Dumas [See cautionary note; abridged versions available.]	Parental decision
Count Who Wished He Were a Peasant, by Morris Philipson	Gr. 8-12
Country of the Hawk, by August Derleth (Aladdin's American Heritage)	Gr. 3-8
Courage in Her Hands, by Iris Noble (Messner)	Gr. 7-12
**Courage to Run*, by Wendy Lawton (Daughters of the Faith)	Gr. 4-8
**Covered Wagon, Bumpy Trails*, by Verla Kay	Gr. K-3
Cowslip [See: *Slave Girl*]	

**Creek*, by Barbara Gray-Kanatiiosh	Gr. 2-5
**Creek Nation*, by Allison Lassieur	Unknown
Cross in the West, by Mark Boesch (Vision)	Gr. 4-10
Cudjo's Cave, by J.T. Trowbridge	Gr. 9-12
**Cut and Assemble a Southern Plantation* (Dover)	Various
Cyclone in Calico, by Nina Brown Baker	Gr. 8-12
Cyrus Holt and the Civil War, by Ann Holt	Gr. 4-8
Cyrus McCormick, by Lavinia Dobler (Childhood)	Gr. 1-6
**Cyrus McCormick and the Mechanical Reaper*, by Lisa Aldrich	Gr. 5-12
**Daily Life in a Covered Wagon*, by Paul Erickson	Gr. 3-8
**Daily Life on a Southern Plantation*, by Paul Erickson	Gr. 3-8
Dan Webster, by Bradford Smith (Childhood)	Gr. 1-6
Dancing Tom, by Elizabeth Coatsworth	Gr. 1-3
Danger at Niagara, by Margaret Goff Clark	Gr. 5-12
Dangerfoot, by Antony Brown	Gr. 5-12
**Daniel Colton* series, by Elaine Schulte	Gr. 4-10
**Daniel Webster*, by Robert Allen (Sower)	Gr. 5-12
Daniel Webster, by Alfred Steinberg	Gr. 6-12
**Daniel Webster: Liberty and Union, Now and Forever*, by Bonnie Harvey	Gr. 5-12
**Daniel's Duck*, by Clyde Robert Bulla	Gr. K-2
**Daring Escape of Ellen Craft*, by Cathy Moore (Carolrhoda On My Own)	Gr. 1-3
Daring Sea Warrior: Franklin Buchanan, by G. Eliot (Messner)	Gr. 9-12
Dark and Bloody Ground, by Phyllis Fenner	Gr. 5-12
David Farragut, by Laura Long (Childhood)	Gr. 1-6
David Farragut: Sea Fighter, by Marie Mudra (Messner)	Gr. 6-12
David Farragut and the Great Naval Blockade, by Russell Shorto	Unknown
**David Farragut, Union Admiral*, by Bruce Adelson (Famous Figures of the...)	Gr. 4-8
David Glasgow Farragut: Our First Admiral, by Jean Lee Latham (Garr. Disc.)	Gr. 1-5
Davy Crockett, by Frank Beals (American Adventures, older series)	Gr. 3-7
Davy Crockett, by Anne Ford (See and Read)	Gr. 1-3
Davy Crockett, by Stewart Holbrook (Landmark)	Gr. 3-8
**Davy Crockett*, by Aileen Parks (Childhood)	Gr. 1-6
Davy Crockett, by Constance Rourke	Gr. 6-12
**Davy Crockett*, by George Sullivan (In Their Own Words)	Unknown
Davy Crockett, by Sanford Tousey	Gr. 3-7
**Davy Crockett: Defender of the Alamo*, by Carl Green & William Sanford	Gr. 4-8
Davy Crockett: Hero of the Wild Frontier, by Elizabeth Mosely (Garr. Discovery)	Gr. 1-5
**Davy Crockett Saves the World*, by Rosalyn Schanzer	Gr. 1-5
**Davy Crockett: Young Pioneer*, by Laurence Santrey (Troll)	Gr. 1-4
Davy Crockett's Earthquake, by William O. Steele	Gr. 2-6
Dawn's Early Light, by Walter Lord [Unknown content.]	Gr. 10+
**Day Lincoln was Shot*, by Jim Bishop	Gr. 9-12
Day of the Arkansas, by Robert Alter	Gr. 7-12
**Day that Changed America: Gettysburg*, by Shelley Tanaka	Gr. 3-7
**Days of Jubilee*, by Patricia McKissack	Gr. 5-12

*_Dear Austin: Letters from the Underground Railroad_, by Elvira Woodruff Gr. 3-7
*_Dear Mr. President: John Quincy Adams: Letters from a Southern Planter's Son_ Gr. 4-9
by Steven Kroll (Dear Mr. President) [See cautionary note.]
Death of Lincoln, by Leroy Hayman Gr. 5-12
Defiance to the Old World: Story of the Monroe Doctrine, by George Dangerfield Gr. 7-12
*_Democracy in America_, by Alexis de Tocqueville Gr. 12+
Deserter, by Peter Burchard Gr. 5-12
Detective Pinkerton and Mr. Lincoln, by William Wise Gr. 2-6
*_Devil and Daniel Webster_, by Stephen Vincent Benét Gr. 6-12
DeWitt Clinton, by Mabel Widdemer (Childhood) Gr. 1-6
*_Diary of an Early American Boy_, by Eric Sloane Gr. 4-12
*_Diary of a Drummer Boy_, by Marlene Brill Gr. 3-6
*_Diary of a Southern Refugee During the War_, by Judith McGuire Unknown
*_Diary of David R. Leeper_, by David Leeper, ed. by the Roops (In My Own...) Gr. 3-6
*_Diary of Sam Watkins, A Confederate Soldier_ (In My Own Words) Unknown
Dick and the Canal Boat, by Sanford Tousey Gr. 1-5
*_Divided in Two_, by James Arnold Unknown
Do Not Annoy the Indians, by Betty Baker Gr. 5-10
*_Dog Jack_, by Florence Biros Gr. 5-12
*_Dog of Discovery_, by Laurence Pringle Gr. 3-6
Dogs of Destiny, by Fairfax Downey Gr. 3-12
Dolley Madison, by Jeannette Covert Nolan (Messner) Gr. 7-12
*_Dolley Madison_, by Jean Patrick (History Makers) Gr. 3-6
*_Dolley Madison_, by Myra Weatherly Gr. 6-12
*_Dolley Madison: Her Life, Letters, and Legacy_, by H. Shulman & D. Mattern Unknown
Dolly Madison, by Jane Mayer (Landmark) Gr. 3-8
Dolly Madison, by Helen Monsell (Childhood) Gr. 1-6
Dolly Madison: Famous First Lady, by Mary Davidson (Garrard Discovery) Gr. 1-5
Donald McKay and the Clipper Ships, by Mary Ellen Chase (North Star) Gr. 7-12
*_Donner Party_, by Marian Calabro Gr. 6-12
*_Donner Party_, by Roger Wachtel (Cornerstones of Freedom II) Gr. 4-8
*_Dorothea Dix: Crusader for the Mentally Ill_, by Amy Herstek (Hist. Am.) Gr. 7-12
Dorothea Dix, by Grace Melin (Childhood) Gr. 1-6
*_Dorothea Dix_, by Barbara Witteman (Let Freedom Ring) Gr. 4-8
Dorothea L. Dix: Hospital Founder, by Mary Malone Unknown
Dorothea Lynde Dix, by Gertrude Norman Gr. 5-12
*_Downright Dencey_, by Caroline Dale Snedeker Gr. 4-12
*_Dred Scott Decision_, by Brendan January (Cornerstones of Freedom) Gr. 3-6
*_Drinking Gourd_, by F.N. Monjo (I Can Read book) Gr. 1-5
Drum-Beat of the Nation, by Charles Coffin [1st in series.] Gr. 7-12
*_Drummer Boy_, by Ann Turner Gr. 1-4
Drummer Boy, by Larry Weinberg Gr. 4-12
*_Drummer Boy at Bull Run_, by Gilbert Morris (Bonnets and Bugles) Gr. 6-12
*_Drummer Boy of Vicksburg_, by G. Clifton Wisler Gr. 5-12
*_Duel! Burr and Hamilton's Deadly War of Words_, by Dennis Fradin Gr. 2-4
*_Duel of the Ironclads_, by Patrick O'Brien Gr. 3-8

Duet: The Story of Clara and Robert Schumann, by Elizabeth Kyle	Gr. 5-12
Dunderhead War, by Betty Baker	Gr. 7-12
**Dvorak in America*, by Joseph Horowitz	Gr. 4-8
Eagle of the Sea, by Bruce Grant	Gr. 3-12
Earliest Americans, by William Scheele [See cautionary note in guide.]	Parental decision
**Early American Industrial Revolution*, by Katie Bagley (Let Freedom Ring)	Gr. 3-8
East of Astoria, by Merritt Parmelee Allen	Gr. 5-12
**Eben Tyne, Powdermonkey*, by Patricia Beatty & Phillip Robbins	Gr. 5-12
**Economics in One Lesson*, by Henry Hazlitt	Gr. 9-12
Edvard Grieg: Boy of the Northland, by Sybil Deucher	Gr. 2-7
Edward Rose: Negro Trail Blazer, by Harold Felton	Gr. 4-12
Eli Whitney, by Judy Alter (First Book)	Gr. 4-7
**Eli Whitney*, by Ann Gaines (Discover the Life of an Inventor)	Gr. 1-4
**Eli Whitney*, by Margaret Hall (Lives and Times)	Gr. 1-3
Eli Whitney, by Dorothea Snow (Childhood)	Gr. 1-6
**Eli Whitney: American Inventor*, by Katie Bagley	Unknown
Eli Whitney and the Machine Age, by Wilma Pitchford Hays	Gr. 3-8
Eli Whitney: Founder of Modern Industry (Immortals of Engineering)	Gr. 8-12
Eli Whitney: Great Inventor, by Jean Lee Latham (Garrard Discovery)	Gr. 1-5
Eli Whitney: Master Craftsman, by Miriam Gilbert (Makers of America)	Gr. 3-7
Elias Howe, by Jean Corcoran (Childhood)	Gr. 1-6
Eliza and the Indian War Pony, by Paul & Beryl Scott	Gr. 5-12
**Elizabeth Barrett Browning*, by Harold Bloom (Bloom's Modern Critical...)	Gr. 10-12
Elizabeth for Lincoln, by Jacqueline McNicol	Gr. 3-12
**Emancipation Proclamation*, by Ann Heinrichs (We the People)	Gr. 5-10
**Emancipation Proclamation*, by Brendan January (Cornerstones)	Gr. 3-8
**Emancipation Proclamation*, by Michael Martin	Unknown
**Emily Brontë*, by Robert Barnard (British Library Writers' Lives)	Gr. 9-12
**Emma and the Civil Warrior*, by Candy Dahl	Gr. 4-10
Emperor and the Drummer Boy, by Ruth Robbins	Gr. 1-6
**Empire Costumes Paper Dolls*, by Tom Tierney	Various
**Empires Lost and Won: The Spanish Heritage in the Southwest*, by Albert Marrin	Gr. 8-12
Empress Josephine, by Marguerite Vance	Gr. 4-12
Engine and the Gun, by James Barbary	Gr. 8-12
Ensign Ronan, by Leonard Burgoyne	Gr. 5-12
Erie Canal, by Samuel Hopkins Adams (Landmark)	Gr. 3-9
**Erie Canal*, by Craig Doherty (Building America)	Gr. 3-7
Erie Canal, by Nicholas Nirgiotis (First Book)	Gr. 7-12
**Erie Canal*, by Andrew Santella (We the People)	Gr. 3-8
**Erie Canal*, by Peter Spier	Gr. K-4
**Erie Canal*, by R. Conrad Stein (Cornerstones II)	Gr. 3-8
**Erie Canal Pirates*, by Eric Kimmel	Gr. 1-4
Escape, by Richard Boning (Incredible series)	Gr. 2-5
Escape by Night, by Helen Wells (Winston Adventure)	Gr. 3-9
**Escape from Home*, by Avi (*Beyond the Western Sea*)	Gr. 7-12

**Escape from Slavery*, by Doreen Rappaport	Gr. 3-8
**Escape from Slavery: Boyhood of Frederick Douglass*, by Douglass & McCurdy	Gr. 2-10
**Escape into the Night*, by Lois Walfrid Johnson (Riverboat Adventures)	Gr. 4-8
**Escape North! Story of Harriet Tubman*, by M. Kulling (Step Into Reading 3)	Gr. 1-3
**Escape to Freedom: Underground Railroad Adventures of Callie and William* by Barbara Brooks-Simon	Unknown
Escape to Freedom, by Ruth Fosdick Jones	Gr. 5-12
**Eugene Delacroix*, by Mike Venezia (Getting to Know the World's Great...)	Gr. 1-6
**Except for Me and Thee*, by Jessamyn West	Gr. 10-12
**Exiled to the Red River*, by Dave & Neta Jackson (Trailblazer)	Gr. 3-8
**Expedition of the Donner Party and Its Tragic Fate*, by Eliza Donner Houghton	Unknown
**Everyone Wears His Name*, by Sondra Henry & Emily Taitz	Gr. 5-12
Eyes and Ears of the Civil War, by G. Allen Foster	Gr. 8-12
**Facing West*, by Kathleen Kudlinski (Once Upon America)	Gr. 2-6
Factories, by Leonard Everett Fisher (Nineteenth Century America)	Gr. 4-12
**Facts the Historians Leave Out: A Confederate Primer*, by John Tilley	Gr. 8-12
**Fair American*, by Elizabeth Coatsworth [Not actually covered in this guide, but mentioned as first in trilogy.]	Gr. 2-8
Famous American Authors, by Sarah Bolton	Gr. 6-12
Famous Authors for Young People, by Ramon Coffmann	Gr. 5-12
Famous Horses of the Civil War, by Fairfax Downey	Gr. 4-12
Famous Indian Tribes, by William Moyers	Gr. 1-6
Famous Mathematicians, by Frances Stonaker	Gr. 3-10
Famous Paintings, by Alice Chase	Gr. 5-12
Famous Pioneers, by Franklin Folsom	Gr. 4-12
Famous Poets for Young People, by Laura Benét	Gr. 5-12
Famous Scientists, by William Stevens	Gr. 6-12
Far-Off Land, by Rebecca Caudill	Gr. 5-12
**Fashions of the Old South Paper Dolls* (Dover)	Various
Father of the Constitution: James Madison, by Katharine Wilkie *et al* (Messner)	Gr.. 8-12
Feather in the Wind, by Beverly Butler	Gr. 7-12
**Fields of Fury: The American Civil War*, by James McPherson	Gr. 5-12
Fifer for the Union, by Lorenzo Allen	Gr. 4-7
Fight for Union, by Margaret Coit	Gr. 7-12
Finlandia: The Story of Sibelius, by Eliot Arnold	Gr. 7-12
Fire in the Night, by Robert Carse	Unknown
Fire Upon the Earth, by Norman Langford	Gr. 4-12
**Firing on Fort Sumter: A Splintered Nation Goes to War*, by Nancy Colbert	Gr. 6-12
First Adventure at Sea, by Ida Rifkin	Gr. 2-6
**First Air Voyage in the United States*, by Alexandra Wallner	Gr. 1-4
First Blue Jeans, by Ricki Dru	Gr. 3-8
First Book of Civil War Naval Actions, by Trevor Dupuy (First Books)	Gr. 4-12
First Book of Pioneers, by Walter Havighurst (First Books)	Gr. 3-8
First Book of the California Gold Rush, by Walter Havighurst (First Books)	Gr. 4-12
First Book of the China Clippers, by Louise Dickinson Rich (First Books)	Gr. 5-12

First Book of the Civil War, by Dorothy Levenson (First Books) Gr. 5-9
First Book of the Confederacy, by Dorothy Levenson (First Books) Gr. 5-9
First Book of the Oregon Trail, by Walter Havighurst (First Books) Gr. 3-8
First Book of the Founding of the Republic, by Richard Morris (First Books) Gr. 6-12
(First Book of) The War of 1812, by Richard Morris (First Book) Gr. 3-8
First Book of the War with Mexico, by Henry Castor (First Books) Gr. 4-9
First Bull Run, by Bruce Palmer (Battle Books) Gr. 7-12
First Overland Mail, by Robert Pinkerton (Landmark) Gr. 3-9
**First Ride: Blazing the Trail for the Pony Express*, by Jacqueline Geis Gr. 1-6
**First Son and President*, by Beverly Gherman (Creative Minds) Gr. 2-5
First Steamboat on the Mississippi, by Sterling North (NorthStar) Gr. 5-12
Fish Hawk's Nest, by Stephen Meader Gr. 5-12
Fishing Fleets of New England, by Mary Ellen Chase (North Star) Gr. 6-12
**Five Bushel Farm*, by Elizabeth Coatsworth Gr. 2-8
Flag for Lafitte, by Frederick Lane (Aladdin's American Heritage) Gr. 3-8
Flag for the Fort, by Carl Carmer Gr. 4-8
**Flag Maker*, by Susan Campbell Bartoletti Gr. 1-4
Flag of the Dreadful Bear, by Robert Howard Gr. 3-8
Flag on the Levee, by Manly Wade Wellman Gr. 7-12
Flatboat Days on Frontier Rivers, by James McCague (Garrard How They Lived) Gr. 3-8
Flatboats and Wagon Wheels, by Mildred Comfort Gr. 1-5
**Fleeing for Freedom: Stories of the Underground Railroad as Told by Levi Coffin...* Gr. 10-12
Flight to Freedom: The Story of the Underground Railroad, by Henrietta Buckmaster Gr. 7-12
**Floating House*, by Scott Russell Sanders Gr. 1-3
**Folks Call Me Appleseed John*, by Andrew Glass Gr. 2-5
Follow My Black Plume, by Geoffrey Trease Gr. 6-12
**Follow the Drinking Gourd*, by Jeanette Winter Gr. K-2
**Following Freedom's Star: Story of the Underground Railroad*, by James Haskins Gr. 4-12
**Food and Recipes of the Civil War*, by George Erdosh Various
**Food and Recipes of the Native Americans*, by George Erdosh Various
Foods the Indian Gave Us, by Wilma Pitchford Hays [Beware cover art.] Various
For Ma and Pa on the Oregon Trail, by Wilma Pitchford Hays Gr. 1-4
Forever Free: The Story of the Emancipation Proclamation, by Dorothy Sterling Gr. 4-12
Forked Lightning: The Story of General Philip H. Sheridan, by Albert Orbaan Gr. 6-12
**Fort Sumter*, by Brendan January (Cornerstones II) Gr. 3-8
**Fort Sumter: The Civil War Begins*, by Michael Uschan (Landmark Events) Unknown
**Forty-Niners*, by Cynthia Mercati (Cover-to-Cover) Gr. 3-5
Fourth of July on the Prairie, by Jean Van Leeuwen Gr. 1-4
**Francis Scott Key*, by David Collins (Sower) Gr. 4-12
Francis Scott Key, by Augusta Stevenson (Childhood) Gr. 1-6
**Francis Scott Key and the "Star Spangled Banner,"* by Lynea Bowdish Gr. K-3
**Francis Scott Key: Patriotic Poet*, by Susan Gregson (Let Freedom Ring) Gr. 3-6
Francis Scott Key: Poet and Patriot, by Lillie Patterson (Garrard Discovery) Gr. 1-5
**Francisco Goya* by Mike Venezia (Getting to Know...) Gr. 1-6
Franz Liszt, by Victor Seroff Gr. 8-12
**Franz Peter Schubert*, by Eric Summerer Unknown

Franz Schubert and His Merry Friends, by Opal Wheeler & Sybil Deucher Gr. 2-7
**Frederic Chopin*, by Jacqueline Dineen (Tell Me About) Gr. 2-6
**Frederic Chopin*, by Mike Venezia (Getting to Know the World's...) Gr. 1-6
Frederic Chopin: Early Years* **and *Frederic Chopin: Later Years*, by Opal Wheeler Gr. 2-7
Frederick Douglass, by Charles Graves (See and Read) Gr. K-2
**Frederick Douglass*, by Norma Jean Lutz (Famous Figures of the Civil War...) Gr. 4-8
Frederick Douglass, by Elisabeth Myers (Childhood) Gr. 1-6
**Frederick Douglass Fights for Freedom*, by Margaret Davidson Gr. 2-7
Frederick Douglass: Freedom Fighter, by Lillie Patterson (Garrard) Gr. 1-5
**Frederick Douglass: In His Own Words*, edited by Milton Meltzer Gr. 6-12
Frederick Douglass: Slave-Fighter-Freeman, by Arna Bontemps Gr. 5-10
**Frederick Douglass: The Last Day of Slavery*, by William Miller Gr. 1-3
**Frederick Douglass You Never Knew*, by James Collier Gr. 3-7
**Freedom Crossing*, by Margaret Goff Clark Gr. 5-12
Freedom Fighter, by Betty Everett Gr. 7-12
**Freedom River*, by Doreen Rappaport Gr. 2-5
Freedom River: Florida, 1845, by M. Douglas Gr. 6-12
**Freedom Roads*, by Joyce Hansen & Gary McGowan Gr. 6-12
**Freedom Train: The Story of Harriet Tubman*, by Dorothy Sterling Gr. 3-12
Freedom Triumphant, by Charles Coffin [4th in series] Gr. 7-12
Freedom Ship of Robert Smalls, by Louise Meriwether Gr. 1-5
Freedom Star, by Marcia Mathews Gr. 2-8
**Freedom's Sons: True Story of the* Amistad *Mutiny*, by Suzanne Jurmain Gr. 5-12
**Freedom's Tremendous Cost*, by Raelene Phillips Unknown
**Freedom's Wings*, by Sharon Wyeth (My America) Gr. 3-7
**Friendly Persuasion*, by Jessamyn West Gr. 10-12
**From Sea to Shining Sea*, by Marshall & Manuel Gr. 6-12
**From Sea to Shining Sea for Children*, by Marshall & Manuel Gr. 1-5
From Spinning Wheel to Spacecraft, by Harry Neal (Messner/Milestones) Gr. 9-12
Frontier Doctors, by Wyatt Blassingame and Richard Glendinning Gr. 7-12
**Frontier Fort on the Oregon Trail*, by Scott Steedman (Inside Story) Gr. 4-10
**Frontier Home*, by Raymond Bial Gr. 3-10
Frontier Leaders and Pioneers, by Dorothy Heiderstadt Gr. 3-10
Frontier Living, by Edwin Tunis Gr. 7-12
**Frontier Village: A Town is Born*, by C. Chambers (Adv. in Frontier Am.) Gr. 2-6
**Frozen Summer*, by Mary Jane Auch Gr. 5-10
Full Hold and Splendid Passage, by B. & G. Bonyun (Living History Library) Gr. 9-12
Fur Trappers of the Old West, by A.M. Anderson (American Adventures, older) Gr. 2-7
**Fyodor Dostoevsky*, by Harold Bloom (Bloom's BioCritiques) Gr. 10-12

Gallant Mrs. Stonewall, by Harnett Kane Gr. 8-12
Garibaldi: Father of Modern Italy, by Marcia Davenport (Landmark) Gr. 4-12
Garibaldi: The Man Who Made a Nation, by Ronald Syme Gr. 6-12
**Gathering of Days*, by Joan Blos Gr. 3-12
General Brock and Niagara Falls, by Samuel Adams (Landmark) Gr. 3-10
General Phil Sheridan and the United States Cavalry, by Milton Lomask Gr. 5-10

**Generals of the Civil War*, by William Davis	Gr. 4-12
**Gentle Annie: The True Story of a Civil War Nurse*, by Mary Shura	Gr. 3-9
**George Gordon Meade, Union General*, by Bruce Adelson	Gr. 4-8
George Shannon: Young Explorer with Lewis and Clark, by Virginia Eifert	Gr. 9-12
George Washington and the First Balloon Flight, by Edmund Lindop	Gr. 2-5
**Get On Board: Story of the Underground Railroad*, by Jim Haskins	Gr. 4-9
**Gettysburg*, by Ruth Ashby	Unknown
**Gettysburg*, by Chris Hughes (Battlefields Across America)	Gr. 5-10
**Gettysburg*, by MacKinlay Kantor (Landmark)	Gr. 3-9
Gettysburg, by F.N. Monjo	Gr. 2-8
**Gettysburg Address*, by Abraham Lincoln, illustrated by Michael McCurdy	All ages
**Gettysburg Address*, by Kenneth Richards (Cornerstones)	Gr. 3-7
Ghost Battalion, by Manly Wade Wellman	Gr. 5-12
**Ghosts of the Civil War*, by Cheryl Harness [See cautionary note.]	Gr. 2-5
Giant of the Rockies, by Elisa Bialk	Gr. 4-12
**Giants on the Hill* trilogy, by Lee Roddy	Gr. 7-12
Gift with a Pen: Charlotte Brontë, by Elisabeth Kyle	Gr. 7-12
Giraffe that Walked to Paris, by Nancy Milton	Gr. 1-6
**Girl Called Boy*, by Belinda Hurmence	Gr. 4-12
Girl of the Alamo, by Rita Kerr	Gr. 5-12
**Girl of the Shining Mountains*, by Peter & Connie Roop	Gr. 7-12
Girl Soldier and Spy: Sarah Emma Edmundson, by Mary Hoehling (Messner)	Gr. 5-12
Git Along, Old Scudder, by Stephen Gammell	Gr. K-3
**Giuseppe Garibaldi*, by Herman & Susan Viola (World Leaders Past...)	Gr. 7-12
**Glass Town*, by Michael Bedard	Gr. 2-7
Glorious Conspiracy, by Joanne Williamson	Gr. 5-12
Glorious Hussar, by Sir Arthur Conan Doyle	Gr. 7-12
**Go Free or Die*, by Jeri Ferris (Carolrhoda Creative Minds)	Gr. 2-8
**Gods and Generals*, by Jeff Shaara	Gr. 10-12
Goethe: Pattern of Genius, by Monroe Stearns (Immortals of Literature)	Gr. 8-12
Gold Fever, by Verla Kay	Gr. K-3
**Gold Fever!* by Catherine McMorrow (Step Into Reading 4)	Gr. 2-4
**Gold Fever!* by Rosalyn Schanzer	Gr. 3-6
Gold in California, by Paul Wellman (North Star)	Gr. 6-12
Gold-Lined Box, by Marjory Hall	Gr. 5-12
**Gold Rush Adventures*, by Edith McCall (Frontiers of America)	Gr. 2-8
**Gold Rush Days*, by Ellen Weiss	Gr. 3-8
**Gold Rush: Hands-On Projects About Mining the Riches of California*, by J. Quasha	Gr. 2-4
Gold Rush of 1849, by Arthur Blake	Gr. 6-12
**Gold Rush! Young Prospector's Guide...*, by James Klein	Various
Golden Book of the Civil War, by Charles Flato	Gr. 7-12
**Gone A-Whaling*, by Jim Murphy	Gr. 6-12
**Good Hunting, Blue Sky*, by Peggy Parish	Gr. K-2
**Good Night for Freedom*, by Barbara Morrow	Gr. 1-3
**Good-bye for Today*, by Peter & Connie Roop	Gr. 2-5
Goya, by Elizabeth Ripley	Gr. 8-12

**Grace's Letter to Lincoln*, by Peter & Connie Roop Gr. 2-5
Granny, Baby, and the Big Gray Wolf **and** *Granny and the Desperadoes*, by P. Parish Gr. K-2
Gray Riders, by Manly Wade Wellman (Aladdin's American Heritage) Gr. 3-10
Great Ambitions, by Elisabeth Kyle Gr. 6-12
Great American Gold Rush, by Rhoda Blumberg Gr. 6-12
**(Great Battles and Sieges:) Trafalgar*, by Richard Balkwill Gr. 5-10
**(Great Battles and Sieges:) Waterloo*, by Philip Sauvain Gr. 4-10
**Great Bridge-Building Contest*, by Bo Zaunders Gr. 1-4
Great Captain, by Honoré Morrow Gr. 9-12
Great Civil War Escapes, by A.I.. Schutzer Gr. 6-12
Great Days of Whaling, by Henry Hough (North Star) Gr. 7-12
Great Doctrine, by Henry Commager Gr. 7-12
Great Evangelical Preachers of Yesterday, by James MacGraw Gr. 11-12
**Great Expedition of Lewis and Clark*, by Judith Edwards Gr. 2-5
**Great Little Madison*, by Jean Fritz Gr. 7-12
Great Proclamation, by Henry Steele Commager Gr. 7-12
Great Rope, by Rosemary Nesbitt Gr. 4-10
Great Turkey Drive, by Charles Wilson Gr. 4-12
Grizzly Adams, by Harry James Gr. 2-7
**Guns of Bull Run*, by Joseph Altsheler Gr. 9-12
**Guns of Shiloh*, by Joseph Altsheler Gr. 7-12
Guns of Vicksburg, by Earl Schenck Miers Gr. 4-12
Guns Over Champlain, by Leon Dean Gr. 4-10
Gunsmith's Boy, by Herbert Best Gr. 5-12

Hank of Lost Nugget Canyon, by H.R. Langdale Gr. 5-12
Hannah Herself, by Ruth Franchere Gr. 6-12
Hannah's Farm, by Michael McCurdy Gr. 1-3
**Harper's Ferry: The Story of John Brown's Raid*, by Tracy Barrett Gr. 5-10
**Harriet and the Promised Land*, by Jacob Lawrence Gr. 1-4
Harriet and the Runaway Book, by Johanna Johnston Gr. 2-7
Harriet Beecher Stowe, by Mabel Widdemer (Childhood) Gr. 1-6
Harriet Beecher Stowe, by Winifred Wise (Lives to Remember) Gr. 6-12
**Harriet Beecher Stowe and the Beecher Preachers*, by Jean Fritz Gr. 6-12
**Harriet Tubman*, by Kathleen Kudlinski (Childhood, reissue) Gr. 1-6
**Harriet Tubman*, by Norma Jean Lutz (Famous Figures of the Civil War) Gr. 4-8
**Harriet Tubman*, by Wil Mara (Rookie Biographies) Gr. 1-4
Harriet Tubman, by Gertrude Winders (Childhood) Gr. 1-6
Harriet Tubman: Conductor on the Underground Railroad, by Ann Petry Gr. 5-12
Harriet Tubman: Flame of Freedom, by F. Humphreville (Piper) Gr. 2-7
**Harriet Tubman: Freedombound*, by Janet & Geoff Benge (Christian Heroes) Gr. 5-12
Harriet Tubman: Guide to Freedom, by Sam & Beryl Epstein (Garr. Am. All) Gr. 3-9
Harriet Tubman: The Road to Freedom, by Ray Baines (Troll) Gr. 1-4
Harvest of the Sea, by Walter Buehr Gr. 3-12
**He Freed Britain's Slaves*, by Charles Ludwig Gr. 7-12
He Wouldn't Be King: The Story of Simon Bolivar, by Nina Brown Baker Gr. 7-12

**Head Full of Notions*, by Andy Brown (Carolrhoda Creative Minds)	Gr. 2-7
Head on Her Shoulders, by G. Bond	Gr. 4-12
Hearthstone in the Wilderness, by Erick Berry	Gr. 5-12
Hello, the Boat, by Phyllis Crawford	Gr. 3-10
Henry Clay, by Helen Monsell (Childhood)	Gr. 1-6
Henry Clay, by Booth Mooney	Gr. 5-12
**Henry Clay*, by Alison Tibbitts (Historical American Biographies)	Unknown
Henry Clay: Leader in Congress, by Helen Peterson (Garrard Discovery)	Gr. 1-5
Henry Clay: Statesman and Patriot, by Regina Kelly (Piper)	Gr. 3-9
**Henry Clay: The Great Compromiser*, by Michael Burgan (Our People)	Unknown
Henry Bergh, by Alvin Harlow (Messner)	Gr. 6-12
Henry's Lincoln, by Louise Neyhart	Gr. 1-6
**Her Piano Sang*, by Barbara Allman (Creative Minds)	Gr. 3-9
Here Comes the Mystery Man, by Scott Russell Sanders	Gr. 1-3
Hero of Trafalgar, by A.B.C. Whipple (Landmark)	Gr. 3-10
**Hero Tales: Vol. I, II, IV*, by Dave & Neta Jackson	Gr. 3-6
**Heroes of the Western Outposts*, by Edith McCall (Frontiers of America)	Gr. 3-7
**Heroic Symphony*, by Anna Celenza	Gr. 1-4
Heroines of the Early West, by Nancy Ross (Landmark)	Gr. 4-12
Hester & Timothy, Pioneers, by Ruth Langland Holberg	Gr. 3-8
Hills Stand Watch, by August Derleth	Gr. 7-12
**History Alive Through Music: Westward Ho!* by Diana Waring	Various
**History Makers of the Scientific Revolution*, by Nina Morgan (History Makers)	Gr. 4-9
**History through the Eyes of Faith*, by Ronald Wells	Gr. 9-12
**Hitty: Her First Hundred Years*, by Rachel Field	Gr. 4-10
**Hog Music*, by M.C. Helldorfer	Gr. 1-3
Homespun, by Erick Berry	Gr. 5-12
Honor Bound, by Frank Bonham	Gr. 9-12
Hornblower in Captivity, by C.S. Forester [See cautionary note in guide.]	Parental decision
Hornblower Takes Command, by C.S. Forester [See cautionary note in guide.]	Parental decision
Horse for General Lee, by Fairfax Downey	Gr. 5-12
Horse that Won the Civil War, by Bern Keating	Gr. 6-12
Horses of Destiny, by Fairfax Downey	Gr. 4-12
**Hospital Sketches*, by Louisa May Alcott	Gr. 7-12
House on Liberty Street, by Mary Ann Weik	Gr. 7-12
How Davy Crockett Got a Bearskin Coat, by Wyatt Blassingame	Gr. 1-5
**How I Survived the Irish Famine*, by L. Wilson	Gr. 5-12
**How Should We Then Live?* by Francis Schaeffer [Book and/or video.]	Gr. 8-12
**How to Draw the Life and Times of John Quincy Adams*, by Betsy Dru Tecco	Various
**How We Crossed the West: Adventures of Lewis & Clark*, by Rosalyn Schanzer	Gr. 2-7
**Hudson Taylor*, by Janet Benge (Christian Heroes, Then and Now)	Gr. 5-12
**Hudson Taylor*, by Vance Christie (Heroes of the Faith)	Gr. 5-12
**Hudson Taylor*, by Susan Miller (Young Reader's Christian Library)	Gr. 1-3
**Hudson Taylor*, by Hudson Taylor (Men of Faith)	Gr. 8-12
Hudson Taylor and Maria, by J.C. Pollock	Gr. 10-12
**Hudson Taylor: Vol. 1 and 2*, by Howard Taylor	Gr. 10-12

*_Hudson Taylor's Spiritual Secret_, by Howard Taylor — Gr. 8-12
*_Hue and Cry_, by Elizabeth Yates — Gr. 6-12
*_Hugh Glass, Mountain Man_, by Robert McClung — Gr. 7-12
Humphry Davy and Chemical Discovery, by Elba Carrier (Immortals of Science) — Gr. 7-12
*_Hunters Blaze the Trails_, by Edith McCall (Frontiers of America) — Gr. 3-7
*_Hunting Neptune's Giants_, by Catherine Gourley — Gr. 4-9
*_Hurry Freedom_, by Jerry Stanley — Gr. 6-12

*_I am Houston_, by Mary Wade — Unknown
I, Jessie, by Ruth Painter Randall — Gr. 7-12
*_I Remember the Alamo_, by D. Anne Love [See cautionary note.] — Gr. 4-7
*_I Thought My Soul Would Rise and Fly_, by Joyce Hansen (Dear America) — Gr. 3-10
I, Varina, by Ruth Randall — Gr. 7-12
*_I Was Born a Slave: The Story of Harriet Jacobs_, by Jennifer Fleischner — Unknown
I Will Be Heard, by Doris Faber — Gr. 7-12
*_If Pigs Could Fly_, by John Lawson [See note in guide.] — Gr. 5-8
*_If You Grew Up with Abraham Lincoln_, by Ann McGovern — Gr. 1-4
*_If You Lived at the Time of the Civil War_, by Kay Moore — Gr. 1-5
*_If You Lived with the Cherokee_, by Peter & Connie Roop — Gr. 2-6
*_If You Lived with the Iroquois_, by Ellen Levine — Gr. 2-6
*_If You Please, President Lincoln_, by Harriette Robinet — Gr. 5-12
*_If You Traveled on the Underground Railroad_, by Ellen Levine — Gr. 1-6
*_If You Traveled West on a Covered Wagon_, by Ellen Levine — Gr. 1-4
*_Illustrated Confederate Reader_, edited by Rod Gragg — Gr. 7-12
*_I'm Sorry, Almira Ann_, by Jane Kurtz — Gr. 2-4
Immortal Wife, by Irving Stone [See note in text.] — Gr. 11-12
In Defense of Freedom: Story of the Monroe Doctrine, by P. Rink (Messner/Milestone) — Gr. 8-12
*_In Praise of Johnny Appleseed_, by Vachel Lindsay — Various
In Scarlet and Blue: The Story of Military Uniforms in America, by D. Gringhuis — Gr. 3-7
*_Incredible Journey of Lewis and Clark_, by R. Blumberg [See caution in guide.] — Gr. 7-12
Indestructible Commodore Matthew Perry, by Arthur Orrmont (Messner) — Gr. 7-12
Indian America: The Black Hawk War, by Miriam Gurko — Gr. 9-12
*_Indian Crafts_, by Keith Brandt — Various
Indian Fishing and Camping, Indian Hunting, etc., by Robert Hofsinde — Gr. 3-12
Indian Harvests, by William Grimm [Some editions have revealing cover.] — Gr. 4-12
Indian Tribes of America, by Marion Gridley — Gr. 3-9
Indians Wars and Warriors—East, by Paul Wellman (North Star) — Gr. 3-10
Indians, by Edwin Tunis — Gr. 6-12
Indians as the Westerners Saw Them, by Ralph Andrews — Gr. 7-12
Indians, Indians, Indians, by Phyllis Fenner — Gr. 3-12
Indians Knew, by Tillie Pine — Various
*_Indian Tribes of North America Coloring Book_ (Dover) — Various
Indians of the Longhouse, by Sonia Bleeker — Gr. 4-12
Indians: The First Americans, by Patricia Miles Martin — Gr. 1-5
*_Industrial America_, by Kitty Shea (We the People) — Gr. 5-12
Industrial Genius: Samuel Slater, by Lewis Miner (Messner) — Gr. 8-12

***Industrial Revolution*, by John D. Clare (Living History) Gr. 4-12
**Industrial Revolution*, by Mary Collins (Cornerstones) Unknown
**Industrial Revolution*, by Andrew Langley (See Through History) Gr. 4-12
**Industrial Revolution*, by Sara Wooten (People at the Center of...) Unknown
**Industrial Revolution Almanac*, by James & Elizabeth Outman Unknown
Indy and Mr. Lincoln, by Natalia Belting Gr. 1-3
**Inside-Outside Book of Washington*, by Roxie Munro Gr. K-3
**Inside the Alamo*, by Jim Murphy Gr. 5-12
**Into the Woods: John James Audubon Lives His Dream*, by Robert Burleigh Gr. 1-5
**Introducing Beethoven*, by Roland Vernon (Introducing Composers) Gr. 5-12
**Introducing Chopin*, by Roland Vernon (Introducing Composers) Gr. 5-12
**Invention*, by Lionel Bender (Eyewitness) Gr. 5-12
Inventors Behind the Inventors, by Roger Burlingame Gr. 7-12
**Invitation to the Classics*, edited by Louise Cowan & Os Guinness Gr. 8-12
**Iron Scouts of the Confederacy*, by Lee McGiffin Gr. 6-12
Ironclad! by Seymour Reit Gr. 4-9
**Ironclads and Blockades in the Civil War*, by Douglas Savage (Untold History...) Gr. 4-8
Iroquois, by Irene Estep Gr. 1-4
**Iroquois*, by Richard Gaines (Native Americans) Gr. 2-5
**Iroquois*, by Virginia Driving Hawk Sneve Gr. 2-5?
**Iroquois Indians*, by Bill Lund Gr. 3-7
**Island Far from Home*, by John Donahue Gr. 4-7
**Island of the Blue Dolphins*, by Scott O'Dell Gr. 4-12
Island on the Border, by Trella Dick Gr. 4-12
**Island Story*, by H.E. Marshall Gr. 3-8

Jack Darby, Able Seaman, by John Clagett Gr. 5-10
Jack Finds Gold, by Sanford Tousey Gr. 2-6
**Jackson and Lee: Legends in Gray*, by James Robertson Unknown
Jacksons of Tennessee, by Marguerite Vance Gr. 7-12
Jacob Brown and the War of 1812, by Frank Latham Gr. 9-12
**James Beckwourth*, by Sean Dolan (Black Americans of Achievement) Unknown
**James Beckwourth*, by Rick Burke (American Lives) Unknown
James Bowie and His Famous Knife, by Shannon Garst (Messner) Gr. 4-12
James Fenimore Cooper, by Isabel Proudfit (Messner) Gr. 5-12
James Fenimore Cooper, by Gertrude Winders (Childhood) Gr. 1-6
**James Longstreet*, by Melanie Le Tourneau Unknown
James Madison, by Susan Clinton (Encyclopedia of the Presidents) Gr. 6-12
**James Madison*, by Brendan January (Encyclopedia of the Presidents II) Unknown
**James Madison*, by Andrew Santella (Profiles of the Presidents) Gr. 3-6?
**James Madison*, by Mike Venezia (Getting to Know the US Presidents) Gr. 1-5
**James Madison: Creating a Nation*, by Zachary Kent Unknown
James Madison: Statesman and President, by Regina Kelly (Piper) Gr. 2-8
James Monroe, by Christine Fitzgerald (Encyclopedia of Presidents) Gr. 5-12
**James Monroe*, by Ann Gaines (Our Presidents) Unknown
**James Monroe*, by Andrew Santella (Encyclopedia of Presidents II) Unknown

**James Monroe*, by Mike Venezia (Getting to Know the U.S. Presidents)	Gr. 1-5
James Monroe, by Mabel Widdemer (Childhood)	Gr. 1-6
**James Monroe: Young Patriot*, by Rae Bains	Gr. 1-3
**James Watt*, by Neil Champion (Groundbreakers)	Gr. 5-7
James Watt: Inventor of a Steam Engine, by Robert Webb (Immortals...)	Gr. 7-12
**James Watt: Master of the Steam Engine*, by Anna Sproule (Giants of Science)	Gr. 5-12
(James Watt:) The Man Who Transformed the World [Also listed as *Man Who Transformed...*]	
**Jane Austen*, by Deirdre Le Faye (British Library Writers' Lives)	Gr. 7-12
**Jane Austen*, by Heather Wagner (Who Wrote That?)	Gr. 7-12
Jane Hope, by Elizabeth Janet Gray	Gr. 8-12
**Jason Lee: Winner of the Northwest*, by Charles Ludwig (Sower)	Gr. 5-12
**Jayhawkers*, by Patricia Beatty	Gr. 6-12
Jeb Stuart, by Lena DeGrummond	Gr. 5-12
Jeb Stuart, by Gertrude Winders (Childhood)	Gr. 1-6
Jed, by Peter Burchard	Gr. 4-12
Jed Smith: Trail Blazer, by Frank Latham (Aladdin's American Heritage)	Gr. 3-9
Jed Smith: Trailblazer and Trapper, by Frank Latham (Garrard Discovery)	Gr. 1-5
Jedediah Smith, by Hal Evarts	Gr. 4-12
**Jedediah Smith*, by Sharlene Nelson	Unknown
**Jedediah Smith and the Mountain Men of the American West*, by John Allen	Unknown
Jedediah Smith: Fur Trapper of the Old West, by Olive Burt (Messner)	Gr. 7-12
Jeff Davis, by Lena DeGrummond (Childhood)	Gr. 1-6
**Jefferson Davis*, by E.J. Carter	Unknown
**Jefferson Davis*, by Joey Frazier (Famous Figures of the Civil War Era)	Gr. 4-8
**Jefferson Davis*, by Scott Ingram	Unknown
Jefferson Davis, by Zachary Kent (Cornerstones)	Gr. 2-7
**Jefferson Davis*, by Perry Scott King (World Leaders Past & Present)	Gr. 6-12
**Jefferson Davis*, by Susan Lee (Heroes of the Civil War)	Gr. 1-3
Jefferson Davis, by Patricia Miles (See and Read)	Gr. K-3
Jerry and the Pony Express, by Sanford Tousey	Gr. 1-4
**Jessica's First Prayer*, by Hesba Stretton (Lamplighter)	Gr. 3-10
**Jessica's Mother Comes Home*, by Hesba Stretton & Mark Hamby (Lamplighter)	Gr. 3-10
Jessie Benton Frémont, by Marguerite Higgins (North Star)	Gr. 7-12
Jessie Frémont, by Jean Wagoner (Childhood)	Gr. 1-6
Jim Beckwourth, by Wyatt Blassingame (Garrard Discovery)	Gr. 1-5
**Jim Beckwourth: Adventures of a Mountain Man*, by Louis Sabin (Troll)	Gr. 1-4
Jim Beckwourth: Negro Mountain Man, by Harold Felton	Gr. 4-12
**Jim Bowie*, by Marianne Johnston (American Legends)	Unknown
Jim Bowie, by Gertrude Winders (Childhood)	Gr. 1-6
**Jim Bowie: Frontier Legend, Alamo Hero*, by J.R. Edmondson	Gr. 5-12
Jim Bridger, by Sanford Tousey	Gr. 2-7
Jim Bridger, by Gertrude Winders (Childhood)	Gr. 1-6
Jim Bridger: Greatest of the Mountain Men, by Shannon Garst	Gr. 4-12
Jim Bridger: Man of the Mountains, by W. & C. Luce (Garrard Discovery)	Gr. 1-5
**J.M.W. Turner*, by Robert Kenner (First Impressions)	Various
Joe Mason: Apprentice to Audubon, by Charlie May Simon	Gr. 5-12

Joe Meek: Man of the West, by Shannon Garst (Messner)	Gr. 6-12
Joel Chandler Harris, by Alvin Harlow (Messner)	Gr. 6-12
Joel Chandler Harris, by Ethel Weddle (Childhood)	Gr. 1-6
**Johannes Brahms*, by Mike Venezia (Getting to Know the World's...)	Gr. 1-6
**Johannes Brahms and the Twilight of Romanticism* (Masters of Music) by Donna Getzinger	Gr. 5-12
John Audubon, by Miriam Mason (Childhood) [Also titled *Young Audubon.*]	Gr. 1-6
John Brown, by Jeannette Covert Nolan (Messner)	Gr. 7-12
**John Brown*, by Thomas Streissguth (Carolrhoda)	Gr. 2-5
John Brown: A Cry for Freedom, by Lorenz Graham	Gr. 8-12
**John Brown: Abolitionist*, by Virginia Brackett (Famous Figures of the...)	Gr. 4-8
John Brown: One Man Against Slavery, by Gwen Everett	Gr. 2-4
**John Brown's Body*.by Stephen Vincent Benét	Gr. 10-12
**John Brown's Raid on Harpers Ferry*, by Brendan January (Cornerstones II)	Gr. 4-10
**John Brown's Raid on Harpers Ferry*, by R. Conrad Stein (In American History)	Gr. 6-12
**John C. Calhoun and the Roots of War*, by Thomas Durwood	Unknown
**John C. Frémont*, by Harold Faber (Great Explorations)	Unknown
**John C. Frémont*, by Hal Marcovitz (Explorers of New Worlds)	Unknown
**John C. Frémont*, by Kristin Petrie	Gr. 3-6
**John C. Frémont*, by D.M. Souza (Watts Library)	Unknown
John C. Frémont, by Sanford Tousey	Gr. 2-7
**John C. Frémont: Soldier and Pathfinder*, by Carl Green & William Sanford	Gr. 4-7
**John Charles Frémont*, by Barbara Witteman (Let Freedom Ring)	Gr. 4-8
John Charles Fremont: Trail Marker..., by Olive Burt (Messner)	Gr. 6-12
John Colter: Man Who Found Yellowstone, by Mark Boesch	Gr. 6-12
John Deere, by Margaret Bare (Childhood)	Gr. 1-6
**John Deere*, by Margaret Hall (Lives and Times)	Gr. 1-3
John Ericsson and the Inventions of War, by Ann Brophy	Gr. 3-10
John Greenleaf Whittier: Fighting Quaker, by Ruth Holberg	Gr. 5-12
John Jacob Astor, by Dorothy Anderson (Childhood)	Gr. 1-6
**John Jacob Astor and the Fur Trade*, by Lewis Parker (American Tycoons)	Unknown
John James Audubon, by Margaret & John Kieran (Landmark)	Gr. 3-9
John James Audubon: Bird Artist, by James Ayars (Garrard Discovery)	Gr. 1-5
**John James Audubon: Wildlife Artist*, by Peter Anderson	Unknown
**John Marshall*, by Stuart Kallen	Gr. 3-5
John Marshall, by Patricia Miles Martin (See and Read)	Gr. 1-3
John Marshall, by Teri Martini	Gr. 3-10
John Marshall, by Helen Monsell (Childhood)	Gr. 1-6
John Marshall, by Alfred Steinberg	Gr. 9-12
John Marshall, by Caroline Tucker	Gr. 9-12
John Quincy Adams, by Milton Lomask	Gr. 7-12
**John Quincy Adams*, by Mike Venezia (Getting to Know the U.S. Presidents)	Gr. 1-5
John Quincy Adams, by Ann Weil (Childhood)	Gr. 1-6
John Sutter, Californian, by Edwin Booth	Gr. 5-12
**John Tabor's Ride*, by Edward Day	Gr. 1-3
**John Wilkes Booth and the Civil War*, by Steven Otfinoski	Gr. 7-12

Johnny Appleseed, by Stephen Vincent Benét — Gr. 1-5
Johnny Appleseed, by David Collins (Sower) — Gr. 5-12
Johnny Appleseed, by Steven Kellogg — Gr. 1-4
Johnny Appleseed, by Reeve Lindbergh — Gr. 1-4
Johnny Appleseed, by Eva Moore — Gr. 2-6
Johnny Appleseed, by Gertrude Norman (See and Read) — Gr. 1-3
Johnny Appleseed, by Louis Sabin — Gr. 1-4
Johnny Appleseed: The Story of a Legend, by Will Moses — Gr. 4-6
Johnny Reb, by Merritt Parmelee Allen — Gr. 5-12
Johnny Reb (Bellerophon) — Various
Johnny Texas, by Carol Hoff — Gr. 2-9
Johnny Texas on the San Antonio Road, by Carol Hoff — Gr. 2-9
Johnny the Confederate Soldier: With 27 Stickers, by A.G. Smith (Dover) — Various
Jonathan Goes West, by Stephen Meader — Gr. 5-12
Josefina Story Quilt, by Eleanor Coerr (I Can Read) — Gr. K-3
Joseph E. Johnston, Confederate General, by Christin Ditchfield — Gr. 7-12
Joseph Priestly: Pioneer Chemist, by Rebecca Marcus (Immortals of Science) — Gr. 7-12
Joseph Turner, by Jayne Woodhouse (Life and Work of...) — Gr. K-2
Josiah True and the Art Maker, by Amy Littlesugar — Gr. 1-4
Journal of Augustus Pelletier, by Kathryn Lasky (My Name is America) — Gr. 5-9
Journal of Brian Doyle, by Jim Murphy (My Name is America) — Gr. 4-9
Journal of Douglas Allen Deeds: Donner Party Expedition (My Name is America) by Rodman Philbrick [See cautionary note] — Gr. 5-8
Journal of James Edmond Pease, by Jim Murphy (My Name is America) — Gr. 4-9
Journal of Jedediah Barstow, by Ellen Levine (My Name is America) — Gr. 4-7
Journal of Rufus Rowe, by Sid Hite (My Name is America) — Gr. 4-9
Journey to Freedom, by Courtni Wright — Gr. 1-4
Journey to Nowhere, by Mary Jane Auch — Gr. 5-10
Journeyman, by Elizabeth Yates — Gr. 6-12
Juanita, by Leo Politi — Gr. 1-3
Jube: Story of a Trapper's Dog, by Thomas Hinkle — Gr. 4-12
Jules Verne: His Life, by Catherine Owens Peare — Gr. 4-10
Jules Verne: Portrait of a Prophet, by Russell Freedman — Gr. 9-12
Jules Verne: The Man Who Invented the Future, by Franz Born — Gr. 8-12
Julia Ann, by Rachel Varble — Gr. 7-12
Jump Ship to Freedom, by James & Christopher Collier — Gr. 3-12
Just a Few Words, Mr. Lincoln, by Jean Fritz — Gr. K-3

Kathleen: Yankee Girl at Gettysburg, by Alice Desmond Curtis — Gr. 3-12
Keelboat Journey, by Zachary Ball — Gr. 7-12
Keep 'Em Rolling, by Stephen Meader — Gr. 4-12
Keep the Wagons Moving! by West Lathrop — Gr. 7-12
Kidnapped Prince: The Life of Olaudah Equiano, by Olaudah Equiano — Gr. 3-8
Kids During the American Civil War, by Lisa Wroble — Gr. 2-4
Kids During the Industrial Revolution, by Lisa Wroble — Gr. 2-4
Killer Angels, by Michael Shaara — Gr. 10-12

**Kindle Me a Riddle*, by Roberta Karim	Gr. 1-4
King of the Clippers, by Edmund Collier (Aladdin's American Heritage)	Gr. 3-8
King's Astronomer, by Deborah Crawford	Gr. 5-12
King's Giraffe, by Mary Jo & Pete Collier	Gr. 2-7
Kit Carson, by Frank Beals (American Adventures, older series)	Gr. 3-8
**Kit Carson*, by Rick Burke	Unknown
**Kit Carson*, by Jan Gleiter (First Biographies)	Gr. 1-3
Kit Carson, by Augusta Stevenson (Childhood)	Gr. 1-6
Kit Carson, by Sanford Tousey	Gr. 2-7
Kit Carson and the Wild Frontier, by Ralph Moody (Landmark)	Gr. 3-9
**Kit Carson: Frontier Scout*, by Carl Green & William Sanford	Gr. 4-8
**Kit Carson: Mountain Man*, by Tracey Boraas (Let Freedom Ring)	Gr. 4-8
Kit Carson: Mountain Scout, by Donald Worcester (Piper)	Gr. 2-7
Kit Carson of the Old West, by Mark Boesch (Vision)	Gr. 4-12
Kit Carson: Pathfinder of the West, by Nardi Campion (Garrard Discovery)	Gr. 1-5
Kit Carson: Trailblazer and Scout, by Shannon Garst (Messner)	Gr. 6-12
**Kit Carson's Autobiography*, by Kit Carson	Unknown
Lad with a Whistle, by Carol Ryrie Brink	Gr. 5-12
Ladd of the Big Swamp, by Cecile Matschat (Winston Adventure)	Gr. 3-9
Ladd of the Lone Star, by Allan Bosworth (Aladdin's American Heritage)	Gr. 3-9
Lafitte the Pirate, by Ariane Dewey	Gr. 1-4
**Lame One: The Story of Sequoyah*, by Jill Wheeler	Unknown
**Land Beyond the Setting Sun*, by Tracy Leininger (Beautiful Girlhood)	Gr. 3-8
Lanterns Aloft, by Mary Andrews	Gr. 5-12
**Last Full Measure*, by Jeff Shaara	Gr. 10-12
Last Stand at the Alamo, by Alden Carter (First Books)	Gr. 5-10
Last Wilderness: The Saga of America's Mountain Men, by N. Gerson (Messner)	Gr. 7-12
**Laura Secord's Brave Walk*, by Connie Brummel Cook	Gr. 2-5
Law or the Gun, by Frank Latham (Aladdin's American Heritage)	Gr. 3-9
**Least of All*, by Carol Purdy	Gr. K-3
**Lee and Grant at Appomattox*, by MacKinlay Kantor (Landmark)	Gr. 3-9
**Lee of Virginia*, by Douglas Southall Freeman	Gr. 10-12
Lee: The Gallant General, by Jeanette Eaton	Gr. 3-6
Lees of Arlington, by Marguerite Vance	Gr. 5-12
Legacy of the Civil War, by Robert Penn Warren	Gr. 10-12
**Legend of Freedom Hill*, by Linda Altman	Gr. 1-4
**Legend of Sleeping Bear*, by Kathy-jo Wargin [Contains Indian religion.]	Gr. 1-4
**Legend of Snowshoe Thompson*, by Cory La Bianca	Gr. 3-8
**Leo Tolstoy*, by Harold Bloom (Bloom's Modern Critical Views)	Gr. 10-12
**Les Misérables*, by Victor Hugo	Various
Let's Be Indians, by Peggy Parish	Various
**Letters from Vinnie*, by Maureen Sappey [See cautionary note.]	Gr. 6-12
**Letzenstein Chronicles* series, by Meriol Trevor (Bethlehem Books)	Gr. 4-12
(*Crystal Snowstorm, Following the Phoenix, Angel & Dragon*, and *Rose & Crown*)	
**Levi Strauss*, by Tiffany Peterson (Lives and Times)	Gr. 1-3

**Levi Strauss: The Blue Jean Man*, by Elizabeth Van Steenwyk	Gr. 5-12
**Levi Strauss: The Man Behind Blue Jeans*, by Carin Ford (Famous Inventors)	Unknown
**Lewis & Papa: Adventure on the Santa Fe Trail*, by Barbara Joosse	Gr. 1-4
Lewis and Clark, by Madge Haines & Leslie Morrill (Makers of America)	Gr. 3-7
**Lewis and Clark*, by Steven Kroll	Gr. 2-5
Lewis and Clark, by Elizabeth Montgomery (Garrard World Explorer)	Gr. 1-5
**Lewis and Clark: A Prairie Dog for the President*, by S. Redmond (Step into...3)	Gr. 1-3
**Lewis and Clark and Me: A Dog's Tale*, by Laurie Myers	Gr. 3-7
**Lewis and Clark Expedition*, by Richard Neuberger (Landmark)	Gr. 3-9
**Lewis and Clark Expedition Coloring Book* (Dover)	Various
**Lewis and Clark for Kids*, by Janis Herbert	Various
**Liberty, Justice, and F'Rall*, by Marjorie Kutchinski	Unknown
**Liberty Street*, by Candice Ransom	Gr. 1-4
Liebeg: Master Chemist, by Louis Kuslan	Gr. 7-12
**Life & Times of Felix Mendelssohn*, by Susan Zannos	Gr. 4-12
**Life & Times of Franz Liszt*, by Jim Whiting (Masters of Music)	Gr. 4-12
**Life & Times of Frederic Chopin*, by Jim Whiting (Masters of Music)	Gr. 4-12
**Life & Times of Giuseppe Verdi*, by Jim Whiting (Masters of Music)	Gr. 4-12
**Life & Times of Johannes Brahms*, by Jim Whiting (Masters of Music)	Gr. 4-12
**Life & Times of Richard Wagner*, by Jim Whiting (Masters of Music)	Gr. 4-12
**Life in a New England Mill Town*, by Sally Isaacs (Picture the Past)	Gr. 2-4
**Life in a Whaling Town*, by Sally Isaacs (Picture the Past)	Gr. 2-4
**Life in an Anishinabe Camp*, by B. Kalman & N. Walker (Native Nations)	Gr. 4-9
Life in Charles Dickens' England, by Diane Yancey (Way People Live)	Gr. 9-12
Life in Lincoln's America, by Helen Reeder Cross (Landmark Giant)	Gr. 5-12
**Light in the Storm*, by Karen Hesse (Dear America)	Gr. 3-9
Life of Andrew Jackson, by Marquis James [See note in guide.]	Gr. 12+
**Life of David Crockett*, by David Crockett	Gr. 8-12
**Life of J.E.B. Stuart*, by Mrs. M.L. Williamson [Included in: **Confederate Trilogy for Young Readers.*]	Gr. 6-12
**Life of Kit Carson*, by Edward Ellis (Lost Classics)	Gr. 5-12
Life of Kit Carson, by C. Richard Schaare [Included in his *Pioneer Stories* too.]	Gr. 2-8
**Life of Robert E. Lee*, by Mrs. M.L. Williamson [Also included in: **Confederate Trilogy for Young Readers.*]	Gr. 7-12
Life on a Barge, by Huck Scarry	Gr. 3-12
**Life on the Oregon Trail*, by Gary Blackwood (Way People Live)	Gr. 5-12
**Life on the Oregon Trail*, by Sally Isaacs (Picture the Past)	Gr. 1-4
**Lightning Time*, by Douglas Rees	Gr. 5-10
**Li'l Dan the Drummer Boy*, by Romare Bearden	Gr. 1-4
**Lincoln: A Photobiography*, by Russell Freedman	Gr. 3-10
Lincoln and Douglas: The Years of Decision, by Regina Kelly (Landmark)	Gr. 3-8
**Lincoln and the Emancipation Proclamation in American History*, by D. Holford	Unknown
**Lincoln-Douglas Debates*, by Michael Burgan (We the People)	Gr. 3-5
**Lincoln-Douglas Debates*, by Brendan January (Cornerstones II)	Gr. 4-8
**Lincoln, Slavery, and the Emancipation Proclamation*, by Carin Ford	Unknown
Lincoln Stories, by Honoré Morrow	Gr. 5-12

Lincoln's Birthday, by Clyde Robert Bulla Gr. 1-6
Lincoln's Little Correspondent, by Hertha Pauli Gr. 2-6
Lincoln's Secret Weapon, by W. Wise Gr. 7-12
**Line in the Sand: Alamo Diary of Lucinda Lawrence*, by S. Garland (Dear Amer.) Gr. 3-8
**Listen for the Whippoorwill*, by Dave & Neta Jackson (Trailblazer) Gr. 2-9
Little Brother of the Wilderness, by Meridel LeSueur Gr. 1-5
Little Giant: Stephen A. Douglas, by Jeannette Covert Nolan (Messner) Gr. 6-12
Little Jonathan, by Miriam Mason Gr. 2-6
Little Maid of New Orleans, by Alice Turner Curtis Gr. 3-8
**Little Runner of the Longhouse*, by Betty Baker Gr. K-3
Little Schubert, by M.B. Goffstein Gr. 1-4
**Little Shepherd of Kingdom Come*, by John Fox, Jr. Gr. 9-12
Lives of Poor Boys Who Became Famous, by Sarah Bolton Gr. 4-12
**Lives of the Artists*, by Kathleen Krull Gr. 5-10
**Lives of the Writers: Comedies, Tragedies (and What the Neighbors Thought)*, by Krull Gr. 3-8
**Log Cabin Christmas*, by Ellen Howard Gr. 1-3
**Log Cabin Church*, by Ellen Howard Gr. 1-3
**Log Cabin Quilt*, by Ellen Howard Gr. 1-3
Lone Hunt, by William O. Steele Gr. 3-12
(Lone Star Leader:) Sam Houston, by Curtis Bishop (Messner) Gr. 7-12
Long Black Schooner (Aladdin's American Heritage) Gr. 3-12
[Also titled **Story of the* Amistad and *Slave Ship.*]
Long Hunt, by Charlie May Simon Gr. 5-12
**Long March*, by Marie-Louise Fitzpatrick Unknown
**Long Road to Gettysburg*, by Jim Murphy Gr. 7-12
Longshanks, by Stephen Meader Gr. 4-12
**Looking at Pictures*, by Joy Richardson Gr. 4-12
**Looking for Pa*, by Geraldine Susi Gr. 4-8
Looking for Orlando, by Frances Browin Gr. 7-12
**Loon Feather*, by Iola Fuller Gr. 10-12
**Lord Kirkle's Money*, by Avi (Beyond the Western Seas) Gr. 7-12
**Lost Cause*, by James Arnold & Roberta Wiener Gr. 5-10
Lost Children of the Shoshones, by Evelyn Nevin Gr. 3-9
Lost Dispatch: Story of Antietam, by Donald Sobol Gr. 7-12
Lost Harpooner, by Leonard Wibberley Gr. 7-12
**Lost in Death Valley*, by Connie Goldsmith Gr. 5-12
Lost Wharf, by Howard Pease Gr. 5-10
Lotta Crabtree, by Marian Place (Childhood) Gr. 1-6
**Lottie's Courage: A Contraband Slave's Story*, by Phyllis Haislip Gr. 4-6
**Loud Emily*, by Alexis O'Neill Gr. 1-3
Louis Braille, by Beverley Birch (People Who Made a Difference) Gr. 5-8
**Louis Braille*, by Margaret Davidson Gr. 3-8
Louis Braille, by Dennis Fradin (Remarkable Children) Gr. 1-4
**Louis Braille*, by Jayne Woodhouse (Lives and Times) Gr. K-2
**Louis Braille: Inventor*, by Jennifer Bryant (Great Achievers) Gr. 4-8
Louisa: Life of Mrs. John Quincy Adams, by Laura Kerr Gr. 8-12

**Louisiana Purchase*, by Gail Sakurai (Cornerstones of Freedom II) Gr. 3-9
Louisiana Purchase, by Robert Tallant (Landmark) Gr. 3-9
Lucinda, a Little Girl of 1860, by Mabel Leigh Hunt Gr. 3-7
Lucretia Mott, by Constance Burnett (Childhood) Gr. 1-6
**Lucretia Mott*, by Lucile Davis (Photo-Illustrated Biography) Gr. 2-5
Lucretia Mott: Foe of Slavery, by Doris Faber (Garrard Discovery) Gr. 1-5
Lucretia Mott: Gentle Warrior, by Dorothy Sterling Gr. 8-12
Ludwig Beethoven and the Chiming Tower Bells, by Opal Wheeler Gr. 1-6
**Ludwig van Beethoven*, by Dynise Balcavage (Great Achievers) Gr. 4-9
Ludwig van Beethoven, by Carol Greene (Rookie) Gr. 1-5
**Ludwig van Beethoven*, by Louis Sabin (Troll) Gr. 1-4
**Ludwig van Beethoven*, by Mike Venezia (Getting to Know...) Gr. 1-6
**Ludwig van Beethoven: Musical Genius*, by Brendan January (Great Life) Unknown

Magnificent Adventure, by Emerson Hough Gr. 8-12
Mail Riders, from Paul Revere to the Pony Express, by Edith McCall (Frontiers...) Gr. 3-8
[This is being reprinted as **Adventures of the Mail Riders.*]
**Make it Three: Story of the CSS H.L. Hunley Civil War Submarine*, by M. Clary Unknown
**Make This Model American Fort* (Usborne) Various
**Make Way for Sam Houston*, by Jean Fritz Gr. 7-12
Make Way for the Brave: The Oregon Quest, by Merritt Parmelee Allen Gr. 6-12
**Maker of Machines: A Story about Eli Whitney*, by Barbara Mitchell (Creative...) Gr. 2-7
Malachy's Gold, by Anico Surany Gr. 1-5
Man of the Monitor, by Jean Lee Latham Gr. 3-12
Man Who Could Read Stones, by Alan Honour Gr. 8-12
Man Who Killed Lincoln, by Philip Stern Gr. 7-12
Man Who Said No, by Sally Edwards Gr. 8-12
Man Who Transformed the World, by William Crane (Messner) Gr. 7-12
Man Who Wouldn't Give Up: Henry Clay, by Katharine Wilkie (Messner) Gr. 7-12
Many Faces of Slavery, by I. E. Levine (Messner) Gr. 7-12
Many Faces of the Civil War, by Irving Werstein (Messner) Gr. 7-12
**Many Thousand Gone*, by Virginia Hamilton Gr. 4-9
Marching to Victory, by Charles Coffin [2nd in series] Gr. 7-12
Marcus and Narcissa Whitman, by James Daugherty Gr. 7-12
Marcus and Narcissa Whitman, by Marian Place (Garrard) Gr. 1-5
**Martha Years* series, by Melissa Wiley Gr. 3-6
Martin and Abraham Lincoln, by Catherine Coblentz Gr. K-3
Marvelous March of Jean François, by John Raymond Gr. 2-6
Mary Elizabeth and Mr. Lincoln, by Margaret Seyler Gr. 3-7
Mary Florence: Little Girl Who Knew Lincoln, by Kathleen Tiffany Gr. 4-12
Mary Montgomery, Rebel, by Helen Daringer Gr. 3-12
**Mary Patten's Voyage*, by Richard Berleth Gr. 2-6
**Mary Todd Lincoln*, by Katharine Wilkie (Childhood) Gr. 1-6
Mary Todd Lincoln: President's Wife, by LaVere Anderson (Garrard Discovery) Gr. 1-5
**Massachusetts 54th*, by Gina DeAngelis (Let Freedom Ring) Gr. 4-8
Master Detective: Allan Pinkerton, by Arthur Orrmont (Messner) Gr. 7-12

**Mathematicians are People Too: Vol. 1 and 2*, by L. & W. Reimer | Gr. 3-10

**Mathematicians are People Too: Vol. 1 and 2*, by L. & W. Reimer	Gr. 3-10
**Mathew Brady: Civil War Photographer*, by Elizabeth Van Steenwyk (First Bk)	Gr. 7-12
**Mathew Brady: His Life and Photographs*, by George Sullivan	Gr. 6-12
Mathew Brady: Historian with a Camera, by James Horan	Gr. 8-12
Matthew Calbraith Perry, by Alexander Scharbach (Childhood)	Gr. 1-6
Me and Willie and Pa, by F.N. Monjo	Gr. 2-6
Mechanical Age: Industrial Revolution in England, by Celia Bland (World Hist)	Gr. 9-12
Medals for Morse: Artist and Inventor, by Jean Lee Latham (Alad. Am. Heritage)	Gr. 4-12
**Meet Abraham Lincoln*, by Barbara Cary (Step-Up Books)	Gr. 1-4
**Meet Addy*, by Connie Porter (American Girls)	Gr. 2-7
Meet Andrew Jackson, by Ormonde de Kay (Step-Up Books)	Gr. K-3
**Meet Josefina*, by Valerie Tripp (and others in this *American Girl* series)	Gr. 1-6
Meet Robert E. Lee, by George Trow (Step-Up Books)	Gr. K-4
**Meet the Allens in Whaling Days*, by John Loeper	Unknown
Meet the North American Indians, by Elizabeth Payne (Step-Up)	Gr. 1-5
Melville in the South Pacific, by Henry Hough (North Star)	Gr. 7-12
Men of Power, by Albert Carr	Gr. 5-12
**Men of Science, Men of God*, by Henry Morris	Gr. 5-12
Mendelssohn, by Michael Hurd	Gr. 7-12
Menominee, by Joan Kalbacken (New True Books)	Gr. 2-5
**Meriwether Lewis*, by Charlotte Bebenroth (Childhood)	Gr. 1-6
**Meriwether Lewis*, by Janet & Geoff Benge (Heroes of History)	Gr. 4-10
**Meriwether Lewis and William Clark*, by D. Petersen (People of Distinction)	Gr. 6-12
Merrie's Miracle, by Florence Musgrave	Gr. 4-10
Message from the Mountains, by Edith McCall	Gr. 4-10
**Messages and Papers of Jefferson Davis and the Confederacy*	Gr. 11-12
**Mexican War*, by Charles Carey (American War)	Gr. 5-12
**Mexican War*, by Alden Carter (newer First Books series)	Gr. 5-10
**Mexican War*, by Bronwyn Mills (America at War)	Unknown
**Mexican War*, by Marc Nobleman (We the People)	Gr. 4-9
**Michael Faraday*, by Ann Fullick (Groundbreakers)	Gr. 5-7
**Michael Faraday*, by Anita Ganeri (What Would You Ask...)	Unknown
**Michael Faraday*, by Stewart Ross (Scientists Who Made History)	Gr. 4-6
Michael Faraday, by Harry Sootin (Messner)	Gr. 6-12
Michael Faraday and the Electric Dynamo, by C. May (Immortals of Science)	Gr. 7-12
Michael Faraday: Apprentice to Science, by Sam & Beryl Epstein	Gr. 2-7
**Michael Faraday: Creative Genius*, by Martin Gutnik	Gr. 7-12
**Michael Faraday: Father of Electronics*, by Charles Ludwig	Gr. 8-12
**Midshipman Quinn Collection*, by Showell Styles	Gr. 7-12
Military Life of Abraham Lincoln, by Trevor Dupuy	Gr. 8-12
Military Life of Napoleon, by Trevor Dupuy	Gr. 8-12
**Mill*, by David Macaulay	Gr. 4-12
Millet Tilled the Soil, by Sybil Deucher and Opal Wheeler	Gr. 3-12
**Millie Cooper's Ride: A True Story from History*, by Marc Simmons	Middle grades
Miney and the Blessing, by Miriam Mason	Gr. 2-5
**Minty: Young Harriet Tubman*, by Alan Schroder	Gr. 1-4

**Mississippi Mud*, by Ann Turner [See cautionary note.] Gr. 1-4
**Moby Dick*, by Herman Melville [There are abridged versions.] Various
**Moccasin Trail*, by Eloise Jarvis McGraw Gr. 7-12
Moccasins through the Rye, by Elaine Egbert Gr. 4-12?
Molly's Hannibal, by Robert Willis Gr. 2-7
**Monitor: Iron Warship that Changed the World*, by G. Thompson (All Aboard 3) Gr. 2-4
Monitor and the Merrimac, by Fletcher Pratt (Landmark) Gr.3-9
**Monitor vs. the Merrimack*, by Bruce Brager (Great Battles Through the Ages) Gr. 6-12
**Monroe Doctrine: An End to European Colonies in America*, by M. Alagna Unknown
**Moon Over Tennessee*, by Craig Crist-Evans Gr. 4-8
More than a Queen: Josephine Bonaparte, by Frances Mossiker Gr. 7-12
**More than Conquerors*, edited by John Woodbridge Gr. 7-12
More than Halfway There, by Janet Ervin Gr. 3-12
**More than Moccasins: A Kid's Activity Guide*, by Laurie Carlson Various
**Mosby and His Rangers: Adventures of the Gray Ghost*, by Susan Beller Unknown
Mosby: Gray Ghost of the Confederacy, by Jonathan Daniels Gr. 4-12
**Moses Austin and Stephen F. Austin*, by Betsy Warren Unknown
Mosquito Fleet, by Gordon Shirreffs Gr. 7-12
Mother Seton and the Sisters of Charity, by Alma Powers-Waters (Vision) Gr. 3-12
**Mothers of Famous Men*, by Archer Wallace (Lamplighter) Gr. 3-12
Mound Builders, by William Scheele [See cautionary note in guide.] Parental decision
Mount Up, by Julia Davis Gr. 9-12
Mountain Man, by Rutherford Montgomery Gr. 6-12
Mountain Men, by Don Berry Gr. 4-12
Mountain Men, by Wyatt Blassingame and Richard Glendinning Gr. 5-10
Mountain Men of the Early West, by Olive Burt Gr. 4-12
Mountain Men: True Grit and Tall Tales, by Andrew Glass Gr. 3-7
**Mr. Blue Jeans: Levi Strauss*, by Maryann Weidt (Carolrhoda's Creative Minds) Gr. 2-7
Mr. Brady's Camera Boy, by Frances Rogers Gr. 7-12
**Mr. Goethe's Garden*, by Diana Cohn [See cautionary note.] Parental decision
Mr. Jefferson's Washington, by Esther Douty (Garrard How They Lived) Gr. 3-8
Mr. Lincoln Speaks at Gettysburg, by Mary Kay Phelan Gr. 6-12
**Mr. Lincoln's Drummer*, by G. Clifton Wisler Gr. 3-12
Mr. Lincoln's Inaugural Journey, by Mary Kay Phelan Gr. 4-12
Mr. Lincoln's Master Spy, by Arthur Orrmont (Messner) Gr. 6-12
Mr. Lincoln's Whiskers, by Burke Davis Gr. 2-8
**Mr. Lincoln's Whiskers*, by Karen Winnick Gr. 1-4
Mr. Madison's War: 1812, by Noel Gerson (Messner/Milestones) Gr. 8-12
**Mrs. Robert E. Lee*, by Rose MacDonald Gr. 10-12
Muddy Road to Glory, by Stephen Meader Gr. 5-12
**My Brother's Keeper*, by Mary Pope Osborne (My America, Civil War) Gr. 3-5
**My Family Shall Be Free! The Life of Peter Still*, by Dennis Fradin Gr. 6-12
**My Name is York*, by Elizabeth Van Steenwyk Gr. K-3
**My Travels with Capts. Lewis and Clark, by George Shannon*, by K. McMullan Gr. 4-10
**Mystery of the Hieroglyphs*, by Carol Donoughue Gr. 6-12
**Mystery of the Periodic Table*, by Benjamin Wiker Gr. 4-9

Naha: Boy of the Seminoles, by Wendell Wright	Gr. 1-4
**Naming the Stones*, by Clara Stites	Gr. 3-7
Nancy Hanks, by Augusta Stevenson (Childhood)	Gr. 1-6
Nancy Hanks of Wilderness Road, by Meridel LeSueur	Gr. 1-5
Nancy Kelsey, by Virginia Evansen	Gr. 7-12
Napoleon, by Manuel Komroff (Messner)	Gr. 7-12
**Napoleon & Josephine: The Sword and the Hummingbird*, by G. Hausman	Gr. 7-12
**Napoleon and Josephine Paper Dolls*, by Tom Tierney	Various
Napoleon and the Battle of Waterloo, by Frances Winwar (Landmark)	Gr. 3-10
**Napoleonic Wars*, by Thomas Streissguth	Gr. 9-12
Napoleon's Hundred Days, by Patrick Pringle	Gr. 7-12
Narcissa Whitman, by Jeanette Eaton	Gr. 4-12
Narcissa Whitman, by Louis Sabin (Troll)	Gr. 1-3
Narcissa Whitman, by Ann Warner (Childhood)	Gr. 1-6
**Narrative of the Life of Frederick Douglass*, by Frederick Douglass	Gr. 7-12
Narrow Escapes of Davy Crockett, by Ariane Dewey	Gr. 1-4
**Nat Turner*, by Terry Bisson (Black Americans of Achievement)	Gr. 7-12
**Nat Turner*, by Susan Gregson (Let Freedom Ring)	Gr. 3-8
Nat Turner, by Judith Griffin	Gr. 2-7
**Nat Turner and the Slave Revolt*, by Tracy Barrett	Unknown
**Nat Turner and the Virginia Slave Revolt*, by Rivvy Neshama	Gr. 3-6
**Nat Turner's Slave Rebellion*, by Judith Edwards (In American History)	Gr. 6-12
Nathaniel Hawthorne: American Storyteller, by Nancy Whitelaw (World Writers)	Gr. 7-12
**Nation Torn*, by Delia Ray (Young Readers' History of the Civil War)	Gr. 5-12
**National Anthem*, by Patricia Quiri (True Book)	Gr. 2-6
**Nations of the Western Great Lakes*, by Kathryn Smithyman (Native Nations)	Gr. 4-9
**Native Americans*, by Andrew Haslam (Make It Work! History)	Various
**Native Americans*, by Gallimard Jeunesse (First Discovery)	Gr. 2-4
Negroes in the Early West, by Olive Burt (Messner)	Gr. 7-12
**Nettie's Trip South*, by Ann Turner	Gr. 2-6
New England Men of Letters, by Wilson Sullivan	Gr. 7-12
**New Orleans*, by King David (Battlefields Across America)	Gr. 5-10
**Next Spring an Oriole*, by Gloria Whelan	Gr. 1-6
Nicholas Arnold, Toolmaker, by Marion Lansing	Gr. 4-12
**Night Journey to Vicksburg*, by Susan Masters	Gr. 3-6
**Night of the Full Moon*, by Gloria Whelan	Gr. 1-6
Nine for California, by Sonia Levitin	Gr. 1-4
Nine Lives of Moses on the Oregon Trail, by Marion Archer	Gr. 5-10
**Nishnawbe*, by Lynne Deur	Gr. 3-8
**No Man's Land*, by Susan Bartoletti	Gr. 5-9
No Other Foundation: The Church Through Twenty Centuries, by Jeremy Jackson	Gr. 11-12
**Noah Webster*, by David Collins (Sower)	Gr. 5-12
Noah Webster, by Helen Higgins (Childhood)	Gr. 1-6
Noah Webster, by Isabel Proudfit (Messner)	Gr. 6-12
**Noah Webster and the First American Dictionary*, by Luisanna Fodde	Unknown
**North and South*, by Elizabeth Gaskell	Gr. 10-12

**North American Indian*, by Doug Murdoch (DK)	Gr. 4-12
North American Indians, by Marie Gorsline	Gr. K-2
North American Indians, by Susan Purdy	Various
North by Night, by Peter Burchard	Gr. 5-12
**North Star to Freedom*, by Gena Gorrell	Gr. 6-12
North Winds Blow Free, by Elizabeth Howard [Two authors bear this name.]	Gr. 5-12
Northern Generals, by Red Reeder	Gr. 8-12
**Northerners*, by John Dunn (Voices from the Civil War)	Unknown
**Nothing Here But Trees*, by Jean Van Leeuwen	Gr. 1-4
**Nowhere to Turn*, by Alan Kay (Young Heroes of History)	Gr. 4-9
Oath of Silence, by Phyllis Bentley	Gr. 5-12
**Obadiah the Bold*, by Brinton Turkle	Gr. 1-3
**Of Courage Undaunted*, by James Daugherty	Gr. 4+
**Off the Map*, edited by Peter & Connie Roop	Gr. 2-8
**Ojibwa Indians*, by Bill Lund	Gr. 3-7
**Old Abe*, by Patrick Young	Gr. 1-4
Old Ironsides, by Harry Hansen (Landmark)	Gr. 3-9
**Old Ironsides*, by David Weitzman	Gr. 3-8
Old Rough and Ready, by Bob & Jan Young (Messner)	Gr. 7-12
Old Whirlwind, by Elizabeth Coatsworth	Gr. 4-8
Old Wilderness Road, by William O. Steele	Gr. 8-12
Oliver Hazard Perry, by Alfred Fenton	Gr. 5-12
Oliver Hazard Perry, by Laura Long (Childhood)	Gr. 1-6
**On the Blockade*, by Oliver Optic	Gr. 7-12
**On the Frontier with Mr. Audubon*, by Barbara Brenner	Gr. 5-12
**On the Long Trail Home*, by Elizabeth Stewart [See cautionary note.]	Gr. 6-10
**On the Trail of John Brown's Body*, by Alan Kay (Young Heroes of History 1)	Gr. 4-9
**On to Oregon!* by Honore Morrow [Also issued as *Seven Alone.*]	Gr. 5-12
On Wings of Song, by Dena Humphreys	Gr. 4-12
**Once on This Island*, by Gloria Whelan	Gr. 3-10
One Gallant Rush, by Peter Burchard	Gr. 10-12
One Long Picnic, by Neta Frazier	Gr. 4-8
**One More Valley, One More Hill: Story of Aunt Clara Brown*, by Linda Lowery	Gr. 6-12
**One of the 28th*, by G.A. Henty	Gr. 7-12
**Only Passing Through: Story of Sojourner Truth*, by Anne Rockwell	Gr. 3-7
Open Gate, by Wilma Pitchford Hays	Gr. 2-6
**Oregon Trail*, by Jean Blashfield (We the People)	Gr. 3-6
**Oregon Trail*, by Leonard Everett Fisher	Gr. 6-12
**Oregon Trail*, by Sally Isaacs (American Adventure)	Gr. 4-7
**Oregon Trail*, by Elizabeth Jaffe (Let Freedom Ring)	Gr. 4-8
**Oregon Trail*, by Francis Parkman [Also titled, *California and Oregon Trail.*]	Various
Oregon Trail, by Laurence Santrey (Troll)	Gr. 2-6
Orphans of the Wind, by Eric Haugaard	Gr. 4-12
Osceola, by Electa Clark (Childhood)	Gr. 1-5
Osceola, by Marion Gridley (See and Read)	Gr. 1-3

**Osceola*, by Rachel Koestler-Grack	Unknown
**Osceola*, by Anne Todd (Native American Biographies)	Unknown
Osceola and the Seminole Wars, by Clifford Alderman (Messner)	Gr. 7-12
Osceola: Seminole Leader, by Ronald Syme	Gr. 2-6
Osceola: Seminole War Chief, by Wyatt Blassingame (Garrard Am. Indians)	Gr. 1-5
Our Blood and Tears, by Ruth Wilson	Gr. 5-12
**Our Flag was Still There*, by Tracy Leininger	Gr. 2-6
**Our Journey West*, by Gare Thompson (National Geographic)	Unknown
**Out of Darkness*, by Russell Freedman	Gr. 6-12
**Out with Garibaldi*, by G.A. Henty	Gr. 7-12
Outlaw Voyage, by Val Gendron	Gr. 6-12
**Outnumbered: Davy Crockett's Final Battle at the Alamo*, by Eric Fein	Unknown
Over the Mormon Trail, by Jones (Frontiers of America) [See note in guide.]	Gr. 3-8
**Ox-Cart Man*, by Donald Hall	Gr. K-4
Paderewski: Pianist and Patriot, by Antoni Gronowicz	Gr. 6-12
Paganini, by Lillian Day	Gr. 3-8
Paganini: Master of the Strings, by Opal Wheeler	Gr. 3-8
Palace Wagon Family: A True Story of the Donner Party, by Margaret Sutton	Gr. 5-12
Panther Lick Creek, by Nelma Haynes	Gr. 3-9
Passage to Texas, by Iris Vinton (Aladdin's American Heritage)	Gr. 3-9
Pat and the Iron Horse, by Polly Angell	Gr. 8-12
Patriotic Rebel: John Calhoun, by William Crane (Messner)	Gr. 5-12
**Patriot's Handbook*, by George Grant	Gr. 9-12
**Patty Reed's Doll*, by Rachel Laurgaard	Gr. 4-12
**Perilous Journey of the Donner Party*, by Marian Calabro	Gr. 6-12
**Perilous Road*, by William O. Steele	Gr. 4-12
**Personal Correspondence of Emma Edmonds and Mollie Turner* (Liberty Letters) by Nancy LeSourd	Gr. 3-8
**Personal Correspondence of Hannah Brown and Sarah Smith* (Liberty Letters) by Nancy LeSourd	Gr. 3-8
**Personal Memoirs*, by Ulysses S. Grant	Gr. 10-12
Peter Cartwright: Pioneer Circuit Rider, by Nancy Veglahn	Gr. 5-12
**Peter Tchaikovsky*, by Mike Venezia (Getting to Know the...)	Gr. 1-6
Peter Tchaikovsky and the Nutcracker Ballet, by Opal Wheeler	Gr. 2-7
**Petticoat Spies: Six Women Spies of the Civil War*, by Peggy Caravantes	Gr. 5-12
**Phantom of the Blockade*, by Stephen Meader	Gr. 4-12
Phebe Fairchild: Her Book, by Lois Lenski	Gr. 3-7
Philippe Pinel: Unchainer of the Insane, by Bernard Mackler (Immortals...)	Gr. 6-12
**Picture Book of Abraham Lincoln*, by David Adler	Gr. K-2
**Picture Book of Davy Crockett*, by David Adler	Gr. K-2
**Picture Book of Frederick Douglass*, by David Adler	Gr. K-2
**Picture Book of Harriet Beecher Stowe*, by David Adler	Gr. K-2
**Picture Book of Harriet Tubman*, by David Adler	Gr. K-2
**Picture Book of Lewis and Clark*, by David Adler	Gr. K-2
**Picture Book of Louis Braille*, by David Adler	Gr. K-2

**Picture Book of Robert E. Lee*, by David Adler	Gr. K-2
**Picture Book of Sacagawea*, by David Adler	Gr. K-2
**Picture Book of Simon Bolivar*, by David Adler	Gr. K-2
**Picture Book of Sojourner Truth*, by David Adler	Gr. K-2
Picture History of Great Inventors, by Gillian Clement	Gr. 2-7
**Picture of Freedom: Diary of Clotee, a Slave Girl*, by P. McKissack (Dear America) [See strong cautionary note.]	Gr. 3-10
**Pictures at an Exhibition*, by Anna Celenza	Gr. 1-4
Pike of Pike's Peak, by Nina Brown Baker	Gr. 3-8
**Pink and Say*, by Patricia Polacco	Gr. 1-3
Pinkerton: America's First Private Eye, by Richard Wormser	Gr. 6-12
**Pioneer Days Lapbook with Study Guide*, by AJTL/Michelle Miller	Various
**Pioneer Days*, by David C. King	Various
**Pioneer Plowmaker: A Story about John Deere*, by David Collins (Carolrhoda)	Gr. 2-7
**Pioneer Recipes*, by Bobbie Kalman	Various
**Pioneer Sampler*, by Barbara Greenwood	Gr. 4-12
Pioneer Stories, by C. Richard Schaare [Also published as separate modules]	Gr. 2-8
**Pioneers Go* West, by George Stewart (Landmark) [also titled, *To California...*]	Gr. 3-9
Pioneers on Early Waterways, by Edith McCall (Frontiers of America) [Now in-print as: **Adventures of the Waterways.*]	Gr. 2-8
Pirate Flag for Monterey, by Lester del Rey (Winston Adventure)	Gr. 3-9
Pirate Lafitte and the Battle of New Orleans, by Robert Tallant (Landmark)	Gr. 3-9
**Pistols and Politics: Alexander Hamilton's Great Duel*, by August Greeley	Unknown
**Pitch in Time*, by Robert Lytle	Gr. 5-8
**Plain Prairie Princess*, by Stephen Bly (1st in *Retta Barre's Oregon Trail* series)	Gr. 4-8
Plenty of Pirates, by Elisabeth Meg	Gr. 4-12
**Pony Bob's Daring Ride*, by Joe Bensen	Unknown
Pony Express, by Samuel Adams (Landmark)	Gr. 3-9
**Pony Express*, by Peter Anderson	Gr. 3-8
**Pony Express*, by Edward Dolan	Unknown
**Pony Express!* by Steven Kroll	Gr. 2-7
**Pony Express*, by Cynthia Mercati (Cover-to-Cover)	Gr. 3-5
**Pony Express*, by Jean Williams (We the People)	Gr. 3-6
Pony Express Goes Through, by Howard Driggs	Gr. 5-12
Poor Felicity, by Sally Watson	Gr. 5-12
Potawatomie Indian Summer, by E. William Oldenburg [See note in guide.]	Gr. 5-10
Pony for Jeremiah, by Robert Miller	Gr. 3-6
Posse of Two, by Gertrude Bell	Gr. 5-12
**Potawatomi*, by Karen Gibson (Native Peoples)	Unknown
Potawatomi, by Suzanne Powell (First Books)	Gr. 5-12
**Potawatomi of Wisconsin*, by Damon Mayrl	Unknown
Powder Boy of the Monitor, by Gordon Shirreffs	Gr. 7-12
Powder Monkey, by B.B. Anderson	Gr. 4-9
**Powder Monkey*, by Carole Campbell (Young American)	Unknown
**Prairie Schooners*, by Glen Rounds	Gr. 3-8
Prairie Schooners West, by Mildred Comfort	Gr. 2-6

**Prelude to War*, by Carter Smith	Gr. 6-12
Presenting Miss Jane Austen, by May Lamberton Becker	Gr. 9-12
President of the Confederacy: Jefferson Davis, by Margaret Green (Messner)	Gr. 6-12
**President of the Underground Railroad*, by Gwenyth Swain (Creative Minds)	Gr. 2-7
President's Lady, by Irving Stone	Gr. 9-12
**Pride and Prejudice Paper Dolls*, by Brenda Mattox	Various
Princess of Siberia, by Christine Sutherland	Gr. 10-12
**Prison Camps of the Civil War*, by Linda Wade	Unknown
**Promise Quilt*, by Candice Ransom	Gr. 1-5
Prophet of Revolution: Karl Marx, by Alfred Apsler (Messner)	Gr. 8-12
Proving Years, by Cateau de Leeuw	Gr. 4-10
**Prudence Crandall*, by Eileen Lucas (On My Own)	Gr. 1-4
Prudence Crandall: Woman of Courage, by Elizabeth Yates	Gr. 4-12
Quest of Michael Faraday, by Tad Harvey	Gr. 7-12
Quick, Annie, Give Me a Catchy Line! by Robert Quackenbush	Gr. 2-7
Quit Pulling My Leg: A Story of Davy Crockett, by Robert Quackenbush	Gr. 2-6
**Rachel and Obadiah*, by Brinton Turkle	Gr. 1-3
Rachel Jackson, by Christine Govan (Childhood)	Gr. 1-6
Railroad to Freedom, by Hildegarde Swift	Gr. 4-12
Railway Engineer: George Stephenson, by Clara Ingram Judson	Gr. 4-12
**Rangers, Jayhawkers, and Bushwhackers in the Civil War* (Untold History of...)	Gr. 4-8
**Ransom's Mark*, by Wendy Lawton (Daughters of the Faith)	Gr. 4-8
Raphael Semmes: Confederate Admiral, by Robert Daly (American Background)	Gr. 5-12
Raphael Semmes, by Dorothea Snow (Childhood)	Gr. 1-6
Rat Hell, by Peter Burchard	Gr. 5-12
Real Book about Indians, by Michael Gorham	Gr. 4-10
**Real Christianity*, by William Wilberforce	Gr. 9-12
Real Johnny Appleseed, by Laurie Lawlor	Gr. 4-8
Reaper Man, by Clara Ingram Judson	Gr. 6-12
Rebel Mail Runner, by Manly Wade Wellman	Gr. 5-12
Rebel on Two Continents, by David Abodaher (Messner)	Gr. 6-12
Rebel Raider: Admiral Semmes, by E. & B. Davis	Gr. 6-12
Rebel Rider, by Lee McGiffin	Gr. 5-12
**Rebel Spy*, by Norma Jean Lutz (American Adventure # 23)	Gr. 3-8
Rebel Trumpet, by Gordon Shirreffs	Gr. 7-12
Rebellion at Christiana, by Margaret Bacon	Gr. 8-12
**Rebels Against Slavery*, by Patricia & Fred McKissack	Gr. 6-12
**Recollections & Letters of Robert E. Lee*, by Robert E. Lee	Gr. 10-12
Red Man in Art, by Rena Coen	Gr. 4-12
**Red Badge of Courage*, by Stephen Crane	Gr. 9-12
**Red Flower Goes West*, by Ann Turner	Gr. 1-4
**Red Fox and His Canoe*, by Nathaniel Benchley (I Can Read)	Gr. K-2
**Red Legs*, by Ted Lewin	Gr. 2-5
Red Pawns, by Leonard Wibberley	Gr. 5-12

Red War Pole, by Louis Capron	Gr. 5-12
Redeeming the Republic, by Charles Coffin [3rd in series]	Gr. 7-12
Redouté: The Man Who Painted Flowers, by Carolyn Croll	Gr. 2-5
**Reflections on the Civil War*, by Bruce Catton	Gr. 12+
Reluctant Warrior: Ulysses S. Grant, by Bob & Jan Young (Messner)	Gr. 7-12
Remember the Alamo! by Robert Penn Warren (Landmark)	Gr. 4-9
Restless Johnny, by Ruth Holberg	Gr. 3-10
Retreat from Moscow, by E.M. Almedingen	Gr. 7-12
Retreat to Glory: Sam Houston, by Jean Lee Latham	Gr. 5-12
**Richard Wagner and German Opera*, by Donna Getzinger	Unknown
Richard Wagner: Titan of Music, by Monroe Stearns (Immortals?)	Gr. 8-12
**Riddle of the Rosetta Stone*, by James Cross Giblin	Gr. 5-12
Ride for Old Glory, by Jacqueline McNicol	Gr. 5-12
Ride for Texas, by Lee McGiffin	Gr. 5-12
**Ride Like the Wind*, by Bernie Fuchs	Gr. 1-4
Ride Proud, Rebel, by André Norton	Gr. 7-12
Ride, Rebels! by Manly Wade Wellman	Gr. 5-12
Ride with the Eagle, by Julia Davis	Gr. 6-12
Riders of the Pony Express, by Ralph Moody (North Star)	Gr. 6-12
Riding the Pony Express, by Clyde Robert Bulla	Gr. 1-5
**Rifles for Watie*, by Harold Keith	Gr. 6-12
**Right Fine Life: Kit Carson on the Santa Fe Trail*, by Andrew Glass	Gr. 1-4
River and Canal, by Edward Boyer	Gr. 4-12
River Boy, by Herbert Arntson	Gr. 4-12
River of Gold, by Gifford Cheshire (Aladdin's American Heritage)	Gr. 3-9
River of the West, by Armstrong Sperry (Winston Adventure)	Gr. 3-9
River Pirates, by Manly Wade Wellman	Gr. 5-12
**River Road: A Story of Abraham Lincoln*, by Meridel LeSueur	Gr. 3-10
**Road to Appomattox*, by Carter Smith (Sourcebook)	Gr. 7-12
Road to Fort Sumter, by Leroy Hayman	Gr. 5-10
Road to Freedom: 1815-1900, by James McCague	Gr. 7-12
**Road to Home*, all by Mary Jane Auch	Gr. 5-10
Roanoke Raiders, by Gordon Shirreffs	Gr. 7-12
**Robert Browning*, by Harold Bloom (Bloom's Major Poets)	Gr. 10-12
Robert E. Lee, by Jonathan Daniels (North Star)	Gr. 4-12
Robert E. Lee, by Guy Emery (Messner)	Gr. 7-12
**Robert E. Lee*, by Grabowski (Famous Figures of the Civil War Era)	Gr. 4-8
**Robert E. Lee*, by David C. King (Triangle)	Gr. 7-12
**Robert E. Lee*, by Helen Monsell (Childhood)	Gr. 1-6
**Robert E. Lee*, by Lee Roddy (Sower)	Gr. 5-12
**Robert E. Lee and His Family Paper Dolls* (Dover)	Various
Robert E. Lee and the Road of Honor, by Hodding Carter (Landmark)	Gr. 3-9
**Robert E. Lee: Brave Leader*, by Rae Bains (Troll)	Gr. 1-5
Robert E. Lee: Hero of the South, by Charles Graves (Garrard Discovery)	Gr. 1-5
**Robert E. Lee: Leader in War and Peace*, by Carol Greene (Rookie)	Gr. 2-4
Robert E. Lee: The South's Great General, by Matthew Grant	Gr. K-3

**Robert E. Lee: Virginia Soldier, American Citizen*, by James Robertson	Unknown
**Robert Fulton*, by Jennifer Gillis (Lives and Times)	Gr. 1-3
Robert Fulton, by Marguerite Henry (Childhood)	Gr. 1-6
Robert Fulton, by Elaine Landau (First Books)	Gr. 4-7
Robert Fulton, by Ruby Radford (See and Read)	Gr. 1-3
**Robert Fulton*, by Lola Schaefer	Unknown
Robert Fulton and the Steamboat, by Ralph Hill (Landmark)	Gr. 3-8
**Robert Fulton: From Submarine to Steamboat*, by Steven Kroll	Gr. 3-6
Robert Fulton: Steamboat Builder, by Joanne Henry (Garrard Discovery)	Gr. 1-5
**Robert Fulton: The Steamboat Man*, by Carin Ford (Famous Inventors)	Unknown
**Robert Henry Hendershot*, by Susan Goodman (Ready-for-Chapter Books)	Gr. 1-5
Robert Louis Stevenson, by Carol Greene (Rookie)	Gr. 1-5
Robert Louis Stevenson, by Eulalie Grover	Gr. 6-12
**Robert Louis Stevenson*, by Francene Sabin (Troll)	Gr. 1-4
Robert Louis Stevenson, by G.B. Stern	Gr. 6-12
Robert Louis Stevenson, by Katharine Wilkie (Piper)	Gr. 2-7
Robert Louis Stevenson: His Life, by Catherine Owens Peare	Gr. 5-12
Robert Schumann and Mascot Ziff, by Opal Wheeler	Gr. 1-6
Robert Todd Lincoln, by LaVere Anderson (Childhood)	Gr. 1-6
**Rock of Chickamauga*, by Joseph Altsheler	Gr. 7-12
Rolling Wheels, by Katharine Grey	Gr. 5-12
Romance of Chemistry, by Keith Irwin	Gr. 7-12
Romance of Physics, by Keith Irwin	Gr. 7-12
Romantic Rebel: Nathaniel Hawthorne, by Hildegarde Hawthorne	Gr. 7-12
**Roots*, by Alex Haley [See cautionary note.]	Gr. 9-12
**Rosa*, by Leo Politi	Gr. 1-3
Rose Greenhow: Confederate Secret Agent, by Dorothy Grant (Amer. Background)	Gr. 5-12
Rose Greenhow: Spy for the Confederacy, by Doris Faber	Gr. 4-12
**Roughing It on the Oregon Trail*, by Diane Stanley	Gr. 2-5
**Roundup of the Street Rovers*, by Dave & Neta Jackson (Trailblazer)	Gr. 3-8
**Roving Commission*, by G.A. Henty	Gr. 7-12
Rum, Slaves, and Molasses, by Clifford Alderman	Gr. 9-12
**Run the Blockade*, by G. Clifton Wisler	Gr. 5-12
Runaway Balloon, by Burke Davis	Gr. 3-7
Runaway Voyage, by Betty Cavanah	Gr. 8-12
Rush for Gold, by Frank Beals (American Adventure, older series)	Gr. 3-8
Sabres of France, by James Finn	Gr. 7-12
**Sac and Fox*, by Nancy Bonvillain	Gr. 5-12
**Sacagawea*, by Liselotte Erdich	Gr. 2-6
**Sacagawea*, by Flora Seymour (Childhood)	Gr. 1-6
Sacajawea, by Virginia Voight (See and Read)	Gr. K-2
Sacajawea: Guide to Lewis and Clark, by Jerry Seibert (Piper)	Gr. 2-8
**Sacajawea: Her True Story*, by Joyce Milton (All Aboard 3)	Gr. 1-3
Sacajawea: Indian Guide, by Wyatt Blassingame (Garrard Am. Indian)	Gr. 1-5
Saga of Andy Burnett, by Stewart Edward White	Gr. 5-12

**Saga of the Sierras* series, by B. Thoene	Gr. 4-12
Sailing the Seven Seas, by Mary Ellen Chase (North Star)	Gr. 6-12
Sailors, Whalers, and Steamers, by Edith Thacher Hurd	Gr. 4-10
**Saint Elizabeth Ann Seton*, by Jeanne Grunwell (Encounter the Saints)	Unknown
**Sally Ann Thunder Ann Whirlwind Crockett*, by Steven Kellogg	Gr. 1-4
Sam Colt and His Gun, by Gertrude Winders [You may also find it as *Samuel Colt and His Gun*.]	Gr. 5-12
Sam Houston, by Paul Hollander (See and Read)	Gr. 1-3
Sam Houston, by Augusta Stevenson (Childhood)	Gr. 1-6
**Sam Houston*, by Lisa Trumbauer (First Biographies)	Gr. 1-4
**Sam Houston: A Leader for Texas*, by Judy Alter	Gr. 3-8
**Sam Houston: American Hero*, by Anne Crawford	Gr. 2-4
Sam Houston: Fighter and Leader, by Frances Wright (Makers of America)	Gr. 2-7
Sam Houston: Friend of the Indians, by Joseph Olgin (Piper)	Gr. 2-7
Sam Houston: Hero of Texas, by Jean Lee Latham (Garrard)	Gr. 1-5
Sam Houston of Texas, by Matthew Grant	Gr. 1-3
**Sam Houston: Soldier and Statesman*, by Tracey Boraas (Let Freedom Ring)	Gr. 4-8
Sam Houston: Texas Hero, by Carl Green & William Sanford	Gr. 4-12
Sam Houston: The Tallest Texan, by William Johnson (Landmark)	Gr. 4-10
Samuel Colt and His Gun, by Gertrude Winders [You may also find it as *Sam Colt and His Gun*.]	Gr. 5-12
**Samuel F.B. Morse*, by John Tiner (Sower)	Gr. 5-12
Samuel F.B. Morse: Artist-Inventor, by Jean Lee Latham (Garrard Discovery)	Gr. 1-5
**Samuel F.B. Morse: Inventor and Code Creator*, by Judy Alter	Unknown
**Samuel Morse*, by Margaret Hall (Lives and Times)	Gr. 1-3
Samuel Morse, by Mona Kerby (First Book)	Gr. 4-7
Samuel Morse, by Dorothea Snow (Childhood)	Gr. 1-6
Samuel Morse and the Telegraph, by Wilma Pitchford Hays	Gr. 4-12
Samuel Slater's Mill and the Industrial Revolution, by Christopher Simonds	Gr. 5-10
Sandy and the Indians, by Margaret Friskey	Gr. 4-10
Santa Fe Trail, by Samuel Adams (Landmark)	Gr. 3-9
**Santa Fe Trail*, by Judy Alter (Cornerstones)	Gr. 2-7
**Santa Fe Trail*, by Jean Blashfield (We the People)	Gr. 3-6
Sapphire Pendant, by Audrey Beyer	Gr. 7-12
**Saving the President*, by Barbara Brenner (What If Mystery)	Gr. 3-8
Scannon: Dog with Lewis and Clark, by Adrien Stoutenberg & L.N. Baker	Gr. 3-8
Scarlet Oak, by Cornelia Meigs	Gr. 5-12
**School for Pompey Walker*, by Michael Rosen	Gr. 4-8
**Schubert*, by Ann Rachlin (Famous Children)	Gr. 3-6
Schubert, by Peggy Woodford	Gr. 7-12
**Schumann*, by Ann Rachlin (Famous Children)	Gr. 3-6
**Science Fiction Pioneer*, by Thomas Streissguth (Carolrhoda's Creative Minds)	Gr. 2-6
Scientists Behind the Inventors, by Roger Burlingame	Gr. 7-12
Scout Who Led an Army, by Lareine Ballantyne (Buckskin)	Gr. 2-8
**Scouts of Stonewall*, by Joseph Altsheler	Gr. 7-12
Sea Lady, by J.F. Batchelor	Gr. 2-5

**Seabird*, by Holling Clancy Holling Gr. 3-9
**Seaman: Dog Who Explored the West with Lewis & Clark*, by Gail Karwoski Gr. 4-7
**Seaman's Journal*, by Patricia Eubank Gr. 1-3
**Seasons Sewn*, by Ann Paul Gr. 2-8
**Seaward Born*, by Lea Wait Gr. 4-7
**Secession: The Southern States Leave the Union*, by Judith Peacock Unknown
Secret of the Rosewood Box, by Helen Fuller Orton Gr. 2-6
Secret on the Potomac, by Eleanor Nolen Gr. 4-12
Secret Sea, by Richard Armstrong Gr. 7-12
**Secret to Freedom*, by Marcia Vaughan Gr. 1-4
Secret Valley, by Clyde Robert Bulla Gr. 1-5
**Secret Weapons in the Civil War*, by Victor Brooks (Untold History of the...) Gr. 4-8
**Secrets of a Civil War Submarine*, by Sally Walker Gr. 4-10
**Seeds of Hope*, by Kristiana Gregory (Dear America) Gr. 3-8
Seeing Fingers, by Etta DeGering Gr. 4-12
**Seeker of Knowledge: The Man Who...*, by James Rumford Gr. 2-7
**Seminole*, by Richard Gaines (Native Americans) Gr. 2-5
Seminole, by Emilie Lepthien (New True Books) Gr. 2-5
**Seminole Diary*, by Dolores Johnson Gr. 3-8
Seminole Indians, by Sonia Bleeker Gr. 4-12
**Seminole Indians*, by Bill Lund Gr. 3-7
**Seminole Indians*, by Caryn Yacowitz Unknown
Seminole Trail, by Dee Dunsing Gr. 6-12
Seminoles, by Irene Estep Gr. 3-8
**Seminoles*, by Virginia Driving Hawk Sneve Gr. 1-5
**Send 'em South*, by Alan Kay (Young Heroes of History 1) Gr. 4-9
**Sequoyah*, by Michelle Levine Unknown
Sequoyah, by Dorothea Snow (Childhood) Gr. 1-6
Sequoyah, by Ruby Radford (See and Read) Gr. 1-3
**Sequoyah*, by Anne Todd Unknown
Sequoyah and the Cherokee Alphabet, by Robert Cwiklik Gr. 5-10
**Sequoyah: Cherokee Hero*, by Joanne Oppenheim (Troll) Gr. 1-5
Sequoyah: Father of the Cherokee Alphabet, by David Peterson Gr. 2-6
**Sequoyah: Inventor of the Cherokee Written Language*, by Diane Shaughnessy Unknown
Sequoyah: Leader of the Cherokees, by Alice Marriott (Landmark) Gr. 3-10
**Sequoyah: Native American Scholar*, by C. Ann Fitterer Unknown
Sequoyah: The Cherokee Who Captured Words, by Lillie Patterson (Gar. Am. Ind.) Gr. 1-4
**Sequoyah's Gift: A Portrait of the Cherokee Leader*, by Janet Klausner Gr. 5-12
Seven Alone, by Honore Morrow [also titled, *On to Oregon!*] Gr. 5-12
**Seven Men Who Rule the World from the Grave*, by Dave Breese Gr. 8-12
**Sewing Quilts*, by Ann Turner Gr. 1-3
Sewing Susie, by Elsie Singmaster Gr. 4-12
**Shades of Gray*, by Carolyn Reeder Gr. 4-12
**Shades of the Wilderness*, by Joseph Altsheler Gr. 7-12
Shamrock Cargo, by Anne Colver (Winston Adventure) Gr. 3-9
**Shanghaied to China*, by Dave & Neta Jackson (Trailblazer) Gr. 3-9

**Shawnee*, by Alice Flanagan (New True Books) Gr. 2-5
**Shawnee*, by Petra Press Unknown
Shawnee Indians, by Sonia Bleeker Gr. 3-12
Sheridan, by Red Reeder Gr. 7-12
**Sheridan's Ride*, by Thomas Read Gr. K-3
Shiloh, by Richard Steins Gr. 4-7
Shipment for Susannah, by Eleanor Nolen Gr. 2-8
**Ships Versus Shore: Civil War Engagements Along Southern Shores and Rivers* by Dave Page Unknown
Shoes for Matt, by Elsa Falk Gr. 2-8
**Shots Fired at Fort Sumter*, by Wendy Vierow (Headlines from History) Unknown
Silver Answer, by Constance Burnett Gr. 7-12
Silver Key, by Beverly Butler Gr. 7-12
Silver Spurs to Monterey, by Page Cooper Gr. 6-12
Silver Wolf, by Merritt Parmelee Allen Gr. 5-12
Simon Bolivar, by Nina Brown Baker Gr. 3-8
Simon Bolivar, by Carol Greene (People of Distinction) Gr. 4-7
Simon Bolivar, by Dennis Wepman (World Leaders Past & Present) Gr. 6-12
Simon Bolivar, by Arnold Whitridge (Landmark) Gr. 3-8
Singing Wire, by Mark Miller (Winston Adventure) Gr. 3-9
Six Feet Six, by Bessie & Marquis James Gr. 5-12
Sketches of America Past, by Eric Sloane Various
**Skillet Bread, Sourdough, and Vinegar Pie*, by Loretta Frances Ichord Various
Slater's Mill, by F.N. Monjo Gr. 5-12
**Slave Dancer*, by Paula Fox Gr. 4-12
**Slave Family*, by Bobbie Kalman Unknown
**Slave Girl* also titled *Cowslip*, by Betsy Haynes Gr. 4-12
**Slave Narratives: Journey to Freedom*, by Elaine Landau (In Their Own Voices) Gr. 6-12
Slave Ship, by Emma Gelders Sterne Gr. 3-12
[Also titled **Story of the* Amistad and *Long Black Schooner*.]
Slave Who Freed Haiti, by Katharine Scherman (Landmark) Gr. 4-10
**Slavery Time When I Was Children*, by Belinda Hurmence Gr. 8-12
Slavonic Rhapsody, by Jan Van Straaten Gr. 6-12
**Small Wolf*, by Nathaniel Benchley (I Can Read) Gr. K-1
**Smithsonian Visual Timeline of Inventions*, by Richard Platt Gr. 5-12
Snowball Fight in the White House, by Louise Davis Gr. 3-8
**Snowbound: Tragic Story of the Donner Party*, by David Lavender Gr. 5-12
**Snowshoe Thompson*, by Nancy Levinson (I Can Read) Gr. 1-3
Snowshoe Thompson, by Adrien Stoutenberg & L. Baker Gr. 7-12
**So Far From Home: Diary of an Irish Mill Girl*, by Barry Denenberg (Dear Am.) Gr. 3-8
[See warning note.]
So Proudly She Sailed, by Olga Cabral Gr. 3-12
Society of Foxes, by Patrick O'Connor/Leonard Wibberley Gr. 9-12
Sod House, by Elizabeth Coatsworth Gr. 3-8
**Soft Rain: A Story of the Cherokee Trail of Tears*, by Cornelia Cornelissen Gr. 3-8
Sojourner Truth, by Aletha Lindstrom (Messner) Gr. 7-12

**Sojourner Truth*, by Peter & Connie Roop	Gr. 3-7
**Sojourner Truth: Abolitionist, Suffragist, and Preacher*, by Norma Jean Lutz	Gr. 6-12
Sojourner Truth: Fearless Crusader, by Helen Peterson (Garrard Americans All)	Gr. 3-9
Sojourner Truth: Freedom-Fighter, by Julian May	Gr. 2-6
Soldier, Statesman, Defendant: Aaron Burr, by Jeannette Nolen (Messner)	Gr. 7-12
**Soldier's Life in the Civil War* (Dover)	Various
**Soldiers of the War of 1812*, by Diane & Henry Smolinski	Unknown
Solomon Juneau, Voyageur, by Marion Lawson	Gr. 5-12
**Solomon Northup's Twelve Years a Slave*, by Sue Eakin	Unknown
Some Plant Olive Trees, by Emma Sterne	Gr. 7-12
Song of the North, by Claire Lee Purdy	Gr. 7-12
**Song of the Swallows*, by Leo Politi	Gr. 1-3
Song of the Voyageur, by Beverly Butler	Gr. 7-12
**Songs and Stories of the Civil War*, by Jerry Silverman	Gr. 5-12
**Sound the Jubilee*, by Sandra Forrester [See cautionary note.]	Gr. 7-12
**Sounding Forth the Trumpet*, by Marshall & Manuel	Gr. 6-12
**Sounding Forth the Trumpet for Children*, by Marshall & Manuel	Gr. 1-5
**Southern Belles Paper Dolls* (Dover)	Various
Southern Generals, by Red Reeder	Gr. 8-12
Southern Yankees, by H. Speicher & K. Borland	Gr. 3-8
**Southerners*, by John Dunn (Voices from the Civil War)	Unknown
**Special Delivery*, by Betty Brandt (On My Own)	Gr. 1-4
Spies for the Blue and the Gray, by Harnett Kane	Gr. 7-12
**Spies in the Civil War*, by Victor Brooks (Untold History of the Civil War)	Gr. 4-8
Spirit of the Eagle, by Merritt Parmelee Allen	Gr. 5-12
**Spiritual Lives of Great Composers*, by Patrick Kavanaugh	Gr. 6-12
Spy for the Confederacy: Rose Greenhow, by Jeannette Covert Nolan (Messner)	Gr. 6-12
Spy in Old New Orleans, by Anne Emery	Gr. 3-12
**Stagecoaches and the Pony Express*, by Sally Isaacs (American Adventure)	Gr. 4-7
Stalwart Men of Early Texas, by Edith McCall (Frontiers of America)	Gr. 3-8
Stand to Horse, by André Norton	Gr. 7-12
**Standing Like a Stone Wall*, by James Robertson	Gr. 5-12
**Star of Gettysburg*, by Joseph Altsheler	Gr. 9-12
**Star-Spangled Banner*, by Deborah Kent (Cornerstones II)	Gr. 3-8
**Star-Spangled Banner*, by Peter Spier	Gr. 1-6
Star-Spangled Banner, by Neil & Anne Swanson	Gr. 5-12
**Star-Spangled Banner*, by Catherine Welch (On My Own)	Gr. 1-3
Star-Spangled Rooster, by Bruce Grant	Gr. 3-10
**Stealing Freedom*, by Elisa Carbone	Gr. 6-12
**Stefan Derksen's Polar Adventure*, by Piet Prins	Unknown
Stephen Decatur, by Bradford Smith (Childhood)	Gr. 1-6
Stephen Decatur: Fighting Sailor, by Wyatt Blassingame (Garrard Discovery)	Gr. 1-5
**Stephen Douglas: Champion of the Union*, by Mike Bonner (Famous Figures...)	Gr. 4-8
**Stephen F. Austin and the Founding of Texas*, by James Haley	Gr. 4-8
Steve Marches with the General, by Marion Renick	Gr. 3-8
**Stillness at Appomattox*, by Bruce Catton	Gr. 10-12

*_Stolen Train_, by Robert Ashley (Winston Adventure) Gr. 3-10
*_Stonewall_, by Jean Fritz Gr. 5-12
Stonewall Jackson, by Jonathan Daniels (Landmark) Gr. 3-10
*_Stonewall Jackson_, by Martha Hewson (Famous Figures of the Civil War Era) Gr. 4-8
*_Stonewall Jackson_, by Chris Hughes Gr. 5-10
*_Stonewall Jackson_, by Charles Ludwig (Sower) Gr. 5-12
*_Stonewall's Courier: Story of Charles Randolph and General Jackson_, by V. Hinkins Gr. 5-12
*_Stories of Napoleon Told to the Children_, by H.E. Marshall Gr. 4-7
Stories of the Early Times in the Great West, by Florence Bass Gr. 3-8
Storm Canvas, by Armstrong Sperry Gr. 5-12
Storming of Fort Wagner, by Irving Werstein Gr. 7-12
Stormy Victory: The Story of Tchaikovsky, by Claire Purdy (Messner) Gr. 6-12
Story Behind Great Inventions, by Elizabeth Montgomery Gr. 6-12
Story of Abraham Lincoln, by Nina Brown Baker (Signature) Gr. 3-8
Story of Andrew Jackson, by Enid LaMonte Meadowcroft (Signature) Gr. 3-8
*_Story of Antietam_, by Zachary Kent (Cornerstones) [Also titled, _Battle of..._] Gr. 3-9
Story of Beethoven, by Helen Kaufmann (Signature) Gr. 3-9
Story of Britain, by R.J. Unstead Gr. 5-12
Story of California, by May McNeer Gr. 4-12
Story of Clara Barton, by Olive Pice (Signature) Gr. 3-9
(Story of) Clara Barton of the Red Cross, by Jeannette Covert Nolan (Messner) Gr. 6-12
Story of Davy Crockett, by Enid LaMonte Meadowcroft (Signature) Gr. 3-8
*_Story of Davy Crockett_, by Walter Retan Gr. 3-8
Story of Eli Whitney, by Jean Lee Latham (Aladdin's American Heritage) Gr. 3-8
Story of Ford's Theater and the Death of Lincoln, by Zachary Kent (Cornerstones) Gr. 2-6
*_Story of Fort Sumter_, by Eugenia Burney (Cornerstones) Gr. 2-7
*_Story of Frederick Douglass_, by Eric Weiner Gr. 3-7
*_Story of Harriet Tubman_, by Kate McMullan Gr. 3-7
Story of Hiawatha, by Longfellow [Or abridged versions; incl. Indian religion.] Various
*_Story of Inventions_, by Michael McHugh & Frank Bachman Gr. 6-12
Story of John Brown's Raid, by Zachary Kent (Cornerstones) Gr. 3-8
Story of John J. Audubon, by Joan Howard (Signature) Gr. 3-8
*_Story of Johnny Appleseed_, by Aliki Gr. 1-4
Story of Kit Carson, by Edmund Collier (Signature) Gr. 3-8
Story of Old Ironsides, by Norman Richards (Cornerstones) Gr. 2-7
Story of Painting for Young People, by H.W. & Dora Janson Gr. 6-12
Story of Robert E. Lee, by Iris Vinton (Signature) Gr. 3-9
Story of Robert Louis Stevenson, by Joan Howard (Signature) Gr. 3-8
*_Story of Sherman's March to the Sea_, by Zachary Kent (Cornerstones) Gr. 2-7
Story of Stephen Decatur, by Iris Vinton (Signature) Gr. 3-9
Story of Tecumseh: Shawnee Chief, by Zachary Kent (Cornerstones) Gr. 2-6
Story of the Alamo, by Norman Richards (Cornerstones) Gr. 2-7
*_Story of the_ Amistad, by Emma Gelders Sterne Gr. 3-12
[Also titled _Slave Ship_ and _Long Black Schooner_.]
*_Story of the Barbary Pirates_, by R. Conrad Stein (Cornerstones) Gr. 2-7
Story of the Battle of Bull Run, by Zachary Kent (Cornerstones) Gr. 3-7

***Story of the Black Hawk War*, by Jim Hargrove (Cornerstones) Gr. 2-6
**Story of the Burning of Washington, D.C.*, by R. Conrad Stein (Cornerstones) Gr. 1-5
**Story of the California Gold Rush Coloring Book* (Dover) Various
Story of the Civil War, by Colonel Red Reeder Gr. 7-12
**Story of the Civil War Coloring Book* (Dover) Various
**Story of the Clipper Ships*, by R. Conrad Stein (Cornerstones) Gr. 2-7
**Story of the Confederate States*, by Joseph Derry Gr. 7-12
**Story of the Election of 1860*, by R. Conrad Stein (Cornerstones) Gr. 2-6
Story of the Erie Canal, by R. Conrad Stein (Cornerstones) Gr. 2-7
**Story of the Gettysburg Address*, by Kenneth Richards (Cornerstones) Gr. 2-8
Story of the Gold at Sutter's Mill, by R. Conrad Stein (Cornerstones) Gr. 2-6
**Story of the Great Republic*, by H.A. Guerber Gr. 4-8
**Story of the H.L. Hunley and Queenie's Coin*, by Fran Hawk Gr. 3-6
**Story of the Lewis and Clark Expedition*, by R. Conrad Stein (Cornerstones) Gr. 1-4
Story of the Louisiana Purchase, by Mary Kay Phelan Gr. 5-12
**Story of the New England Whalers*, by R. Conrad Stein (Cornerstones) Gr. 2-6
**Story of the Oregon Trail*, by R. Conrad Stein (Cornerstones) Gr. 2-6
**Story of the Pony Express*, by R. Conrad Stein (Cornerstones) Gr. 2-7
Story of the Seminoles, by Marion Gridley Gr. 3-8
Story of the Southwest, by May McNeer Gr. 4-10
**Story of the Star-Spangled Banner*, by Natalie Miller (Cornerstones) Gr. 2-6
**Story of the Surrender at Appomattox Courthouse*, by Z. Kent (Cornerstones) Gr. 2-7
**Story of the Trail of Tears*, by R. Conrad Stein (Cornerstone) Gr. 2-6
**Story of the Underground Railroad*, by R. Conrad Stein (Cornerstones) Gr. 1-7
Story of the U.S. Capitol, by Marilyn Prolman (Cornerstones) Gr. 1-6
Story of the War of 1812, by Colonel Red Reeder Gr. 7-12
**Story of the White House*, by Natalie Miller (Cornerstones) Gr. 1-6
**Story of the White House*, by Kate Waters Gr. 1-4
**Story of the World: Volume 3*, by Susan Wise Bauer Gr. 3-6
Some families enjoy this book's scope, so ask us to cite it; others seek different worldview; so, parental decision.
**Story of the World: Volume 4*, by Susan Wise Bauer Gr. 3-6
Some families enjoy this book's scope, so ask us to cite it; others seek different worldview; so, parental decision.
Story of Ulysses S. Grant, by Jeannette Nolan (Signature) Gr. 3-9
**Story of Whaling Coloring Book*, by Peter Copeland (Dover) Various
Story-Lives of American Composers, by Katherine Bakeless Gr. 8-12
Story-Lives of Great Composers, by Katherine Bakeless Gr. 8-12
**Stout-Hearted Seven*, by Neta Frazier Gr. 6-12
Strange Island, by Marion Havighurst Gr. 5-12
Stranger in the Storm, by Charles May Gr. 3-10
**Streams to the River, River to the Sea*, by Scott O'Dell Gr. 5-12
**Strength of These Arms*, by Raymond Bial Gr. 3-7
Strike the Tent, by Jeffrey Baker Gr. 4-12
**Striking it Rich!* by Stephen Krensky (Ready-to-Read 3) Gr. 2-3
Summer is for Growing, by Ann Nolan Clark Gr. 5-12

Sun Trail, by Merritt Parmelee Allen Gr. 5-12
Sunday in Centreville: The Battle of Bull Run, by G. Allen Foster Gr. 7-12
Sunrise Over the Harbor, by Louise Mandrell & Ace Collins Gr. 3-6
**Sunsets of the West*, by Tony Johnston Gr. 1-4
**Surrender at Appomattox*, by Tom McGowen (Cornerstones II) Gr. 3-9
Susan Peck, Late of Boston, by Carmel Martinez Gr. 5-10
Susanna and Tristam, by Marjorie Allee Gr. 5-12
**Susanna of the Alamo*, by John Jakes Gr. 1-5
Susannah: The Pioneer Cow, by Miriam Mason Gr. 1-5
Susie King Taylor: Civil War Nurse, by Simeon Booker Gr. 5-12
Sutter's Fort: Empire on the Sacramento, by W. & C. Luce (Garrard How They...) Gr. 3-9
**Swamp Angel*, by Anne Isaacs Gr. 1-4
Sweeper of the Skies, by Frances Higgins Gr. 6-12
**Sweet Betsy from Pike*, by Glen Rounds Various
**Sweet Clara and the Freedom Quilt*, by Deborah Hopkinson Gr. 1-6
Sweet Land of Michigan, by August Derleth Gr. 7-12
**Sweetwater Run: Story of Buffalo Bill and the Pony Express*, by Andrew Glass Gr. 2-6
**Sword of Antietam*, by Joseph Altsheler Gr. 9-12
Swords, Stars and Bars, by Lee McGiffin Gr. 6-12
Sycamore Tree, by Marion Havighurst Gr. 5-10
**Sylvia Stark*, by Victoria Scott [See cautionary note.] Gr. 4-10

Tad Lincoln: Abe's Son, by LaVere Anderson (Garrard Discovery) Gr. 1-5
Tad Lincoln and the Green Umbrella, by Margaret Friskey Gr. 3-10
Tad Lincoln: White House Wildcat, by David Collins Gr. 1-6
**Take Command, David Farragut!* by Peter & Connie Roop Gr. 3-6
**Taken by the Enemy*, by Oliver Optic Gr. 7-12
**(Taking) Wagons Over the Mountains*, by Edith McCall (Frontiers of America) Gr. 3-8
[The original was titled *Wagons...*; the reprint is titled *Taking Wagons...*]
**Tales for Hard Times*, by David Collins (Carolrhoda's Creative Minds) Gr. 2-5
**Tales of Uncle Remus*, by Julius Lester Gr. 3-12
Tales from the Vienna Woods, by David Ewen Gr. 5-12
Talking Bones, by William O. Steele [See cautionary note.] Parental decision
Talking Leaves: The Story of Sequoyah, by Bernice Kohn Gr. 1-5
Talleyrand, by Manuel Komroff (Messner) Gr. 7-12
**Tamarack Tree*, by Patricia Clapp Gr. 5-12
**Tchaikovsky*, by Greta Cencetti (World of Composers) Gr. 2-6
**Tchaikovsky*, by Ann Rachlin (Famous Children) Gr. 3-6
**Tchaikovsky Discovers America* (Classical Kids) Dramatizations-all ages; Book-Gr. 2-7
Tears for a King, by Ron Rendleman Gr. 7-12
**Tecumseh*, by Rachel Koestler-Grack Unknown
Tecumseh, by Augusta Stevenson (Childhood) Gr. 1-6
**Tecumseh: Chief of the Shawnee*, by C. Ann Fitterer (Our People) Unknown
Tecumseh: Destiny's Warrior, by David Cooke (Messner) Gr. 7-12
**Tecumseh: Shawnee Leader*, by Susan Gregson (Let Freedom Ring) Gr. 3-6
Tecumseh: Shawnee Rebel, by Robert Cwiklik (N. Am. Indians of Achievement) Gr. 5-10

**Tecumseh: Shawnee War Chief*, by Jane Fleischer	Gr. 1-5
Tecumseh: Shawnee Warrior-Statesman, by James McCague (Garrard Am. Ind.)	Gr. 1-5
Teenagers Who Made History, by Russell Freedman	Gr. 4-12
Texan Scouts, Texan Star,* **and *Texan Triumph*, all by Joseph Altsheler	Gr. 8-12
**Texas Jack at the Alamo*, by James Rice	Gr. K-3
Thaddeus Lowe: America's One Man Air Corps, by Mary Hoehling (Messner)	Gr. 6-12
Thaddeus Lowe: Uncle Sam's First Airman, by Lydel Sims	Gr. 7-12
Thaddeus Stevens and the Fight for Negro Rights, by Milton Meltzer	Gr. 9-12
**Thank You Very Much, Captain Ericsson*, by Connie Wooldridge	Unknown
**Thanksgiving in the White House*, by Gary Hines	Gr. 1-3
**Thar She Blows!* by Susan Kessirer (Smithsonian Odyssey)	Gr. 1-4
**Thee, Hannah*, by Marguerite de Angeli	Gr. 2-7
Their Shining Hour, by Ramona Mahler	Gr. 7-12
Then Was the Future, by Douglas Miller (Living History Library)	Gr. 8-12
Theodosia: Daughter of Aaron Burr, by Anne Colver	Gr. 7-12
**They Loved to Laugh*, by Kathryn Worth	Gr. 4-12
They Rode the Frontier, by Wyatt Blassingame	Gr. 4-12
**They're Off! The Story of the Pony Express*, by Cheryl Harness	Gr. 2-7
**Thieves of Tyburn Square*, by Dave & Neta Jackson (Trailblazer)	Gr. 3-8
**This Country of Ours*, by H.E. Marshall	Gr. 3-8
This is Washington, D.C., by Miroslav Sasek	Gr. 2-5
This Hallowed Ground, by Bruce Catton	Gr. 6-10
This is Washington, D.C., by Miroslav Sasek	Gr. 2-5
This Slender Reed, by Milton Lomask	Gr. 6-12
Thousand for Sicily, by Geoffrey Trease	Gr. 6-12
Thread of Victory, by Helen Lobdell	Gr. 9-12
**Three Against the Tide*, by D. Anne Love	Gr. 4-7
Three Days with Robert E. Lee at Gettysburg, by Paxton Davis	Gr. 7-12
**Three Little Indians*, by George Stuart	Gr. 1-4
**Three Stalks of Corn*, by Leo Politi	Gr. 1-3
**Through Russian Snows*, by G.A. Henty	Gr. 7-12
**Thunder at Gettysburg*, by Patricia Gauch	Gr. 4-8
Thundermaker: General Thomas Meagher, by William Lamers	Gr. 6-12
**Thy Friend, Obadiah*, by Brinton Turkle	Gr. 1-3
Timothy O'Dowd and the Big Ditch, by Len Hilts	Gr. 3-7
Tippecanoe and Tyler Too, by Stanley Young (Landmark)	Gr. 3-12
To Be a Pioneer, by Paul Burns	Gr. 3-8
**To Be a Slave*, by Julius Lester	Gr. 7-12
To California by Covered Wagon, by George Stewart (Landmark) [Reprinted as **Pioneers Go West.*]	Gr. 3-9
**To Fly with the Swallows*, by Debbie Heller (Stories of America)	Unknown
To Hold This Ground, by Susan Beller	Gr. 6-12
To the Shores of Tripoli, by Berta Briggs (Winston Adventure)	Gr. 3-12
Torrie, by Annabel Johnson	Gr. 7-12
Touch of Light, by Anne Neimark	Gr. 4-12
Toussaint: Black Liberator, by Ronald Syme	Gr. 4-10

**Toussaint L'Ouverture: Lover of Liberty*, by Laurence Santrey	Gr. 2-6
**Toussaint L'Overture*, by Walter Dean Myers	Gr. 3-6
**Traditional Native American Arts & Activities*, by Arlette Braman	Various
**Trafalgar*, by Richard Balkwill (Great Battles and Sieges)	Gr. 5-10
**Tragic Tale of Narcissa Whitman and a Faithful History of the Oregon Trail*	Gr. 4-8
Trail of Apple Blossoms, by Irene Hunt	Gr. 4-12
**Trail of Tears*, by Joseph Bruchac (Step Into Reading 5)	Gr. 2-4
Trail of Tears, by Marlene Brill	Gr. 5-12
**Trail of Tears*, by Sally Isaacs (American Adventure)	Gr. 4-7
Trail to Oklahoma, by Jim Booker	Gr. 4-9
Trail to Santa Fe, by David Lavender (North Star)	Gr. 4-12
Trails West, by George Cory Franklin	Gr. 3-9
Trails West and the Men Who Made Them, by E. Dorian & W. Wilson	Gr. 4-12
Trappers and Traders of the Far West, by James Daugherty (Landmark)	Gr. 3-8
Treasure Hunter: The Story of Robert Louis Stevenson, by Isabel Proudfit (Messner)	Gr. 6-12
Treasure in the Covered Wagon, by Vera Graham	Gr. 4-12
Treasure in the Little Trunk, by Helen Fuller Orton	Gr. 4-8
**Tree in the Trail*, by Holling Clancy Holling	Gr. 3-8
**Tree of Appomattox*, by Joseph Altsheler	Gr. 9-12
Tree Wagon, by Evelyn Lampman	Gr. 7-12
**Trial and Triumph: Stories from Church History*, by Richard Hannula	Gr. 5-12
**Trouble for Lucy*, by Carla Stevens	Gr. 2-5
**True Adventure of Daniel Hall*, by Diane Stanley	Gr. 3-8
True Adventures of Grizzly Adams, by Robert McClung	Unknown
True Book of Indians, by Teri Martini	Gr. K-3
True Book of Pioneers, by Mabel Harmer (True Books)	Gr. K-3
True Story of Lord Nelson, by Richard Houghton	Gr. 7-12
True Story of Napoleon, by Anthony Corley	Gr. 7-12
**True Tale of Johnny Appleseed*, by Margaret Hodges	Gr. 1-4
**Truth about Sacajawea*, by Kenneth Thomasma	Gr. 5-10
Truth about the Man Behind the Book, by Frances Cavanah	Gr. 7-12
**Turn Homeward, Hannalee*, by Patricia Beatty	Gr. 7-12
**Turner*, by Emily Cottrill (Picture Study Portfolios)	All ages
Tuscarora, by Jill Duvall (New True Books)	Gr. 2-5
Twelve Pioneers of Science, by Harry Sootin	Gr. 7-12
**Twins, the Pirates and the Battle of New Orleans*, by Harriette Robinet	Gr. 4-7
Two Flags Flying, by Donald Sobol	Gr. 2-8
**Two Little Confederates*, by Thomas Page	Gr. 3-10
**Two Little Savages*, by Ernest Thompson Seton	Unknown
Two Logs Crossing, by Walter Edmonds	Gr. 3-7
Two Scarlet Songbirds, by Carole Lexa Schaefer	Gr. 1-4
**Two Tickets to Freedom*, by Florence Freedman	Gr. 3-12
**Two Years Before the Mast*, by Richard Dana	Gr. 9-12
U.S. Grant, by Augusta Stevenson (Childhood)	Gr. 1-6
**Ulysses S. Grant*, by Susan Aller	Unknown

Ulysses S. Grant, by Bill Bentley (First Books)	Gr. 7-12
**Ulysses S. Grant*, by Zachary Kent	Gr. 4-12
**Ulysses S. Grant*, by David C. King	Gr. 7-12
**Ulysses S. Grant*, by Steven O'Brien	Gr. 6-12
**Ulysses S. Grant*, by Tim O'Shei (Famous Figures of the Civil War Era)	Gr. 4-8
Ulysses S. Grant, by Henry Thomas	Gr. 5-9
**Ulysses S. Grant and His Family Paper Dolls* (Dover)	Various
Ulysses S. Grant: Horseman and Fighter, by Col. Red Reeder (Garr. Discovery)	Gr. 1-5
Uncle Remus stories, by Joel Chandler Harris [There are many versions.]	Various
**Uncle Tom's Cabin*, by Harriet Beecher Stowe	Gr. 9-12
**Unconditional Surrender*, by Albert Marrin	Gr. 7-12
**Under a Strong Wind*, by Dorothy Morrison	Unknown
Under the Hawthorn Tree, by Marita Conlon-McKenna	Gr. 5-12
**Under the Quilt of Night*, by Deborah Hopkinson	Gr. 1-6
**Under Wellington's Command*, by G.A. Henty	Gr. 7-12
**Underground Man*, by Milton Meltzer	Unknown
**Underground Railroad*, by Raymond Bial	Gr. 4-9
**Underground Railroad*, by R. Conrad Stein (Cornerstones II)	Gr. 4-7
**Underground Railroad for Kids: From Slavery to Freedom with 21 Activities* by Mary Kay Carson	Various
**Understanding the Times*, by David Noebel	Gr. 9-12
**Undying Glory*, by Clinton Cox	Gr. 5-12
**Unfading Beauty*, by Tracy Leininger (Beautiful Girlhood)	Gr. 3-8
**Union Army Paper Soldiers* (Dover)	Various
**Union Soldiers*, by John Dunn (Civil War Voices)	Unknown
Uprising at Dawn, by Lee Roddy (Between Two Flags)	Gr. 4-9
Valiant Few: Crisis at the Alamo, by Lon Tinkle (Macmillan Battle Books)	Gr. 7-12
Valiant Virginian: Stonewall Jackson, by Felix Sutton (Messner)	Gr. 6-12
**Valley of the Moon*, by Sherry Garland (Dear America)	Gr. 3-8
Value of Adventure: Sacajawea, by Ann Johnson (ValueTales)	Gr. 1-4
Value of Helping: Harriet Tubman, by Anne Johnson (ValueTales)	Gr. 1-4
Value of Imagination: Charles Dickens, by Spencer Johnson (ValueTales)	Gr. 1-5
Value of Kindness, by Spencer Johnson (ValueTales)	Gr. 3-8
Value of Love: Johnny Appleseed, by Anne Johnson (ValueTales)	Gr. 1-4
Value of Respect: Abraham Lincoln, by Johnson (ValueTales)	Gr. 1-4
Vaughan Williams, by Michael Hurd	Gr. 7-12
**Verdi*, by Greta Cencetti (World of Composers)	Gr. 2-6
**Vicksburg*, by Mary Ann Fraser	Gr. 5-12
Vicksburg Veteran, by F.N Monjo	Gr. K-4
**Victor Lopez at the Alamo*, by James Rice	Gr. 5-8
**Vinnie and Abraham*, by Dawn FitzGerald and Catherine Stock	Gr. 1-4
Vinnie Ream, by Gordon Hall	Gr. 5-12
Violet for Bonaparte, by Geoffrey Trease	Gr. 7-12
**Virginia's General: Robert E. Lee*, by Albert Marrin	Gr. 8-12
**Visit to William Blake's Inn*, by Nancy Willard	Gr. 1-8

**Visual Dictionary of the Civil War*, by John Stanchak (DK) Gr. 5-12
**Voice of Freedom: A Story about Frederick Douglass*, by M. Weidt (Creat. Minds) Gr. 2-7
**Voices from the Civil War*, edited by Milton Meltzer Gr. 9-12
**Voices of the Alamo*, by Sherry Garland Gr. 5-12
**Voyage of Patience Goodspeed*, by Heather Frederick [See cautionary note.] Gr. 5-10
**Voyage of the Javelin*, by Stephen Meader Gr. 4-12
**Voyage of the Ludgate Hill*, by Nancy Willard Gr. 1-3

**Wagner*, by Greta Cencetti (World of Composers) Gr. 2-6
**Wagon Train*, by Sydelle Kramer (All Aboard) Gr. 1-3
**Wagons Ho!* by Cynthia Mercati (Cover-to-Cover) Gr. 3-5
Wagons Over the Mountains, by Edith McCall (Frontiers of America) Gr. 3-8
Wagons to the Wilderness, by Samuel Adams (Winston Adventure) Gr. 3-9
**Wagons West*, by Roy Gerrard Gr. 1-4
**Wait for Me, Watch for Me, Eula Bee*, by Patricia Beatty Gr. 4-12
**Walking the Road to Freedom*, by Jeri Ferris (Creative Minds) Gr. 2-8
Waltz King, by Kurt Pahlen Gr. 7-12
**Wanted Dead or Alive: The Story of Harriet Tubman*, by Ann McGovern Gr. 1-3
War Between the States, by Eric Barnes Gr. 4-8
War Chant, by Dee Dunsing Gr. 6-12
War Chief of the Seminoles, by May McNeer (Landmark) Gr. 3-9
War Eagle: Civil War Mascot, by Edmund Lindop Gr. 1-6
**War of 1812*, by Alden Carter Gr. 5-12
**War of 1812*, by Kathlyn & Martin Gay (Voices from the Past) Gr. 5-8
War of 1812, by Donald Lawson Gr. 6-12
**War of 1812*, by Richard Morris (First Book) Gr. 3-8
**War of 1812*, by Andrew Santella (Cornerstones of Freedom II) Gr. 3-7
**War with Mexico*, by William Jay Jacobs (Spotlight on American History) Gr. 5-10
War with Mexico, by Irving Werstein Gr. 7-12
**War's End*, by Norma Jean Lutz (American Adventure # 24) Gr. 3-8
**Warm as Wool*, by Scott Sanders Gr. 1-3
Washington Adventure, by Stockton Banks Gr. 4-10
**Washington City is Burning*, by Harriette Robinet Gr. 4-9
**Washington, D.C.*, KIDS Discover Magazine, March, 1997 Gr. 2-10
Washington, D.C., by Howard K. Smith (Landmark Giant) Gr. 6-12
**Washington, D.C.: A Scrapbook*, by Laura Lee Benson Gr. 2-8
Washington Irving, by Anya Seton (North Star) Gr. 6-12
Washington Irving, by Mabel Widdemer (Childhood) Gr. 1-6
Washington Irving: His Life, by Catherine Owens Peare Gr. 3-9
**Washington Irving: Storyteller for a New Nation*, by David Collins (World Writers) Gr. 6-12
Watergate: A Story of the Irish on the Erie Canal, by Herbert Best (Land of the Free) Gr. 5-12
**Waterloo*, by Philip Sauvain (Great Battles and Sieges) Gr. 4-10
Waterway West: The Story of the Erie Canal, by Mary Kay Phelan Gr. 8-12
Watt Got You Started, Mr. Fulton? by Robert Quackenbush Gr. 2-7
**Way West*, by Amelia Knight Gr. 2-6
We Were There at the Battle of Gettysburg, by Alida Malkus (We Were There) Gr. 3-8

We Were There at the Battle of the Alamo, by Margaret Cousins Gr. 3-8
We Were There at the Opening of the Erie Canal (We Were There) Gr. 3-8
**We Were There on the Oregon Trail*, by William Steele (We Were There) Gr. 3-8
We Were There on the Santa Fe Trail, by Ross Taylor (We Were There) Gr. 3-8
We Were There when Grant met Lee at Appomattox, by Earl Miers (We Were...) Gr. 3-8
We Were There with Jean Lafitte, by Iris Vinton (We Were There) Gr. 3-8
We Were There with Lewis and Clark, by James Munves (We Were There) Gr. 3-8
We Were There with Lincoln in the White House, by Earl Miers (We Were There) Gr. 3-8
We Were There with the California Forty-Niners, by Stephen Holt (We Were....) Gr. 3-8
We Were There with the California Rancheros, by Stephen Holt (We Were...) Gr. 3-8
We Were There with the Pony Express, by William O. Steele (We Were There) Gr. 3-8
**Wealth of Nations*, by Adam Smith Gr. 11-12
West to Danger, by Isabelle Lawrence Gr. 5-12
Western Star, by Merritt Parmelee Allen Gr. 4-12
Western Stories of Bret Harte [adapted] Gr. 5-12
Westward Adventure, by William O. Steele Gr. 6-12
Westward with American Explorers, by Walter Buehr Gr. 4-12
Whale Hunters, by Joseph Phelan Gr. 5-12
**Whaler 'Round the Horn*, by Stephen Meader Gr. 5-12
**Whalers*, by Peter Chrisp (Remarkable World) Gr. 4-8
**Whaling Days*, by Carol Carrick Gr. 3-9
**What Do You Mean?* by Jeri Ferris (Creative Minds) Gr. 2-7
What the Dickens! by Jane Curry Gr. 4-6
**What Was Cooking in Dolley Madison's White House?* by Tanya Larkin Various
**What Was Cooking in Mary Todd Lincoln's White House*, by Tanya Larkin Various
**What's the Deal?* by Rhoda Blumberg Gr. 6-12
**Whatever Happened to Penny Candy?* by Richard Maybury Gr. 7-12
Wheat Won't Wait, by Adele Nathan (Aladdin's American Heritage) Gr. 3-8
Wheels West, by Evelyn Lampman Gr. 5-12
**When Abraham Lincoln Talked to the Trees*, by Elizabeth Van Steenwyk Gr. 2-5
When Clipper Ships Ruled the Seas, by James McCague (Garr. How They Lived) Gr. 3-9
When Guns Thundered at Tripoli, by Charles Finger Gr. 8-12
**When Johnny Went Marching Home: Young Americans Fight the Civil War* Gr. 5-12
by G. Clifton Wisler
When Lincoln Went to Gettysburg, by Adele Nathan Gr. 2-8
When Mountain Men Trapped Beaver, by R. Glendinning (Gar. How They Lived) Gr. 3-8
When Nantucket Men Went Whaling, by Enid Meadowcroft (Gar. How They...) Gr. 3-9
When Pioneers Pushed West to Oregon, by Elizabeth Montgomery (Garr. How...) Gr. 3-8
**When Pioneer Wagons Rumbled West*, by Christine Graham Gr. 1-3
When Rebels Rode, by Grace Huffard Gr. 3-7
When Wagon Trains Rolled to Santa Fe, by Erick Berry (Gar. How They Lived) Gr. 3-8
**When Will This Cruel War Be Over?* by Barry Denenberg (Dear America) Gr. 3-10
[See cautionary note.]
Where is Papa Now? by Celeste Conway Gr. 1-4
**Where Lincoln Walked*, by Raymond Bial Gr. 2-12
**Where the Buffalo Roams*, by Jacqueline Geis Gr. 1-7

**Which Way Freedom?* by Joyce Hansen	Gr. 4-12
Whistle for the Crossing, by Marguerite de Angeli	Gr. 2-7
White Feather, by Merritt Parmelee Allen	Gr. 5-12
White Feather, by Ruth Eitzen	Gr. 1-4
White Sails to China, by Clyde Robert Bulla	Gr. 1-5
**Whitman Massacre of 1847*, by Catherine Sager	Unknown
**Who Comes with Cannons?* by Patricia Beatty	Gr. 2-10
**Who Let Muddy Boots into the White House?* by Robert Quackenbush	Gr. 3-8
Who Owns the Sun? by Stacy Chbosky	Gr. 1-4
Who Rides in the Dark? by Stephen Meader	Gr. 7-12
Who Said There's No Man on the Moon? by Robert Quackenbush	Gr. 2-7
Who'd Believe John Colter? by Mary Blount Christian	Gr. 3-7
Wide World of Aaron Burr, by Helen Orlob	Gr. 5-12
Wildcat, the Seminole, by Electa Clark (Aladdin's American Heritage)	Gr. 3-9
Wilderness Pioneer, by Carol Hoff	Gr. 4-12
Will Clark, by Katharine Wilkie (Childhood)	Gr. 1-6
William Bent and His Adobe Empire, by Shannon Garst (Messner)	Gr. 7-12
**William Blake*, by Harold Bloom	Gr. 10-12
William Blake, by James Daugherty	Gr. 7-12
**William Carey*, by Janet Benge (Christian Heroes, Then and Now)	Gr. 5-12
**William Carey*, by Basil Miller (Men of Faith)	Gr. 8-12
**William Carey: Father of Modern Missions*, by Sam Wellman (Heroes of the F...)	Gr. 5-12
**William Henry Harrison*, by Steven Otfinoski (Enc. of Presidents II)	Gr. 5-12
**William Henry Harrison*, by Howard Peckham (Childhood/Young Patriots)	Gr. 1-6
**William Henry Harrison*, by Mike Venezia (Getting to Know the US Presi...)	Gr. 1-5
William McGuffey, by Barbara Williams (Childhood)	Gr. 1-6
William T. Sherman, by Marsha Landreth (Great American Generals)	Gr. 7-12
William Tecumseh Sherman, by Wyatt Blassingame (Hall of Fame)	Gr. 6-12
William Tecumseh Sherman, by Charles Graves	Gr. 3-12
**William Tecumseh Sherman, Union General*, by Henna Remstein (Famous Fig...)	Gr. 4-8
William Warren, by Will Antell	Gr. 5-12
**Willie McLean and the Civil War Surrender*, by Candice Ransom (On My Own)	Gr. 1-3
Winged Moccasins: The Story of Sacajawea, by Frances Farnsworth (Messner)	Gr. 5-12
Wish on Capitol Hill, by Esther Brady	Gr. 3-10
With Bolivar Over the Andes, by C.M. Nelson	Gr. 5-12
**With Every Drop of Blood*, by James & Christopher Collier [See cautionary note.]	Gr. 5-12
**With Lee in Virginia*, by G.A. Henty	Gr. 7-12
**With Moore at Corunna*, by G. A. Henty	Gr. 7-12
**With Open Hands: A Story about Biddy Mason*, by Jeri Ferris (Creative Minds)	Gr. 3-6
**Within the Enemy Lines*, by Oliver Optic	Gr. 7-12
Woman with a Sword, by Hollister Noble	Gr. 8-12
**Women Civil War Spies of the Confederacy*, by Larissa Phillips	Unknown
Wonderful Voyage, by Ruth Langland Holberg	Gr. 3-9
**Working in the First Factories*, by Patrice Coupry	Gr. 3-8
**World at His Fingertips*, by Barbara O'Connor (Creative Minds)	Gr. 3-8

Yankee Clippers: The Story of Donald McKay, by Clara Ingram Judson Gr. 5-12
**Yankee Girl at Fort Sumter*, by Alice Desmond Curtis Gr. 4-12
Yankee in the White House, by Mary Hoehling (Messner) Gr. 7-12
Yankee Spy: Elizabeth Van Lew, by Jeannette Nolan (Messner) Gr. 4-12
Yankee Thunder, by Irwin Shapiro (Messner) Gr. 4-12
Yankee Traitor, Rebel Spy, by Elinor Case Gr. 4-12
Yankees on the Run, by John Brick Gr. 5-12
Year of the Big Snow, by Steve Frazee Gr. 7-12
Year of the Horseless Carriage: 1801, by Genevieve Foster Gr. 4-9
Young Tennyson, by Charlotte Hope Gr. 7-12
**Young Abe Lincoln: The Frontier Days, 1809-1837*, by Cheryl Harness Gr. 1-4
**Young Abraham Lincoln*, by Woods (Troll First-Start) Gr. K-1
Young Audubon, by Miriam Mason (Childhood) Gr. 1-6
[This may also have been published as *John Audubon.*]
Young Brahms, by Sybil Deucher Gr. 2-7
Young Brontës, by Phyllis Bentley Gr. 7-12
**Young Buglers*, by G.A. Henty Gr. 7-12
Young Dickens, by Patrick Pringle Gr. 7-12
Young Edgar Allan Poe, by Laura Benét Parental discretion
Young Elizabeth Barrett Browning, by Clare Abrahall Gr. 7-12
Young Elizabeth Fry, by Patrick Pringle Gr. 7-12
Young Faraday, by Patrick Pringle Gr. 7-12
**Young Frederick Douglass: Fight for Freedom*, by Laurence Santrey (Troll) Gr. K-2
Young Generals, by James Norman Gr. 7-12
**Young Harriet Tubman*, by Anne Benjamin (Troll First-Start) Gr. K-2
Young Hickory, by Stanley Young Gr. 5-12
Young Jane Austen, by Rosemary Sisson Gr. 7-12
(Young) Jed Smith, by Olive Burt (Childhood) Gr. 1-6
**Young John Quincy*, by Cheryl Harness Gr. 1-4
Young Keats, by Jean Haynes Gr. 7-12
Young Mac of Fort Vancouver, by Mary Jane Carr Gr. 5-12
Young Man in a Hurry, by Iris Clinton [About William Carey.] Gr. 4-12
Young Mr. Meeker and His Exciting Journey to Oregon, by Miriam Mason Gr. 2-8
Young Napoleon, by Leonard Cooper Gr. 7-12
Young Nelson, by Ronald Syme Gr. 7-12
Young People's Story of Architecture: Gothic-Modern, by Hillyer & Huey Gr. 2-8
Young People's Story of Fine Art: Last Two Hundred Years, by Hillyer & Huey Gr. 3-12
[Originally printed as: *Child's History of Art*, by Hillyer & Huey.]
**Young Pony Express Rider*, by Charles Coombs Gr. 3-9
Young Robert Louis Stevenson, by Ian Finlay Gr. 7-12
Young Squire Morgan, by Manly Wade Wellman Gr. 7-12
Young Stonewall, by Helen Monsell (Childhood) Gr. 1-6
Young United States, by Edwin Tunis Gr. 7-12
Young Walter Scott, by Elizabeth Jane Gray Gr. 7-12
Young Wordsworth, by Trudy West Gr. 7-12

Zachary Taylor, by Patricia Miles Martin (See and Read)	Gr. 1-3
**Zachary Taylor*, by Mike Venezia (Getting to Know the....)	Gr. 1-5
Zach Taylor, by Katharine Wilkie (Childhood)	Gr. 1-6
Zachary, the Governor's Pig, by Bruce Grant	Gr. 3-10
Zeb Pike, by Augusta Stevenson (Childhood)	Gr. 1-6
Zebulon Pike, by Bern Keating	Gr. 4-12
Zebulon Pike, by Faith Knoop (Real People)	Gr. 3-7
**Zebulon Pike: Explorer of the Southwest*, by William Sanford & Carl Green	Gr. 4-7
Zebulon Pike: Soldier and Explorer, by Leonard Wibberley	Gr. 7-12
**Zebulon Pike: Soldier and Explorer*, by Barbara Witteman (Let Freedom Ring)	Gr. 4-8
**Zia*, by Scott O'Dell	Gr. 4-12

Films

Parental discretion is always advised. Some films have portions which should be omitted.

**Abraham Lincoln*, very old film starring Walter Huston
**Amazing Grace*, starring Ioan Gruffudd
**Barretts of Wimpole Street*, starring Frederic March
**Beethoven Lives Upstairs* (Classical Kids)
**Candle in the Dark*
**Civil War Diary*
**Davy Crockett: King of the Wild Frontier*, starring Fess Parker
**Five Mile Creek*
**Friendly Persuasion*
**Gettysburg*, starring Martin Sheen and Sam Elliott
**Ghosts of Dickens' Past: The Untold Story of a Simple Act of Charity*
**Great Locomotive Chase*, starring Fess Parker
**How Should We Then Live?* by Francis Schaeffer [Also in book version.]
**Kit Carson*, by Richard "Little Bear" Wheeler
**Last of Mrs. Lincoln*
**Lewis & Clark*, produced by Ken Burns
**Liszt's Rhapsody* (Composers' Specials)
**Miss Austen Regrets*, starring Olivia Williams
**North and South*, starring Daniela Deby-Ashe and Richard Armitage
**Nutcracker*
**Origin of the Indians*, by Richard "Little Bear" Wheeler
**Rossini's Ghost* (Composers' Specials)
**Seven Alone*
**Shenandoah*, starring Jimmy Stewart
**Strauss: The King of 3/4 Time* (Composers' Specials)
**Uncle Tom's Cabin*, starring Phylicia Rashad
**William Wilberforce*, produced by Gateway/Vision Video
**Young Mr. Lincoln*, Henry Fonda plays Lincoln as a young, country lawyer

Audios

**Beethoven Lives Upstairs* (Classical Kids)	Various
**Escape*, by Sharon Gayle (Smithsonian/Soundprints)	Various
**Historical Devotionals: Volume XII*, by Mantle Ministries	Various
**History Alive Through Music: Westward Ho!* by Diana Waring	Various
**Nutcracker*	Various
**Tchaikovsky Discovers America* (Classical Kids)	Various
**Wanted: A Few Bold Riders*, by Darice Bailer [Book/tape combo.]	Various
**We Hold These Truths to be Self-Evident*, narrated by Max McLean	Various
**Young Harriet Tubman*, by Anne Benjamin [Book/tape combo.]	Various
**Your Story Hour: Volume 6*	Various
**Your Story Hour: Volume 7*	Various

Bibliography

Breese, Dave. *Seven Men Who Rule the World from the Grave.* Chicago: Moody, 1990.

Carson, Clarence. *The Beginning of the Republic, 1775-1825—A Basic History of the United States, Volume II.*

Wadley, AL: American Textbook Committee, 1984.

__________. *The Sections and the Civil War, 1826-1877—A Basic History of the United States, Volume III.* Wadley, AL: American Textbook Committee, 1985.

Coolidge, Olivia. *The Statesmanship of Abraham Lincoln.* New York: Charles Scribner's Sons, 1976.

Cowan, Louise and Os Guinness. *Invitation to the Classics.* Grand Rapids, MI: Baker, 1998.

Galbraith, John Kenneth. *The Age of Uncertainty.* Boston: Houghton Mifflin, 1977.

Grant, R.G. *1848: Year of Revolution.* New York: Thomson Learning, 1995.

Gridley, Marion. *Indian Tribes of America.* Northbrook, IL: Hubbard Press, 1973.

Grun, Bernard. *The Timetables of History.* New York: Touchstone Books, published by Simon & Schuster, 1991.

Hotchkiss, Jeanette. *American Historical Fiction and Biography for Children and Young People.* Metuchen, NJ: Scarecrow Press, 1973.

__________. *European Historical Fiction for Children and Young People.* Metuchen, NJL Scarecrow Press, 1967.

Jackson, Jeremy. *No Other Foundation: The Church Through Twenty Centuries.* Westchester, IL: Cornerstone, 1980.

Lord, John. *Beacon Lights of History, Volume 4: Warriors and Statesmen.* New York: Fords, Howard, and Hulbert, 1885.

Marshall, Peter and David Manuel. *From Sea to Shining Sea.* Grand Rapids, MI: Revell, 1986.

__________. *Sounding Forth the Trumpet.* Grand Rapids, MI: Revell, 1997.

Merriam Webster's Encyclopedia of Literature (Springfield, MA: Merriam-Webster, Inc., 1995) 1099.

Metzner, Seymour. *American History in Juvenile Books.* New York: H.N. Wilson, 1966.
__________. *World History in Juvenile Books.* New York: H.N. Wilson, 1973.

Miller, Douglas. *Then Was the Future: The North in the Age of Jackson, 1815-1850.* New York: Knopf, 1973.

Morris, Richard. *Encyclopedia of American History.* New York: Harper & Brothers, 1953.

Potter, William. *The Boy's Guide to the Historical Adventures of G.A. Henty.* Bulverde, TX: Vision Forum, 2000.

Rowley, Gill (editor). *The Book of Music.* Englewood Cliffs, NJ: Prentice-Hall, 1978.

Schaeffer, Francis. *How Should We Then Live?* Old Tappan, NJ: Revell, 1976.

Unstead, R.J. *The Story of Britain.* New York: Thomas Nelson, 1970.

Webster's Biographical Dictionary. Springfield, MA: G. & C. Merriam, 1943.

Webster's New Collegiate Dictionary. Springfield, MA: G. & C. Merriam, 1977.

Werstein, Irving. *Storming of Fort Wagner.* New York: Scholastic, 1970.